Subjectivity
and
Relations

D1340930

Subjectivity
and
Social Relations

A Reader edited by
Veronica Beechey and James Donald
at the Open University

OPEN UNIVERSITY PRESS

Milton Keynes : Philadelphia

Open University Press
Open University Educational Enterprises Limited
12 Cofferidge Close
Stony Stratford
Milton Keynes MK11 1BY, England
and
242 Cherry Street
Philadelphia, PA 19106, USA

First Published 1985

British Library Cataloguing in Publication Data
Subjectivity and social relations.
    "One of three readers designed for the Open University courses 'Beliefs and
ideologies' "—Pref.
    Bibliography: p.
    Includes index.
    1. Social interaction. 2. Social institutions.
3. Subjectivity. 4. Ideology. 5. Family. I. Beechey,
Veronica. II. Donald, James. III. Open University.
HM291.S855 1985   302   85-11600

ISBN 0-335-15106-X
ISBN 0-335-15105-1 (pbk)

Library of Congress Cataloging in Publication Data
Subjectivity and social relations: a reader.
    1. Social interaction
    I. Beechey, Veronica   II. Donald, James
    302   HM291

ISBN 0-335-15106-X
ISBN 0-335-15105-1 Pbk

311136

Typeset by Gilbert Composing Services
Printed in Great Britain at the Alden Press, Oxford.

Contents

Section III: The regulation of sexuality   **155**

Section IV: Schooling: norms and differences   **213**

Acknowledgements

1   Reprinted from P. Hirst & P. Woolley, *Social Relations and Human Attributes*, Tavistock, 1982, copyright © Paul Hirst and Penny Woolley 1982, by permission of Associated Book Publishers (UK) Ltd.

2   Reprinted from S. Hall, 'The rediscovery of "ideology" ' in M. Gurevitch, A. Bennett, J. Curran & J. Woollacott (Eds), *Culture, Society and the Media*, Methuen, 1982, by permission of Associated Book Publishers (UK) Ltd.

3   Reprinted from L. Althusser (trans. B. Brewster), *Lenin and Philosophy and other essays*, New Left Books, 1971, pp 121–173, by permission of Verso.

4   (a) Reprinted from M. Foucault, *Power/Knowledge: Selected interviews and other writings 1972–1977*, Harvester Press, 1980, pp 109–133, by permission of the Harvester Press Ltd.
    (b) Reprinted from M. Foucault, 'The West and the truth of sex' in *Substance* no. 20, 1978, pp 5–8, by permission of the University of Wisconsin Press.

5   Reprinted from O. Harris, 'Households as Natural Units' in K. Young, C. Walkowitz & R. McCullagh (Eds), *Of Marriage and the Market*, pp 136–153, CSE books 1981, second edition Routledge & Kegan Paul 1984, by permission of Routledge & Kegan Paul plc.

6   Original article by Veronica Beechey, © The Open University 1985, by permission of The Open University.

7   Reprinted from D. Riley, *War in the Nursery: Theories of the Child and Mother*, Virago, 1983, chapter 6, copyright © Denise Riley, by permission of Virago Press.

8   Reprinted from R. Coward, *Female Desire: Women's Sexuality Today*, Paladin, pp 163–171, copyright © Rosalind Coward, by permission of Granada Publishing Ltd.

9   Original article by Nancy Wood, © The Open University 1985, by permission of The Open University.

10   Reprinted from J. Walkowitz, 'Male Vice and Feminist Virtue' in *History Workshop* no. 13, 1982, pp 79–93, by permission of Routledge & Kegan Paul plc.

11   Reprinted from G. Weeks, *Sex, Politics and Society: The Regulation of Sexuality since 1880*, Longman, 1981, chapter 7, by permission of the Longman Group Ltd.

12   Reprinted from F. Mort, 'Sexuality: Regulation and Contestation' in the Gay Liberation Collective (Eds), *Homosexuality, Power and Politics*, Allison & Busby, pp 38–51, by permission of Allison & Busby Ltd.

13   Original article by James Donald, © The Open University 1985, by permission of The Open University.

14   Reprinted from J. Rose, *The Case of Peter Pan*, Macmillan, 1984, pp 115–129, copyright © Jacqueline Rose, by permission of Macmillan, London and Basingstoke and of Salem House.

Figures 7 and 8 are reproduced by permission of the Metropolitan Borough of Stockport, Leisure Services Division, Library of Local Studies Photographic Collection. Figure 9 is reproduced by permission of Barnardo's Photographic Library.

Preface

Subjectivity and Social Relations is one of three readers designed for the Open University course *Beliefs and Ideologies*, the others being *Religion and Ideology* (Bocock and Thompson, 1985) and *Politics and Ideology* (Donald and Hall, 1985). Here the focus is not on the role of supernatural beliefs, spectacular rituals and religious movements as mechanisms of social cement or resistance, nor on the political mobilization of such ideological categories as 'the nation' or 'the people'. The concerns of this volume are, in a sense, more mundane, more everyday and more intimate. But they are none the less important for that, nor are they beyond the grip of relations of power. On the contrary, they raise very clearly a question at the heart of any theory of ideology or of society: how is it that subjects – people, individuals, social agents, human beings – are formed not only within but *by* the social and cultural world they inhabit?

In seeking some possible ways of answering that question, we focus on three areas of everyday life – the representation and organization of families, the definition and regulation of sexuality, and the ideological implications of schooling. The readings which analyse these issues draw on a number of approaches – not only sociology, but also, for example, anthropology, history, psychoanalysis and the 'genealogy' associated with Michel Foucault. Even this apparently eclectic range nowhere near exhausts the range of perspectives that have been brought to bear on the question of subjectivity in recent decades, and concepts deriving from philosophy, political science, semiotics and aesthetic theory are also frequently brought into play. This diversity is a testament, perhaps, to a process of realignment within the traditional disciplines as well as to the importance of ideology in current academic and political debates.

The book is divided into four sections. The first marks out the conceptual terrain that is explored in more empirical detail in the other three, which deal with the family, the regulation of sexuality, and schooling. Each of these sections contains an article specially written for this volume, along with a selection of articles or extracts from books which represent the best recent work on the topic. In trying to include as comprehensive a range of material as possible, we have inevitably had to shorten many of these. Our hope is that this collection will encourage readers to return to the originals to follow through the arguments and debates more fully. In many cases, especially in some of the historical essays, we have not included detailed references, especially to primary sources. That is because what is important in this context is the *argument*; again, readers who want to explore those sources should refer back to the original publications. Editorial cuts have been marked by three dots in square brackets: [. . .]. Editorial interpolations are placed in square brackets.

Although this book has been designed with the needs of Open University students principally in mind, we hope that it will also be of wider interest – not only to students of the social sciences and humanities, but also to people wanting an introduction to the exciting work now being done on topics that are of concern to us all, both politically and in our personal lives.

For their advice and assistance in the preparation of this book, we would like to thank Cora Kaplan, John Eldridge, Robert Bocock, Stuart Hall, Kenneth Thompson, Keith Stribley, Tom Hunter, Joan Higgs, Marie Day, Carol Johns and Jo Mathieson. We are also indebted to the authors of the readings for allowing us to publish their work in abbreviated form.

Veronica Beechey
James Donald

References

Bocock, R. and Thompson, K. (1985) *Religion and Ideology*, Manchester, Manchester University Press.

Donald, J. and Hall, S. (1985) *Politics and Ideology*, Milton Keynes, Open University Press.

Introduction

The question of how (or whether) subjectivity is constituted by the social domain has always been at the heart of sociological inquiry. The premise of Marx's conception of ideology, for example, was that: 'It is not the consciousness of men that determines their being, but, on the contrary, their social being that determines their consciousness.' This is because the social and cultural world in which they live always already exists: 'men make their own history, but they do not make it as they please; they do not make it under circumstances chosen by themselves, but under circumstances directly encountered, given and transmitted from the past.'

The Durkheimian tradition

Consciousness is presented by Marx as historically and culturally variable. He did not have much to say about *how* 'social being' determines 'consciousness', though. Nor did he perceive that the idea of *consciousness* as the definitive characteristic of being a person is itself of comparatively recent origin. In his 1938 lecture on 'A Category of the Human Mind: the Notion of Person, the Notion of "Self"', for example, Durkheim's collaborator Marcel Mauss argued that the equation between person and self, and between self and consciousness was made possible only by the definitions of individual freedom, responsibility and consciousness developed by sectarian religious movements in the seventeenth and eighteenth centuries. For Mauss, what defines the category of 'the person' is not the fact of consciousness but the specific cultural definitions produced through religion, kinship, the law, language and so forth. Tracing the genealogy of the modern Western conception of selfhood from Greek rituals and Roman conceptions of the *persona* through the development of Christian civilization, he identified a sequence of transformations – 'from a mere masquerade to the mask, from a role to a person, to a name, to an individual, from the last to a being with a metaphysical and ethical value, from a moral consciousness to a sacred being, from the latter to a fundamental form of thought and action' (1979, p.90).

As Mauss realized, the idea that the person or the self is a culturally and historically malleable category is probably one of the most scandalous axioms of the social sciences. It offends not only common sense, but also our sense of who and what we are. It calls into question the very integrity and coherence of ourselves as conscious, rational, self-directed beings. But, as Mauss suggested, our conception of what it is to be a person is a metaphysical fiction. Anthropological evidence as well as historical researches underline its fragility and its transience. 'Who knows even if this "category", which all of us here today believe to be well founded, will always be recognized as such? It was formed only for us, among us' (1979, p.90). (For an exposition of Mauss's argument, and a more extended discussion of the category of the person, see Hirst and Woolley, 1982, esp. Chapter 6.)

In his lecture, Mauss concentrated on the social definition of the *category* of the person rather than on a detailed analysis of how this modern 'consciousness' is formed. As a follower of Durkheim, it is clear that he saw this process in terms of the subject's internalization and negotiation of the 'collective representations' embodied in social relations, practices and rules. This perspective is not dissimilar from Marx's conception of consciousness being formed by 'circumstances directly encountered, given and transmitted from the past', although Mauss emphasizes their symbolic power more than Marx.

The critical edge of this approach has often been lost as it was appropriated into mainstream structural-functionalist sociology by Talcott Parsons and his followers. The idea of collective *representations* was translated by these sociologists into a notion of shared norms and values acting as the primary mechanism for maintaining social order. This led to what Dennis Wrong called, in a famous critique, an 'oversocialized conception' of man in modern sociology (Wrong, 1961). George Herbert Mead also took for granted the existence of a consensual social order which is internalized by the individual, but his symbolic interactionism was more sensitive to the importance of the production of *meaning* than functionalist sociologists. Like Marx and Durkheim, Mead started from the premise that 'the social process' pre-exists 'the self conscious individual' both temporally and logically. From there, rather as Althusser was to do later, he went on to pose the question of how subjectivity is formed in relation to the pre-existing social order – a question which he formulated in terms of how the 'socialization' process works so as to produce the socialized citizen in which 'the "me" is the organized set of attitudes of others' which the self has to take on (Mead, 1934, p.26; see also Henriques *et al*, pp.18,23).

Such explanations of the formation of subjectivity in terms of socialization have been called into question by a number of disciplines and perspectives. Cultural anthropology and historical research have shown how varied and diverse are the ways that 'the person' and 'selfhood' can be categorized in different societies and epochs. Psychoanalysis, linguistics and semiotics have all produced accounts of the production of subjectivity which differ fundamentally from the socialization approach. So, too, have Marxist approaches to ideology, organized around Gramsci's conception of hegemony, which attempt to explain how and why subjects 'consent' to existing social relations.

Some of the intellectual co-ordinates for these critical discussions about the relationship between culture and subjectivity are charted in the contributions to the first section of this volume by Paul Hirst and Penny Woolley and by Stuart Hall. One reference point for both of them is the strand of structuralist thought that has developed in the wake of the anthropological studies of Claude Lévi-Strauss. This, in turn, bore the imprint of Durkheim's emphasis on the social importance of the symbolic, although Lévi-Strauss reworked it through the model of structural linguistics proposed by Saussure. Just as people use grammatical rules which they cannot formulate and of which they are largely unconscious when they speak, so Lévi-Strauss argues that culture should be approached as a field of possibilities for the production of meaning. This linguistic analogy has remained a characteristic feature of subsequent structuralist analyses of ideology – and also of many, like those of Althusser and Foucault, in which the structuralist label is explicitly denied.

Althusser and Foucault

It is within the diverse and often conflicting terms of this critical paradigm, rather than those of sociological accounts of socialization, that the family, sexuality and schooling are analysed in the case studies that follow. The fact that all these contributions have been written in the 1970s and 1980s shows how central the question of ideology became after the political upheavals of 1968 – the events which prompted Althusser's essay on 'Ideology and ideological state apparatuses', the bulk of which was written in that year and which is republished in this volume.

However often this essay has been criticized, it has remained the principal reference point for most of the subsequent discussions and controversies. More recently, however, its centrality has been to some extent displaced by the approach to the history and formation of discourse pioneered by Michel Foucault, who has declared himself to be sceptical about the explanatory value of the concept of ideology. The tension between the Althusserian and Foucaultian positions informs all three case studies. It may therefore be useful to indicate what is at stake in it by recapitulating Althusser's conceptualization of ideology and outlining how and why Foucault questions it.

In his earlier books, *For Marx* and *Reading Capital*, Althusser developed his theory of ideology in the context of a critical discussion of Marx's early writings. One aspect of this was his attempt to establish firm epistemological boundaries between ideology and science, assigning Marx's early writings to ideology and the later ones to science. This was bound up with the controversy that dominated the left in post-war France, in which a number of writers, including Merleau-Ponty and Sartre, were attempting to formulate a humanistic Marxism. It was against this that Althusser's 'anti-humanist' polemic was directed. The premise of Althusser's anti-humanist conception of the subject is that it is the structure of a social formation that determines the individual's behaviour and make-up. If this was, in one way, a restatement of Marx's principle that 'social being' determines 'consciousness', it was now reformulated in structuralist terms. Like Lévi-Strauss, Althusser conceptualized ideology in terms of the themes, concepts and representations through which people 'live', in an imaginary relation, their relation to the real conditions of their existence. This concept of an 'imaginary relation' is quite distinct from notions like 'false consciousness' because it takes ideologies to refer not to ideas or the contents of consciousness, but to the unconscious categories through which the real relations of existence are represented and experienced. It is these unconscious structures that enable people to act 'as if' the ideological were real:

> In truth, ideology has very little to do with 'consciousness', even supposing this term to have an unambiguous meaning. It is profoundly *unconscious* [. . .] Ideology is indeed a system of representations, but in the majority of cases these representations have nothing to do with 'consciousness': they are usually images and occasionally concepts, but it is above all as *structures* that they impose on the vast majority of men, not via their 'consciousness'. They are perceived-accepted-suffered cultural objects and they act functionally on men via a process that escapes them.
> (Althusser, 1977, p.233)

Althusser's earlier formulations were called into question in the late 1960s – especially the epistemological knots he tied himself up in around the science/ideology distinction. Criticism (and not least his self-criticism) came from two directions. Partly, it stemmed from the type of work on subjectivity being developed within psychoanalysis, semiotics and the study of discourse, but it was also prompted by the failure of the political events of 1968 (or, more specifically, of the French Communist Party) to bring about revolutionary change. This cruelly exposed mechanistic conceptions of class struggle or over-sanguine expectations of the Party. While hanging onto his fundamental anti-humanism, therefore, Althusser proposed in his essay on the ideological state apparatuses (the ISAs) a more complex account of the relationship between ideology, subjectivity and class struggle. This can be summarized briefly in three major propositions, the first two of which are developed in the first part of the essay, while the third is spelt out in the latter part.

(1) Ideology should be approached through the problematic of reproduction.

Althusser wanted to break from the overly deterministic accounts of ideology which often flowed from the classical Marxist question, how is the ideological superstructure determined by the economic base? Althusser argued that Marxist writers had taken the base/superstructure metaphor too literally. He therefore reformulated the base/superstructure relationship, emphasizing the functioning of ideology rather than its determination. Althusser's question was, therefore, how does ideology function to reproduce the social division of labour necessary for the continuation of capitalism? He argued that this reproduction is carried out through a number of institutions, among them some which work primarily through ideology. These are the ideological state apparatuses. Following Gramsci's analysis, Althusser argues that these may be part of 'the state' or 'civil society', located within either 'public' or 'private' spheres. Under feudalism, according to Althusser, the most significant of these institutions was the Church. It was supposed to convince people that the fixed hierarchy of monarch, lord and peasant was natural, inevitable and, if possible, just. In the equally exploitative but much more complex social relations of capitalism, however, the Church has been displaced by what Althusser calls the school-family couplet. These institutions have a particular economic role to play through the reproduction of labour power, although they also help to mould people's beliefs. As they pass through the family and the school, children learn not only the skills and know-how necessary for the positions they will occupy in the labour market, but also the self-perceptions, attitudes and rules of conduct which are part and parcel of the dominant ideology. Working-class children learn to submit to these rules, according to Althusser, while those destined for more prestigious jobs learn to manipulate them. Thus through the family and the school people are distributed in roughly the right proportions into various categories required by the division of labour-administrators, technicians, white- and blue-collar workers, and so forth.

(2) Ideology refers to the formation of human subjectivity through
the practices of a network of institutions (the ISAs).
The ISAs *function for* the economic but, according to Althusser, their *mode of functioning* is ideological. Their purpose is to ensure that people's apparently freely chosen patterns of conduct coincide with the systematic requirements of capitalist social (i.e. class) relations. This is achievable because of the imaginary relation through which people live these social relations. They do not experience themselves as determined by them, but as if they were each a self-determining, conscious agent freely making subjective judgements and choices. This 'as if' relationship is tied up with bourgeois legal and political categories of 'the person'–citizenship, contractual obligation, individual rights and responsibilities, freedom of the individual, equality of opportunity and so forth. This sense of selfhood is also produced in our daily negotiation of the images and conceptual patterns inscribed in the daily routines and rituals of school, family, firm, union, mass media, church and so on. The problem, however, is *how* the individual is bound into them.

(3) Individuals are transformed into subjects through the
mechanism of interpellation.
Interpellation refers to the way people identify themselves as being addressed by ideological systems. As we noted earlier, Althusser takes the structuralist view that ideology is concerned primarily not with consciousness, but with securing the unconscious structures which make people responsive to particular representations. This model is derived from a proposition in the psychoanalyst Jacques Lacan's reading of Freud: that the infant takes up a position within the symbolic order of culture (i.e. becomes a subject) as it perceives itself being addressed as a separate, finite subject by the Mother. The subject can only recognize itself *as a subject* in the 'reflection' provided by the image of the Other, which for Althusser

becomes the Subject with a capital S. It is this process of reflection and recognition that makes up the specular mechanism of ideology. Althusser illustrates his argument with reference to Christianity, in which God is the addressing Subject, the believer the subject addressed. It applies equally to the state's address to the citizen, the teacher's address to the student, television's address to the viewer and so on.

Foucault's scepticism

Foucault's differences from Althusser, like the self-critical changes in Althusser's own work, can in part be explained by broader political and intellectual struggles – particularly Foucault's rejection of claims by the Communist (or any other) Party to speak for or represent oppressed groups. This history is charted in a pair of useful articles by Peter Dews (1979; 1980); what matters here are Foucault's theoretical objections to an Althusserian conception of ideology. In his 1977 interview 'Truth and power', extracts from which are republished in this volume, Foucault declares that the notion of ideology is 'difficult to make use of' for three reasons (p.91).

(1) 'Like it or not, [ideology] always stands in virtual opposition to something else which is supposed to count as truth.'
This objection is to the binary opposition between the ideological and what is true or rational that governs most sociological and Marxist analysis. Although the ISAs essay represents a partial revision and loosening of Althusser's earlier theory, which drew a particularly rigid distinction between science and ideology, it still presents ideology as an imaginary *distortion* of people's *real* conditions of existence. This presupposes the possibility of a non-distorted account of that relationship – which would be the 'true' or 'real' knowledge of science. For Althusser, science is true, but everywhere people labour under the illusion that ideology is true.

Foucault rejects this distinction between 'scientific' truth and 'ideological' distortion. Instead of trying to trace back the epistemological basis of what is accepted as true, it is more profitable in his view to study in historical detail 'how effects of truth are produced within discourses which are themselves neither true nor false'. Foucault, in short, is a pragmatist. He refuses to engage with epistemological questions (to the rage and despair of his critics) because, from his perspective, there is little of interest to say about Truth with a capital T. Despite strenuous efforts over many centuries, philosophers and scientists still have not managed to get behind discourse to reveal something which it 'corresponds' to, which it is 'grounded' in, or which it 'expresses'. So instead of banging his head against the brick wall of epistemology, Foucault examines how truth is produced in discourse, how it is implicated and deployed in social practices, and how 'regimes of truth' can have profound social and cultural consequences.

(2) 'The concept of ideology refers, necessarily I think, to something of the order of a subject.'

This statement condenses two objections. One derives from the anti-humanism that Foucault shares with Althusser. Both reject the attempt to trace ideas and beliefs to an origin in human consciousness. Both attempt to explain how the subject is *produced* in historically specific forms through cultural practices. But they provide very different accounts of how this production is achieved.

Althusser, as we have seen, attempts both to identify the apparently eternal and universal mechanisms of the unconscious which are the precondition for subjectivity and also to show how ideology creates subjects in the forms necessary for historically variable relations of production – an impossible task, as critics have pointed out. Foucault does not attempt to emulate this juggling trick. Rather than propose a better theory for linking social relations to psychic mechanisms, he focuses historically on the techniques of subjectification which have emerged in the modern era. This approach to subjectification does not require a theory of ideology, he claims: ' . . . power relations can materially penetrate the body in depth, without depending even on the mediation of the subject's own representations. If power takes hold in the body, this isn't through its having first to be interiorised in people's consciousness' (1980, p.196). Here, of course, Foucault implies a definition of ideology in terms of consciousness – which is just the sort of conception that Althusser for one explicitly rejected.

The other aspect of Foucault's objection to the ideology/subject link turns on his refusal to root theories, strategies and practices in subjectivized social forces like 'the ruling class', 'the State' or 'society'. This sort of reference back to an originating source, common to most perspectives in the sociology of knowledge and especially prevalent in Marxism, conflicts with Foucault's insistence that such categories are themselves constructed within particular discursive regimes, and his emphasis on the dispersal and diffusion of power through institutional techniques and the human sciences. That does not mean that Foucault denies the existence of social classes, but simply that, for him, these cannot be accepted theoretically as the subjects and origin of history. In a 1977 interview, for example, Foucault indicates the nature and the limits of his objection:

> . . . one can say that the strategy of moralising the working class is that of the bourgeoisie. One can even say that it's the strategy which allows the bourgeois class to be the bourgeois class and exercise its domination. But what I don't think one can say is that it's the bourgeois class on the level of its ideology or its economic project which, as a sort of at once real and fictive subject, invented and forcibly imposed this strategy on the working class . . . And yet [the moralization of the working class] was accomplished, because it met the urgent need to master a vagabond, floating labour force. So the objective existed and the strategy was developed, with ever-growing coherence, but without it being necessary to attribute it to a subject which makes the law, pronouncing in the form of 'Thou shalt' and 'Thou shalt not'.
> (Foucault, 1980, pp.203–4)

In the 'Truth and power' interview, Foucault argues in a similar vein – and perhaps as an implied riposte to Althusser's overextended version of the state in the ISAs essay – that relations of power 'necessarily extend beyond the limits of the State' (p.92). Jacques Donzelot, who shares Foucault's perspective, has made the point even more emphatically. Power, he argues, must be considered 'as a specific phenomenon, irreducible to a subject (the State)'. This does not mean that the state is irrelevant or unimportant, but rather that the usual way of thinking about it should be turned back on its feet: ' . . . the State would never be a subject of history as such but a support for technologies and a resultant effect of governmental strategies' (Donzelot, 1979, pp.76, 78). Such questions about the diffusion of power and about whether techniques of subjectification can be systematically linked to political and economic factors have proved perhaps the greatest bone of contention between Foucault and even his most sympathetic Marxist critics. They are also central to his third objection to the concept of ideology.

(3) 'Ideology stands in a secondary position relative to something
which functions as its infrastructure, as its material, economic
determinant, etc.'
With this comment, Foucault not only rejects (like Althusser) notions about the ideological superstructure 'reflecting' or 'corresponding to' the economic or class base. He also calls into question Althusser's alternative formulation of ideology as representations and structures determined by the functional requirements of the capitalist economy. This is because he sees knowledge and power as indivisible. Discourses are powers in themselves; they therefore have no need to derive their power from some external source.

The main criticism of this line of thinking is that it can lead to an oversimplified and overblown view of power. The generalized assertion that 'power is everywhere' (1979, p.93) leaves no space for alternatives outside the rationality of existing forms of power. Although Foucault claims retrospectively to have been 'analysing power relations through the antagonism of strategies' (1982, p.211), his histories do not in practice allow for the possibility of such dialogue – for such oppositional strategies would have to be *coming from* somewhere, and Foucault insists that power is not *based* anywhere. His images of power saturating and oozing from every nook and cranny of the social formation, swallowing up everything in its path, can even suggest that power itself is the generative principle of social relations – in the sense that historical phenomena are seen as no more than the concretized instances of a power that precedes them.

But if power is conceived as less fluid than Foucault makes out – if, like mud, it sticks – then it is possible to argue that the strategies and techniques whose detailed ebb and flow Foucault charts may gradually produce more enduring institutional sedimentations and formations of power and resistance. If these processes are explored in conjunction with the productivity of economic and political relations, then a more familiar topography organized around the state, social classes and other condensations of social antagonisms once again becomes visible. To insist that these features are the outcomes and not the origins of a number of different practices and discourses does not necessarily mean that they cannot become sites and centres for the exercise of power.

In 'The subject and power' (1982), Foucault seems to edge closer to this sort of position. He identifies three types of struggle:

... either against forms of domination (ethnic, social and religious); against forms of exploitation which separate individuals from what they produce; or against that which ties the individual to himself and submits him to others in this way (struggles against subjection, against forms of subjectivity and submission).

In their historical manifestations, he argues, these can be 'either isolated from each other, or mixed together.' Nowadays, however, 'the struggle against the forms of subjection – against the submission of subjectivity – is becoming more and more important, even though the struggles against forms of domination and exploitation have not disappeared. Quite the contrary' (1981, pp.212–3). This division is clearly similar to the conventional distinction between political, economic and ideological instances in a social formation. What Foucault still remains silent about – the question begged by the vague notion of different struggles being 'mixed together' – is whether there is any systematic logic to the relationship between them. Thus Stuart Hall, for example, has accused Foucault of

> so thoroughgoing a scepticism about any determinacy or relationship between practices, other than the largely contingent, that we are entitled to see him, not as an agnostic on these questions, but as deeply committed to the necessary non-correspondence of all practices (Hall, 1980a, p.71).

> His 'power' is dispersed precisely so that it cannot, theoretically, be traced back to any single organizing instance, such as 'the state'. It voids the question of the economic precisely because it cannot, in his view, be crystallized into any set of global relations – e.g. class relations (Hall, 1980b, p.67).

From the other side of the debate, Donzelot shares Hall's view that Foucault cannot be integrated into the framework of classical Marxism:

> ... those who would see in this new level of analysis nothing more than the refined and obliging demonstration of the tentacular excrescences of the State are performing the same hasty recycling operated by the interpreters of Freud, relocating a subversive discovery within the terrain of the already-said and of practices which are current and popular.
> (Donzelot, 1979, p.76)

As Hall and Donzelot both suggest in their different ways, there is little to be gained from attempting to create a spurious synthesis between Althusser and Foucault. Nevertheless, it is equally true that the positions they represent still, to a considerable degree, define the field of debate about subjectivity and social relations. Indeed, this is reflected in the case studies around which this volume is organized – the couplet of the family and school to which Althusser attributed such importance in the ISAs essay and the history of sexuality to which Foucault's studies were devoted in the years before his death. Similarly, many of the authors of the readings explicitly or implicitly orientate themselves in relation to these positions. Some question the functionalist tendencies in both Althusser and Foucault – their apparent assumption, despite references to the unconscious or to corporeally-based resistances, that the processes of interpellation or subjection/subjectification actually work – by referring to the psychoanalytical premise that 'the unconscious constantly reveals the "failure" of identity' (Rose, 1983, p.9). The focus of the case studies is therefore not on ideology as a process of social cementation, but as a site of struggle. The approach of most of the readings is to work through the conceptual and methodological questions in the concrete analysis of specific historical instances of such struggles–instances, in other words, of social and symbolic 'circumstances directly encountered, given and transmitted from the past'.

References

ALTHUSSER, L. (1969) *For Marx* (1977 edn) London, New Left Books

ALTHUSSER, L. (1970) *Reading Capital*, London, New Left Books

DEWS, P. (1979) 'The Nouvelle Philosophie and Foucault', *Economy and Society*, vol. 8 no. 2

DEWS, P. (1980) 'The "New Philosophers" and the end of Leftism', *Radical Philosophy*, no. 24

DONZELOT, J. (1979) 'The poverty of political culture', *Ideology and Consciousness*, no 5

FOUCAULT, M. (1979) *The History of Sexuality*, vol. 1, London, Allen Lane

FOUCAULT, M. (1980) *Power/Knowledge: Selected interviews and other writings* (ed C. Gordon), Brighton, Harvester

FOUCAULT, M. (1982) 'The subject and power', Afterword to DREYFUS, H. L. and RABINOW, P. *Michel Foucault: Beyond Structuralism and Hermeneutics*, Brighton, Harvester

HALL, S. (1980a) 'Cultural studies: two paradigms', *Media, Culture and Society*, no. 2, 1980

HALL, S. (1980b) 'Nicos Poulantzas: State, Power, Socialism', *New Left Review*, no. 119

HENRIQUES, J., HOLLWAY, W., URWIN, C., VENN, C. and WALKERDINE, V. (1984) *Changing the Subject: Psychology, social regulation and subjectivity*, London, Methuen

HIRST, P. and WOOLLEY, P. (1982) *Social Relations and Human Attributes*, London, Tavistock

MAUSS, M. (1979) *Sociology and Psychology*, London, Routledge and Kegan Paul

MEAD, G. H. (1934) *Mind, Self and Society*, Chicago, University of Chicago Press

ROSE, J. (1983) 'Femininity and its discontents', *Feminist Review*, no. 14

WRONG, D. H. (1961) 'The oversocialized conception of man in modern sociology', *American Sociological Review*, vol. 26, no. 2, April

PART I

Subjects, Institutions, Social Relations

1 Psychoanalysis and Social Relations

Paul Hirst and Penny Woolley

From Paul Hirst and Penny Woolley *Social Relations and Human Attributes*, 1982. Reprinted by permission of the publisher, Tavistock Publications.

Psychoanalysis began as a revolutionary 'discovery' on the frontiers of medico-psychiatric practice, a frontier which involved the clinical treatment of 'hysteria' by means of hypnosis. But Freud's discovery took him outside of the clinical field in his therapeutic methods, and it forced him to create a new theoretical discipline which touches and disturbs all the human sciences. Freud's discovery had four linked components: that hysteria was a complex psychical formation, a neurosis, linked to the sexual history of the individual; that the 'symptom' was no mere physical register of mental disorder but was part of a pattern of significance; that these signs and the pathological formation could only be unravelled and made intelligible by bringing to light repressed unconscious psychic material; and that the means for doing so was the speech of the neurotic in a special relationship with the analyst, 'transference'. The comprehension of the therapeutic efficacy of this method, transference, took longest of all to recognize and work out. Baldly stated it appears compromising and sordid, that the analyst becomes the object of the analysand's libido and the pathological components of this sexual organization are worked out through their projection onto the analytic relationship. This libidinal attachment is crucial to the overcoming of the resistances to the unconscious expression of repressed sexual desires.

It is transference more than anything else which has limited the role of analysis proper in clinical-medical psychiatry. Other methods, developed initially in schism from Freud's own, have proved more adaptable to a hospital context, especially in the USA. Freud never became an 'anti-psychiatrist', never castigated the clinic or medical psychiatry as such. Psychiatry has tended to shun or to marginalize Freud, but not merely for reasons of distaste or fear of ideas like the unconscious, infantile sexuality, and so on. The 'transference neuroses', the primary object of analytic therapy, form a definite and limited class of mental pathologies. Freud tried strenuously to extend analytic *concepts* to cover and explain the psychoses, but psychoanalysis, as a therapeutic *method*, has faced a fundamental problem in dealing with psychosis, the difficulty of establishing a relation of transference. The reason is given by the classic analytic account of psychosis, a pathological and chronic narcissistic fixation of the patient's libido on his own ego and a withdrawal from reality into an internal psychic world or a delusional system.

Freud's discovery remained centred on a therapeutic practice and retained the concept of *pathology*. Neuroses resulted from a failure to successfully repress certain sexual desires, which remained active in the unconscious and found their expression, against conscious censorship, in the form of the symptom. The symptom is not a stable 'abnormal' sexual organization, thwarted and stigmatized by social norms, but an instance of failed repression. The irruption of unconscious wishes generates guilt, and secondary mechanisms of repression and denial which are necessarily ineffective and in turn generate further defence mechanisms. Neurosis is an economy of failed repression; a pattern of developing, transforming and migrating symptoms – often of baffling complexity. Analysis is thus often an equally complex process of uncovering successive diffuse pathological mechanisms and resistances; consequently analysis is often protracted and frequently broken off or terminated too soon. As a therapeutic practice, analysis has no simple measure of its efficacy. The challenges of psychologists like Eysenck, who claim it has a low rate of 'cure' and a high rate of 'relapse', are therefore largely beside the point. Analysis has never been nor claimed to be a therapeutic 'magic bullet', a psychic equivalent of penicillin.

Freud never conceived analysis as a practice of adaptation to accepted social norms, the conversion of neurotics into 'normal' family men or conventional wives and mothers. All too often neurotics are outwardly just this to begin with. It is the acceptance by the neurotic of the highest standards of current sexual morality and social life which poses the problem, for therein lies the source of guilt and self-reproach. Freud did not seek to convert the homosexual, for example, into a conventional paterfamilias, but, rather, to enable him to come to terms with his own, socially condemned, sexuality and to lead the fullest and most creative life, to overcome immobilizing guilt and fear.

However, Freud never assumed, as many psychiatric radicals do, that it was possible to create a social order in which all sexual desires could be met, in which repression, dissatisfaction, and pathology could be overcome. Indeed, he has often been criticized for this, for example, by the Marxist philosopher Herbert Marcuse in *Eros and Civilization* (1955). But Freud retained the concepts of pathology and perversion, not because he wished to enforce the prevailing notions of sexual discipline and normality, but because he argued that *all* human society necessarily repressed and directed sexual desires towards certain ends. Infantile sexuality is polymorphous and perverse. The child, far from being an asexual innocent, begins life as a demanding, narcissistic, and auto-erotic animal who is gradually forced to accept the existence of others, and certain socially sanctioned organizations of its sexual needs. The child is forced to recognize the demands of an extra-psychic 'reality', in the form of the necessities of association with others and the attainment of a pattern of sexual objects and gratification ('genitality') which will make possible the reproduction of new members of the species, themselves in turn subject to social necessities and the needs of the species. Freud retained throughout his work the concepts of a sexual *energy*, which must be directed and harnessed to certain objects ('cathexis'), and an evolutionary-biological notion of men as a species of animals who adapt to their environment through the information of certain psychic structures which produce the effect of reproduction. Culture, in organizing psychic life, attains the effects served by instinctively patterned behaviour in less complex and developed species.

It is the process of repression, denying and directing sexual desires and drives, which creates the split between conscious and unconscious mental systems. Central to this gradual process, a process of psychic development which does not correspond to an orderly succession of 'stages' based on physical maturation, is the taboo on incest, the forbidding of the mother or the father, brother or sister, to children of the opposite sex. Genital sexuality is established as the end to which psychical development is directed. Were this 'end' the culmination of a simple biological process, then the repressions, disasters, and failures of human sexuality would have no place, no conditions of existence.

Culture has a psychic kernel for Freud, the taboo on incest, and the triadic relationship between the father who imposes the law, who forbids the child the mother as a sexual object with the threat of castration, and who thereby forces the child to seek satisfaction in the foundation of a family of its own.[1] Human children are born with no *psychical* sexual identity; the sexual drives of the infant are bisexual, polymorphous, and perverse. It is through the 'Oedipus complex' and its resolution that sexual differences and sexual identities, men and women with distinct and complementary patterns of object choice, are produced. Sexuality, for Freud, is culturally implanted and enforced. The Oedipus complex is the universal kernel of all human culture. Culture is no given attribute of the species, it is something which is far from inevitable and is painfully attained in the development of man.

It is here that Freud goes beyond the limits of a new therapeutic method. Freud claimed to have discovered in analysis of neurotic patients something which went beyond the domain of pathology and which underlay it. Pathology was no particular defect to be located in the life history or biology of the individual. On the contrary, the neurotic individual was a product of a process which concerned the foundation of all human subjects. The neurotic differed from other men not in possessing repressed sexual wishes, but in the *failure* of this process of repression, not in the desire for his mother, but in the *failure* of its resolution and redirection.

It is here that Freud challenges and comes into conflict with the established human sciences of sociology and anthropology. Where, behind particular social norms and family institutions, Freud supposes a universal psychic kernel, a triadic nuclear relationship, the social sciences recognize only a diversity of family structures, customs, and institutions, and in place of his common human civilization they recognize distinct and radically different patterns of behaviour, ideas, and affect. Bronislaw Malinowski was the first social scientist to clearly draw attention to this dichotomy in the suppositions and concepts of those two bodies of knowledge concerned with human social relations and the attributes which follow from them. His *Sex and Repression in Savage Society* (1937) is an honest attempt to reveal the paradox for psychoanalysis of the existence of distinct family institutions. As he presents them, the familial institutions of the Trobriand Islanders have no place for the 'nuclear complex' which is the kernel of human civilization in Freud's theory. We will consider this debate here, not in order to plead the claims of one discipline against the other, nor to resolve the paradox in some higher synthesis, for such is not to be had, but to show how two theories of human civilization are both necessary, both produce valuable knowledges, and yet contain incompatible suppositions and irresoluble contradictions. As matters stand, the analysis of social relations and human attributes can be reduced to no theoretically consistent order, nor should we expect the 'progress of knowledge' necessarily to lead to some resolution. The idea that knowledges or sciences ultimately form some single rational order corresponding to the unity of 'reality' is a metaphysical proposition. It is one we must learn to lay on one side if we are to exploit all that psychoanalysis and cultural anthropology have to offer.

Before we turn to Malinowski we must consider in greater detail how and why Freud is led to the theory of a universal Oedipus complex.

Sexual instincts and the Oedipal order

Freud's theory of neuroses is concerned with the vicissitudes that befall the organization of human sexual desires in the process of psychical development. It is necessary therefore to consider what Freud means by sexual energy, or 'libido', and sexual 'instincts'.

Freud thinks of sexuality as based on an 'instinct'. His developed concept of *Sexualtriebe* is the product of a cautious and partial differentiation by him between *drives* (*Triebe*) and *instincts* (*Instinkte*). Freud does not simply reproduce contemporary biological conceptions of instinct in his conception of sexuality.[2] The biological concept of instinct refers to organically determined patterned behaviour. It is a response of the organism governed by its nervous system and identified with and triggered by a specific context of sensory information. A *drive*, by contrast, is a more complex somatic/psychological formation: the behaviour of the organism is not patterned by the organic elements which provide its conditions of existence. The context of expression, its objects, and the resultant pattern of behaviour are psychically shaped and determined. Drives, nevertheless, do have a definite somatic foundation and functional effect for the organism: drives are conceived by Freud as a determinate form of somatic *pressure* and as directed toward needs of the organism (self-preservation, release of tension, etc.). Freud never abandoned the *somatic* element in the drives; this element has a conditional and causative role, it has effects on the psychical apparatus (but *through* psychical representation) independent of any conscious choice on the part of the subject. Nor did he abandon the functional equilibrium of the organism (including its equilibrium of internal stimuli and its equilibrium in relation to the environment, its threats and excitations) as a crucial point of reference. Thus Freud remains within the field of the biological theory of instincts, although differentiated from it. Thus 'instincts' (drives) might be considered as a concept substituted for instinct (in the strict biological sense) in the analysis of an animal with higher psychical functions, Homo Sapiens. Freud attempted to retain contact with the evolutionary biology of the nervous system, the growth and enlargement of the cortex and the diminution of the relative role of autonomic nervous reactions in human behaviour.

In his concept of sexual instinct Freud is careful to avoid two other possible theoretical options. The first is *pan-sexualism*, the reduction of behaviour to a single sexual instinct as the foundation and source of all others, to a single determinative principle. Freud is far from 'reducing everything to sex' as ill-informed critics often claim. Pan-sexualism is generally accompanied by the essentialization and biologization of sexuality; it is closer to the conception of 'sexologists' like the Englishman Havelock Ellis than to Freud's view. Freud insists on the multiplicity of instincts. In the first stage of theorization, before 1920, Freud is concerned with two broad groups of instincts, those of self-preservation (corresponding to the 'reality principle' and the demands of the environment, demands mediated by the ego) and those of sexuality (corresponding to the pleasure principle, the economy of excitation and release of tension in the organism, an economy whose demands are mediated by the unconscious). In the second stage of theorization, inaugurated by *Beyond the Pleasure Principle* (1920), the opposition and antagonism is between the 'life instincts' (subsuming the first two groups) and 'death instincts' (instincts which seek release of tension through destruction and which are expressed in aggressiveness, whether directed towards others or the self). The death 'instinct' is not merely a metaphorical concept, it is not a simple biological *drive* but a complex tendency observed in organized matter and psychic life.

Freud thus avoids reducing human behaviour to sexual needs and motives conceived in the narrow sense, of genital and perverse adult sexuality. The sexual instinct is somatic in foundation but it has no given form. In the beginning it is polymorphous and perverse, and need not be expressed in terms of objects or ends commonly regarded as 'sexual'. It is not directed toward the preservation and perpetuation of the organism, and its demands for satisfaction expressed by the unconscious pay no regard to the reality principle or to socially accepted or recognized modes of gratification.

The second rejected theoretical option is the multiplication of instincts or drives, the identification of distinct patterns of behaviour–eating, sexuality, aggression, etc.–and the ascription of each to a distinct motivating instinct. Freud thus avoids the forms of circularity to be found in the explanations of human behaviour by contemporaries like William McDougall.

In his major theoretical work on the theory of sexual instincts and their organization, *Three Essays on the Theory of Sexuality* (1905), Freud considers the different combinations of the *object*, *aim* and *source* of the drive. Sexuality is in no sense confined to genitality. Freud considers all the various complexities of infantile sexual development and the possibilities of its partial, or 'arrested', resolution, the aberrant or perverse forms of adult sexuality. The object, aim, and source of the sexual instincts are in no sense given, and distinct combinations of these three components are possible. 'The *object* of an instinct is the thing in regard to which or through which the instinct is able to achieve its aim.' The *aim* is a specific form of pressure and release of tension (pressure), psychically encoded. The *source* is the bodily site or process of excitation. Virtually any orifice, organ, or function can serve as the source of a sexual aim. Freud here radically rejects any automatic process of sexual excitation or any given associated behaviour. He is unable to locate this diverse and complex somatic pressure in any specific physiological mechanism, in any gland, secretion, or hormone (but he *would* have done so *had* such biological knowledges been available to him – they are no more available to us). *But,* the *Three Essays* should not be regarded as a monument to relativism, as contending that sexual desire is merely conventional and a matter of personal preference. The notion of somatic basis remains crucial. Freud constantly gives expression to this in the 'economic' metaphors of pressure/tension and the necessity of its release through cathexis on objects. The somatic component of the instinct (or drive) is necessary to its insistence on the psyche and to the non-voluntary nature of its pressure and effects.

Sexuality is thus in the first instance a somatically definite but expressionally diffuse *pressure*. It is a pressure because energy is bound in it and seeks expression through it. Somatic sexual energy is the basis of *all* psychic energy, libido serves as the 'fuel' of the psychic engine. Libido serves as the foundation of *all* psychical functions: complex thought, art, science, and industry are 'sublimated' sexual energy. The objective of the *Three Essays*, the different organizations of the object, aim, and source, arises from the fact that sexuality is *psychically constructed*: libidinal energy is psychically bound into definite forms of excitation and discharge. This binding takes place through the developmental history of the individual, through the intersection between an inherited instinctual 'constitution' (individuals differ in their predispositions and capacities), and the particular circumstances of his or her family, experiences, and so on. The diffuseness of the instinct, its construction through psychical forms, and the consequent 'binding' of energy to particular psychic contents create the space for a wide range of possible combinations of object, aim, and source. The somatic diffuseness of the drive gives rise to psychically patterned difference. It is this crucial intervention of psychic significance in the direction and formation of the drive which distinguishes it from any given sexual 'need' and it is the binding of somatic energy which gives a necessity and consistency to the psychical pattern thus established which goes beyond any matter of conscious choice or any mere attribution of social value or cultural significance.

But sexual energy, however necessary to the economy of the whole somatic-psychical system, is diffuse. The somatic component of the sexual instincts, because the behaviour of the organism is largely determined by the autonomous activity of the higher brain centres, cannot be effective in and as itself. How does what is without direct psychical organization (somatic pressure/energy), and, therefore, without psychical effectiveness, acquire it? The libido becomes effective, becomes organized and, therefore, a psychically effective pressure through what Freud calls the *'psychical representative'* of the drive. Sexuality is constructed in its psychical representations, and these always take the form of a definite organization of the instincts toward certain objects and sources of pleasure. Thus there is no pre-given sexual 'aim'; sexuality can invest virtually any object, organ, or activity. The development of a particular personal organization of the instincts proceeds through two linked processes:

1   Through attachment to the functions of the 'life instincts' – a process Freud called 'anaclisis' or propping. The sexual instincts attach themselves to, or are propped up by, other sources of excitation and spheres of activity. Thus the infant comes to derive pleasure from the necessary activity of sucking at the mother's breast; bodily functions (feeding, thumb-sucking, defecating, etc.) become the school and model for the excitation of sexual instincts. Sexuality is *always* a derived form, there is no original or primal sexuality. Thus the auto-eroticism of the infant is not something it is born with, it is a development subsequent to an anaclitic constitution of the sexual instincts. (For a discussion of 'propping', see Laplanche, 1976, pp. 15–18.)

2   Through phantasy. Propping provides linkages between sexual instinct and the order of excitation and activity. Phantasy is the primary form in which sexual instincts become organized through their 'psychical representatives'. Phantasy is the psychical construction of desire, the construction of imagined sexual objects and means of satisfaction. Infantile and unconscious adult phantasies bear no relation to 'reality' in the sense of sanctioned adult genital sexual activity. The desire constructed in phantasy must be repressed and attached to the sanctioned genital order.

But this order is not easily attained. The child's sexuality must be both directed and yet repressed in the considerable period before it becomes capable of adult sexual activity. At the same time the child must be formed as a social agent or subject, capable of playing its part in social relations. Thus the organization of the instincts cannot be random, the field of object choice must be rigidly structured. The child must identify with his father before he can *be* a father, and he must identify with something more than the particular individual who confronts him. In other words, genitality must take a symbolic form. 'Father' must be a symbolic category with a power and significance greater than the child's immediate and stronger rival for the mother. It is the father-as-symbol who wields the threat of castration, a compulsion which forces the child to relinquish a phantastic (but perfectly real and 'satisfiable' – in displaced forms) sexual aim. It is the father-as-symbol with whom the child can identify long before he can become a real father. Genitality is thus a *psychical end* imposed on the process of the child's development from the beginning, an end he is brought to recognize and adopt as his destiny long before it can be 'attained'. It is imposed on all children long before and irrespective of their biological capacities to become mothers or fathers; the woman who will be sterile, the man who will be impotent are no less subject to this regime.

Thus for Freud this 'end' (genitality) is a symbolic one, part of the child's development as a social subject, and not a given somatic process of maturation.

The decisive stage of this process of sexual identification takes place long before puberty. But this does not mean that genitality should be conceived of as a social norm which is imposed upon the child, a 'role' with which he or she identifies and acts out. Freud's theory is as opposed to socially normative conceptions of genitality as it is to biological reductionism. Because the symbolic father exceeds the real father, because he wields a threat (castration) which social rules in the form of law actually proscribe the real father, the child cannot identify in the way he would with a social 'role'. In a sense *no* man can actually occupy the place of the father. Equally, the child does not choose or happen to identify with the sexual norm, or, on the contrary, choose to adopt some 'deviant' pattern. The biological and sociologistic conceptions of genitality fit very well together; for the sociological relativist genital sexuality is a merely given biological capability which may be accepted or rejected by individuals in their adoption of sexual roles. Genitality is, on the contrary, for Freud, a symbolic construct which dominates *all* organizations of the sexual instincts.

Genitality, the law of the father, is the symbolic matrix which governs *all* object choices. The *Three Essays*, as we have said, might appear on a casual reading to offer a relativistic theory of different and parallel object choices. Freud set no great store by social norms or conventions as such. We have seen that he clearly regarded the stigmatization of homosexuals as barbarous and unjust. This is because the law of the father is *not* a social norm; the homosexual's object 'choice' is a vicissitude of his sexual history and not merely an act of 'deviance', it has a psychic necessity which renders notions of 'deviant behaviour' absurd. Freud retains in the *Three Essays* the concept of pathology and perversion. They exist however in another register from concepts of deviation from the average or from social norms. Genitality is not a social norm from which other organizations of the sexual instincts deviate in the form of being *different*, since they are no less subject to its symbolic order. Genitality is the psychical end which dominates the symbolic and the process of development of the child as a social agent. Perversions and neuroses are developments under the sign of genitality, failures to resolve the Oedipus complex and, therefore, as much under the sway of this psychical end and symbolic order as 'normal' instinctual organizations.

The Oedipal structure, what Malinowski calls the 'nuclear complex', is the symbolic system of places (Father-Mother, Brother-Sister) necessary to the constitution of genital sexual difference, to the construction of 'men' and 'women' who can in turn stand in the places of this symbolic system. We have stressed Freud's commitment to a sexual *instinct* with a somatic referent and have shown how, paradoxically, this makes the symbolic order – culture – necessary to the construction of sexual differences and identities. The libido is polymorphous, perverse, and bisexual. Sexual difference is psychically constituted and *physical* differences are both recognized and given significance on this basis. Physical differences in themselves cannot give rise to sexual identity: a biologically fully developed man whose libido is narcissistically fixated on his own ego simply confirms this point. Children's sexual identities are formed before physical sexual maturation. The significance of the male and female sexual organs is recognized before puberty and through the threat of (in the case of the boy) or recognition of (in the case of the girl) castration. Freud contends that both male and female infants believe they possess a *phallus*, the boy identifies it with his as yet tiny penis, the girl lives in expectation that hers will grow. These infantile imaginings are rudely shaken. But it is the symbolic phallus that makes recognition of sexual identity possible – through the threat of castration in the case of the boy it links the penis that is (and the Oedipal desire that must remain a phantasy) with the penis that will be. Sexual identity, far from being an 'obvious' physical matter, is symbolically constructed.

We can now recapitulate the elements of the symbolic-cultural order necessary to the formation of genital sexual identities. Central are a series of terms which give the father primacy: the phallus and the threat of castration, the denial of the mother *and* the sister to the male child. These terms make the incest taboo necessary. It is the proscription of the mother and the sister which installs the father in the primary place in the Oedipal system. The taboo on incest is the linch-pin of the whole system. For Freud the taboo on incest, the primacy of the father, and the Oedipus complex are necessarily human features of human culture. Now we have seen that the father is a symbol exceeding the 'real' father, who may be a weakling, absent, or dead, while the threat wielded by this father or spoken in the father's name by the mother, relative, or nurse is an act which, if carried out, would put its perpetrator in gaol as a violator of human laws. Freud's all-powerful and savage father, like the god of the Hebrews, might be said to dwell among us in at best a symbolic sense.

Totem and Taboo

But for Freud this symbol must be vivid, alive, and effective in the human psyche and the family of the Oedipus complex – Father, Mother, Brother, Sister – must underlie all forms of the human family. It is in *Totem and Taboo* (1913) that Freud tries to explain this psychic presence at the back of all human institutions and culture. In the book Freud tries to explain why all human societies, and savage peoples in particular, evince a horror of incest and also why primitive peoples practise certain rites in respect of totem animals which serve as the symbols for the clan. He denies that the taboo on incest is practised for eugenic reasons; custom prohibits sexual relations between persons where no threat of inbreeding is pertinent. Instead Freud links the taboo on incest with totemism. Incest and totemism form a system: the prohibition of incest is evidence of a repressed wish to commit precisely this act, whilst the ritual consumption of the normally forbidden totem animal in a common meal by members of the clan reveals an ambivalence towards it which shows that it symbolizes far more than a mere emblem of the clan. The key to this system is to be found in what Freud calls ' . . . a hypothesis which may seem fantastic' (*SE* XIII, p.141).

Freud links together three elements to form this hypothesis. Two are anthropological theses. Darwin's thesis in *The Descent of Man* is based on deductions from the behaviour of the higher apes, that early man too lived in 'hordes', in which a single dominant male kept all the females to himself and ruthlessly excluded his sons and rivals. W. Robertson Smith's thesis in *Lectures on the Religion of the Semites* is that the ritual killing and communal consumption of the totem animal was an important part of the totemic stage of the development of religion. The third element is based on Freud's contention that it is legitimate to draw a parallel between the results of the analysis of neurotics and the customs of primitive peoples, that the former can be used to illuminate and interpret the latter. Freud takes a case of his own, Little Hans, and one of Sandor Ferenczi's, Little Árpád, to argue that animals are symbols for the father. The totem animal is the symbol of the father, and the totem meal a ritual consumption of the body of the father.

This meal Freud argues is a symbolic memory of a *real* act. Freud proceeds to convert Darwin's hypothesis into a real event, a 'primal horde' dominated by an all-powerful father who kept the women to himself, who drove out or castrated any of his sons who dared to challenge him. The sons were driven to combine to kill and devour their father. But the feelings of the sons to their father were ambivalent – they hated and feared him, and yet they loved and admired him too. This ambivalence was the basis of a sense of guilt which they shared in common. From this guilt and remorse came a 'deferred obedience' to the father. This is an obedience possible *because* of his death, in which he became more formidable than ever he could be alive. The father they symbolized by the totem animal. And they united under the totem to institute the law against incest. This law ended the war of all against all for the women of the horde. Henceforward, a man may not possess a woman of his own clan, that is, a woman of the blood of the father-totem.

Freud was aware that his hypothesis was 'fantastic' and that 'this earliest state of society has never been an object of observation' (*SE* XIII, p.141). Even the simplest human societies are already divided into clans and already have a long history behind them (*SE* XIII, pp.162–63). Freud's hypothesis has been savaged by anthropologists – Freud himself was driven to refer to it as a 'Just-So Story' and a 'scientific myth' (*SE* XVII, pp. 122 and 135). But Freud retained it to his dying day. He also thought the memory of this 'primal event' remained with all of us to this day, that the Oedipus complex operated in its shadow. Freud was well aware that this involved the concept of a 'collective mind', such that the contents of the psyche were not a matter of happenstance, education, and experience in the individual but rather all individuals were connected with one interpenetrating psychic domain. This 'memory' of an event did not necessarily involve an inherited 'racial mind', and, therefore, the inheritance of acquired characteristics. Ontogeny (individual development) did not only recapitulate phylogeny (development of the species) as a biological process, through inheritance, but *within culture*.

Freud argued that this common psychic domain operated at the level of the unconscious and that the 'primary process' was universal in its basic contents and mechanisms:

no generation is able to conceal any of its more important mental processes from its successor. For psycho-analysis has shown us that everyone possesses in his unconscious mental activity an apparatus which enables him to interpret other people's reactions, that is, to undo the distortions which other people have imposed on the expression of their feelings. An unconscious understanding such as this of all the customs, conventions, ceremonies and dogmas left behind by the original relation to the father may have made it possible for later generations to take over their heritage of emotion.
(Freud, *SE* XIII, p.159)

The unconscious is thus only in part 'personal', and men's psyches interpenetrate in ways which conscious thought and custom cannot control and censor. A Viennese member of the liberal professions and an aboriginal denizen of the Australian deserts are linked, under the vast differences of culture and knowledge, by similar mechanisms of unconscious thought and similar desires. It is the universality of the primary process, its mechanisms of entering conscious mental activity, of evading censorship in the complex and displaced forms of symbolization we find in dreams of parapraxes, for example, which explains how it is possible to interpret dreams and other forms of symbolism across differences of culture and personal experience.[3]

Although Freud treats the murder of the primal father as a real event, he is clear that psychoanalysis itself provides the means to challenge this presupposition. Neurotics are tormented by guilt concerning impulses and desires which are 'always *psychical* realities and never *factual* ones' (*SE* XIII, p.159). The reports of childhood scenes of seduction, incest, and so on, given by neurotics in analysis generally turn out to be phantasies. For primitive man:

> the mere hostile *impulse* against the father, the mere existence of a wishful phantasy of killing and devouring him, would have been enough to produce the moral reaction that created totemism and taboo. In this way we should avoid the necessity for deriving the origin of our cultural legacy, of which we justly feel so proud, from a hideous crime, revolting to all our feelings. No damage would thus be done to the causal chain stretching from the beginning to the present day, for psychical reality would be strong enough to bear the weight of these consequences.
> (Freud, *SE* XIII, p.160)

This explanation has the advantage that it does not suppose a single 'event' transmitted in memory to the present day and constantly recreated. But it has the defect that it presupposes the Oedipal-symbolic order *ab initio* – for the symbolic father is never the *real* father and the threat of castration was never *really* carried out. This explanation cannot serve to explain the *origin* of the symbolic system of the Oedipus complex.[4]

Before turning to criticisms of Freud's views, a number of points of clarification need to be made. Firstly, in *Totem and Taboo* Freud is not offering an explanation of the origin of human social life or association as such. Freud is indifferent to sociological considerations, and does not differentiate and characterize social relations as phenomena distinct from the psychic. Freud's concepts of social organization proper are generally hazy – he tends to refer to 'civilization'.

Malinowski is, therefore, wrong to suppose that Freud considers the 'primal horde' to be in a pure state of nature.[5] We have seen that sexuality is in no sense 'natural' for Freud – he is not concerned with the transition from nature to culture, from pure instinct to law. Men exist in definite relations of psychic association *before* the institution of totemic clans; in an ambivalent relation to their father, and a bond (with a libidinal-homosexual component) one to another. Freud is explaining the origin of the incest taboo, *not society*, so that whilst the brothers enter into a social contract which institutes the taboo, they already share relations of association and co-operation with one another. This is confirmed by Freud's later remarks on *Totem and Taboo*. In *Group Psychology and the Analysis of the Ego* (1921) Freud treats the primal horde as a 'group' – the brothers are bound in a common affective tie to the dominant father just as the members of a group are to their leader (*SE* XVIII, pp. 122-3). In *Civilization and its Discontents* the horde is regarded as a 'family', a stable association, lacking but 'one essential feature of civilization, that is, the arbitrary will of its head, the father, was unrestricted' (*SE* XXI, pp. 99-100).

Secondly, Freud is not concerned to explain institutions in the way a sociologist or anthropologist would. He derives religion, law, and custom directly from the dynamics of the psyche. He explains institutions as resulting from collective psychic states; thus a 'sense of guilt' (*SE* XIII, p.143) leads the brothers to venerate the father in the form of the totem.

It should be said straight away that the explanatory devices used in *Totem and Taboo* are in no sense peculiar to Freud. *Totem and Taboo* has all the defects of contract theories: an institution is explained as the product of an instituting *event*: men came together and agreed to make it so. Contract theories are no fabulous relic of the pre-history of scientific social thought. The generation of social relations from the 'interaction' of individuals continues to be a theoretical device: Talcott Parsons uses the interaction of an abstract Ego and Alter to explain the development of patterned expectations of conduct in *The Social System* (1951); Peter Berger and Thomas Luckmann in *The Social Construction of Reality* (1967) are forced to invent their own 'Just-So Story', the interaction of two isolated individuals, to explain the origin of language. But Freud's totemic contract does echo some of the traditional features of classical contract theory. John Locke in his *Second Treatise of Government* explained the development of *political* society, or government and instituted law, by means of a social contract but this contract is possible because it is made by the members of an already existing human society or association. Freud explains the formation of the Oedipal order but to do so he presupposes elements of the things to be explained or instituted by this order, sexual identities and the place of the Father. Far from explaining the origin of the symbolic, *Totem and Taboo* surreptitiously presupposes it. The consequences of the murder serve in effect to recognize and formalize the already existing patterns of emotion and psychic states. This defect of contract theory has been recognized since Rousseau, but these defective 'Just-So Stories' constantly recur when it is a matter of the explanation of *origins*. We have seen why Freud is driven to explain the Oedipal order in an *event*. It is no immediate out-growth of biology and yet it underlies all human psychic formations, it is present beneath the differences of custom and institution. The event, shattering and horrible, persists as a memory in the collective unconscious, with all its charges of guilt and ambivalence.

Psychic states give rise directly to institutions–to the incest taboo and the totemic religion. These institutions are fundamental, they underlie all the varied forms of kinship organization and all the later developed theologies and Churches. Thus Freud says:

> Totemic religion arose from the filial sense of guilt, in an attempt to allay that feeling and appease the father by deferred obedience to him. All later religions are seen to be attempts at solving the same problem. They vary according to the stage of civilization at which they arise and according to the methods which they adopt; but all have the same end in view and are reactions to the same great event in which civilization began and which, since it occurred, has not allowed mankind a moment's rest.
> (Freud, *SE* VIII, p.145)

This direct derivation of institutions from psychic states is fraught with problems. Institutions become mere effects of collective psychic states, a mere medium for projecting and resolving psychic conflicts.[6] But Freud in no way shows *how* psychic states give rise to institutions–why does *guilt* lead to the phenomenon of totemism in particular rather than some other institution? Freud in answering such a question would be forced to presuppose a common 'mentality' in which the germinal ideas of the Oedipal family and totemic religion are already present.

Freud's account is clearly unacceptable to any theory which is concerned to demonstrate the specific effects on thought and conduct of different institutional arrangements and the different consequences in conduct of elaborated belief systems and the kinds of entities postulated in them. Yet it is not without its parallels in sociology and anthropology. The famous sociologist Emile Durkheim considered all religion as in essence the veneration of a special class of things, the 'sacred' as distinct from the 'profane'. The 'sacred' transcends commonplace experience and special rites surround it, thereby reinforcing its uniqueness and mystery. In *The Elementary Forms of the Religious Life*–a book published in 1912, shortly before Freud's own–Durkheim too was concerned with the *origin* of religion. He thought its essential features were to be observed in its simplest forms and these were presented to us in the rituals of the Australian aborigines. Durkheim ends up explaining what he claims to be a category of the 'collective consciousness' by means of the *psychic states* of the individual members associated in collective rituals. Individuals form the idea of the transcendent or sacred in a state of exultation through experience of clan rituals in which they are 'taken out of themselves' (see Durkheim, 1915, pp.218–19). Thus Freud's work is no more absurd or bizarre than that of other men of his generation who sought to explain the origins of the family or of religion.

Freud had the misfortune to write just as one form of anthropological theorizing and investigative practice was about to give way to another, to base himself on the work of men like Fraser and Robertson-Smith. The new cultural anthropology based upon systematic field-work methods was about to confront him with materials which could not but be embarrassing. Bronislaw Malinowski's *Sex and Repression in Savage Society* has become an anthropological classic whilst *Totem and Taboo* has become an embarrassment and a scandal. To see why, to have catalogued all the anthropological errors and deficiencies of explanation, one has only to turn to the 1920 review by A. L. Kroeber of the English translation (in Kroeber, 1952, ch. 37).

Social relations and the psychical

Malinowski clearly draws out what is at stake in his challenge to Freud's thesis of the universality of the Oedipus complex: to psychoanalysis

> the Oedipus complex is something absolute, the primordial source . . . the *fons et origo* of everything. To me on the other hand, the nuclear family complex is a functional formation dependent upon the structure and upon the culture of a society. It is necessarily determined by the manner in which sexual restrictions are moulded in a community and by the manner in which authority is apportioned.
> (Malinowski, 1937, p.143)

Malinowski is here asserting that social institutions differ in their specific effects and that cultures mould individuals in terms of the types of entity and patterns of conduct they posit [. . .]

Malinowski points out that in the Trobriand Islands in Melanesia the family structure is radically different from that presupposed in the Oedipus complex. The Trobrianders reckon descent through the female line, the male child inherits property and social status from his maternal uncle, *not* from his father. The maternal uncle is an authority figure for the child, he represents discipline and social sanction. Relations with the uncle are reserved and difficult. The father, on the contrary, acts as a nurse and playmate. Relations with the father are intimate and affectionate. The child does not come into conflict with the uncle as a sexual rival, or with the father as a source of discipline. Infantile sexuality is not denied or repressed as it is in Europe – children and adolescents are allowed to engage in sexual play. Indeed, Malinowski contends that the Trobrianders are ignorant of the role of the father in procreation. They believe that children are conceived by the spirits of dead ancestors, Baloma, entering the mother, whilst she is swimming in the sea, for example. They have no reason to relate the orders of sexuality and paternity. This does not mean that Trobriand sexuality is without its conflicts or forbidden objects. The male child is forbidden the female members of his uncle's clan and, in particular, his sister. This form of incest prohibition is a consequence of the matrilineal system and the form of exogamy it presupposes. Trobriand society thus gives rise to a special and distinct form of 'complex', in which sexual-emotional conflicts can arise; these centre on the relation between brother and sister. The elements of conflict which are superimposed in the Oedipal structure are separated in the Trobriands, since even though the uncle upholds the incest taboo, he is not a direct sexual rival, while the father is not in sexual competition with the child nor does he represent social authority.

> In the Trobriands there is no friction between father and son, and all the infantile craving of the child for its mother is allowed gradually to spend itself *in a natural spontaneous manner*. The ambivalent attitude of veneration and dislike is felt between a man and his mother's brother, while the repressed sexual attitude of incestuous temptation can be formed only towards his sister.
> (Malinowski, 1937, p.80, our emphasis)

Malinowski proposes a theory in which culture moulds and mediates biological needs and instincts. Patterns of sentiment are created within the particular institutions of a culture; impulses and emotions are systematically organized in a particular social context. Culture meets biological needs and impulses but it determines the form in which they are met and socially expressed. Malinowski says: 'Thus the building up of the sentiments, the conflicts which this implies, depend largely upon the sociological mechanism which works in a given society' (1937, p.277).

The problem with Malinowski's account arises less from its attempt to assert the specificity of effects of social institutions or doctrines of entity than from its conception of sexuality. Malinowski recognizes *infantile* sexuality but only as a form of playing at genitality. Malinowski is clear that there is no given, biologically determined sexual behaviour – sexuality is organized and regulated by custom, not instinct – but he treats sexuality as *inherently* genital. He fails to consider sexual instincts as polymorphous and perverse. In a sense therefore human sexuality is given and unified at the biological level: sexual instincts are 'needs' which culture must both organize and meet. Sexuality is natural and the infantile attachments of the child for its mother cease 'in a natural spontaneous manner' when other sexual objects become available. Genitality is thus a natural outcome. Freud, as we have seen, is forced to explain the unity of sexuality at the level of its 'psychical representation' – to explain how genitality is attained as a *psychical* end.

Malinowski also refuses Freud's concept of the unconscious. He equates the concept of 'collective unconscious' with the group mind, and considers it a 'metaphysical' conception (Malinowski, 1937, p.277). Now this objection is an epistemological one: Malinowski here uses positivist criteria of the validity of forms of knowledge to eliminate a concept against which he has no other arguments to marshal. It is metaphysical and occult because it is not observable or an inference from observation. But the collective unconscious is *by definition* not an observable phenomenon, certainly not one which can be derived from the conscious testimony of informants. It is indeed a supra-observational concept but one which attempts to account for and explain definite 'observations' (which are far from being a *brutum factum*, since they are dependent on the practice of analysis, but then, nothing ever is). *All* complex concepts are 'metaphysical'. 'Culture', 'institution', 'rule' etc., concepts necessary to cultural anthropology, are not observables, but means of organizing and analysing statements of native informants. The collective unconscious is a correlate of the notion of an individual unconscious: it follows from the theses of the universality of the primary process and of the interpenetration of the unconscious thoughts of individuals despite conscious censorship. The unconscious cannot simply be bidden by social norms. The unconscious provides an independent dynamic element in subjects' connections with social institutions, one which is subject neither to considerations of physical necessity nor to those of the rules and conventions on which institutions depend. In ignoring this psychic level, Malinowski can treat sentiments as merely the effects of a pattern of culture. Men are united in their physical, biological, needs which cultures must in their different ways recognize and meet. But in respect of sentiments and thoughts they are different, artefacts of culture. Now this thesis has its place and its value in challenging biologistic and psychologistic conceptions of 'human nature' – of which the various sociobiologies are merely the latest variant. However, Freud's position has no affinity with these reductionisms, while Malinowski's theory of instincts and sentiments has all the defects of the culturalism it tries to avoid. Culture becomes a series of inexplicable and given differences. Each culture, moreover, imposes itself on its inhabitants as a universe, a totality, in which thought and action are specified in ways which happen to be distinct from elsewhere.

If Freud makes social relations the unmediated results of psychic states, Malinowski makes social relations, in the last instance, patterns of culture. Both positions have different faults. *Totem and Taboo* has a thousand weaknesses, it is neither convincing nor consistent. Yet Freud does in that book and in later works indicate that social relations, kinship structures, law, religion, etc. must mobilize and manage psychic forms that they did not create and on which they depend. In *Group Psychology and the Analysis of the Ego* (1921) and *Civilization and its Discontents* (1930) Freud considers the psychic foundations of complex human associations. Freud argues in the former work that groups are sustained by libidinal ties, that the members' libidinal energies are in part directed at the leader or at one another. This may appear absurd, and, indeed, Freud's account of the Church and the army treats them merely as bodies of individuals tied to a common leader. This would be a fatuous analysis of complex organizations if that was all one could say about them. To *ignore* this element in groups is, however, equally fatuous. Small army units are built on close ties and a sublimated homosexuality; willingness to face danger and ignore privation are based on more than discipline, belief in the purposes of the war, or fear of shame. Love for one's comrades, concentrated by isolation and suffering, leads to commitments on the part of masses of men which exceed duty or prudence. The intense attachments formed by English soldiers in the First World War, the development of paternal feelings on the part of the officers for the men despite differences of education and social class, and the estrangement from people at home are all instances of such libidinal ties, commonly reported in memoirs [such as Siegfried Sassoon's *Memoirs of an Infantry Officer*]. Political parties and similar groups can also provide such attachments, as can groups of religious disciples. To ignore the degree to which Nazi ideology and practices fostered this libidinization would be a serious error, since it clearly played an important part in attracting support and preserving unquestioning adherence to Hitler. Certain ideologies and party practices create favourable conditions for the formation of such ties: bourgeois centre parties are probably least effective in this respect.

In *Civilization and its Discontents* Freud considered another aspect of the question: man's 'unease' in civilization. Freud argues that social relations cannot be measured by the standard of the happiness of the individual:

> Here by far the most important thing is the aim of creating a unity out of individual human beings . . . . It almost seems as if the creation of a great human community would be most successful if no attention were paid to the happiness of the individual. (Freud, *SE* XXI, p.140)

Freud argues 'that necessity alone, the advantages of work in common' (*SE* XXI, p.122) will not hold men together. The reason is the Death Instinct. An inherent aggressiveness is the main derivative and manifestation of this tendency to seek release of tension in the destruction of the organism rather than in pleasure. This aggressivity is 'inherent' in that it is unrelated to circumstances; it reflects neither the functional biological needs of the organism, for territory, for food, self-defence, etc., nor social interests which need to be defended by violence. It is quite unlike what is postulated in modern ethological theories of aggression or territoriality in animals in that it has no adaptive or preservative function. It, like sexuality, exists in the form of psychical representation; it therefore exceeds in its capacity for negativity and destructiveness any biological instinct toward violent behaviour which would be confined to certain motivating stimuli and definite circumstances. Freud introduced this concept at a relatively late stage in his work and with some reluctance. It first appears in *Beyond the Pleasure Principle* (1920); he introduced it to account for what he called a 'compulsion to repeat'—in which distressing situations are reproduced or relived compulsively. Neither release of tension nor adjustment to reality could explain this phenomenon widely observed in survivors from the First World War.

Social relations depend on the libidinal binding of individuals into groups. In a group the members are united in ties of love which inhibit and deflect aggression one to another. The aggressive instincts are harnessed to the work of civilization as well. Civilization opposes aggressiveness by utilizing it, aggression is introjected, internalized and directed toward the ego. Aggression is linked with morality and governs the psyche in the form of the 'super-ego'. Civilization, because it inhibits the outward expression of the aggressive instincts, must constantly reinforce them in their direction against the individual in the form of a sense of guilt. 'Conscience' is far from being a purely social matter, it is tied to psychical forces which go beyond any particular set of customs and taboos. Morality, far from being merely functional to the social order, imposes too great demands on the ego precisely when it is most civilized and demands the highest standards of conduct. Freud argues both that the Christian commandment, 'Love thy neighbour as thyself', is the strongest defence against aggressiveness and that the civilized super-ego imposes unrealistic demands on the ego, requiring it to have unlimited mastery over the unconscious or id. This is the general paradox of civilization, not merely of Christian ethics, that its means of control of aggression produce both psychic unhappiness and the perpetual revolt of repressed unconscious wishes. Freud is thus far from regarding either custom or sentiments purely as a matter of social relations: social relations, the customs and institutions of particular peoples, intersect with a general psychic domain which is far from neutral.

We see here two quite different forms of theory and investigative practice brought into confrontation, one based on a practice of uncovering the unconscious of civilized European neurotics and the other on recording through intensive field-work studies the manifest reported culture and observable customs of 'primitive' peoples. Malinowski radically misunderstands, as we have seen, Freud's conceptions of sexuality and the unconscious. He is far from being a psychoanalytic ignoramus but he is trapped by his own theses and his own practice. Aware that his attempts to collect and interpret Trobrianders' dreams are doomed to analytic irrelevancy, he is stuck with a paucity of dreams, with a relation to his respondents very different from the analyst's relation of transference and, therefore, stuck with the 'manifest content'. Now the 'manifest content' of dreams is affected by the processes in which the unconscious wishes (the 'latent content') avoid censorship; dreams are like a complex code. The manifest content of *Europeans'* dreams could just as easily be used to 'refute' Freud. Analysts like Ernest Jones (1964) and Géza Róheim (1950; see esp. pp.29–30, p.159 and ch.3) have thus interpreted Trobriand customs and dreams very differently from Malinowski, and both find lurking behind them the structures of the Oedipus complex. Jones, for example, treats matriarchy as a derivative form from the Oedipal structure, a form of repression of its conflicts in the form of social relations. Now not only does this tend to reduce the Oedipal structure from a psychic-symbolic structure to a pattern of manifest institutions overlain by others, but, as Malinowski argues, there is no possible evidence, derived from field-work, which can substantiate it. Psychoanalytic anthropological interpretation suffers from a serious defect: where analysis includes a means, the 'transference', for bringing repressed material to light and at the same time a test on its interpretation, this is lacking in work like Róheim's, which–however interesting–is always impossible to assess. We cannot as things stand do what Freud wished to do, bring the materials revealed by the analysis of neurotics to the interpretation of the customs of 'primitive' peoples or, rather, we cannot rigorously and reliably do so.

The problem of relating the two practices does not lie merely on the analytic side. Anthropology has committed itself to a thesis and a method strongly represented in Malinowski's work. The thesis is that sentiments and activities are artefacts of culture. Conduct and belief are primarily determined by the particular institutions and culture of a people, although for Malinowski cultures must meet biological needs. This view is re-echoed against Freud, some decades after Malinowski, by Claude Lévi-Strauss. He argues, correctly, against the derivation of institutions from individual psychic states:

> social constraints, whether positive or negative, cannot be explained, either in their origin or in their persistence, as the effects of impulses or emotions which appear

again and again, with the same characteristics and during the course of centuries and millennia, in different individuals.
(Lévi-Strauss, 1964, p.69)

He goes on to say:

We do not know, and never shall know, anything about the first origin of beliefs and customs the roots of which plunge into the distant past; but, as far as the present is concerned, it is certain that social behaviour is not produced spontaneously by each individual, under the influence of the emotions of the moment . . . Customs are given as external norms before giving rise to internal sentiments, and these non-sentient norms determine the sentiments of individuals as well as the circumstances in which they may, or must, be displayed.
(Lévi-Strauss, 1964, p.70)

[We] are clearly in sympathy with this thesis. It is directed against reductionist theories which seek to explain social relations in terms of biology or psychology–a given human nature. But psychoanalysis, as we have tried to present it, is neither of these. The psychic-symbolic domain interpenetrates with culture and social relations. 'Civilization' in Freud's terms, is *more* than particular cultures or societies. Here is Freud's most radical point of contradiction with contemporary cultural anthropology. For anthropology sentiments and activities are particular to a culture, conceived as a limited and exclusive totality of social life. Anthropology in its thesis of cultural determination leaves no space for Freud's psychic-symbolic domain.

[Although we maintain that social relations have specific and radical effects in psychic life, at the same time we recognize] that social relations do not wholly encapsulate the psychic domain. It too has a specific effectiveness which cannot be reduced to biology or individual psychology. It has a collective and symbolic character. 'Culture', in the anthropological sense, is a totality which encloses and determines the way of life, sentiments, and actions of a people. It tends therefore to deny any place for Freud's form of analysis. We would argue that social relations do not form an inclusive totality in this sense. It should also be said that this psychic domain, postulated by psychoanalysis, is neither fully defined nor explained by it. *Totem and Taboo* represents a signal failure to do so. It has the negative merit of most clearly revealing the problematic nature of the relations between psychoanalysis and cultural anthropology.

Psychoanalysis provides the means to question a central concept of anthropology, the opposition between nature and culture. Lévi-Strauss attempts to use this opposition in his own explanation of the incest taboo, taking the incest taboo to be the foundation of *all* social rules (see Lévi-Strauss, 1969, p.XXIX and chs. 1,2; also 1971). He argues that the human family is based on institutional rules which deny nature, and it is precisely *because* it is a denial of nature, of a perfectly possible biological relationship, that the taboo on incest is the origin of culture. The rule establishes the first oppositions, between the possible and the instituted, from which follow all other oppositions and cultural differences. But if Freud is right about human sexuality, there is no given 'nature', a biological realm of possible actions, to be denied. It is not merely that 'incest' is a cultural category. *All* organization of the sexual instincts is psychical and symbolic. 'Nature' is a cultural category too. Freud's arguments lead us to recognize that there is no 'nature' *separate* from the psychic and symbolic, which can be opposed and denied. It is this implication of Freud's theory which makes it particularly difficult to put psychoanalysis and anthropology together as complementary human sciences. They are condemned for the foreseeable future to coexist in tension. We should try to make that tension productive rather than sterile. Recognizing mutual incompatibilities and limitations may be one route to doing so.

Notes

1 For purposes of economy in exposition we will treat the child as a male. It is often contended that Freud cannot account fully for the development of female sexuality with his concept of the 'Oedipus complex'. Juliet Mitchell in *Psychoanalysis and Feminism* (1975) argues that this is not the case; we can do no better than refer the reader to her work.

2 Sexual 'instincts' would thus better be rendered as sexual 'drives' but we retain here the usage of the Standard Edition of Freud's works edited by James Strachey, and continue to refer to *Sexualtriebe* as 'sexual instincts'.

3 Géza Róheim, whose anthropological work among the Australian Aborigines was supported by Freud and other analysts, strenuously argues this thesis in *Psychoanalysis and Anthropology* (1950) among other works. He gives interesting examples of virtually identical dream symbolism occurring in cultures as diverse as New York and the Normanby Islands.

4 Freud thus founded the characteristic element of the formation of human sexual identities on an *event*. Freud does not treat the murder of the primal father as pre-given or inevitable. The basic components of the Oedipo-symbolic have been transmitted in memory and myth from that day to this. Freud's explanation is thus neither evolutionary – involving a necessary succession of 'stages' – nor does it involve a concept of progress. Freud's account differs radically from writers like Morgan and Engels who set up a primitive promiscuity, matriarchy, and patriarchy as successive stages of culture – each more advanced than the preceding one. Matriarchy is not a stage *prior* to patriarchy for Freud – human sexuality is constituted by the law of the father throughout history in *Totem and Taboo*.

5 See Freud's discussion of the emancipation of sexuality from instinct, from direct excitation by olfactory stimuli. 'Civilization' is not an even but a gradual process: 'The fateful process of civilization would thus not have set in with man's adoption of an erect posture' (*SE* XXI: 90–100n). The 'horde', thus, is hardly natural or pre-social.

6 Malinowski observes at this point: 'As we saw, we are asked to believe that the totemic crime produces remorse which is expressed in the sacrament of endocannibalistic totemic feast, and in the institution of sexual taboo. This implies the primordial sons had a conscience. But conscience is a most unnatural mental trait imposed on man by culture' (1937: 165). As we shall see, Freud thought 'conscience' to be a far from unproblematic cultural imposition, that guilt has its own psychic dynamics.

22   *Paul Hirst and Penny Woolley*

References

BERGER, P. and LUCKMANN, T. (1967) *The Social Construction of Reality*, London, Allen Lane.

DURKHEIM, E. (1915) *The Elementary Forms of the Religious Life*, London, Allen and Unwin.

FREUD, S. *Complete Psychological Works*, *(SE)*, *(Standard Edition)*, ed. J. Strachey, London, Hogarth Press.

FREUD, S. (1905) *Three Essays on the Theory of Sexuality*, in *SE* VII.

FREUD, S. (1913) *Totem and Taboo*, in *SE* VIII.

FREUD, S. (1920) *Beyond the Pleasure Principle*, in *SE* XVII.

FREUD, S. (1921) *Group Psychology and the Analysis of the Ego*, in *SE* XVII.

FREUD, S. (1930) *Civilization and its Discontents*, in *SE* XXI.

JONES, E. (1964) 'Mother Right and the sexual ignorance of savages', in *Essays in Applied Psychoanalysis*, Vol 2, New York, International Universities Press.

KROEBER, A. L. (1952) *The Nature of Culture*, Chicago, Chicago University Press.

LAPLANCHE, J. (1967) *Life and Death in Psychoanalysis*, Baltimore, Johns Hopkins University Press.

LÉVI-STRAUSS, C. (1964) *Totemism*, London, Merlin.

LÉVI-STRAUSS, C. (1969) *The Elementary Structures of Kinship*, London, Eyre and Spottiswoode.

LÉVI-STRAUSS, C. (1971) 'The family' in H. L. Shapiro (ed.) *Man, Culture and Society*, London, Oxford University Press.

MALINOWSKI, B. (1937) *Sex and Repression in Savage Society*, London, Routledge and Kegan Paul.

MARCUSE, H. (1955) *Eros and Civilization*, New York, Vintage.

MITCHELL, J. (1975) *Psychoanalysis and Feminism*, Harmondsworth, Penguin.

PARSONS, T. (1951) *The Social System*, London, Routledge and Kegan Paul.

RÓHEIM, G. (1950) *Psychoanalysis and Anthropology*, New York, International Universities Press.

2   The Rediscovery of 'Ideology': Return of the Repressed in Media Studies

Stuart Hall

From M. Gurevitch, T. Bennett, J. Curran and J. Woollacott (eds) *Culture, Society and the Media*, 1982. Reprinted by permission of the publisher, Methuen Ltd.

Mass communications research has had, to put it mildly, a somewhat chequered career. Since its inception as a specialist area of scientific inquiry and research – roughly, the early decades of the twentieth century – we can identify at least three distinct phases. The most dramatic break is that which occurred between the second and third phases. This marks off the massive period of research conducted within the sociological approaches of 'mainstream' American behavioural science, beginning in the 1940s and commanding the field through into the 1950s and 1960s, from the period of its decline and the emergence of an alternative, 'critical' paradigm. This [article] attempts to chart this major paradigm-shift in broad outline and to identify some of the theoretical elements which have been assembled in the course of the formation of the 'critical' approach. Two basic points about this break should be made at this stage in the argument. First, though the differences between the 'mainstream' and the 'critical' approaches might appear, at first sight, to be principally methodological and procedural, this appearance is, in our view, a false one. Profound differences in theoretical perspective and in political calculation differentiate the one from the other. These differences first appear in relation to media analysis. But, behind this immediate object of attention, there lie broader differences in terms of how societies or social formations in general are to be analysed. Second, the simplest way to characterize the shift from 'mainstream' to 'critical' perspectives is in terms of the movement from, essentially, a behavioural to an ideological perspective.

'Dream come true':
Pluralism, the Media and the Myth of Integration

The 'mainstream' approach was behavioural in two senses. The central question that concerned American media sociologists during this period was the question of

23

the media's effects. These effects – it was assumed – could best be identified and analysed in terms of the changes which the media were said to have effected in the behaviour of the individuals exposed to their influence. The approach was also 'behavioural' in a more methodological sense. Speculation about media effects had to be subject to the kinds of empirical test which characterized positivistic social science. This approach was installed as the dominant one in the flowering of media research in the United States in the 1940s. Its ascendancy paralleled the institutional hegemony of American behavioural science on a world scale in the hey-day of the 1950s and early 1960s. Its decline paralleled that of the paradigms on which that intellectual hegemony had been founded. Though theoretical and methodological questions were of central importance in this change of direction, they certainly cannot be isolated from their historical and political contexts. This is one of the reasons why the shifts between the different phases of research can, without too much simplification, also be characterized as a sort of oscillation between the American and the European poles of intellectual influence.

To understand the nature of media research in the period of the behavioural mainstream hegemony, and its concern with a certain set of effects, we must understand the way it related, in turn, to the first phase of media research. For, behind this concern with behavioural effects lay a longer, less scientific and empirical tradition of thought, which offered, in a speculative mode, a set of challenging theses about the impact of the modern media on modern industrial societies. Basically European in focus, this larger debate assumed a very powerful, largely unmediated set of effects attributable to the media. The premise of the work was the assumption that, somewhere in the period of later industrial capitalist development, modern societies had become 'mass societies'. The mass media were seen both as instruments in this evolution, and as symptomatic of its most troubling tendencies. The 'mass society/mass culture' debate really goes back as far, at least, as the eighteenth century. Its terms were first defined in the period of the rise of an urban commercial culture, interpreted at the time as posing a threat, because of its direct dependence on cultural production for a market, to traditional cultural values. But the debate was revived in a peculiarly intense form at the end of the nineteenth century. It is common, nowadays – and we agree with this view – largely to discount the terms in which these cultural and social problems associated with the development of industrial capitalism were debated. Nonetheless, the mass culture debate did indeed identify a deep and qualitative shift in social relations which occurred in many advanced industrial capitalist societies in this period. Although the nature of these historical transformations could not be adequately grasped or properly theorized within the terms of the 'mass society' thesis, these were indeed the terms which prevailed when the 'debate' came to the fore again at the commencement of what, nowadays, we would want to characterize as the transition to monopoly forms of advanced capitalist development.

The effects which most concerned this more speculative approach can be grouped under three rough headings. Some were defined as cultural: the displacement, debasement and trivialization of high culture as a result of the dissemination of the mass culture associated with the new media. Some were defined as political: the vulnerability of the masses to the false appeals, propaganda and influence of the media. Some were defined as social: the break-up of community ties, of *Gemeinschaft*, of intermediary face-to-face groups and the exposure of the masses to the commercialized influences of élites, via the media. A very specific historical image came to dominate this scenario: the breakdown of European societies under the double assault of economic depression and fascism: the latter seen in terms of the unleashing of irrational political forces, in which the propaganda media had played a key role.

The Frankfurt School gave this critique its most biting philosophical elaboration [. . .] When, in the wake of fascism, the Frankfurt School was dispersed, and its members took refuge in the United States, they brought their pessimistic forebodings about mass society with them. Briefly, their message was: 'it can happen here, too'. In a way, American behavioural science – which had already taken issue with the early versions of this mass society critique – continued, in the 1940s and 1950s, to develop a sort of displaced reply to this challenge. It argued that, though some of the tendencies of mass society were undoubtedly visible in the United States, there were strong countervailing tendencies. Primary groups had not disintegrated. Media effects were not direct, but mediated by other social processes. Essentially, to the charge that American society displayed symptoms of a sort of creeping totalitarianism, American social scientists made the optimistic response: 'pluralism works here'.

Perhaps more important than the distinction between 'pessimistic' and 'optimistic' social predictions about media effects, were the distinctions between the theoretical and methodological approaches of the two schools. The European approach was historically and philosophically sweeping, speculative, offering a rich but over-generalized set of hypotheses. The American approach was empirical, behavioural and scientistic. In fact, hypotheses proposed within one framework were often tested, refined and found wanting in an altogether different one. It is little wonder that hypotheses and findings were not commensurable. Only those who believe that there is a given and incontrovertible set of facts, innocent of the framework of theory in which they are identified, which can be subject to empirical verification according to a universal scientific method, would have expected that to be so. But this is exactly what American behavioural science offered itself as doing. There are some intriguing transitional moments here which are worth remarking – in lieu of a fuller account. They can be encapsulated in the history of two émigrés. Lazarsfeld, a distinguished European methodologist, linked with, though not a subscribing member of, the Frankfurt School, became in fact the doyen and leading luminary of behavioural methodology in the American context. (It has been speculated that his success at the latter task may have had something to do with his early sensitization to more speculative European questions: certainly, he was a more theoretically sophisticated methodologist than his more technical colleagues.) Adorno, on the other hand, the most formidable of the Frankfurt School theorists, attempted, without any conspicuous success, to adapt his speculative critique to empirical procedures. *The Authoritarian*

Personality (1950) was a hybrid monster of just this kind – the product of a mixed but unholy parentage.

In the approach which succeeded the European critique, the main focus was on behavioural change. If the media had 'effects' these, it was argued, should show up empirically in terms of a direct influence on individuals, which would register as a switch of behaviour. Switches of choice – between advertised consumer goods or between presidential candidates – were viewed as a paradigm case of measurable influence and effect. The model of power and influence being employed here was paradigmatically empiricist and pluralistic: its primary focus was the individual; it theorized power in terms of the direct influence of A on B's behaviour; it was preoccupied (as so-called 'political science' in this mould has been ever since) with the process of decision making. Its ideal experimental test was a before/after one: its ideal model of influence was that of the campaign. Political campaign studies conceived politics largely in terms of voting, and voting largely in terms of campaign influences and the resulting voter choices. The parallel with advertising campaigns was exact. Not only was a great deal of the research funded for the purpose of identifying how to deliver specific audiences to the advertisers – loftily entitled 'policy research' – but the commercial model tended to dominate the theory, even in the more rarified atmosphere of Academia. Larger historical shifts, questions of political process and formation before and beyond the ballot-box, issues of social and political power, of social structure and economic relations, were simply absent, not by chance, but because they were *theoretically outside the frame of reference*. But that was because the approach, though advanced as empirically-grounded and scientific, was predicated on a very specific set of political and ideological presuppositions. These presuppositions, however, were not put to the test, within the theory, but framed and underpinned it as a set of unexamined postulates. It should have asked, 'does pluralism work?' and 'how does pluralism work?' Instead, it asserted, 'pluralism works' – and then went on to measure, precisely and empirically, just how well it was doing. This mixture of prophecy and hope, with a brutal, hard-headed, behaviouristic positivism provided a heady theoretical concoction which, for a long time, passed itself off as 'pure science'.

In this model, power and influence were identical and interchangeable terms: both could be empirically demonstrated at the point of decision making. Occasionally, this reductionism was projected on to a larger canvas and the impact of the media was discussed in terms of 'society' as a whole. But this connection was made in a very specific way. And society was defined in a very limited manner. A largely cultural definition of society was assumed. Class formations, economic processes, sets of institutional power-relations were largely unacknowledged. What held society together it was agreed were its norms. In a pluralist society, a fundamental broadly-based consensus on norms was assumed to prevail throughout the population. The connection between the media and this normative consensus, then, could only be established at the level of values. This was a tricky term. In Parson's 'social system' (Parsons, 1951) such values played an absolutely pivotal role; for around them the integrative mechanisms which held the social order together were organized. Yet what these values were – their content and structure – or how they were produced, or how, in a highly differentiated and dynamic modern industrial capitalist society, an inclusive consensus on 'the core value system' had spontaneously arisen, were questions that were not and could not be explained. Value consensus, however, was assumed. Culturally, Edward Shils (a collaborator of Parsons) argued, this broad band of values was so widely shared as to have accreted to itself the power of the sacred (Shils, 1961a, p. 117). If some groups were, unaccountably, not yet fully paid-up members of the consensus club, they were well on the way to integration within it. The core would gradually absorb the more 'brutal' cultures of the periphery (Shils, 1961b). Thus the democratic enfranchisement of all citizens within political society, and the economic enfranchisement of all consumers within the free-enterprise economy, would rapidly be paralleled by the cultural absorption of all groups into the culture of the centre. Pluralism rested on these three mutually reinforcing supports. In its purest form, pluralism assumed that no structural barriers or limits of class would obstruct this process of cultural absorption: for, as we all 'knew', America was no longer a class society. Nothing prevented the long day's journey of the American masses to the centre. This must have been very good news to blacks, Hispanics, Chicanos, American Injuns, New York Italians, Boston Irish, Mexican wetbacks, California Japanese, blue-collar workers, hard-hats, Bowery bums, Southern poor-whites and other recalcitrant elements still simmering in the American melting pot. What is more (a comforting thought in the depths of the Cold War) all other societies were well on their way along the 'modernizing' continuum. Pluralism thus became, not just a way of defining American particularism, but *the model* of society as such, written into social science. Despite the theoretical form in which the ramshackle construction was advanced, and the refined methodologies by which its progress was empirically confirmed, there is no mistaking the political and ideological settlement which underpinned it. Daniel Bell assured us, in *The End of Ideology* (1960), that the classical problem of 'ideology' had at last been superseded. There would be a range of pluralistic conflicts of interest and value. But they could all be resolved within the framework of the pluralistic consensus and its 'rules of the game'. This was essentially because, as another apologist, Seymour Lipset, forcefully put the matter:

> the fundamental political problems of the industrial revolution have been solved: the workers have achieved industrial and political citizenship; the conservatives have accepted the welfare state; and the democratic left has recognized that an increase in overall state power carries with it more dangers to freedom than solutions for economic problems.
> (Lipset, 1963, p.406)

The installation of pluralism as *the* model of industrial social order represented a moment of profound theoretical and political closure. It was not, however, destined to survive the testing times of the ghetto rebellions, campus revolts, counter-cultural upheavals and anti-war movements of the late 1960s. But, for a time, it prevailed. It became a global ideology, backed by the credentials of social science. It was exported with a will around the globe. Some of its force arose from the fact that what, in theory, ought to be the case, could be shown so convincingly and empirically to be, in fact, the case. The American Dream had been empirically verified. A whole number of decisive interventions in developing countries were made in the name of hastening them along this modernizing pathway. It is sometimes asked what a moment of political settlement and theoretical hegemony looks like: this would certainly be one good candidate.

The media were articulated to this general social scientific model in, principally, two ways. In the campaign/decision-making framework, its influences were traced: directly, in behaviour changes amongst individuals; indirectly, in its influences on opinion which led, in a second step, to empirically-observable behavioural differences. Here, media messages were read and coded in terms of the intentions and biases of the communicators. Since the message was assumed as a sort of empty linguistic construct, it was held to mirror the intentions of its producers in a relatively simple way. It was simply the means by which the intentions of communicators effectively influenced the behaviour of individual receivers. Occasionally, moves were announced to make the model of media influence more fully societal. But these, largely, remained at the level of unfulfilled programmatic purposes. The methods of coding and processing a vast corpus of messages in an objective and empirically-verifiable way (content analysis) were vastly sophisticated and refined. But, conceptually, the media message, as a symbolic sign vehicle or a structured discourse, with its own internal structuration and complexity, remained theoretically wholly undeveloped.

At the broader level, the media were held to be largely reflective or expressive of an achieved consensus. The finding that, after all, the media were not very influential was predicated on the belief that, in its wider cultural sense, the media largely reinforced those values and norms which had already achieved a wide consensual foundation. Since the consensus was a 'good thing', those reinforcing effects of the media were given a benign and positive reading. The notion of selective perception was subsequently introduced, to take account of the fact that different individuals might bring their own structure of attention and selectivity to what the media offered. But these differential interpretations were not related back either to a theory of reading or to a complex map of ideologies. They were, instead, interpreted functionally. Different individuals could derive different satisfactions and fulfil different needs from the different parts of the programming. These needs and satisfactions were assumed to be universal and trans-historical. The positive assumption arising from all this was, in sum, that the media–though open to commercial and other influences–were, by and large, functional for society, because they functioned in line with and strengthened the core value system of society. They underwrote pluralism.

Deviants and the Consensus

We can identify two kinds of breaks within this theoretical synthesis which began to occur towards the closing years of the paradigm's dominance, but before it was more profoundly challenged from outside its confines. The first may be summed up as the problematizing of the term 'consensus' itself. As we suggested, the presumption of an integral and organic consensus did leave certain empirically identifiable groups beyond the pale. Since, at first, these groups were not conceived to be organized around conflicting structural or ideological principles, they were defined exclusively in terms of their deviation from the consensus. To be outside the consensus was to be, not in an alternative value-system, but simply outside of norms as such: normless – therefore, anomic. In mass society theory, anomie was viewed as a condition peculiarly vulnerable to over-influence by the media. But when these deviant formations began to be studied more closely, it became clear that they did often have alternative foci of integration. These enclaves were then defined as 'sub-cultural'. But the relation of sub-cultures to the dominant culture continued to be defined culturally. That is, sub-cultural deviation could be understood as learning or affiliating or subscribing to a 'definition of the situation' different or deviant from that institutionalized within the core value system. The career deviant in a sub-culture had subscribed positively to, say, a definition of drug-taking which the dominant consensus regarded as outside the rules (with the exception of alcohol and tobacco which, unaccountably, were given a high and positive premium within the American central value system). For a time, these different 'definitions of the situation' were simply left lying side by side. Sub-cultural theorists set about investigating the rich underlife of the deviant communities, without asking too many questions about how they connected with the larger social system. Robert Merton is one of the few sociologists who, from a position within the structural functionalist or 'anomie' perspective, took this question seriously (Merton, 1957).

But this theoretical pluralism could not survive for long. For it soon became clear that these differentiations between 'deviant' and 'consensus' formations were not natural but socially defined – as the contrast between the different attitudes towards alcohol and cannabis indicated. Moreover, they were historically variable: sub-cultural theorists were just old enough to recall the days of Prohibition, and could contrast them with the period when the positive definitions of American masculinity appeared to require a steady diet of hard liquor and king-sized filter-tips. What mattered was the power of the alcohol-takers to define the cannabis-smokers as deviant. In short, matters of cultural and social power – the power to define the rules of the game to which everyone was required to subscribe – were involved in the transactions between those who were consensus-subscribers and those who were labelled deviant. There was what Howard Becker, one of the early 'appreciators' of deviance, called a 'hierarchy of credibility' (Becker, 1967). Moreover, such 'definitions' were operational. Deviants were positively identified and labelled: the labelling process served to mobilize moral censure and social sanction against them. This had – as those who now recalled the forgotten parts of Durkheim's programme acknowledged – the consequence of reinforcing the internal solidarity of the moral community. As Durkheim puts it: 'Crime brings together upright consciences and concentrates them' (Durkheim, 1960, p.102).

But it also served to enforce greater conformity to society's 'rules' by punishing and stigmatizing those who departed from them. Beyond the limit of moral censure were, of course, all those sterner practices of legal processing and enforcement which punished, on behalf of society, deviant infractors. The question then arose: who had the power to define whom? And, more pertinently, in the interest of what was the disposition of power between definers and defined secured? In what interest did the consensus 'work'? What particular type of social order did it sustain and underpin?

In fact, what was at issue here was the problem of social control, and the role of social control in the maintenance of the social order. But this was no longer simply that form of social order expressly revealed in the spontaneous 'agreement to agree on fundamentals' of the vast majority: it was not simply the 'social bond' which was enforced. It was consent to a particular kind of social order; a consensus around a particular form of society: integration within and conformity to the rules of a very definite set of social, economic and political structures. It was for these – in a direct or indirect sense – that the rules could be said to 'work'. Social order now looked like a rather different proposition. It entailed the enforcement of social, political and legal discipline. It was articulated to that which existed: to the given dispositions of class, power and authority: to the established institutions of society. This recognition radically problematized the whole notion of 'consensus'.

What is more, the question could now be asked whether the consensus did indeed spontaneously simply arise or whether it was the result of a complex process of social construction and legitimation. A society, democratic in its formal organization, committed at the same time by the concentration of economic capital and political power to the massively unequal distribution of wealth and authority, had much to gain from the continuous production of popular consent to its existing structure, to the values which supported and underwrote it, and to its continuity of existence. But this raised questions concerning the social role of the media. For if the media were not simply reflective or 'expressive' of an already achieved consensus, but instead tended to reproduce those very definitions of the situation which favoured and legitimated the existing structure of things, then what had seemed at first as merely a reinforcing role had now to be reconceptualized in terms of the media's role in the process of consensus formation.

A second break, then, arose around the notion of 'definitions of the situation'. What this term suggested was that a pivotal element in the production of consent was how things were defined. But this threw into doubt the reflexive role of the media – simply showing things as they were – and it put in question the transparent conception of language which underpinned their assumed naturalism. For reality could no longer be viewed as simply a given set of facts: it was the result of a particular way of constructing reality. The media defined, not merely reproduced, 'reality'. Definitions of reality were sustained and produced through all those linguistic practices (in the broad sense) by means of which selective definitions of 'the real' were represented. But representation is a very different notion from that of reflection. It implies the active work of selecting and presenting, of structuring and shaping: not merely the transmitting of an already-existing meaning, but the more active labour of *making things mean*. It was a practice, a production, of meaning: what subsequently came to be defined as a 'signifying practice'. The media were signifying agents. A whole new conception of the symbolic practices through which this purpose of signification was sustained intervened in the innocent garden of 'content analysis'. The message had now to be analysed, not in terms of its manifest 'message', but in terms of its ideological structuration. Several questions then followed: how was this ideological structuration accomplished? How was its relation to the other parts of the social structure to be conceptualized? In the words of Bachrach and Baratz, did it matter that the media appeared to underwrite systematically 'a set of predominant values, beliefs, rituals, and institutional procedures ("rules of the game") that operate systematically and consistently to the benefit of certain persons and groups at the expense of others?' (Bachrach and Baratz, 1970, pp.43–4). In this move to take seriously the power of the media to signify reality and to define what passed as 'the real', the so-called 'end of ideology' thesis was also radically problematized.

In part, what was involved in these questions was a return of the problem of power to the powerless universe of mainstream pluralism, but also, a shift in the very conception of power. Pluralism, as Lukes has suggested (Lukes, 1975), did retain a model of power, based around the notion of 'influence'. A influenced B to make decision X. Certainly, this was a form of power. Pluralism qualified the persistence of this form of power by demonstrating that, because, in any decision-making situation, the As were different, and the various decisions made did not cohere within any single structure of domination, or favour exclusively any single interest, therefore power itself had been relatively 'pluralized'. The dispersal of power plus the randomness of decisions kept the pluralist society relatively free of an identifiable power-centre. (Various gaps in this random-power model were unconvincingly plugged by the discreet deployment of a theory of 'democratic élitism' to up-date the 'pure' pluralist model and make it square more with contemporary realities.) Lukes observes that this is a highly behaviouristic and one-dimensional model of power. But the notion of power which arose from the critique of consensus-theory, and which Bachrach and Baratz, for example, proposed, was of a very different order: 'Power is also exercised when A devotes energies to creating or reinforcing social and political values and institutional practices that limit the scope of the political process to public consideration of only those issues which are comparatively innocuous to A' (Bachrach and Baratz, 1970, p.7)–a modest way of putting the ideological question. Lukes puts this two-dimensional model even more clearly when he refers to that power exercised 'by influencing, shaping and determining [an individual's] very wants' (Lukes, 1975, p.16). In fact, this is a very different order of question altogether–a three-dimensional model, which has thoroughly broken with the behaviourist and pluralist assumptions. It is the power which arises from 'shaping perceptions, cognitions and preferences in such a way that they [i.e. social agents] accept their role in the existing order of things, either because they can see or imagine no alternative to it, or because they see it as natural and unchangeable, or because they value it as divinely ordained or beneficial' (Lukes, 1975, p.24). This is an 'ideological' model of power, by whatever other name it is called. The move from the pluralist to the critical model of media research centrally involved a shift from a one- to the two- and three-dimensional models of power in modern societies. From the viewpoint of the media, what was at issue was no longer specific message-injunctions, by A to B, to do this or that, but a shaping of the whole ideological environment: a way of representing the order of things which endowed its limiting perspectives with that natural or divine inevitability which makes them appear universal, natural and coterminous with 'reality' itself. This movement – towards the winning of a universal validity and legitimacy for accounts of the world which are partial and particular, and towards the grounding of these particular constructions in the taken-for-grantedness of 'the real' – is indeed the characteristic and defining mechanism of 'the ideological'.

The Critical Paradigm

It is around the rediscovery of the ideological dimension that the critical paradigm in media studies turned. Two aspects were involved: each is dealt with separately below. How does the ideological process work and what are its mechanisms? How is 'the ideological' to be conceived in relation to other practices within a social formation? The debate developed on both these fronts, simultaneously. The first, which concerned the production and transformation of ideological discourses, was powerfully shaped by theories concerning the symbolic and linguistic character of ideological discourses – the notion that the elaboration of ideology found in language (broadly conceived) its proper and privileged sphere of articulation. The second, which concerned how to conceptualize the ideological instance within a social formation, also became the site of an extensive theoretical and empirical development.

In our discussion of these two supporting elements of the critical paradigm, I shall not be concerned with identifying in detail the specific theoretical inputs of particular disciplines – linguistics, phenomenology, semiotics, psychoanalysis, for example – nor with the detailed internal arguments between these different approaches. Nor shall I attempt to offer a strict chronological account of how the succession of concepts and disciplines were integrated in sequences into the paradigm. I shall rather be concerned exclusively with identifying the broad lines through which the reconceptualization of 'the ideological' occurred, and the integration of certain key theoretical elements into the general framework of the paradigm as such.

Cultural Inventories

I shall first examine how ideologies work. Here we can begin with the influence of the Sapir-Whorf hypothesis in linguistic anthropology: an idea which, though never picked up in detail, suggests some important continuities between the new paradigm and some previous work, especially in social anthropology. The Sapir-Whorf hypothesis suggested that each culture had a different way of classifying the world. These schemes would be reflected, it argued, in the linguistic and semantic structures of different societies. Lévi-Strauss worked on a similar idea, though he gradually became less interested in the cultural specificity of each society's classification system, and more involved with outlining the universal 'laws' of signification – a universal transformational cultural 'grammar', common to all cultural systems – associated with the cognitive function, the laws of the mind, and with thinking as such. Lévi-Strauss performed such an analysis on the cultural systems and myths of so-called 'primitive' societies – 'societies without history', as he called them. These examples were well fitted to his universalism, since their cultural systems were highly repetitive, consisting often of the weaving together of different transformations on the same, very limited classificatory 'sets'. Though the approach did not, clearly, hold so well for societies of more continuous and extensive historical transformation, the general idea proved a fruitful one: it showed how an apparently 'free' construction of particular ideological discourses could be viewed as transformations worked on the same, basic, ideological grid. In this, Lévi-Strauss was following Saussure's (1960) call for the development of a general 'science of signs' – semiology: the study of 'the life of signs at the heart of social life' (Lévi-Strauss, 1967, p.16). Potentially, it was argued, the approach could be applied to all societies with a great variety of cultural systems. The name most prominently associated with this broadening of 'the science of signs' was that of Roland Barthes, whose work on modern myths, *Mythologies*, is a *locus classicus* for the study of the intersection of myth, language and ideology. The further extrapolation – that whole societies and social practices apart from language could also be analysed 'on the model of a language' – was subsequently much developed, especially in Marxist structuralism: though the germ of the idea was to be found in Lévi-Strauss, who analysed kinship relations in primitive societies in just this way (i.e. on a communicative model – the exchange of goods, messages and women) (Lévi-Strauss, 1969).

The structuralist strand is, clearly, the most significant one, theoretically, in this development. But we should note that similar pointers could be found in theoretical approaches far removed from the universe of structuralism. It was also present in the 'social construction of reality' approach, developed by Berger and Luckmann (1966). Interactionist deviancy theory, which we earlier suggested first identified the question of 'the definition of the situation' and 'who defines whom?' also moved, though more tentatively, in the same direction. David Matza's book, *Becoming Deviant*, concluded with a strange and wayward section, intriguingly entitled 'Signification' (Matza, 1969). Also relevant was the work of the ethnomethodologists, with their concern for the strategies involved in the understanding of everyday situations, the form of practical accounting by means of which societal members produced the social knowledge they used to make themselves understood, and their increasing attention to conversational strategies.

In the structuralist approach, the issue turned on the question of signification.

This implies, as we have already said, that things and events in the real world do not contain or propose their own, integral, single and intrinsic meaning, which is then merely transferred through language. Meaning is a social production, a practice. The world has to be *made to mean*. Language and symbolization is the means by which meaning is produced. This approach dethroned the referential notion of language, which had sustained previous content analysis, where the meaning of a particular term or sentence could be validated simply by looking at what, in the real world, it referenced. Instead, language had to be seen as the medium in which specific meanings are produced. What this insight put at issue, then, was the question of which kinds of meaning get systematically and regularly constructed around particular events. Because meaning was not given but produced, it followed that different kinds of meaning could be ascribed to the same events. Thus, in order for one meaning to be regularly produced, it had to win a kind of credibility, legitimacy or taken-for-grantedness for itself. That involved marginalizing, down-grading or de-legitimating alternative constructions. Indeed, there were certain kinds of explanation which, given the power and credibility acquired by the preferred range of meanings were literally unthinkable or unsayable (see Hall *et al.*, 1977). Two questions followed from this. First, how did a dominant discourse warrant itself as *the* account, and sustain a limit, ban or proscription over alternative or competing definitions? Second, how did the institutions which were responsible for describing and explaining the events of the world – in modern societies, the mass media, *par excellence* – succeed in maintaining a preferred or delimited range of meanings in the dominant systems of communication? How was this active work of privileging or giving preference practically accomplished?

This directed attention to those many aspects of actual media practice which had previously been analysed in a purely technical way. Conventional approaches to media content had assumed that questions of selection and exclusion, the editing of accounts together, the building of an account into a 'story', the use of particular narrative types of exposition, the way the verbal and visual discourses of, say, television were articulated together to make a certain kind of sense, were all merely technical issues. They abutted on the question of the social effects of the media only in so far as bad editing or complex modes of narration might lead to incomprehension on the viewer's part, and thus prevent the pre-existing meaning of an event, or the intention of the broadcaster to communicate clearly, from passing in an uninterrupted or transparent way to the receiver. But, from the viewpoint of signification, these were all elements or elementary forms of a social practice. They were the means whereby particular accounts were constructed. Signification was a social practice because, within media institutions, a particular form of social organization had evolved which enabled the producers (broadcasters) to employ the means of meaning production at their disposal (the technical equipment) through a certain practical use of them (the combination of the elements of signification identified above) in order to produce a product (a specific meaning) (see Hall, 1975). The specificity of media institutions therefore lay precisely in the way a *social practice* was organized so as to produce a *symbolic product.* To construct *this* rather than *that* account required the specific choice of certain means (selection) and their articulation together through the practice of meaning production (combination). Structural linguists like Saussure and Jakobson had, earlier, identified selection and combination as two of the essential mechanisms of the general production of meaning or sense. Some critical researchers then assumed that the description offered above – producers, combining together in specific ways, using determinate means, to work up raw materials into a product – justified their describing signification as exactly similar to any other media labour process. Certain insights were indeed to be gained from that approach. However, signification differed from other modern labour processes precisely because the product which the social practice produced was a discursive object. What differentiated it, then, as a practice was precisely the articulation together of social and symbolic elements – if the distinction will be allowed here for the purposes of the argument. Motor cars, of course, have, in addition to their exchange and use values, a symbolic value in our culture. But, in the process of meaning construction, the exchange and use values depend on the symbolic value which the message contains. The symbolic character of the practice is the dominant element although not the only one. Critical theorists who argued that a message could be analysed as just another kind of commodity missed this crucial distinction (Garnham, 1979; Golding and Murdock, 1979).

The Politics of Signification

As we have suggested, the more one accepts that how people act will depend in part on how the situations in which they act are defined, and the less one can assume either a natural meaning to everything or a universal consensus on what things mean – then, the more important, socially and politically, becomes the process by means of which certain events get recurrently signified in particular ways. This is especially the case where events in the world are problematic (that is, where they are unexpected); where they break the frame of our previous expectations about the world; where powerful social interests are involved; or where there are starkly opposing or conflicting interests at play. The power involved here is an ideological power: the power to signify events in a particular way.

To give an obvious example: suppose that every industrial dispute could be signified as a threat to the economic life of the country, and therefore against 'the national interest'. Then such significations would construct or define issues of economic and industrial conflict in terms which would consistently favour current economic strategies, supporting anything which maintains the continuity of production, whilst stigmatizing anything which breaks the continuity of production, favouring the general interests of employers and shareholders who have nothing to gain from production being interrupted, lending credence to the specific policies of governments which seek to curtail the right to strike or to weaken the bargaining position and political power of the trade unions. (For purposes of the later argument, note that such significations depend on taking-for-granted what the national interest is. They are predicated on an assumption that we all live in a society where the bonds which bind labour and capital together are stronger, and more legitimate, than the grievances which divide us into labour versus capital. That is to say, part of the function of a signification of this kind is to construct a subject to which the discourse applies: e.g. to translate a discourse whose subject is 'workers versus employers' into a discourse whose subject is the collective 'we, the people'.) That, on the whole, industrial disputes are indeed so signified is a conclusion strongly supported by the detailed analyses subsequently provided by, for example, the Glasgow Media Group research published in *Bad News* (1976) and *More Bad News* (1980). Now, of course, an industrial dispute has no singular, given meaning. It could, alternatively, be signified as a necessary failure of all capitalist economies, part of the inalienable right of workers to withdraw their labour, and a necessary defence of working-class living standards – the very purpose of the trade unions, for which they have had to fight a long and bitter historic struggle. So, by what means is the first set of significations recurrently preferred in the ways industrial disputes are constructed in our society? By what means are the alternative definitions which we listed excluded? And how do the media, which are supposed to be impartial, square their production of definitions of industrial conflict which systematically favour one side in such disputes, with their claims to report events in a balanced and impartial manner? What emerges powerfully from this line of argument is that the power to signify is not a neutral force in society. Significations enter into controversial and conflicting social issues as a real and positive social force, affecting their outcomes. The signification of events is part of what has to be struggled over, for it is the means by which collective social understandings are created – and thus the means by which consent for particular outcomes can be effectively mobilized. Ideology, according to this perspective, has not only become a 'material force', to use an old expression – real because it is 'real' in its effects. It has also become a site of struggle (between competing definitions) and a stake – a prize to be won – in the conduct of particular struggles. This means that ideology can no longer be seen as a dependent variable, a mere reflection of a pre-given reality in the mind. Nor are its outcomes predictable by derivation from some simple determinist logic. They depend on the balance of forces in a particular historical conjuncture: on the 'politics of signification'.

Central to the question of how a particular range of privileged meanings was sustained was the question of classification and framing. Lévi-Strauss, drawing on models of transformational linguistics, suggested that signification depended, not on the intrinsic meaning of particular isolated terms, but on the organized set of interrelated elements within a discourse. Within the colour spectrum, for example, the range of colours would be subdivided in different ways in each culture. Eskimos have several words for the thing which we call 'snow'. Latin has one word, *mus*, for the animal which in English is distinguished by two terms, 'rat' and 'mouse'. Italian distinguishes between *legno* and *bosco* where English only speaks of a 'wood'. But where Italian has both *bosco* and *foresta*, German only has the single term, *wald*. (The examples are from Eco's essay, 'Social life as a sign system' (1973).) These are distinctions, not of Nature but of Culture. What matters, from the viewpoint of signification, is not the integral meaning of any single colour-term, – mauve, for example – but the system of differences between all the colours in a particular classificatory system; and where, in a particular language, the point of difference between one colour and another is positioned. It was through this play of difference that a language system secured an equivalence between its internal system (signifiers) and the systems of reference (signifieds) which it employed. Language constituted meaning by punctuating the continuum of Nature into a cultural system; such equivalences or correspondences would therefore be differently marked. Thus there was no natural coincidence between a word and its referent: everything depended on the conventions of linguistic use, and on the way language intervened in Nature in order to make sense of it. We should note that at least two, rather different epistemological positions can be derived from this argument. A Kantian or neo-Kantian position would say that, therefore, nothing exists except that which exists in and for language or discourse. Another reading is that, though the world does exist outside language, we can only make sense of it through its appropriation in discourse. There has been a good deal of epistemological heavy warfare around these positions in recent years.

What signified, in fact, was the positionality of particular terms within a set. Each positioning marked a pertinent difference in the classificatory scheme involved. To this Lévi-Strauss added a more structuralist point: that it is not the particular utterance of speakers which provides the object of analysis, but the classificatory system which underlies those utterances and from which they are produced, as a series of variant transformations. Thus, by moving from the surface narrative of particular myths to the generative system or structure out of which they were produced, one could show how apparently different myths (at the surface level) belonged in fact to the same family or constellation of myths (at the deep-structure level). If the underlying set is a limited set of elements which can be variously combined, then the surface variants can, in their particular sense, be infinitely varied, and spontaneously produced. The theory closely corresponds in certain aspects to Chomsky's theory of language, which attempted to show how language could be both free and spontaneous, and yet regular and 'grammatical'. Changes in meaning, therefore, depended on the classificatory systems involved, and the ways different elements were selected and combined to make different meanings. Variations in the surface meaning of a statement, however, could not in themselves resolve the question as to whether or not it was a transformation of the same classificatory set.

This move from content to structure or from manifest meaning to the level of code is an absolutely characteristic one in the critical approach. It entailed a redefinition of what ideology was – or, at least, of how ideology worked. The point is clearly put by Veron:

> If ideologies are structures . . . then they are not 'images' nor 'concepts' (we can say, they are not contents) but are sets of rules which determine an organization and the functioning of images and concepts . . . Ideology is a system of coding reality and not

a determined set of coded messages . . . in this way, ideology becomes autonomous
in relation to the consciousness or intention of its agents: these may be conscious of
their points of view about social forms but not of the semantic conditions (rules and
categories or codification) which make possible these points of view . . . . From this
point of view, then, an 'ideology' may be defined as a system of semantic rules to
generate messages . . . it is one of the many levels of organization of messages, from
the viewpoint of their semantic properties . . .
(Veron, 1971, p.68)

Critics have argued that this approach forsakes the content of particular
messages too much for the sake of identifying their underlying structure. Also,
that it omits any consideration of how speakers themselves interpret the
world – even if this is always within the framework of those shared sets of meanings
which mediate between individual actors/speakers and the discursive formations
in which they are speaking. But, provided the thesis is not pushed too far in a
structuralist direction, it provides a fruitful way of reconceptualizing ideology.
Lévi-Strauss regarded the classificatory schemes of a culture as a set of 'pure',
formal elements (though, in his earlier work, he was more concerned with the
social contradictions which were articulated in myths, through the combined
operations on their generative sets). Later theorists have proposed that the
ideological discourses of a particular society function in an analogous way. The
classificatory schemes of a society, according to this view, could therefore be said
to consist of ideological elements or premises. Particular discursive formulations
would, then, be ideological, not because of the manifest bias or distortions of their
surface contents, but because they were generated out of, or were transformations
based on, a limited ideological matrix or set. Just as the myth-teller may be
unaware of the basic elements out of which his particular version of the myth is
generated, so broadcasters may not be aware of the fact that the frameworks and
classifications they were drawing on reproduced the ideological inventories of
their society. Native speakers can usually produce grammatical sentences in their
native language but only rarely can they describe the rules of syntax in use which
make their sentences orderly, intelligible to others and grammatical in form. In the
same way, statements may be unconsciously drawing on the ideological
frameworks and classifying schemes of a society and reproducing them – so that
they appear ideologically 'grammatical' – without those making them being aware
of so doing. It was in this sense that the structuralists insisted that, though speech
and individual speech-acts may be an individual matter, the language-system
(elements, rules of combination, classificatory sets) was a social system: and
therefore that speakers were as much 'spoken' by their language as speaking it. The
rules of discourse functioned in such a way as to position the speaker as if he or she
were the intentional author of what was spoken. The system on which this
authorship depended remained, however, profoundly unconscious. Subsequent
theorists noticed that, although this de-centered the authorial 'I', making it
dependent on the language systems speaking through the subject, this left an
empty space where, in the Cartesian conception of the subject, the all-
encompassing 'I' had previously existed. In theories influenced by Freudian and

Lacanian psychoanalysis (also drawing on Lévi-Strauss), this question of how the speaker, the subject of enunciation, was positioned in language became, not simply one of the mechanisms through which ideology was articulated, but the principal mechanism of ideology itself (Coward and Ellis, 1977). More generally, however, it is not difficult to see how Lévi-Strauss's proposition – 'speakers produce meaning, but only on the basis of conditions which are not of the speaker's making, and which pass through him/her into language, unconsciously' – could be assimilated to the more classic Marxist proposition that 'people make history, but only in determinate conditions which are not of their making, and which pass behind their backs'. In later developments, these theoretical homologies were vigorously exploited, developed – and contested.

Historicizing the Structures

Of course, in addition to the homologies with Lévi-Strauss's approach, there were also significant differences. If the inventories from which particular significations were generated were conceived, not simply as a formal scheme of elements and rules, but as a set of ideological elements, then the conceptions of the ideological matrix had to be radically historicized. The 'deep structure' of a statement had to be conceived as the network of elements, premises and assumptions drawn from the long-standing and historically-elaborated discourses which had accreted over the years, into which the whole history of the social formation had sedimented, and which now constituted a reservoir of themes and premises on which, for example, broadcasters could draw for the work of signifying new and troubling events. Gramsci, who referred, in a less formal way, to the inventory of traditional ideas, the forms of episodic thinking which provide us with the taken-for-granted elements of our practical knowledge, called this inventory 'common sense'.

> What must be explained is how it happens that in all periods there coexist many systems and currents of philosophical thought, how these currents are born, how they are diffused, and why in the process of diffusion they fracture along certain lines and in certain directions . . . it is this history which shows how thought has been elaborated over the centuries and what a collective effort has gone into the creation of our present method of thought which has subsumed and absorbed all this past history, including all its follies and mistakes.
> (Gramsci, 1971, p.327)

In another context, he argued:

> Every social stratum has its own 'common sense' and its own 'good sense', which are basically the most widespread conception of life and of men. Every philosophical current leaves behind a sedimentation of 'common sense': this is the document of its historical effectiveness. Common sense is not something rigid and immobile, but is continually transforming itself, enriching itself with scientific ideas and with philosophical opinions which have entered ordinary life . . . Common sense creates the folklore of the future, that is as a relatively rigid phase of popular knowledge at a given place and time.
> (Gramsci, 1971, p.326)

The formalist conception of the 'cultural inventory' suggested by structuralism was not, in my view, available as a theoretical support for the elaboration of an adequate conception of ideology until it had been thoroughly historicized in this way. Only thus did the preoccupation, which Lévi-Strauss initiated, with the universal 'grammars' of culture begin to yield insights into the historical grammars which divided and classified the knowledge of particular societies into their distinctive ideological inventories.

The structural study of myth suggested that, in addition to the ways in which knowledge about the social world was classified and framed, there would be a distinctive logic about the ways in which the elements in an inventory could yield certain stories or statements about the world. It was, according to Lévi-Strauss, the 'logic of arrangement' rather than the particular contents of a myth which 'signified'. It was at this level that the pertinent regularities and recurrences could best be observed. By 'logic' he did not, certainly, mean logic in the philosophical sense adopted by western rationalism. Indeed, his purpose was to demonstrate that western rationalism was only one of the many types of discursive arrangement possible; no different intrinsically, in terms of how it worked, from the logic of so-called pre-scientific thinking or mythic thought. Logic here simply meant an apparently necessary chain of implication between statement and premise. In western logic, propositions are said to be logical if they obey certain rules of inference and deduction. What the cultural analyst meant by logic was simply that all ideological propositions about the social world were similarly premised, predicated or inferenced. They entailed a framework of linked propositions, even if they failed the test of logical deduction. The premises had to be assumed to be true, for the propositions which depended on them to be taken as true. This notion of 'the entailment of propositions', or, as the semanticists would say, the embeddedness of statements, proved of seminal value in the development of ideological analysis. To put the point in its extreme form, a statement like 'the strike of Leyland tool-makers today further weakened Britain's economic position' was premised on a whole set of taken-for-granted propositions about how the economy worked, what the national interest was, and so on. For it to win credibility, the whole logic of capitalist production had to be assumed to be true. Much the same could be said about any item in a conventional news bulletin, that, without a whole range of unstated premises or pieces of taken-for-granted knowledge about the world, each descriptive statement would be literally unintelligible. But this 'deep structure' of presuppositions, which made the statement ideologically 'grammatical', were rarely made explicit and were largely unconscious, either to those who deployed them to make sense of the world or to those who were required to make sense of it. Indeed, the very declarative and descriptive form of the statement rendered invisible the implied logic in which it was embedded. This gave the statement an unchallenged obviousness, and obvious truth-value. What were in fact propositions about how things were, disappeared into and acquired the substantive affirmation of merely descriptive statements: 'facts of the case'. The logic of their entailment being occluded, the statements seemed to work, so to speak, by themselves. They appeared as proposition-free – natural and spontaneous affirmations about 'reality'.

The Reality Effect

In this way, the critical paradigm began to dissect the so-called 'reality' of discourse. In the referential approach, language was thought to be transparent to the truth of 'reality itself' – merely transferring this originating meaning to the receiver. The real world was both origin and warrant for the truth of any statement about it. But in the conventional or constructivist theory of language, reality came to be understood, instead, as the result or effect of how things had been signified. It was because a statement generated a sort of 'recognition effect' in the receiver that it was taken or 'read' as a simple empirical statement. The work of formulation which produced it secured this closing of the pragmatic circle of knowledge. But this recognition effect was not a recognition of the reality behind the words, but a sort of confirmation of the obviousness, the taken-for-grantedness of the way the discourse was organized and of the underlying premises on which the statement in fact depended. If one regards the laws of a capitalist economy as fixed and immutable, then its notions acquire a natural inevitability. Any statement which is so embedded will thus appear to be merely a statement about 'how things really are'. Discourse, in short, had the effect of sustaining certain 'closures', of establishing certain systems of equivalence between what could be assumed about the world and what could be said to be true. 'True' means credible, or at least capable of winning credibility as a statement of fact. New, problematic or troubling events, which breached the taken-for-granted expectancies about how the world should be, could then be 'explained' by extending to them the forms of explanation which had served 'for all practical purposes', in other cases. In this sense, Althusser was subsequently to argue that ideology, as opposed to science, moved constantly within a closed circle, producing, not knowledge, but a recognition of the things we already knew. It did so because it took as already established fact exactly the premises which ought to have been put in question. Later still, this theory was to be complemented by psychoanalytic theories of the subject which tried to demonstrate how certain kinds of narrative exposition construct a place or position of empirical knowledge for each subject at the centre of any discourse – a position or point of view from which alone the discourse 'makes sense'. It, accordingly, defined such narrative procedures, which established an empirical-pragmatic closure in discourse, as all belonging to the discourse of 'realism'.

More generally, this approach suggested, discourses not only referenced themselves in the structure of already objectivated social knowledge (the 'already known') but established the viewer in a complicitous relationship of pragmatic knowledge to the 'reality' of the discourse itself. 'Point of view' is not, of course, limited to visual texts – written texts also have their preferred positions of knowledge. But the visual nature of the point-of-view metaphor made it particularly appropriate to those media in which the visual discourse appeared to be dominant. The theory was therefore most fully elaborated in relation to film:

but it applied, *tout court*, to television as well – the dominant medium of social discourse and representation in our society. Much of television's power to signify lay in its visual and documentary character – its inscription of itself as merely a 'window on the world', showing things as they really are. Its propositions and explanations were underpinned by this grounding of its discourse in 'the real' – in the evidence of one's eyes. Its discourse therefore appeared peculiarly a naturalistic discourse of fact, statement and description. But in the light of the theoretical argument sketched above, it would be more appropriate to define the typical discourse of this medium not as naturalistic but as *naturalized*: not grounded in nature but producing nature as a sort of guarantee of its truth. Visual discourse is peculiarly vulnerable in this way because the systems of visual recognition on which they depend are so widely available in any culture that they appear to involve no intervention of coding, selection or arrangement. They appear to reproduce the actual trace of reality in the images they transmit. This, of course, is an illusion – the 'naturalistic illusion' – since the combination of verbal and visual discourse which produces this effect of 'reality' requires the most skilful and elaborate procedures of coding: mounting, linking and stitching elements together, working them into a system of narration or exposition which 'makes sense'.

This argument obviously connects with the classical materialist definition of how ideologies work. Marx, you will recall, argued that ideology works because it appears to ground itself in the mere surface appearance of things. In doing so, it represses any recognition of the contingency of the historical conditions on which all social relations depend. It represents them, instead, as outside of history: unchangeable, inevitable and natural. It also disguises its premises as already known facts. Thus, despite its scientific discoveries, Marx described even classical political economy as, ultimately, 'ideological' because it took the social relations and the capitalist form of economic organization as the only, and inevitable, kind of economic order. It therefore presented capitalist production 'as encased in eternal natural laws independent of history'. Bourgeois relations were then smuggled in 'as the inviolable laws on which society in the abstract is founded'. This eternalization or naturalization of historical conditions and historical change he called 'a forgetting'. Its effect, he argued, was to reproduce, at the heart of economic theory, the categories of vulgar, bourgeois common sense. Statements about economic relations thus lost their conditional and premised character, and appeared simply to arise from 'how things are' and, by implication, 'how they must forever be'. But this 'reality-effect' arose precisely from the circularity, the presupposition-less character, the self-generating and self-confirming nature, of the process of representation itself.

The 'class struggle in language'

Later, within the framework of a more linguistic approach, theorists like Pêcheux were to demonstrate how the logic and sense of particular discourses depended on the referencing, within the discourse, of these preconstructed elements (Pêcheux, 1975). Also, how discourse, in its systems of narration and exposition, signalled its conclusions forward, enabling it to realize certain potential meanings within the chain or logic of its inferences, and closing off other possibilities. Any particular discursive string, they showed, was anchored within a whole discursive field or complex of existing discourses (the 'inter-discourse'); and these constituted the pre-signifieds of its statements or enunciations. Clearly, the 'pre-constituted' was a way of identifying, linguistically, what, in a more historical sense, Gramsci called the inventory of 'common sense'. Thus, once again, the link was forged, in ideological analysis, between linguistic or semiological concerns, on the one hand, and the historical analysis of the discursive formations of 'common sense' on the other. In referencing, within its system of narration, 'what was already known', ideological discourses both warranted themselves in and selectively reproduced the common stock of knowledge in society.

Because meaning no longer depended on 'how things were' but on how things were signified, it followed, as we have said, that the same event could be signified in different ways. Since signification was a practice, and 'practice' was defined as 'any process of transformation of a determinate raw material into a determinate product, a transformation effected by a determinate human labour, using determinate means (of "production")' (Althusser, 1969, p.166), it also followed that signification involved a determinate form of labour, a specific 'work': the work of meaning-production, in this case. Meaning was, therefore, not determined, say, by the structure of reality itself, but conditional on the work of signification being successfully conducted through a social practice. It followed, also, that this work need not necessarily be successfully effected: because it was a 'determinate' form of labour it was subject to contingent conditions. The work of signification was a social accomplishment – to use ethnomethodological terminology for a moment. Its outcome did not flow in a strictly predictable or necessary manner from a given reality. In this, the emergent theory diverged significantly, both from the reflexive or referential theories of language embodied in positivist theory, and from the reflexive kind of theory also implicit in the classical Marxist theory of language and the superstructures.

Three important lines of development followed from this break with early theories of language. Firstly, one had to explain how it was possible for language to have this multiple referentiality to the real world. Here, the polysemic nature of language – the fact that the same set of signifiers could be variously accented in those meanings – proved of immense value. Volosinov put this point best when he observed:

Existence reflected in the sign is not merely reflected but refracted. How is this refraction of existence in the ideological sign determined? By an intersecting of differently oriented social interests in every ideological sign. Sign becomes an arena of class struggle. This social multi-accentuality of the ideological sign is a very crucial aspect . . . A sign that has been withdrawn from the pressures of the social struggle – which, so to speak, crosses beyond the whole of the class struggle – inevitably loses force, degenerates into allegory, becoming the object not

of a live social intelligibility but of a philological comprehension.
(Volosinov, 1973, p.23)

The second point is also addressed as an addendum, in Volosinov's remark. Meaning, once it is problematized, must be the result, not of a functional reproduction of the world in language, but of a social struggle–a struggle for mastery in discourse–over which kind of social accenting is to prevail and to win credibility. This reintroduced both the notion of 'differently oriented social interests' and a conception of the sign as 'an arena of struggle' into the consideration of language and of signifying 'work'.

Althusser, who transposed some of this kind of thinking into his general theory of ideology, tended to present the process as too uni-accentual, too functionally adapted to the reproduction of the dominant ideology (Althusser, 1971). Indeed, it was difficult, from the base-line of this theory, to discern how anything but the 'dominant ideology' could ever be reproduced in discourse. The work of Volosinov and Gramsci offered a significant correction to this functionalism by reintroducing into the domain of ideology and language the notion of a 'struggle over meaning' (which Volosinov substantiated theoretically with his argument about the multi-accentuality of the sign). What Volosinov argued was that the mastery of the struggle over meaning in discourse had, as its most pertinent effect or result, the imparting of a 'supraclass, eternal character to the ideological sign, to extinguish or drive inward the struggle between social value judgements which occurs in it, to make the sign uni-accentual' (1973, p.23). To go back for a moment to the earlier argument about the reality-effect: Volosinov's point was that uni-accentuality–where things appeared to have only one, given, unalterable and 'supraclass' meaning–was the result of a practice of closure: the establishment of an *achieved system of equivalence* between language and reality, which the effective mastery of the struggle over meaning produced as its most pertinent effect. These equivalences, however, were not given in reality, since, as we have seen, the same reference can be differently signified in different semantic systems; and some systems can constitute differences which other systems have no way of recognizing or punctuating. Equivalences, then, were secured through discursive practice. But this also meant that such a practice was conditional. It depended on certain conditions being fulfilled. Meanings which had been effectively coupled could also be un-coupled. The 'struggle in discourse' therefore consisted precisely of this process of discursive articulation and disarticulation. Its outcomes, in the final result, could only depend on the relative strength of the 'forces in struggle', the balance between them at any strategic moment, and the effective conduct of the 'politics of signification'. We can think of many pertinent historical examples where the conduct of a social struggle depended, at a particular moment, precisely on the effective dis-articulation of certain key terms, e.g. 'democracy', the 'rule of law', 'civil rights', 'the nation', 'the people', 'Mankind', from their previous couplings, and their extrapolation to new meanings, representing the emergence of new political subjects.

The third point, then, concerned the mechanisms within signs and language, which made the 'struggle' possible. Sometimes, the class struggle in language occurred between two different terms: the struggle, for example, to replace the term 'immigrant' with the term 'black'. But often, the struggle took the form of a different accenting of the *same* term: e.g. the process by means of which the derogatory colour 'black' became the enhanced value 'Black' (as in 'Black is Beautiful'). In the latter case, the struggle was not over the term itself but over its connotative meaning. Barthes, in his essay on 'Myth Today', argued that the associative field of meanings of a single term – its connotative field of reference – was, *par excellence*, the domain through which ideology invaded the language system. It did so by exploiting the associative, the variable, connotative, 'social value' of language. For some time, this point was misunderstood as arguing that the denotative or relatively fixed meanings of a discourse were not open to multiple accentuation, but constituted a 'natural' language system; and only the connotative levels of discourse were open to different ideological inflexion. But this was simply a misunderstanding. Denotative meanings, of course, are not uncoded; they, too, entail systems of classification and recognition in much the same way as connotative meanings do; they are not natural but 'motivated' signs. The distinction between denotation and connotation was an analytic, not a substantive one (see Camargo, 1980; Hall, 1980a). It suggested, only, that the connotative levels of language, being more open-ended and associative, were peculiarly vulnerable to contrary or contradictory ideological inflexions.

Hegemony and Articulation

The real sting in the tail did not reside there, but in a largely unnoticed extension of Volosinov's argument. For if the social struggle in language could be conducted over the same sign, it followed that signs (and, by a further extension, whole chains of signifiers, whole discourses) could not be assigned, in a determinate way, permanently to any one side in the struggle. Of course, a native language is not equally distributed amongst all native speakers regardless of class, socio-economic position, gender, education and culture: nor is competence to perform in language randomly distributed. Linguistic performance and competence is socially distributed, not only by class but also by gender. Key institutions – in this respect, the family-education couple – play a highly significant role in the social distribution of cultural 'capital', in which language played a pivotal role, as educational theorists like Bernstein and social theorists like Bourdieu have demonstrated. But, even where access for everyone to the same language system could be guaranteed, this did not suspend what Volosinov called the 'class struggle in language'. Of course, the same term, e.g. 'black', belonged in both the vocabularies of the oppressed and the oppressors. What was being struggled over was not the 'class belongingness' of the term, but the inflexion it could be given, its connotative field of reference. In the discourse of the Black movement, the denigratory connotation 'black=the despised race' could be inverted into its opposite: 'black=beautiful'. There was thus a 'class struggle in language'; but not one in which whole discourses could be unproblematically assigned to whole social classes or social groups. Thus Volosinov argued:

Class does not coincide with the sign community i.e. with the community which is the totality of users of the same set of signs of ideological communication. Thus various different classes will use one and the same language. As a result, differently oriented accents intersect in every ideological sign. Sign becomes an arena of class struggle.
(Volosinov, 1973, p.23)

This was an important step: the ramifications are briefly traced through below. But one could infer, immediately, two things from this. First, since ideology could be realized by the semantic accenting of the same linguistic sign, it followed that, though ideology and language were intimately linked, they could not be one and the same thing. An analytic distinction needed to be maintained between the two terms. This is a point which later theorists, who identified the entry of the child into his/her linguistic culture as one and the same mechanism as the entry of the child into the ideology of its society neglected to show. But the two processes, though obviously connected (one cannot learn a language without learning something of its current ideological inflexions), cannot be identified or equated in that perfectly homologous way. Ideological discourses can win to their ways of representing the world already-languaged subjects, i.e. subjects already positioned within a range of existing discourses, fully-social speakers. This underlined the necessity to consider, instead, the 'articulation' of ideology in and through language and discourse.

Second, though discourse could become an arena of social struggle, and all discourses entailed certain definite premises about the world, this was not the same thing as ascribing ideologies to classes in a fixed, necessary or determinate way. Ideological terms and elements do not necessarily 'belong' in this definite way to classes: and they do not necessarily and inevitably flow from class position. The same elementary term, 'democracy' for example, could be articulated with other elements and condensed into very different ideologies: democracy of the Free West and the German Democratic Republic, for example. The same term could be disarticulated from its place with one discourse and articulated in a different position: the Queen acknowledging the homage of 'her people', for example, as against that sense of 'the people' or 'the popular' which is oppositional in meaning to everything which connotes the élite, the powerful, the ruler, the power bloc. What mattered was the way in which different social interests or forces might conduct an ideological struggle to disarticulate a signifier from one, preferred or dominant meaning-system, and rearticulate it within another, different chain of connotations. This might be accomplished, formally, by different means. The switch from 'black=despised' to 'black=beautiful' is accomplished by inversion. The shift from 'pig=animal with dirty habits' to 'pig=brutal policeman' in the language of the radical movements of the 1960s to 'pig=male-chauvinist pig' in the language of feminism, is a metonymic mechanism – sliding the negative meaning along a chain of connotative signifiers. This theory of the 'no necessary class belongingness' of ideological elements and the possibilities of ideological struggle to articulate/disarticulate meaning, was an insight drawn mainly from Gramsci's work, but considerably developed in more recent writings by theorists like Laclau (1977).

But the 'struggle over meaning' is not exclusively played out in the discursive condensations to which different ideological elements are subject. There was also the struggle over access to the very means of signification: the difference between those accredited witnesses and spokesmen who had a privileged access, as of right, to the world of public discourse and whose statements carried the representativeness and authority which permitted them to establish the primary framework or terms of an argument; as contrasted with those who had to struggle to gain access to the world of public discourse at all; those 'definitions' were always more partial, fragmentary and delegitimated; and who, when they did gain access, had to *perform with the established terms of the problematic in play*.

A simple but recurrent example of this point in current media discourse is the setting of the terms of the debate about black immigrants to Britain as a problem 'about numbers'. Liberal or radical spokesmen on race issues could gain all the physical access to the media which they were able to muster. But they would be powerfully constrained if they then had to argue within the terrain of a debate in which 'the numbers game' was accepted as *the privileged* definition of the problem. To enter the debate on these terms was tantamount to giving credibility to the dominant problematic: e.g. 'racial tension is the result of too many black people in the country, not a problem of white racialism'. When the 'numbers game' logic is in play, opposing arguments can be put as forcefully as anyone speaking is capable of: but the terms define the 'rationality' of the argument, and constrain how the discourse will 'freely' develop. A counter argument – that the numbers are *not* too high – makes an opposite case: but inevitably, it *also reproduces the given terms of the argument*. It accepts the premise that the argument is 'about numbers'. Opposing arguments are easy to mount. Changing the terms of an argument is exceedingly difficult, since the dominant definition of the problem acquires, by repetition, and by the weight and credibility of those who propose or subscribe to it, the warrant of 'common sense'. Arguments which hold to this definition of the problem are accounted as following 'logically'. Arguments which seek to change the terms of reference are read as 'straying from the point'. So part of the struggle is over the way the problem is formulated: the terms of the debate, and the 'logic' it entails.

A similar case is the way in which the 'problem of the welfare state' has come, in the era of economic recession and extreme monetarism, to be defined as 'the problem of the scrounger', rather than the 'problem of the vast numbers who could legally claim benefits, and need them, but don't'. Each framework, of course, has real social consequences. The first lays down a base-line from which public perceptions of the 'black problem' can develop – linking an old explanation to a new aspect. The next outbreak of violence between blacks and whites is therefore seen as a 'numbers problem' too – giving credence to those who advance the political platform that 'they should all be sent home', or that immigration controls should be strengthened. The definition of the welfare state as a 'problem of the illegal claimant' does considerable duty in a society which needs convincing that 'we cannot afford welfare', that it 'weakens the moral fibre of the nation', and therefore, that public welfare spending ought to be drastically reduced. Other aspects of the same process – for example, the establishment of the range of issues which demand public attention (or as it is more commonly known, the question of 'who sets the national agenda?') – were elaborated as part of the same concern with extending and filling out precisely what we could mean by saying that signification was a site of social struggle.

The fact that one could not read off the ideological position of a social group or individual from class position, but that one would have to take into account how the struggle over meaning was conducted, meant that ideology ceased to be a mere reflection of struggles taking place or determined elsewhere (for example, at the level of the economic struggle). It gave to ideology a relative independence or 'relative autonomy'. Ideologies ceased to be simply the independent variable in social struggle: instead, ideological struggle acquired a specificity and a pertinence of its own – needing to be analysed in its own terms, and with real effects on the outcomes of particular struggles. This weakened, and finally overthrew altogether, the classic conception of ideas as wholly determined by other determining factors (e.g. class position). Ideology might provide sets of representations and discourses through which we lived out, 'in an imaginary way, our relation to our real conditions of existence' (Althusser, 1969, p.233). But it was every bit as 'real' or 'material', as so-called non-ideological practices, because it affected their outcome. It was 'real' because it was *real in its effects*. It was determinate, because it depended on other conditions being fulfilled. 'Black' could not be converted into 'black=beautiful' simply by wishing it were so. It had to become part of an organized practice of struggles requiring the building up of collective forms of black resistance as well as the development of new forms of black consciousness. But, at the same time, ideology was also determining, because, depending on how the ideological struggle was conducted, material outcomes would be positively or negatively affected. The traditional role of the trade unions is to secure and improve the material conditions of their members. But a trade-union movement which lost the ideological struggle, and was successfully cast in the folk-devil role of the 'enemy of the national interest', would be one which could be limited, checked and curtailed by legal and political means: one, that is, in a weaker position relative to other forces on the social stage; and thus less able to conduct a successful struggle in the defence of working-class standards of living. In the very period in which the critical paradigm was being advanced, this lesson had to be learned the hard way. The limitations of a trade-union struggle which pursued economic goals exclusively at the expense of the political and ideological dimensions of the struggle were starkly revealed when obliged to come to terms with a political conjuncture where the very balance of forces and the terms of struggle had been profoundly altered by an intensive ideological campaign conducted with peculiar force, subtlety and persistence by the radical Right. The theory that the working class was permanently and inevitably attached to democratic socialism, the Labour Party and the trade-union movement, for example, could not survive a period in which the intensity of the Thatcher campaigns preceding the General Election of 1979 made strategic and decisive inroads, precisely into major sectors of the working-class vote (Hall, 1979; Hall,

1980b). And one of the key turning-points in the ideological struggle was the way the revolt of the lower-paid public-service workers against inflation, in the 'Winter of Discontent' of 1978-9, was successfully signified, not as a defence of eroded living standards and differentials, but as a callous and inhuman exercise of overweening 'trade-union power', directed against the defenceless sick, aged, dying and indeed the dead but unburied 'members of the ordinary public'.

Ideology in the Social Formation

This may be a convenient point in the argument to turn, briefly, to the second strand: concerning the way ideology was conceived in relation to other practices in a social formation. Many of the points in this part of the argument have already been sketched in. Complex social formations had to be analysed in terms of the economic, political and ideological institutions and practices through which they were elaborated. Each of these elements had to be accorded a specific weight in determining the outcomes of particular conjunctures. The question of ideology could not be extrapolated from some other level – the economic, for example – as some versions of classical Marxism proposed. But nor could the question of value-consensus be assumed, or treated as a dependent process merely reflecting in practice that consensus already achieved at the level of ideas, as pluralism supposed. Economic, political and ideological conditions had to be identified and analysed before any single event could be explained. Further, as we have already shown, the presupposition that the reflection of economic reality at the level of ideas could be replaced by a straightforward 'class-determination', also proved to be a false and misleading trail. It did not sufficiently recognize the relative autonomy of ideological processes, or the real effects of ideology on other practices. It treated classes as 'historical givens' – their ideological 'unity' already given by their position in the economic structure – whereas, in the new perspective, classes had to be understood only as the complex result of the successful prosecution of different forms of social struggle at all the levels of social practice, including the ideological. This gave to the struggle around and over the media – the dominant means of social signification in modern societies – a specificity and a centrality which, in previous theories, they had altogether lacked. It raised them to a central, relatively independent, position in any analysis of the question of the 'politics of signification'.

Though these arguments were cast within a materialist framework, they clearly departed radically from certain conventional ways of putting the Marxist question. In their most extended text on the question, *The German Ideology*, Marx and Engels had written, 'The ideas of the ruling classes are in every epoch the ruling ideas i.e. the class which is the ruling material force is at the same time its ruling intellectual force' (1970, p.64). The passage is, in fact, more subtle and qualified than that classic and unforgettable opening suggests. But, in the simple form in which it appeared, it could no longer – for reasons partly sketched out earlier – be sustained. Some theorists took this to mean that any relationship between ruling-

class and dominant ideas had therefore to be abandoned. My own view is that this
threw the baby out with the bath water, in two senses. It was based on the
unsupported, but apparently persuasive idea that, since 'ideas' could not be given
a *necessary* 'class belongingness', therefore there could be no relation of any kind
between the process through which ideologies were generated in society and the
constitution of a dominant alliance or power bloc based on a specific configuration
of classes and other social forces. But clearly it was not necessary to go so far in
breaking the theory of ideology free of a necessitarian logic. A more satisfactory
approach was to take the point of 'no necessary class belongingness': and then to
ask under what circumstances and through what mechanisms certain class
articulations of ideology might be actively secured. It is clear, for example, that
even though there is no necessary belongingness of the term 'freedom' to the
bourgeoisie, historically, a certain class articulation of the term has indeed been
effectively secured, over long historical periods: that which articulated 'freedom'
with the liberty of the individual, with the 'free' market and liberal political values,
but which disarticulated it from its possible condensations in a discourse
predicated on the 'freedom' of the worker to withdraw his labour or the 'freedom-
fighter'. These historical traces are neither necessary nor determined in a final
fashion. But such articulations have been historically secured. And they do have
effects. The equivalences having been sustained, they are constantly reproduced
in other discourses, in social practices and institutions, in 'free societies'. These
traditional couplings, or 'traces' as Gramsci called them, exert a powerful
traditional force over the ways in which subsequent discourses, employing the
same elements, can be developed. They give such terms, not an absolutely
determined class character, but a tendential class articulation. The question as to
how the articulation of ideological discourses to particular class formations can be
conceptualized, without falling back into a simple class reductionism, is a matter on
which important work has since been done (the work of Laclau referred to earlier
here is, once again, seminal).

Second, to lose the ruling-class/ruling-ideas proposition altogether is, of
course, also to run the risk of losing altogether the notion of 'dominance'. But
dominance is central if the propositions of pluralism are to be put in question.
And, as we have shown, the critical paradigm has done a great deal of work in
showing how a non-reductionist conception of dominance can be worked out in
the context of a theory of ideology. However, important modifications to our way
of conceiving dominance had to be effected before the idea was rescuable. That
notion of dominance which meant the direct imposition of one framework, by
overt force or ideological compulsion, on a subordinate class, was not sophisticated
enough to match the real complexities of the case. One had also to see that
dominance was accomplished at the unconscious as well as the conscious level: to
see it as a property of the system of relations involved, rather than as the overt and
intentional biases of individuals; and to recognize its play in the very activity of
regulation and exclusion which functioned through language and discourse before
an adequate conception of dominance could be theoretically secured. Much of this
debate revolved around the replacement of all the terms signifying the external

imposition of ideas or total incorporation into 'ruling ideas' by the enlarged concept of 'hegemony'. Hegemony implied that the dominance of certain formations was secured, not by ideological compulsion, but by cultural leadership. It circumscribed all those processes by means of which a dominant class alliance or ruling bloc, which has effectively secured mastery over the primary economic processes in society, extends and expands its mastery over society in such a way that it can transform and re-fashion its ways of life, its *mores* and conceptualization, its very form and level of culture and civilization in a direction which, while not directly paying immediate profits to the narrow interests of any particular class, favours the development and expansion of the dominant social and productive system of life as a whole. The critical point about this conception of 'leadership'–which was Gramsci's most distinguished contribution–is that hegemony is understood as accomplished, not without the due measure of legal and legitimate compulsion, but principally by means of winning the active consent of those classes and groups who were subordinated within it.

From the 'reflection of consensus' to the 'production of consent'

This was a vital issue – and a critical revision. For the weakness of the earlier Marxist positions lay precisely in their inability to explain the role of the 'free consent' of the governed to the leadership of the governing classes under capitalism. The great value of pluralist theory was precisely that it included this element of consent – though it gave to it a highly idealist and power-free gloss or interpretation. But, especially in formally democratic class societies, of which the US and Britain are archetypal cases, what had to be explained was exactly the *combination* of the maintained rule of powerful classes *with* the active or inactive consent of the powerless majority. The ruling-class/ruling-ideas formula did not go far enough in explaining what was clearly the most stabilizing element in such societies – consent. 'Consensus theory' however, gave an unproblematic reading to this element – recognizing the aspect of consent, but having to repress the complementary notions of power and dominance. But hegemony attempted to provide the outlines, at least, of an explanation of how power functioned in such societies which held both ends of the chain at once. The question of 'leadership' then, became, not merely a minor qualification to the theory of ideology, but the principal point of difference between a more and a less adequate explanatory framework. The critical point for us is that, in any theory which seeks to explain both the monopoly of power and the diffusion of consent, the question of the place and role of ideology becomes absolutely pivotal. It turned out, then, that the consensus question, in pluralist theory, was not so much wrong as incorrectly or inadequately posed. As is often the case in theoretical matters, a whole configuration of ideas can be revealed by taking an adequate premise and showing the unexamined conditions on which it rested. The 'break', therefore, occurred precisely at the point where theorists asked, 'but who produces the consensus?' 'In what interests does it function?' 'On what conditions does it depend?' Here, the media and other signifying institutions came back into the question – no longer as the institutions which merely reflected and sustained the consensus, but as the institutions which helped to produce consensus and which manufactured consent.

This approach could also be used to demonstrate how media institutions could be articulated to the production and reproduction of the dominant ideologies, while at the same time being 'free' of direct compulsion, and 'independent' of any direct attempt by the powerful to nobble them. Such institutions powerfully secure consent precisely because their claim to be independent of the direct play of political or economic interests, or of the state, is not wholly fictitious. The claim is ideological, not because it is false but because it does not adequately grasp all the conditions which make freedom and impartiality possible. It is ideological because it offers a partial explanation as if it were a comprehensive and adequate one – it takes the part for the whole (fetishism). Nevertheless, its legitimacy depends on that part of the truth, which it mistakes for the whole, being real in fact, and not merely a polite fiction.

This insight was the basis of all of that work which tried to demonstrate how it could be true that media institutions were both, in fact, free of direct compulsion and constraint, and yet freely articulate themselves systematically around definitions of the situation which favoured the hegemony of the powerful. The complexities of this demonstration cannot be entered into here and a single argument, relating to consensus, will have to stand. We might put it this way. Formally, the legitimacy of the continued leadership and authority of the dominant classes in capitalist society derives from their accountability to the opinions of the popular majority – the 'sovereign will of the people'. In the formal mechanisms of election and the universal franchise they are required to submit themselves at regular intervals to the will or consensus of the majority. One of the means by which the powerful can continue to rule with consent and legitimacy is, therefore, if the interests of a particular class or power bloc can be aligned with or made equivalent to the general interests of the majority. Once this system of equivalences has been achieved, the interests of the minority and the will of the majority can be 'squared' because they can both be represented as coinciding in the consensus, on which all sides agree. The consensus is the medium, the regulator, by means of which this necessary alignment (or equalization) between power and consent is accomplished. But if the consensus of the majority can be so shaped that it squares with the will of the powerful, then particular (class) interests can be represented as identical with the consensus will of the people. This, however, requires the shaping, the education and tutoring of consent: it also involves all those processes of representation which we outlined earlier.

Now consider the media – the means of representation. To be impartial and independent in their daily operations, they cannot be seen to take directives from the powerful, or consciously to be bending their accounts of the world to square with dominant definitions. But they must be sensitive to, and can only survive legitimately by operating within, the general boundaries or framework of 'what everyone agrees' to: the consensus. When the late Director General of the BBC,

Sir Charles Curran, remarked that 'the BBC could not exist outside the terms of parliamentary democracy', what he was pointing to was the fact that broadcasting, like every other institution of state in Britain, must subscribe to the fundamental form of political regime of the society, since it is the foundation of society itself and has been legitimated by the will of the majority. Indeed, the independence and impartiality on which broadcasters pride themselves depends on this broader coincidence between the formal protocols of broadcasting and the form of state and political system which licenses them. But, in orienting themselves in 'the consensus' and, at the same time, attempting to shape up the consensus, operating on it in a formative fashion, the media become part and parcel of that dialectical process of the 'production of consent' – shaping the consensus while reflecting it – which orientates them within the field of force of the dominant social interests represented within the state.

Notice that we have said 'the state', not particular political parties or economic interests. The media, in dealing with continuous public or political issues, would be rightly held to be partisan if they systematically adopted the point of view of a particular political party or of a particular section of capitalist interests. It is only in so far as (a) these parties or interests have acquired legitimate ascendancy in the state, and (b) that ascendancy has been legitimately secured through the formal exercise of the 'will of the majority' that their strategies can be represented as coincident with the 'national interest' – and therefore form the legitimate basis or framework which the media can assume. The 'impartiality' of the media thus requires the mediation of the state – that set of processes through which particular interests become generalized, and, having secured the consent of 'the nation', carry the stamp of legitimacy. In this way a particular interest is represented as 'the general interest' and 'the general interest as "ruling"'. This is an important point, since some critics have read the argument that the operations of the media depend on the mediation of the state in too literal a way – as if it were merely a matter of whether the institution is state-controlled or not. The argument is then said to 'work better for the BBC than for ITV'. But it should be clear that the connections which make the operations of the media in political matters legitimate and 'impartial' are not institutional matters, but a wider question of the role of the state in the mediation of social conflicts. It is at this level that the media can be said (with plausibility – though the terms continue to be confusing) to be 'ideological state apparatuses'. (Althusser, however, whose phrase this is, did not take the argument far enough, leaving himself open to the charge of illegitimately assimilating all ideological institutions into the state, and of giving this identification a functionalist gloss.)

This connection is a systematic one: that is, it operates at the level where systems and structures coincide and overlap. It does not function, as we have tried to show, at the level of the conscious intentions and biases of the broadcasters. When in phrasing a question, in the era of monetarism, a broadcasting interviewer simply takes it for granted that rising wage demands are the sole cause of inflation, he is both 'freely formulating a question' on behalf of the public and establishing a logic which is compatible with the dominant interests in society. And this would be the case regardless of whether or not the particular broadcaster was a lifelong supporter of some left-wing Trotskyist sect. This is a simple instance; but its point is to reinforce the argument that, in the critical paradigm, ideology is a function of the discourse and of the logic of social processes, rather than an intention of the agent. The broadcaster's consciousness of what he is doing – how he explains to himself his practice, how he accounts for the connection between his 'free' actions and the systematic inferential inclination of what he produces–is, indeed, an interesting and important question. But it does not substantially affect the theoretical issue. The ideology has 'worked' in such a case because the discourse has spoken itself through him/her. Unwittingly, unconsciously, the broadcaster has served as a support for the reproduction of a dominant ideological discursive field.

The critical paradigm is by no means fully developed; nor is it in all respects theoretically secure. Extensive empirical work is required to demonstrate the adequacy of its explanatory terms, and to refine, elaborate and develop its infant insights. What cannot be doubted is the profound theoretical revolution which it has already accomplished. It has set the analysis of the media and media studies on the foundations of a quite new problematic. It has encouraged a fresh start in media studies when the traditional framework of analysis had manifestly broken down and when the hard-nosed empirical positivism of the halcyon days of 'media research' had all but ground to a stuttering halt. This is its value and importance. And at the centre of this paradigm shift was the rediscovery of ideology and the social and political significance of language and the politics of sign and discourse: the *re*-discovery of ideology, it would be more appropriate to say – the return of the repressed.

References

ADORNO, T.W. *et al.* (1950) *The Authoritarian Personality*, New York, Harper & Row.

ALTHUSSER, L. (1969) *For Marx*, London, Allen Lane.

ALTHUSSER, L. (1971) 'Ideology and ideological state apparatuses', in *Lenin and Philosophy and Other Essays*, London, New Left Books.

BACHRACH, P. AND BARATZ, M. (1970) *Power and Poverty, Theory and Practice*, Oxford, Oxford University Press.

BARTHES, R. (1972) *Mythologies*, London, Jonathan Cape.

BECKER, H. (1967) 'Whose side are we on?', *Social Problems*, 14, Winter.

BELL, D. (1960) *The End of Ideology*, New York, Free Press.

BERGER, P. AND LUCKMANN, T. (1966) *The Social Construction of Reality*, Harmondsworth, Penguin.

CAMARGO, M. (1980) 'Ideological dimension of media messages', in Hall, S. *et al.* (eds) *Culture, Media, Language*, London, Hutchinson.

COWARD, R. AND ELLIS, J. (1977) *Language and Materialism*, London, Routledge & Kegan Paul.

DURKHEIM, E. (1960) *The Division of Labour in Society*, Glencoe, Free Press.

ECO, U. (1973) 'Social life as a sign system', in Robey, D. (ed.) *Structuralism: An Introduction*, Oxford, Clarendon Press.

GARNHAM, N. (1979) 'Contribution to a political economy of mass communication', *Media, Culture and Society*, 1(2), April.

GLASGOW UNIVERSITY MEDIA GROUP (1976), *Bad News*, London, Routledge & Kegan Paul.

GLASGOW UNIVERSITY MEDIA GROUP (1980), *More Bad News*, London, Routledge & Kegan Paul.

GOLDING, P. AND MURDOCK, G. (1979) 'Ideology and mass communication: the question of determination', in Barrett, M., Corrigan, P., Kuhn, A. and Wolff, J. (eds) *Ideology and Cultural Reproduction*, London, Croom Helm.

GRAMSCI, A. (1971) *Selections from the Prison Notebooks*, London, Lawrence & Wishart.

HALL, S. (1975) 'Encoding and decoding in the television discourse', *Education and Culture*, 6, Council of Europe, Strasbourg.

HALL, S. (1979) 'The great right moving show', *Marxism Today*, January.

HALL, S. (1980a) 'Encoding and decoding' (revised extract), in Hall, S. *et al.* (eds) *Culture, Media, Language*, London, Hutchinson.

HALL, S. (1980b) 'Popular democratic vs authoritarian populism', in Hunt, A. (ed.) *Marxism and Democracy*, London, Lawrence & Wishart.

HALL, S., CONNELL, I. AND CURTI, L. (1977) 'The "unity" of current affairs television', *Cultural Studies*, 9.

LACLAU, E. (1977) *Politics and Ideology in Marxist Theory*, London, New Left Books.

LÉVI-STRAUSS, C. (1967) *The Scope of Anthropology*, London, Jonathan Cape.

LÉVI-STRAUSS, C. (1969) *The Elementary Structures of Kinship*, London, Eyre & Spottiswoode.

LIPSET, S. (1963) *Political Man*, London, Heinemann.

LUKES, S. (1975) *Power: A Radical View*, London, Macmillan.

MARX, K. AND ENGELS, F. (1970), *The German Ideology*, London, Lawrence & Wishart.

MATZA, D. (1969) *Becoming Deviant*, New Jersey, Prentice Hall.

MERTON, R. (1957) *Social Theory and Social Structure*, New York, Free Press.

PARSONS, T. (1951) *The Social System*, New York, Free Press.

PÊCHEUX, P. (1975) *Les Verités de la Palice*, Paris, Maspero.

SAUSSURE, F. de (1960) *Course in General Linguistics*, London, P. Owen.

SHILS, E. (1961a) 'Centre and periphery', in *The Logic of Personal Knowledge*, London Routledge & Kegan Paul.

SHILS, E. (1961b) 'Mass society and its culture' in Jacobs, N. (ed.) *Culture For the Millions*, New York, Van Nostrand.

VERON, E. (1971) 'Ideology and the social sciences', *Semiotica*, III(2), Mouton.

VOLOSINOV, V. N. (1973) *Marxism and the Philosophy of Language*, New York, Seminar Press.

3 Ideology and Ideological State Apparatuses (Notes towards an Investigation)

Louis Althusser

From *Lenin and Philosophy and other essays* by Louis Althusser, 1971. Translated by Ben Brewster. Copyright *La Penseé* 1970. Reprinted by permission of the publisher, NLB.

On the Reproduction of the Conditions of Production

I must now expose more fully something which was briefly glimpsed in my analysis when I spoke of the necessity to renew the means of production if production is to be possible. That was a passing hint. Now I shall consider it for itself.

As Marx said, every child knows that a social formation which did not reproduce the conditions of production at the same time as it produced would not last a year. The ultimate condition of production is therefore the reproduction of the conditions of production. This may be 'simple' (reproducing exactly the previous conditions of production) or 'on an extended scale' (expanding them). Let us ignore this last distinction for the moment.

What, then, is *the reproduction of the conditions of production?*

Here we are entering a domain which is both very familiar (since *Capital* Volume Two) and uniquely ignored. The tenacious obviousnesses (ideological obviousnesses of an empiricist type) of the point of view of production alone, or even of that of mere productive practice (itself abstract in relation to the process of production) are so integrated into our everyday 'consciousness' that it is extremely hard, not to say almost impossible, to raise oneself to the *point of view of reproduction*. Nevertheless, everything outside this point of view remains abstract (worse than one-sided: distorted) – even at the level of production, and, *a fortiori*, at that of mere practice.

Let us try and examine the matter methodically.

To simplify my exposition, and assuming that every social formation arises from a dominant mode of production, I can say that the process of production sets to work the existing productive forces in and under definite relations of production.

56

It follows that, in order to exist, every social formation must reproduce the conditions of its production at the same time as it produces, and in order to be able to produce. It must therefore reproduce:

1 the productive forces,
2 the existing relations of production.

Reproduction of the Means of Production
Everyone (including the bourgeois economists whose work is national accounting, or the modern 'macro-economic' 'theoreticians') now recognizes, because Marx compellingly proved it in *Capital* Volume Two, that no production is possible which does not allow for the reproduction of the material conditions of production: the reproduction of the means of production.

The average economist, who is no different in this than the average capitalist, knows that each year it is essential to foresee what is needed to replace what has been used up or worn out in production: raw material, fixed installations (buildings), instruments of production (machines), etc. I say the average economist=the average capitalist, for they both express the point of view of the firm, regarding it as sufficient simply to give a commentary on the terms of the firm's financial accounting practice.

But thanks to the genius of Quesnay who first posed this 'glaring' problem, and to the genius of Marx who resolved it, we know that the reproduction of the material conditions of production cannot be thought at the level of the firm, because it does not exist at that level in its real conditions. What happens at the level of the firm is an effect, which only gives an idea of the necessity of reproduction, but absolutely fails to allow its conditions and mechanisms to be thought.

A moment's reflection is enough to be convinced of this: Mr X, a capitalist who produces woollen yarn in his spinning-mill, has to 'reproduce' his raw material, his machines, etc. But *he* does not produce them for his own production – other capitalists do: an Australian sheep-farmer, Mr Y, a heavy engineer producing machine-tools, Mr Z, etc., etc. And Mr Y and Mr Z, in order to produce those products which are the condition of the reproduction of Mr X's conditions of production, also have to reproduce the conditions of their own production, and so on to infinity – the whole in proportions such that, on the national and even the world market, the demand for means of production (for reproduction) can be satisfied by the supply.

In order to think this mechanism, which leads to a kind of 'endless chain', it is necessary to follow Marx's 'global' procedure, and to study in particular the relations of the circulation of capital between Department I (production of means of production) and Department II (production of means of consumption), and the realization of surplus-value, in *Capital*, Volumes Two and Three.

We shall not go into the analysis of this question. It is enough to have mentioned the existence of the necessity of the reproduction of the material conditions of production.

Reproduction of Labour-Power

However, the reader will not have failed to note one thing. We have discussed the reproduction of the means of production – but not the reproduction of the productive forces. We have therefore ignored the reproduction of what distinguishes the productive forces from the means of production, i.e. the reproduction of labour power.

From the observation of what takes place in the firm, in particular from the examination of the financial accounting practice which predicts amortization and investment, we have been able to obtain an approximate idea of the existence of the material process of reproduction, but we are now entering a domain in which the observation of what happens in the firm is, if not totally blind, at least almost entirely so, and for good reason: the reproduction of labour power takes place essentially outside the firm.

How is the reproduction of labour power ensured?

It is ensured by giving labour power the material means with which to reproduce itself: by wages. Wages feature in the accounting of each enterprise, but as 'wage capital', not at all a condition of the material reproduction of labour power.

However, that is in fact how it 'works', since wages represents only that part of the value produced by the expenditure of labour power which is indispensable for its reproduction: sc., indispensable to the reconstitution of the labour power of the wage-earner (the wherewithal to pay for housing, food and clothing, in short to enable the wage-earner to present himself again at the factory gate the next day – and every further day God grants him); and we should add: indispensable for raising and educating the children in whom the proletarian reproduces himself (in n models where n=0, 1, 2, etc. . . .) as labour power.

Remember that this quantity of value (wages) necessary for the reproduction of labour power is determined not by the needs of a 'biological' Guaranteed Minimum Wage (*Salaire Minimum Interprofessionnel Garanti*) alone, but by the needs of a historical minimum (Marx noted that English workers need beer while French proletarians need wine) – i.e. a historically variable minimum.

I should also like to point out that this minimum is doubly historical in that it is not defined by the historical needs of the working class 'recognized' by the capitalist class, but by the historical needs imposed by the proletarian class struggle (a double class struggle: against the lengthening of the working day and against the reduction of wages).

However, it is not enough to ensure for labour power the material conditions of its reproduction if it is to be reproduced as labour power. I have said that the available labour power must be 'competent', i.e. suitable to be set to work in the complex system of the process of production. The development of the productive forces and type of unity historically constitutive of the productive forces at a given moment produce the result that the labour power has to be (diversely) skilled and therefore reproduced as such. Diversely: according to the requirements of the socio-technical division of labour, its different 'jobs' and 'posts'.

How is this reproduction of the (diversified) skills of labour power provided for in a capitalist regime? Here, unlike social formations characterized by slavery or serfdom, this reproduction of the skills of labour power tends (this is a tendential law) decreasingly to be provided for 'on the spot' (apprenticeship within production itself), but is achieved more and more outside production: by the capitalist education system, and by other instances and institutions.

What do children learn at school? They go varying distances in their studies, but at any rate they learn to read, to write and to add – i.e. a number of techniques, and a number of other things as well, including elements (which may be rudimentary or on the contrary thoroughgoing) of 'scientific' or 'literary culture', which are directly useful in the different jobs in production (one instruction for manual workers, another for technicians, a third for engineers, a final one for higher management, etc.). Thus they learn 'know-how'.

But besides these techniques and knowledges, and in learning them, children at school also learn the 'rules' of good behaviour, i.e. the attitude that should be observed by every agent in the division of labour, according to the job he is 'destined' for: rules of morality, civic and professional conscience, which actually means rules of respect for the socio-technical division of labour and ultimately the rules of the order established by class domination. They also learn to 'speak proper French', to 'handle' the workers correctly, i.e. actually (for the future capitalists and their servants) to 'order them about' properly, i.e. (ideally) to 'speak to them' in the right way, etc.

To put this more scientifically, I shall say that the reproduction of labour power requires not only a reproduction of its skills, but also, at the same time, a reproduction of its submission to the rules of the established order, i.e. a reproduction of submission to the ruling of ideology for the workers, and a reproduction of the ability to manipulate the ruling ideology correctly for the agents of exploitation and repression, so that they, too, will provide for the domination of the ruling class 'in words'.

In other words, the school (but also other State institutions like the Church, or other apparatuses like the Army) teaches 'know-how', but in forms which ensure *subjection to the ruling ideology* or the mastery of its 'practice'. All the agents of production, exploitation and repression, not to speak of the 'professionals of ideology' (Marx), must in one way or another be 'steeped' in this ideology in order to perform their tasks 'conscientiously' – the tasks of the exploited (the proletarians), of the exploiters (the capitalists), of the exploiters' auxiliaries (the managers), or of the high priests of the ruling ideology (its 'functionaries'), etc.

The reproduction of labour power thus reveals as its *sine qua non* not only the reproduction of its 'skills' but also the reproduction of its subjection to the ruling ideology or of the 'practice' of that ideology, with the proviso that it is not enough to say 'not only but also', for it is clear that *it is in the forms and under the forms of ideological subjection that provision is made for the reproduction of the skills of labour power.*

But this is to recognize the effective presence of a new reality: *ideology.*

Here I shall make two comments.

The first is to round off my analysis of reproduction.

I have just given a rapid survey of the forms of the reproduction of the productive forces, i.e. of the means of production on the one hand, and of labour power on the other.

But I have not yet approached the question of the *reproduction of the relations of production*. This is a *crucial question* for the Marxist theory of the mode of production. To let it pass would be a theoretical omission – worse, a serious political error.

I shall therefore discuss it. But in order to obtain the means to discuss it, I shall make another long detour.

The second comment is that in order to make this detour, I am obliged to re-raise my old question: what is a society?

Infrastructure and Superstructure

On a number of occasions I have insisted on the revolutionary character of the Marxist conception of the 'social whole' insofar as it is distinct from the Hegelian 'totality'. I said (and this thesis only repeats famous propositions of historical materialism) that Marx conceived the structure of every society as constituted by 'levels' or 'instances' articulated by a specific determination: the *infrastructure*, or economic base (the 'unity' of the productive forces and the relations of production) and the *superstructure*, which itself contains two 'levels' or 'instances': the politico-legal (law and the State) and ideology (the different ideologies, religious, ethical, legal, political, etc.).

Besides its theoretico-didactic interest (it reveals the difference between Marx and Hegel), this representation has the following crucial theoretical advantage: it makes it possible to inscribe in the theoretical apparatus of its essential concepts what I have called their *respective indices of effectivity*. What does this mean?

It is easy to see that this representation of the structure of every society as an edifice containing a base (infrastructure) on which are erected the two 'floors' of the superstructure, is a metaphor, to be quite precise, a spatial metaphor: the metaphor of a topography (*topique*). Like every metaphor, this metaphor suggests something, makes something visible. What? Precisely this: that the upper floors could not 'stay up' (in the air) alone, if they did not rest precisely on their base.

Thus the object of the metaphor of the edifice is to represent above all the 'determination in the last instance' by the economic base. The effect of this spatial metaphor is to endow the base with an index of effectivity known by the famous terms: the determination in the last instance of what happens in the upper 'floors' (of the superstructure) by what happens in the economic base.

Given this index of effectivity 'in the last instance', the 'floors' of the superstructure are clearly endowed with different indices of effectivity. What kind of indices?

It is possible to say that the floors of the superstructure are not determinant in the last instance, but that they are determined by the effectivity of the base; that if they are determinant in their own (as yet undefined) ways, this is true only insofar as they are determined by the base.

Their index of effectivity (or determination), as determined by the determination in the last instance of the base, is thought by the Marxist tradition in two ways: (1) there is a 'relative autonomy' of the superstructure with respect to the base; (2) there is a 'reciprocal action' of the superstructure on the base.

We can therefore say that the great theoretical advantage of the Marxist topography, i.e. of the spatial metaphor of the edifice (base and superstructure) is simultaneously that it reveals that questions of determination (or of index of effectivity) are crucial; that it reveals that it is the base which in the last instance determines the whole edifice; and that, as a consequence, it obliges us to pose the theoretical problem of the types of 'derivatory' effectivity peculiar to the superstructure, i.e. it obliges us to think what the Marxist tradition calls conjointly the relative autonomy of the superstructure and the reciprocal action of the superstructure on the base.

The greatest disadvantage of this representation of the structure of every society by the spatial metaphor of an edifice is obviously the fact that it is metaphorical: i.e. it remains *descriptive*.

It seems to me that it is possible and desirable to represent things differently. NB, I do not mean by this that I want to reject the classical metaphor, for that metaphor itself requires that we go beyond it. And I am not going beyond it in order to reject it as outworn. I simply want to attempt to think what it gives us in the form of a description.

I believe that it is possible and necessary to think what characterizes the essential of the existence and nature of the superstructure *on the basis of reproduction*. Once one takes the point of view of reproduction, many of the questions whose existence was indicated by the spatial metaphor of the edifice, but to which it could not give a conceptual answer, are immediately illuminated.

My basic thesis is that it is not possible to pose these questions (and therefore to answer them) *except from the point of view of reproduction*.

I shall give a short analysis of Law, the State and Ideology *from this point of view*. And I shall reveal what happens both from the point of view of practice and production on the one hand, and from that of reproduction on the other.

The State

The Marxist tradition is strict, here: in the *Communist Manifesto* and the *Eighteenth Brumaire* (and in all the later classical texts, above all in Marx's writings on the Paris Commune and Lenin's on *State and Revolution*), the State is explicitly conceived as a repressive apparatus. The State is a 'machine' of repression, which enables the ruling classes (in the nineteenth century the bourgeois class and the 'class' of big landowners) to ensure their domination over the working class, thus enabling the former to subject the latter to the process of surplus-value extortion (i.e. to capitalist exploitation).

The State is thus first of all what the Marxist classics have called *the State apparatus*. This term means: not only the specialized apparatus (in the narrow sense) whose existence and necessity I have recognized in relation to the requirements of legal practice, i.e. the police, the courts, the prisons; but also the army, which (the proletariat has paid for this experience with its blood) intervenes directly as a supplementary repressive force in the last instance, when the police and its specialized auxiliary corps are 'outrun by events'; and above this ensemble, the head of State, the government and the administration.

Presented in this form, the Marxist-Leninist 'theory' of the State has its finger on the essential point, and not for one moment can there be any question of rejecting the fact that this really is the essential point. The State apparatus, which defines the State as a force of repressive execution and intervention 'in the interests of the ruling classes' in the class struggle conducted by the bourgeoisie and its allies against the proletariat, is quite certainly the State, and quite certainly defines its basic 'function'.

From Descriptive Theory to Theory as such

Nevertheless, here too, as I pointed out with respect to the metaphor of the edifice (infrastructure and superstructure), this presentation of the nature of the State is still partly descriptive.

As I shall often have occasion to use this adjective (descriptive), a word of explanation is necessary in order to remove any ambiguity.

Whenever, in speaking of the metaphor of the edifice or of the Marxist 'theory' of the State, I have said that these are descriptive conceptions or representations of their objects, I had no ulterior critical motives. On the contrary, I have every ground to think that great scientific discoveries cannot help but pass through the phase of what I shall call *descriptive 'theory'*. This is the first phase of every theory, at least in the domain which concerns us (that of the science of social formations). As such, one might – and in my opinion one must – envisage this phase as a transitional one, necessary to the development of the theory. That it is transitional is inscribed in my expression: 'descriptive theory', which reveals in its conjunction of terms the equivalent of a kind of 'contradiction'. In fact, the term theory 'clashes' to some extent with the adjective 'descriptive' which I have attached to it. This means quite precisely: (1) that the 'descriptive theory' really is, without a shadow of a doubt, the irreversible beginning of the theory; but (2) that the 'descriptive' form in which the theory is presented requires, precisely as an effect of this 'contradiction', a development of the theory which goes beyond the form of 'description'.

Let me make this idea clearer by returning to our present object: the State.

When I say that the Marxist 'theory' of the State available to us is still partly 'descriptive', that means first and foremost that this descriptive 'theory' is without the shadow of a doubt precisely the beginning of the Marxist theory of the State, and that this beginning gives us the essential point, i.e. the decisive principle of every later development of the theory.

Indeed, I shall call the descriptive theory of the State correct, since it is perfectly possible to make the vast majority of the facts in the domain with which it is concerned correspond to the definition it gives of its object. Thus, the definition of the State as a class State, existing in the repressive State apparatus, casts a brilliant light on all the facts observable in the various orders of repression whatever their domains: from the massacres of June 1848 and of the Paris Commune, of Bloody Sunday, May 1905 in Petrograd, of the Resistance, of Charonne, etc., to the mere (and relatively anodyne) interventions of a 'censorship' which has banned Diderot's *La Religieuse* or a play by Gatti on Franco; it casts light on all the direct or indirect forms of exploitation and extermination of the masses of the people (imperialist wars); it casts light on that subtle everyday domination beneath which can be glimpsed, in the forms of political democracy, for example, what Lenin, following Marx, called the dictatorship of the bourgeoisie.

And yet the descriptive theory of the State represents a phase in the constitution of the theory which itself demands the 'suppression' of this phase. For it is clear that if the definition in question really does give us the means to identify and recognize the facts of oppression by relating them to the State, conceived as the repressive State apparatus, this 'interrelationship' gives rise to a very special kind of obviousness, about which I shall have something to say in a moment: 'Yes, that's how it is, that's really true!' And the accumulation of facts within the definition of the State may multiply examples, but it does not really advance the definition of the State, i.e. the scientific theory of the State. Every descriptive theory thus runs the risk of 'blocking' the development of the theory, and yet that development is essential.

That is why I think that, in order to develop this descriptive theory into theory as such, i.e. in order to understand further the mechanisms of the State in its functioning, I think that it is indispensable to *add* something to the classical definition of the State as a State apparatus.

The Essentials of the Marxist Theory of the State

Let me first clarify one important point: the State (and its existence in its apparatus) has no meaning except as a function of *State power*. The whole of the political class struggle revolves around the State. By which I mean around the possession, i.e. the seizure and conservation of State power by a certain class or by an alliance between classes or class fractions. This first clarification obliges me to distinguish between State power (conservation of State power or seizure of State power), the objective of the political class struggle on the one hand, and the State apparatus on the other.

We know that the State apparatus may survive, as is proved by bourgeois 'revolutions' in nineteenth-century France (1830, 1848), by *coups d'état* (2 December, May 1958), by collapses of the State (the fall of the Empire in 1870, of the Third Republic in 1940), or by the political rise of the petty bourgeoisie (1890–95 in France), etc., without the State apparatus being affected or modified: it may survive political events which affect the possession of State power.

Even after a social revolution like that of 1917, a large part of the State apparatus survived after the seizure of State power by the alliance of the proletariat and the small peasantry: Lenin repeated the fact again and again.

It is possible to describe the distinction between State power and State apparatus as part of the 'Marxist theory' of the State, explicitly present since Marx's *Eighteenth Brumaire* and *Class Struggles in France*.

To summarize the 'Marxist theory of the State' on this point, it can be said that the Marxist classics have always claimed that (1) the State is the repressive State apparatus, (2) State power and State apparatus must be distinguished, (3) the objective of the class struggle concerns State power, and in consequence the use of the State apparatus by the classes (or alliance of classes or of fractions of classes) holding State power as a function of their class objectives, and (4) the proletariat must seize State power in order to destroy the existing bourgeois State apparatus and, in a first phase, replace it with a quite different, proletarian, State apparatus, then in later phases set in motion a radical process, that of the destruction of the State (the end of State power, the end of every State apparatus).

In this perspective, therefore, what I would propose to add to the 'Marxist theory' of the State is already there in so many words. But it seems to me that even with this supplement, this theory is still in part descriptive, although it does now contain complex and differential elements whose functioning and action cannot be understood without recourse to further supplementary theoretical development.

The State Ideological Apparatus
Thus, what has to be added to the 'Marxist theory' of the State is something else.

Here we must advance cautiously in a terrain which, in fact, the Marxist classics entered long before us, but without having systematized in theoretical form the decisive advances implied by their experiences and procedures. Their experiences and procedures were indeed restricted in the main to the terrain of political practice.

In fact, i.e. in their political practice, the Marxist classics treated the State as a more complex reality than the definition of it given in the 'Marxist theory of the State', even when it has been supplemented as I have just suggested. They recognized this complexity in their practice, but they did not express it in a corresponding theory.[1]

I should like to attempt a very schematic outline of this corresponding theory. To that end, I propose the following thesis.

In order to advance the theory of the State it is indispensable to take into account not only the distinction between *State power* and *State apparatus*, but also another reality which is clearly on the side of the (repressive) State apparatus, but must not be confused with it. I shall call this reality by its concept: *the ideological State apparatuses*.

What are the ideological State apparatuses (ISAs)?

They must not be confused with the (repressive) State apparatus. Remember that in Marxist theory, the State Apparatus (SA) contains: the Government, the Administration, the Army, the Police, the Courts, the Prisons, etc., which constitute what I shall in future call the Repressive State Apparatus. Repressive suggests that the State Apparatus in question 'functions by violence' – at least ultimately (since repression, e.g. administrative repression, may take non-physical forms).

I shall call Ideological State Apparatuses a certain number of realities which present themselves to the immediate observer in the form of distinct and specialized institutions. I propose an empirical list of these which will obviously have to be examined in detail, tested, corrected and reorganized. With all the reservations implied by this requirement, we can for the moment regard the following institutions as Ideological State Apparatuses (the order in which I have listed them has no particular significance):

-the religious ISA (the system of the different Churches),
-the educational ISA (the system of the different public and private 'Schools'),
-the family ISA,[2]
-the legal ISA,[3]
-the political ISA (the political system, including the different Parties), ~c the PCF?
-the trade-union ISA, ~ this equally a part of the state?
-the communications ISA (press, radio and television, etc.),
-the cultural ISA (Literature, the Arts, sports, etc.).

I have said that the ISAs must not be confused with the (Repressive) State Apparatus. What constitutes the difference?

As a first moment, it is clear that while there is *one* (Repressive) State Apparatus, there is a *plurality* of Ideological State Apparatuses. Even presupposing that it exists, the unity that constitutes this plurality of ISAs as a body is not immediately visible.

As a second moment, it is clear that whereas the –unified– (Repressive) State Apparatus belongs entirely to the *public* domain, much the larger part of the Ideological State Apparatuses (in their apparent dispersion) are part, on the contrary, of the *private* domain. Churches, Parties, Trade Unions, families, some schools, most newspapers, cultural ventures, etc., etc., are private.

We can ignore the first observation for the moment. But someone is bound to question the second, asking me by what right I regard as Ideological *State* Apparatuses, institutions which for the most part do not possess public status, but are quite simply *private* institutions. As a conscious Marxist, Gramsci already forestalled this objection in one sentence. The distinction between the public and the private is a distinction internal to bourgeois law, and valid in the (subordinate) domains in which bourgeois law exercises its 'authority'. The domain of the State escapes it because the latter is 'above the law': the State, which is the State *of* the ruling class, is neither public nor private; on the contrary, it is the precondition for any distinction between public and private. The same thing can be said from the starting-point of our State Ideological Apparatuses. It is unimportant whether the institutions in which they are realized are 'public' or 'private'. What matters is how they function. Private institutions can perfectly well 'function' as Ideological State Apparatuses. A reasonably thorough analysis of any one of the ISAs proves it.

But now for what is essential. What distinguishes the ISAs from the (Repressive) State Apparatus is the following basic difference: the Repressive

State Apparatus functions 'by violence', whereas the Ideological State Apparatuses *function 'by ideology'*.

I can clarify matters by correcting this distinction. I shall say rather that every State Apparatus, whether Repressive or Ideological, 'functions' both by violence and by ideology, but with one very important distinction which makes it imperative not to confuse the Ideological State Apparatuses with the (Repressive) State Apparatus.

This is the fact that the (Repressive) State Apparatus functions massively and predominantly *by repression* (including physical repression), while functioning secondarily by ideology. (There is no such thing as a purely repressive apparatus.) For example, the Army and the Police also function by ideology both to ensure their own cohesion and reproduction, and in the 'values' they propound externally.

In the same way, but inversely, it is essential to say that for their part the Ideological State Apparatuses function massively and predominantly *by ideology*, but they also function secondarily by repression, even if ultimately, but only ultimately, this is very attentuated and concealed, even symbolic. (There is no such thing as a purely ideological apparatus.) Thus Schools and Churches use suitable methods of punishment, expulsion, selection, etc., to 'discipline' not only their shepherds, but also their flocks. The same is true of the Family ... The same is true of the cultural IS Apparatus (censorship, among other things), etc.

Is it necessary to add that this determination of the double 'functioning' (predominantly, secondarily) by repression and by ideology, according to whether it is a matter of the (Repressive) State Apparatus or the Ideological State Apparatuses, makes it clear that very subtle explicit or tacit combinations may be woven from the interplay of the (Repressive) State Apparatus and the Ideological State Apparatuses? Everyday life provides us with innumerable examples of this, but they must be studied in detail if we are to go further than this mere observation.

Nevertheless, this remark leads us towards an understanding of what constitutes the unity of the apparently disparate body of the ISAs. If the ISAs 'function' massively and predominantly by ideology, what unifies their diversity is precisely this functioning, insofar as the ideology by which they function is always in fact unified, despite its diversity and its contradictions, *beneath the ruling ideology*, which is the ideology of the ruling class? Given the fact that the 'ruling class' in principle holds State power (openly or more often by means of alliances between classes or class fractions), and therefore has at its disposal the (Repressive) State Apparatus, we can accept the fact that this same ruling class is active in the Ideological State Apparatuses insofar as it is ultimately the ruling ideology which is realized in the Ideological State Apparatuses, precisely in its contradictions. Of course, it is a quite different thing to act by laws and decrees in the (Repressive) State Apparatus and to 'act' through the intermediary of the ruling ideology in the Ideological State Apparatuses. We must go into the details of this difference – but it cannot mask the reality of a profound identity. To my knowledge, *no class can hold State power over a period without at the same time exercising its hegemony over and in the State Ideological Apparatuses.* I only need one example and proof of this: Lenin's anguished concern to revolutionize the educational Ideological State Apparatus (among others), simply to make it possible for the Soviet proletariat, who had seized State power, to secure the future of the dictatorship of the proletariat and the transition to socialism.

This last comment puts us in a position to understand that the Ideological State Apparatuses may be not only the *stake*, but also the *site* of class struggle, and often of bitter forms of class struggle. The class (or class alliance) in power cannot lay down the law in the ISAs as easily as it can in the (repressive) State apparatus, not only because the former ruling classes are able to retain strong positions there for a long time, but also because the resistance of the exploited classes is able to find means and occasions to express itself there, either by the utilization of their contradictions, or by conquering combat positions in them in struggle.

Let me run through my comments.

If the thesis I have proposed is well-founded, it leads me back to the classical Marxist theory of the State, while making it more precise in one point. I argue that it is necessary to distinguish between State power (and its possession by . . .) on the one hand, and the State Apparatus on the other. But I add that the State Apparatus contains two bodies: the body of institutions which represent the Repressive State Apparatus on the one hand, and the body of institutions which represent the body of Ideological State Apparatuses on the other.

But if this is the case, the following question is bound to be asked, even in the very summary state of my suggestions: what exactly is the extent of the role of the Ideological State Apparatuses? What is their importance based on? In other words: to what does the 'function' of these Ideological State Apparatuses, which do not function by repression but by ideology, correspond?

On the Reproduction of the Relations of Production

I can now answer the central question which I have left in suspense for many long pages: *how is the reproduction of the relations of production secured?*

In the topographical language (Infrastructure, Superstructure), I can say: for the most part, it is secured by the legal-political and ideological superstructure.

But as I have argued that it is essential to go beyond this still descriptive language, I shall say: for the most part, it is secured by the exercise of State power in the State Apparatuses, on the one hand the (Repressive) State Apparatus, on the other the Ideological State Apparatuses.

What I have just said must also be taken into account, and it can be assembled in the form of the following three features:

1 All the State Apparatuses function both by repression and by ideology, with the difference that the (Repressive) State Apparatus functions massively and predominantly by repression, whereas the Ideological State Apparatuses function massively and predominantly by ideology.

2   Whereas the (Repressive) State Apparatus constitutes an organized whole whose different parts are centralized beneath a commanding unity, that of the politics of class struggle applied by the political representatives of the ruling classes in possession of State power, the Ideological State Apparatuses are multiple, distinct, 'relatively autonomous' and capable of providing an objective field to contradictions which express, in forms which may be limited or extreme, the effects of the clashes between the capitalist class struggle and the proletarian class struggle, as well as their subordinate forms.

3   Whereas the unity of the (Repressive) State Apparatus is secured by its unified and centralized organization under the leadership of the representatives of the class in power executing the politics of the class struggle of the classes in power, the unity of the different Ideological State Apparatuses is secured, usually in contradictory forms, by the ruling ideology, the ideology of the ruling class.

Taking these features into account, it is possible to represent the reproduction of the relations of production in the following way, according to a kind of 'division of labour'.

The role of the repressive State apparatus, insofar as it is a repressive apparatus, consists essentially in securing by force (physical or otherwise) the political conditions of the reproduction of relations of production which are in the last resort *relations of exploitation*. Not only does the State apparatus contribute generously to its own reproduction (the capitalist State contains political dynasties, military dynasties, etc.), but also and above all, the State apparatus secures by repression (from the most brutal physical force, via mere administrative commands and interdictions, to open and tacit censorship) the political conditions for the action of the Ideological State Apparatuses.

In fact, it is the latter which largely secure the reproduction specifically of the relations of production, behind a 'shield' provided by the repressive State apparatus. It is here that the role of the ruling ideology is heavily concentrated, the ideology of the ruling class, which holds State power. It is the intermediation of the ruling ideology that ensures a (sometimes teeth-gritting) 'harmony' between the repressive State apparatus and the Ideological State Apparatuses, and between the different Ideological State Apparatuses.

We are thus led to envisage the following hypothesis, as a function precisely of the diversity of ideological State apparatuses in their single, because shared, role of the reproduction of the relations of production.

Indeed we have listed a relatively large number of ideological State apparatuses in contemporary capitalist social formations: the educational apparatus, the religious apparatus, the family apparatus, the political apparatus, the trade-union apparatus, the communications apparatus, the 'cultural' apparatus, etc.

But in the social formations of that mode of production characterized by 'serfdom' (usually called the feudal mode of production), we observe that although there is a single repressive State apparatus which, since the earliest known Ancient States, let alone the Absolute Monarchies, has been formally very similar to the one we know today, the number of Ideological State Apparatuses is smaller and their individual types are different. For example, we observe that during the Middle Ages, the Church (the religious ideological State apparatus) accumulated a number of functions which have today developed on to several distinct ideological State apparatuses, new ones in relation to the past I am invoking, in particular educational and cultural functions. Alongside the Church there was the family Ideological State Apparatus, which played a considerable part, incommensurable with its role in capitalist social formations. Despite appearances, the Church and the Family were not the only Ideological State Apparatuses. There was also a political Ideological State Apparatus (the Estates General, the *Parlement*, the different political factions and Leagues, the ancestors of the modern political parties, and the whole political system of the free Communes and then of the *Villes*). There was also a powerful 'proto-trade-union' Ideological State Apparatus, if I may venture such an anachronistic term (the powerful merchants' and bankers' guilds and the journey-men's associations, etc.). Publishing and Communications, even, saw an indisputable development, as did the theatre; initially both were integral parts of the Church, then they became more and more independent of it.

In the pre-capitalist historical period which I have examined extremely broadly, it is absolutely clear that *there was one dominant Ideological State Apparatus, the Church,* which concentrated within it not only religious functions, but also educational ones, and a large proportion of the functions of communications and 'culture'. It is no accident that all ideological struggle, from the sixteenth to the eighteenth century, starting with the first shocks of the Reformation, was *concentrated* in an anti-clerical and anti-religious struggle; rather this is a function precisely of the dominant position of the religious ideological State apparatus.

The foremost objective and achievement of the French Revolution was not just to transfer State power from the feudal aristocracy to the merchant-capitalist bourgeoisie, to break part of the former repressive State apparatus and replace it with a new one (e.g., the national popular Army)–but also to attack the number-one Ideological State Apparatus: the Church. Hence the civil constitution of the clergy, the confiscation of ecclesiastical wealth, and the creation of new ideological State apparatuses to replace the religious ideological State apparatus in its dominant role.

Naturally, these things did not happen automatically: witness the Concordat, the Restoration and the long class struggle between the landed aristocracy and the industrial bourgeoisie throughout the nineteenth century for the establishment of bourgeois hegemony over the functions formerly fulfilled by the Church: above all by the Schools. It can be said that the bourgeoisie relied on the new political, parliamentary-democratic, ideological State apparatus, installed in the earliest years of the Revolution, then restored after long and violent struggles, for a few months in 1848 and for decades after the fall of the Second Empire, in order to conduct its struggle against the Church and wrest its ideological functions away from it, in other words, to ensure not only its own political hegemony, but also the ideological hegemony indispensable to the reproduction of capitalist relations of production.

That is why I believe that I am justified in advancing the following Thesis, however precarious it is. I believe that the ideological State apparatus which has been installed in the *dominant* position in mature capitalist social formations as a result of a violent political and ideological class struggle against the old dominant ideological State apparatus, is the *educational ideological apparatus.*

This thesis may seem paradoxical, given that for everyone, i.e. in the ideological representation that the bourgeoisie has tried to give itself and the classes it exploits, it really seems that the dominant ideological State apparatus in capitalist social formations is not the Schools, but the political ideological State apparatus, i.e. the regime of parliamentary democracy combining universal suffrage and party struggle.

However, history, even recent history, shows that the bourgeoisie has been and still is able to accommodate itself to political State apparatuses other than parliamentary democracy: the First and Second Empires, Constitutional Monarchy (Louis XVIII and Charles X), Parliamentary Monarchy (Louis-Philippe), Presidential Democracy (de Gaulle), to mention only France. In England this is even clearer. The Revolution was particularly 'successful' there from the bourgeois point of view, since unlike France, where the bourgeoisie, partly because of the stupidity of the petty aristocracy, had to agree to being carried to power by peasant and plebeian *'journées révolutionnaires'*, something for which it had to pay a high price, the English bourgeoisie was able to 'compromise' with the aristocracy and 'share' State power and the use of the State apparatuses with it for a long time (peace among all men of good will in the ruling classes!). In Germany it is even more striking, since it was behind a political ideological State apparatus in which the imperial Junkers (epitomized by Bismarck), their army and their police provided it with a shield and leading personnel, that the imperialist bourgeoisie made its shattering entry into history, before 'traversing' the Weimar Republic and entrusting itself to Nazism.

Hence I believe I have good reasons for thinking that behind the scenes of its political Ideological State Apparatus, which occupies the front of the stage, what the bourgeoisie has installed as its number-one, i.e. as its dominant ideological State apparatus, is the educational apparatus, which has in fact replaced in its functions the previously dominant ideological State apparatus, the Church. One might even add: the School-Family couple has replaced the Church-Family couple.

Why is the educational apparatus in fact the dominant ideological State apparatus in capitalist social formations, and how does it function?

For the moment it must suffice to say:

1   All ideological State apparatuses, whatever they are, contribute to the same result: the reproduction of the relations of production, i.e. of capitalist relations of exploitation.

2   Each of them contributes towards this single result in the way proper to it. The political apparatus by subjecting individuals to the political State ideology, the 'indirect' (parliamentary) or 'direct' (plebiscitary or fascist) 'democratic' ideology.

ie = particular discourse.

The communications apparatus by cramming every 'citizen' with daily doses of nationalism, chauvinism, liberalism, moralism, etc, by means of the press, the radio and television. The same goes for the cultural apparatus (the role of sport in chauvinism is of the first importance), etc. The religious apparatus by recalling in sermons and the other great ceremonies of Birth, Marriage and Death, that man is only ashes, unless he loves his neighbour to the extent of turning the other cheek to whoever strikes first. The family apparatus . . . but there is no need to go on.

3   This concert is dominated by a single score, occasionally disturbed by contradictions (those of the remnants of former ruling classes, those of the *lacs* proletarians and their organizations): the score of the Ideology of the current ruling class which integrates into its music the great themes of the Humanism of the Great Forefathers, who produced the Greek Miracle even before Christianity, and afterwards the Glory of Rome, the Eternal City, and the themes of Interest, particular and general, etc. nationalism, moralism and economism.

4   Nevertheless, in this concert, one ideological State apparatus certainly has the dominant role, although hardly anyone lends an ear to its music: it is so silent! This is the School.

It takes children from every class at infant-school age, and then for years, the years in which the child is most 'vulnerable', squeezed between the family State apparatus and the educational State apparatus, it drums into them, whether it uses new or old methods, a certain amount of 'know-how' wrapped in the ruling ideology (French, arithmetic, natural history, the sciences, literature) or simply the ruling ideology in its pure state (ethics, civic instruction, philosophy). Somewhere around the age of sixteen, a huge mass of children are ejected 'into production': these are the workers or small peasants. Another portion of scholastically adapted youth carries on: and, for better or worse, it goes somewhat further, until it falls by the wayside and fills the posts of small and middle technicians, white-collar workers, small and middle executives, petty bourgeois of all kinds. A last portion reaches the summit, either to fall into intellectual semi-employment, or to provide, as well as the 'intellectuals of the collective labourer', the agents of exploitation (capitalists, managers), the agents of repression (soldiers, policemen, politicians, administrators, etc.) and the professional ideologists (priests of all sorts, most of whom are convinced 'laymen').

Each mass ejected *en route* is practically provided with the ideology which suits the role it has to fulfil in class society: the role of the exploited (with a 'highly-developed' 'professional', 'ethical', 'civic', 'national' and apolitical conscious-ness); the role of the agent of exploitation (ability to give the workers orders and speak to them: 'human relations'), of the agent of repression (ability to give orders and enforce obedience 'without discussion', or ability to manipulate the demagogy of a political leader's rhetoric), or of the professional ideologist (ability to treat consciousnesses with the respect, i.e. with the contempt, blackmail, and demagogy they deserve, adapted to the accents of Morality, of Virtue, of 'Transcendence', of the Nation, of France's World Role, etc.).

Of course, many of these contrasting Virtues (modesty, resignation, submissiveness on the one hand, cynicism, contempt, arrogance, confidence, self-importance, even smooth talk and cunning on the other) are also taught in the Family, in the Church, in the Army, in Good Books, in films and even in the football stadium. But no other ideological State apparatus has the obligatory (and not least, free) audience of the totality of the children in the capitalist social formation, eight hours a day for five or six days out of seven.

But it is by an apprenticeship in a variety of know-how wrapped up in the massive inculcation of the ideology of the ruling class that the *relations of production* in capitalist social formation, i.e. the relations of exploited to exploiters and exploiters to exploited, are largely reproduced. The mechanisms which produce this vital result for the capitalist regime are naturally covered up and concealed by a universally reigning ideology of the School, universally reigning because it is one of the essential forms of the ruling bourgeois ideology: an ideology which represents the School as a neutral environment purged of ideology (because it is . . . lay), where teachers respectful of the 'conscience' and 'freedom' of the children who are entrusted to them (in complete confidence) by their 'parents' (who are free, too, i.e. the owners of their children) open up for them the path to the freedom, morality and responsibility of adults by their own example, by knowledge, literature and their 'liberating' virtues.

I ask the pardon of those teachers who, in dreadful conditions, attempt to turn the few weapons they can find in the history and learning they 'teach' against the ideology, the system and the practices in which they are trapped. They are a kind of hero. But they are rare and how many (the majority) do not even begin to suspect the 'work' the system (which is bigger than they are and crushes them) forces them to do, or worse, put all their heart and ingenuity into performing it with the most advanced awareness (the famous new methods!). So little do they suspect it that their own devotion contributes to the maintenance and nourishment of this ideological representation of the School, which makes the School today as 'natural', indispensable-useful and even beneficial for our contemporaries as the Church was 'natural', indispensable and generous for our ancestors a few centuries ago.

In fact, the Church has been replaced today *in its role as the dominant Ideological State Apparatus* by the School. It is coupled with the Family just as the Church was once coupled with the Family. We can now claim that the unprecedentedly deep crisis which is now shaking the education system of so many States across the globe, often in conjunction with a crisis (already proclaimed in the *Communist Manifesto*) shaking the family system, takes on a political meaning, given that the School (and the School-Family couple) constitutes the dominant Ideological State Apparatus, the Apparatus playing a determinant part in the reproduction of the relations of production of a mode of production threatened in its existence by the world class struggle.

On Ideology

When I put forward the concept of an Ideological State Apparatus, when I said that the ISAs 'function by ideology', I invoked a reality which needs a little discussion: ideology.

It is well known that the expression 'ideology' was invented by Cabanis, Destutt de Tracy and their friends, who assigned to it as an object the (genetic) theory of ideas. When Marx took up the term fifty years later, he gave it a quite different meaning, even in his Early Works. Here, ideology is the system of the ideas and representations which dominate the mind of a man or a social group. The ideologico-political struggle conducted by Marx as early as his articles in the *Rheinische Zeitung* inevitably and quickly brought him face to face with this reality and forced him to take his earliest intuitions further.

However, here we come upon a rather astonishing paradox. Everything seems to lead Marx to formulate a theory of ideology. In fact, *The German Ideology* does offer us, after the *1844 Manuscripts*, an explicit theory of ideology, but . . . it is not Marxist (we shall see why in a moment). As for *Capital*, although it does contain many hints towards a theory of ideologies (most visibly, the ideology of the vulgar economists), it does not contain that theory itself, which depends for the most part on a theory of ideology in general.

I should like to venture a first and very schematic outline of such a theory. The theses I am about to put forward are certainly not off the cuff, but they cannot be sustained and tested, i.e. confirmed or rejected, except by much thorough study and analysis.

Ideology has no History

One word first of all to expound the reason in principle which seems to me to found, or at least justify, the project of a theory of ideology *in general*, and not a theory of particular ideolog*ies*, which, whatever their form (religious, ethical, legal, political), always express *class positions*.

It is quite obvious that it is necessary to proceed towards a theory of ideolog*ies* in the two respects I have just suggested. It will then be clear that a theory of ideolog*ies* depends in the last resort on the history of social formations, and thus of the modes of production combined in social formations, and of the class struggles which develop in them. In this sense it is clear that there can be no question of a theory of ideolog*ies in general*, since ideolog*ies* (defined in the double respect suggested above: regional and class) have a history, whose determination in the last instance is clearly situated outside ideologies alone, although it involves them.

On the contrary, if I am to put forward the project of a theory of ideology *in general*, and if this theory really is one of the elements on which theories of ideolog*ies* depend, that entails an apparently paradoxical proposition which I shall express in the following terms: *ideology has no history*.

As we know, this formulation appears in so many words in a passage from *The German Ideology*. Marx utters it with respect to metaphysics, which, he says, has no more history than ethics (meaning also the other forms of ideology).

In *The German Ideology*, this formulation appears in a plainly positivist context. Ideology is conceived as a pure illusion, a pure dream, i.e. as nothingness. All its reality is external to it. Ideology is thus thought as an imaginary construction whose status is exactly like the theoretical status of the dream among writers before Freud. For these writers, the dream was the purely imaginary, i.e. null, result of the 'day's residues', presented in an arbitrary arrangement and order, sometimes even 'inverted', in other words, in 'disorder'. For them the dream was the imaginary, it was empty, null and arbitrarily 'stuck together' (*bricolé*), once the eyes had closed, from the residues of the only full and positive reality, the reality of the day. This is exactly the status of philosophy and ideology (since in this book philosophy is ideology *par excellence*) in *The German Ideology*.

Ideology, then, is for Marx an imaginary assemblage (*bricolage*), a pure dream, empty and vain, constituted by the 'day's residues' from the only full and positive reality, that of the concrete history of concrete material individuals materially producing their existence. It is on this basis that ideology has no history in *The German Ideology*, since its history is outside it, where the only existing history is, the history of concrete individuals, etc. In *The German Ideology*, the thesis that ideology has no history is therefore a purely negative thesis, since it means both:

1   ideology is nothing insofar as it is pure dream (manufactured by who knows what power: if not by the alienation of the division of labour, but that, too, is a *negative* determination);

2   ideology has no history, which emphatically does not mean that there is no history in it (on the contrary, for it is merely the pale, empty and inverted reflection of real history) but that it has no history *of its own*.

Now, while the thesis I wish to defend formally speaking adopts the terms of *The German Ideology* ('ideology has no history'), it is radically different from the positivist and historicist thesis of *The German Ideology*.

For on the one hand, I think it is possible to hold that ideolog*ies have a history of their own* (although it is determined in the last instance by the class struggle); and on the other, I think it is possible to hold that ideology *in general has no history*, not in a negative sense (its history is external to it), but in an absolutely positive sense.

This sense is a positive one if it is true that the peculiarity of ideology is that it is endowed with a structure and a functioning such as to make it a non-historical reality, i.e. an *omni-historical* reality, in the sense in which that structure and functioning are immutable, present in the same form throughout what we can call history, in the sense in which the *Communist Manifesto* defines history as the history of class struggles, i.e. the history of class societies.

To give a theoretical reference-point here, I might say that, to return to our example of the dream, in its Freudian conception this time, our proposition: ideology has no history, can and must (and in a way which has absolutely nothing arbitrary about it, but, quite the reverse, is theoretically necessary, for there is an organic link between the two propositions) be related directly to Freud's proposition that the *unconscious is eternal*, i.e. that it has no history.

If eternal means, not transcendent to all (temporal) history, but omnipresent, trans-historical and therefore immutable in form throughout the extent of history, I shall adopt Freud's expression word for word, and write *ideology is eternal*, exactly like the unconscious. And I add that I find this comparison theoretically justified by the fact that the eternity of the unconscious is not unrelated to the eternity of ideology in general.

That is why I believe I am justified, hypothetically at least, in proposing a theory of ideology *in general*, in the sense that Freud presented a theory of the unconscious *in general*.

To simplify the phrase, it is convenient, taking into account what has been said about ideologies, to use the plain term ideology to designate ideology in general, which I have just said has no history, or, what comes to the same thing, is eternal, i.e. omnipresent in its immutable form throughout history (=the history of social formations containing social classes). For the moment I shall restrict myself to 'class societies' and their history.

Ideology is a 'Representation' of the Imaginary Relationship of Individuals to their Real Conditions of Existence

In order to approach my central thesis on the structure and functioning of ideology, I shall first present two theses, one negative, the other positive. The first concerns the object which is 'represented' in the imaginary form of ideology, the second concerns the materiality of ideology.

THESIS 1: Ideology represents the imaginary relationship of individuals to their real conditions of existence.

We commonly call religious ideology, ethical ideology, legal ideology, political ideology, etc., so many 'world outlooks'. Of course, assuming that we do not live one of these ideologies as the truth (e.g. 'believe' in God, Duty, Justice, etc. . . . .), we admit that the ideology we are discussing from a critical point of view, examining it as the ethnologist examines the myths of a 'primitive society', that these 'world outlooks' are largely imaginary, i.e. do not 'correspond to reality'.

However, while admitting that they do not correspond to reality, i.e. that they constitute an illusion, we admit that they do make allusion to reality, and that they need only be 'interpreted' to discover the reality of the world behind their imaginary representation of that world (ideology=*illusion/allusion*).

There are different types of interpretation, the most famous of which are the *mechanistic* type, current in the eighteenth century (God is the imaginary representation of the real King), and the '*hermeneutic*' interpretation, inaugurated by the earliest Church Fathers, and revived by Feuerbach and the theologico-philosophical school which descends from him, e.g. the theologian Barth (to Feuerbach, for example, God is the essence of real Man). The essential point is that on condition that we interpret the imaginary transposition (and inversion) of ideology we arrive at the conclusion that in ideology 'men represent their real conditions of existence to themselves in an imaginary form'.

Unfortunately, this interpretation leaves one small problem unsettled: why do men 'need' this imaginary transposition of their real conditions of existence in order to 'represent to themselves' their real conditions of existence?

The first answer (that of the eighteenth century) proposes a simple solution: Priests or Despots are responsible. They 'forged' the Beautiful Lies so that, in the belief that they were obeying God, men would in fact obey the Priests and Despots, who are usually in alliance in their imposture, the Priests acting in the interests of the Despots or *vice versa*, according to the political positions of the 'theoreticians' concerned. There is therefore a cause for the imaginary transposition of the real conditions of existence: that cause is the existence of a small number of cynical men who base their domination and exploitation of the 'people' on a falsified representation of the world which they have imagined in order to enslave other minds by dominating their imaginations.

The second answer (that of Feuerbach, taken over word for word by Marx in his Early Works) is more 'profound', i.e. just as false. It, too, seeks and finds a cause for the imaginary transposition and distortion of men's real conditions of existence, in short, for the alienation in the imaginary of the representation of men's conditions of existence. This cause is no longer Priests or Despots, nor their active imagination and the passive imagination of their victims. This cause is the material alienation which reigns in the conditions of existence of men themselves. This is how, in *The Jewish Question* and elsewhere, Marx defends the Feuerbachian idea that men make themselves an alienated (=imaginary) representation of their conditions of existence because these conditions of existence are themselves alienating (in the *1844 Manuscripts*: because these conditions are dominated by the essence of alienated society – '*alienated labour*').

All these interpretations thus take literally the thesis which they presuppose, and on which they depend, i.e. that what is reflected in the imaginary representation of the world found in an ideology is the conditions of existence of men, i.e. their real world.

Now I can return to a thesis which I have already advanced: it is not their real conditions of existence, their real world, that 'men' 'represent to themselves' in ideology, but above all it is their relation to those conditions of existence which is represented to them there. It is this relation which is at the centre of every ideological, i.e. imaginary, representation of the real world. It is this relation that contains the 'cause' which has to explain the imaginary distortion of the ideological representation of the real world. Or rather, to leave aside the language of causality it is necessary to advance the thesis that it is the *imaginary nature of this relation* which underlies all the imaginary distortion that we can observe (if we do not live in its truth) in all ideology.

To speak in a Marxist language, if it is true that the representation of the real conditions of existence of the individuals occupying the posts of agents of production, exploitation, repression, ideologization and scientific practice, does in the last analysis arise from the relations of production, and from relations deriving from the relations of production, we can say the following: all ideology represents in its necessarily imaginary distortion not the existing relations of production (and the other relations that derive from them), but above all the (imaginary) relationship of individuals to the relations of production and the relations that derive from them. What is represented in ideology is therefore not the system of the real relations which govern the existence of individuals, but the imaginary relation of those individuals to the real relations in which they live.

If this is the case, the question of the 'cause' of the imaginary distortion of the real relations in ideology disappears and must be replaced by a different question: why is the representation given to individuals of their (individual) relation to the social relations which govern their conditions of existence and their collective and individual life necessarily an imaginary relation? And what is the nature of this imaginariness? Posed in this way, the question explodes the solution by a 'clique', by a group of individuals (Priests or Despots) who are the authors of the great ideological mystification, just as it explodes the solution by the alienated character of the real world. We shall see why later in my exposition. For the moment I shall go no further.

THESIS II: Ideology has a material existence.

I have already touched on this thesis by saying that the 'ideas' or 'representations', etc., which seem to make up ideology do not have an ideal (*idéale* or *idéelle*) or spiritual existence, but a material existence. I even suggested that the ideal (*idéale, idéelle*) and spiritual existence of 'ideas' arises exclusively in an ideology of the 'idea' and of ideology, and let me add, in an ideology of what seems to have 'founded' this conception since the emergence of the sciences, i.e. what the practicians of the sciences represent to themselves in their spontaneous ideology as 'ideas', true or false. Of course, presented in affirmative form, this thesis is unproven. I simply ask that the reader be favourably disposed towards it, say, in the name of materialism. A long series of arguments would be necessary to prove it.

This hypothetical thesis of the not spiritual but material existence of 'ideas' or other 'representations' is indeed necessary if we are to advance in our analysis of the nature of ideology. Or rather, it is merely useful to us in order the better to reveal what every at all serious analysis of any ideology will immediately and empirically show to every observer, however critical.

While discussing the ideological State apparatuses and their practices, I said that each of them was the realization of an ideology (the unity of these different regional ideologies – religious, ethical, legal, political, aesthetic, etc. – being assured by their subjection to the ruling ideology). I now return to this thesis: an ideology always exists in an apparatus, and its practice, or practices. This existence is material.

Of course, the material existence of the ideology in an apparatus and its practices does not have the same modality as the material existence of a paving-stone or a rifle. But, at the risk of being taken for a Neo-Aristotelian (NB Marx had a very high regard for Aristotle), I shall say that 'matter is discussed in many senses', or rather that it exists in different modalities, all rooted in the last instance in 'physical' matter.

Having said this, let me move straight on and see what happens to the 'individuals' who live in ideology, i.e. in a determinate (religious, ethical, etc.) representation of the world whose imaginary distortion depends on their imaginary relation to their conditions of existence, in other words, in the last instance, to the relations of production and to class relations (ideology=an imaginary relation to real relations). I shall say that this imaginary relation is itself endowed with a material existence.

Now I observe the following.

An individual believes in God, or Duty, or Justice, etc. This belief derives (for everyone, i.e. for all those who live in an ideological representation of ideology, which reduces ideology to ideas endowed by definition with a spiritual existence) from the ideas of the individual concerned, i.e. from him as a subject with a consciousness which contains the ideas of his belief. In this way, i.e. by means of the absolutely ideological 'conceptual' device (*dispositif*) thus set up (a subject endowed with a consciousness in which he freely forms or freely recognizes ideas in which he believes), the (material) attitude of the subject concerned naturally follows.

The individual in question behaves in such and such a way, adopts such and such a practical attitude, and, what is more, participates in certain regular practices which are those of the ideological apparatus on which 'depend' the ideas which he has in all consciousness freely chosen as a subject. If he believes in God, he goes to Church to attend Mass, kneels, prays, confesses, does penance (once it was material in the ordinary sense of the term) and naturally repents and so on. If he believes in Duty, he will have the corresponding attitudes, inscribed in ritual practices 'according to the correct principles'. If he believes in Justice, he will submit unconditionally to the rules of the Law, and may even protest when they are violated, sign petitions, take part in a demonstration, etc.

Throughout this schema we observe that the ideological representation of ideology is itself forced to recognize that every 'subject' endowed with a 'consciousness' and believing in the 'ideas' that his 'consciousness' inspires in him and freely accepts, must '*act* according to his ideas', must therefore inscribe his own ideas as a free subject in the actions of his material practice. If he does not do so, 'that is wicked'.

Indeed, if he does not do what he ought to do as a function of what he believes, it is because he does something else, which, still as a function of the same idealist scheme, implies that he has other ideas in his head as well as those he proclaims, and that he acts according to these other ideas, as a man who is either 'inconsistent' ('no one is willingly evil') or cynical, or perverse.

In every case, the ideology of ideology thus recognizes, despite its imaginary distortion, that the 'ideas' of a human subject exist in his actions, or ought to exist in his actions, and if that is not the case, it lends him other ideas corresponding to the actions (however perverse) that he does perform. This ideology talks of actions: I shall talk of actions inserted into *practice*. *And* I shall point out that these practices are governed by the *rituals* in which these practices are inscribed, within the *material existence of an ideological apparatus,* be it only a small part of that apparatus: a small mass in a small church, a funeral, a minor match at a sports' club, a school day, a political party meeting, etc.

Besides, we are indebted to Pascal's defensive 'dialectic' for the wonderful formula which will enable us to invert the order of the notional schema of ideology. Pascal says more or less: 'Kneel down, move your lips in prayer, and you will believe.' He thus scandalously inverts the order of things, bringing, like Christ, not peace but strife, and in addition something hardly Christian (for woe to him who brings scandal into the world!)—scandal itself. A fortunate scandal which makes him stick with Jansenist defiance to a language that directly names the reality.

I will be allowed to leave Pascal to the arguments of his ideological struggle with the religious ideological State apparatus of his day. And I shall be expected to use a more directly Marxist vocabulary, if that is possible, for we are advancing in still poorly explored domains.

I shall therefore say that, where only a single subject (such and such an individual) is concerned, the existence of the ideas of his belief is material in that *his ideas are his material actions inserted into material practices governed by material rituals which are themselves defined by the material ideological apparatus from which derive the ideas of that subject.* Naturally, the four inscriptions of the adjective 'material' in my proposition must be affected by different modalities: the materialities of a displacement for going to mass, of kneeling down, of the gesture of the sign of the cross, or of the *mea culpa*, of a sentence, of a prayer, of an act of contrition, of a penitence, of a gaze, of a hand-shake, of an external verbal discourse or an 'internal' verbal discourse (consciousness), are not one and the same materiality. I shall leave on one side the problem of a theory of the differences between the modalities of materiality.

It remains that in this inverted presentation of things, we are not dealing with an 'inversion' at all, since it is clear that certain notions have purely and simply disappeared from our presentation, whereas others on the contrary survive, and new terms appear.

Disappeared: the term *ideas.*

Survive: the terms *subject, consciousness, belief, actions.*

Appear: the terms *practices, rituals, ideological apparatus.*

It is therefore not an inversion or overturning (except in the sense in which one might say a government or a glass is overturned), but a reshuffle (of a non-ministerial type), a rather strange reshuffle, since we obtain the following result.

Ideas have disappeared as such (insofar as they are endowed with an ideal or spiritual existence), to the precise extent that it has emerged that their existence is inscribed in the actions or practices governed by rituals defined in the last instance by an ideological apparatus. It therefore appears that the subject acts insofar as he is acted on by the following system (set out in the order of its real determination): ideology existing in a material ideological apparatus, prescribing material practices governed by a material ritual, which practices exist in the material actions of a subject acting in all consciousness according to his belief.

But this very presentation reveals that we have retained the following notions: subject, consciousness, belief, actions. From this series I shall immediately extract the decisive central term on which everything else depends: the notion of the *subject.*

And I shall immediately set down two conjoint theses:

1   there is no practice except by and in an ideology;
2   there is no ideology except by the subject and for subjects.

I can now come to my central thesis.

Ideology Interpellates Individuals as Subjects
This thesis is simply a matter of making my last proposition explicit: there is no ideology except by the subject and for subjects. Meaning, there is no ideology except for concrete subjects, and this destination for ideology is only made possible by the subject: meaning, *by the category of the subject* and its functioning.

By this I mean that, even if it only appears under this name (the subject) with the rise of bourgeois ideology, above all with the rise of legal ideology, the category of the subject (which may function under other names: e.g., as the soul in Plato, as God, etc.) is the constitutive category of all ideology, whatever its determination (regional or class) and whatever its historical date – since ideology has no history.

I say: the category of the subject is constitutive of all ideology, but at the same time and immediately I add that *the category of the subject is only constitutive of all ideology insofar as all ideology has the function (which defines it) of 'constituting' concrete individuals as subjects.* In the interaction of this double constitution exists the functioning of all ideology, ideology being nothing but its functioning in the material forms of existence of that functioning.

In order to grasp what follows, it is essential to realize that both he who is writing these lines and the reader who reads them are themselves subjects, and therefore ideological subjects (a tautological proposition), i.e. that the author and the reader of these lines both live 'spontaneously' or 'naturally' in ideology in the sense in which I have said that 'man is an ideological animal by nature'.

That the author, insofar as he writes the lines of a discourse which claims to be scientific, is completely absent as a 'subject' from 'his' scientific discourse (for all scientific discourse is by definition a subject-less discourse, there is no 'Subject of science' except in an ideology of science) is a different question which I shall leave on one side for the moment.

As St Paul admirably put it, it is in the 'Logos', meaning in ideology, that we 'live, move and have our being'. It follows that, for you and for me, the category of the subject is a primary 'obviousness' (obviousnesses are always primary): it is clear that you and I are subjects (free, ethical, etc. . . .). Like all obviousnesses, including those that make a word 'name a thing' or 'have a meaning' (therefore including the obviousness of the 'transparency' of language), the 'obviousness' that you and I are subjects – and that that does not cause any problems – is an ideological effect, the elementary ideological effect. It is indeed a peculiarity of ideology that it imposes (without appearing to do so, since these are 'obviousnesses') obviousnesses as obviousnesses, which we cannot *fail to recognize* and before which we have the inevitable and natural reaction of crying out (aloud or in the 'still, small voice of conscience'): 'That's obvious! That's right! That's true!'

At work in this reaction is the ideological *recognition* function which is one of the two functions of ideology as such (its inverse being the function of *misrecognition–méconnaissance*).

To take a highly 'concrete' example, we all have friends who, when they knock on our door and we ask, through the door, the question 'Who's there?', answer (since it's obvious') 'It's me'. And we recognize that 'it is him', or 'her'. We open the door, and 'it's true, it really was she who was there'. To take another example, when we recognize somebody of our (previous) acquaintance ((*re*)-*connaissance*) in the street, we show him that we have recognized him (and have recognized that he has recognized us) by saying to him 'Hello, my friend', and shaking his hand (a material ritual practice of ideological recognition in everyday life – in France, at least; elsewhere, there are other rituals).

In this preliminary remark and these concrete illustrations, I only wish to point out that you and I are *always already* subjects, and as such constantly practice the rituals of ideology recognition, which guarantee for us that we are indeed concrete, individual, distinguishable and (naturally) irreplaceable subjects. The writing I am currently executing and the reading you are currently performing are also in this respect rituals of ideological recognition, including the 'obviousness' with which the 'truth' or 'error' of my reflections may impose itself on you.

But to recognize that we are subjects and that we function in the practical rituals of the most elementary everyday life (the hand-shake, the fact of calling you by your name, the fact of knowing, even if I do not know what it is, that you 'have' a name of your own, which means that you are recognized as a unique subject, etc.) – this recognition only gives us the 'consciousness' of our incessant (eternal) practice of ideological recognition – its consciousness, i.e. its *recognition* – but in no sense does it give us the (scientific) *knowledge* of the mechanism of this recognition. Now it is this knowledge that we have to reach, if you will, while speaking in ideology, and from within ideology we have to outline a discourse which tries to break with ideology, in order to dare to be the beginning of a scientific (i.e. subjectless) discourse on ideology.

Thus in order to represent why the category of the 'subject' is constitutive of ideology, which only exists by constituting concrete subjects as subjects, I shall employ a special mode of exposition: 'concrete' enough to be recognized, but abstract enough to be thinkable and thought, giving rise to a knowledge.

As a first formulation I shall say: *all ideology hails or interpellates concrete individuals as concrete subjects*, by the functioning of the category of the subject.

This is a proposition which entails that we distinguish for the moment between concrete individuals on the one hand and concrete subjects on the other, although at this level concrete subjects only exist insofar as they are supported by a concrete individual.

I shall then suggest that ideology 'acts' or 'functions' in such a way that it 'recruits' subjects among the individuals (it recruits them all), or 'transforms' the individuals into subjects (it transforms them all) by that very precise operation which I have called *interpellation* or hailing, and which can be imagined along the lines of the most commonplace everyday police (or other) hailing: 'Hey, you there!'

Assuming that the theoretical scene I have imagined takes place in the street, the hailed individual will turn round. By this mere one-hundred-and-eighty-degree physical conversion, he becomes a *subject*. Why? Because he has recognized that the hail was 'really' addressed to him, and that 'it was *really him* who was hailed' (and not someone else). Experience shows that the practical telecommunication of hailings is such that they hardly ever miss their man: verbal call or whistle, the one hailed always recognizes that it is really him who is being hailed. And yet it is a strange phenomenon, and one which cannot be explained solely by 'guilt feelings', despite the large numbers who 'have something on their consciences'.

Naturally for the convenience and clarity of my little theoretical theatre I have had to present things in the form of a sequence, with a before and an after, and thus in the form of a temporal succession. There are individuals walking along. Somewhere (usually behind them) the hail rings out: 'Hey, you there!' One individual (nine times out of ten it is the right one) turns round, believing/suspecting/knowing that it is for him, i.e. recognizing that 'it really is he' who is meant by the hailing. But in reality these things happen without any succession. The existence of ideology and the hailing or interpellation of individuals as subjects are one and the same thing.

I might add: what thus seems to take place outside ideology (to be precise, in the street), in reality takes place in ideology. What really takes place in ideology seems therefore to take place outside it. That is why those who are in ideology believe themselves by definition outside ideology: one of the effects of ideology is the practical *denegation* of the ideological character of ideology by ideology: ideology never says, 'I am ideological'. It is necessary to be outside ideology, i.e. in scientific knowledge, to be able to say: I am in ideology (a quite exceptional case) or (the general case): I was in ideology. As is well known, the accusation of being in ideology only applies to others, never to oneself (unless one is really a Spinozist or a Marxist, which, in this matter, is to be exactly the same thing). Which amounts to saying that ideology *has no outside* (for itself), but at the same time *that it is nothing but outside* (for science and reality).

Spinoza explained this completely two centuries before Marx, who practised it but without explaining it in detail. But let us leave this point, although it is heavy with consequences, consequences which are not just theoretical, but also directly political, since, for example, the whole theory of criticism and self-criticism, the golden rule of the Marxist-Leninist practice of the class struggle, depends on it.

Thus ideology hails or interpellates individuals as subjects. As ideology is eternal, I must now suppress the temporal form in which I have presented the functioning of ideology, and say: ideology has always-already interpellated individuals as subjects, which amounts to making it clear that individuals are always-already interpellated by ideology as subjects, which necessarily leads us to one last proposition: *individuals are always-already subjects*. Hence individuals are 'abstract' with respect to the subjects which they always-already are. This proposition might seem paradoxical.

That an individual is always-already a subject, even before he is born, is nevertheless the plain reality, accessible to everyone and not a paradox at all. Freud shows that individuals are always 'abstract' with respect to the subjects they always-already are, simply by noting the ideological ritual that surrounds the expectation of a 'birth', that 'happy event'. Everyone knows how much and in what way an unborn child is expected. Which amounts to saying, very prosaically, if we agree to drop the 'sentiments', i.e. the forms of family ideology (paternal/maternal/conjugal/fraternal) in which the unborn child is expected: it is certain in advance that it will bear its Father's Name, and will therefore have an identity and be irreplaceable. Before its birth, the child is therefore always-already a subject, appointed as a subject in and by the specific familial ideological configuration in which it is 'expected' once it has been conceived. I hardly need add that this familial ideological configuration is, in its uniqueness, highly structured, and that it is in this implacable and more or less 'pathological' (presupposing that any meaning can be assigned to that term) structure that the former subject-to-be will have to 'find' 'its' place, i.e. 'become' the sexual subject (boy or girl) which it already is in advance. It is clear that this ideological constraint and pre-appointment, and all the rituals of rearing and then education in the family, have some relationship with what Freud studied in the forms of the pre-genital and genital 'stages' of sexuality, i.e. in the 'grip' of what Freud registered by its effects as being the unconscious. But let us leave this point, too, on one side.

Let me go one step further. What I shall now turn my attention to is the way the 'actors' in this *mise en scène* of interpellation, and their respective roles, are reflected in the very structure of all ideology.

An Example: The Christian Religious Ideology
As the formal structure of all ideology is always the same, I shall restrict my analysis to a single example, one accessible to everyone, that of religious ideology, with the proviso that the same demonstration can be produced for ethical, legal, political, aesthetic ideology, etc.

Let us therefore consider the Christian religious ideology. I shall use a rhetorical figure and 'make it speak', i.e. collect into a fictional discourse what it 'says' not only in its two Testaments, its Theologians, Sermons, but also in its practices, its rituals, its ceremonies and its sacraments. The Christian religious ideology says something like this:

It says: I address myself to you, a human individual called Peter (every individual is called by his name, in the passive sense, it is never he who provides his own name), in order to tell you that God exists and that you are answerable to Him. It adds: God addresses himself to you through my voice (Scripture having collected the Word of God, Tradition having transmitted it, Papal Infallibility fixing it for ever on 'nice' points). It says: this is who you are: you are Peter! This is your origin, you were created by God for all eternity, although you were born in the 1920th year of Our Lord! This is your place in the world! This is what you must do! By these means, if you observe the 'law of love' you will be saved, you, Peter, and will become part of the Glorious Body of Christ! Etc. . . .

Now this is quite a familiar and banal discourse, but at the same time quite a surprising one.

Surprising because if we consider that religious ideology is indeed addressed to individuals, in order to 'transform them into subjects', by interpellating the individual, Peter, in order to make him a subject, free to obey or disobey the appeal, i.e. God's commandments; if it calls these individuals by their names, thus recognizing that they are always-already interpellated as subjects with a personal identity (to the extent that Pascal's Christ says: 'It is for you that I have shed this drop of my blood!'); if it interpellates them in such a way that the subject responds: '*Yes, it really is me!*'; if it obtains from them the *recognition* that they really do occupy the place it designates for them as theirs in the world, a fixed residence: 'It really is me, I am here, a worker, a boss or a soldier!' in this vale of tears; if it obtains from them the recognition of a destination (eternal life or damnation) according to the respect or contempt they show to 'God's Commandments', Law become Love; – if everything does happen in this way (in the practices of the well-known rituals of baptism, confirmation, communion, confession and extreme unction, etc. . .), we should note that all this 'procedure' to set up Christian religious subjects is dominated by a strange phenomenon: the fact that there can only be such a multitude of possible religious subjects on the absolute condition that there is a Unique, Absolute, *Other Subject*, i.e. God.

It is convenient to designate this new and remarkable Subject by writing Subject with a capital S to distinguish it from ordinary subjects, with a small s.

It then emerges that the interpellation of individuals as subjects presupposes the 'existence' of a Unique and central Other Subject, in whose Name the religious ideology interpellates all individuals as subjects. All this is clearly written in what is rightly called the Scriptures. 'And it came to pass at the time that God the Lord (Yahweh) spoke to Moses in the cloud. And the Lord cried to Moses, "Moses!" And Moses replied "It is (really) I! I am Moses thy servant, speak and I shall listen!" And the Lord spoke to Moses and said to him, "*I am that I am*"'.

God thus defines himself as the Subject *par excellence*, he who is through himself and for himself ('I am that I am'), and he who interpellates his subject, the individual subjected to him by his very interpellation, i.e. the individual named Moses. And Moses, interpellated-called by his Name, having recognized that it 'really' was he who was called by God, recognizes that he is a subject, a subject *of* God, a subject subjected to God, *a subject through the Subject and subjected to the Subject*. The proof: he obeys him, and makes his people obey God's commandments.

God is thus the Subject, and Moses and the innumerable subjects of God's people, the Subject's interlocutors-interpellates: his *mirrors*, his *reflections*. Were not men made *in the image* of God? As all theological reflection proves, whereas He 'could' perfectly well have done without men, God needs them, the Subject needs the subjects, just as men need God, the subjects need the Subject. Better: God needs men, the great Subject needs subjects, even in the terrible inversion of his image in them (when the subjects wallow in debauchery, i.e. sin).

Better: God duplicates himself and sends his Son to the Earth, as a mere subject 'forsaken' by him (the long complaint of the Garden of Olives which ends in the Crucifixion), subject but Subject, man but God, to do what prepares the way for the final Redemption, the Resurrection of Christ. God thus needs to 'make himself' a man, the Subject needs to become a subject, as if to show empirically, visibly to the eye, tangibly to the hands (see St Thomas) of the subjects, that, if they are subjects, subjected to the Subject, that is solely in order that finally, on

Judgement Day, they will re-enter the Lord's Bosom, like Christ, i.e. re-enter the Subject.

Let us decipher into theoretical language this wonderful necessity for the duplication of *the Subject into subjects* and of *the Subject itself into a subject-Subject*.

We observe that the structure of all ideology, interpellating individuals as subjects in the name of a Unique and Absolute Subject is *speculary*, i.e. a mirror-structure, and *doubly* speculary: this mirror duplication is constitutive of ideology and ensures its functioning. Which means that all ideology is *centred*, that the Absolute Subject occupies the unique place of the Centre, and interpellates around it the infinity of individuals into subjects in a double mirror-connexion such that it *subjects* the subjects to the Subject, while giving them in the Subject in which each subject can contemplate its own image (present and future) the *guarantee* that this really concerns them and Him, and that since everything takes place in the Family (the Holy Family: the Family is in essence Holy), 'God will *recognize* his own in it', i.e. those who have recognized God, and have recognized themselves in Him, will be saved.

Let me summarize what we have discovered about ideology in general.

The duplicate mirror-structure of ideology ensures simultaneously:

1   the interpellation of 'individuals' as subjects;

2   their subjection to the Subject;

3   the mutual recognition of subjects and Subject, the subjects' recognition of each other, and finally the subject's recognition of himself;

4   the absolute guarantee that everything really is so, and that on condition that the subjects recognize what they are and behave accordingly, everything will be all right: Amen – '*So be it*'.

Result: caught in this quadruple system of interpellation as subjects, of subjection to the Subject, of universal recognition and of absolute guarantee, the subjects 'work', they 'work by themselves' in the vast majority of cases, with the exception of the 'bad subjects' who on occasion provoke the intervention of one of the detachments of the (repressive) State apparatus. But the vast majority of (good) subjects work all right 'all by themselves', i.e. by ideology (whose concrete forms are realized in the Ideological State Apparatuses). They are inserted into practices governed by the rituals of the ISAs. They 'recognize' the existing state of affairs (*das Bestehende*), that 'it really is true that it is so and not otherwise', and that they must be obedient to God, to their conscience, to the priest, to de Gaulle, to the boss, to the engineer, that thou shalt 'love thy neighbour as thyself', etc. Their concrete, material behaviour is simply the inscription in life of the admirable words of the prayer: '*Amen – So be it*'.

Yes, the subjects 'work by themselves'. The whole mystery of this effect lies in the first two moments of the quadruple system I have just discussed, or, if you prefer, in the ambiguity of the term *subject*. In the ordinary use of the term, subject in fact means: (1) a free subjectivity, a centre of initiatives, author of and responsible for its actions; (2) a subjected being, who submits to a higher authority, and is therefore stripped of all freedom except that of freely accepting his submission. This last note gives us the meaning of this ambiguity, which is merely a reflection of the effect which produces it: the individual *is interpellated as a (free) subject in order that he shall submit freely to the commandments of the Subject, i.e. in order that he shall (freely) accept his subjection*, i.e. in order that he shall make the gestures and actions of his subjection 'all by himself'. *There are no subjects except by and for their subjection*. That is why they 'work all by themselves'.

'*So be it!* . . . ' This phrase which registers the effect to be obtained proves that it is not 'naturally' so ('naturally': outside the prayer, i.e. outside the ideological intervention). This phrase proves that it *has* to be so if things are to be what they must be, and let us let the words slip: if the reproduction of the relations of production is to be assured, even in the processes of production and circulation, every day, in the 'consciousness', i.e. in the attitudes of the individual-subjects occupying the posts which the socio-technical division of labour assigns to them in production, exploitation, repression, ideologization, scientific practice, etc. Indeed, what is really in question in this mechanism of the mirror recognition of the Subject and of the individuals interpellated as subjects, and of the guarantee given by the Subject to the subjects if they freely accept their subjection to the Subject's 'commandments'? The reality in question in this mechanism, the reality which is necessarily *ignored (méconnue)* in the very forms of recognition (ideology=misrecognition/ignorance) is indeed, in the last resort, the reproduction of the relations of production and of the relations deriving from them.

January–April 1969

P.S. If these few schematic theses allow me to illuminate certain aspects of the functioning of the Superstructure and its mode of intervention in the Infrastructure, they are obviously *abstract* and necessarily leave several important problems unanswered, which should be mentioned:

1   The problem of the *total process* of the realization of the reproduction of the relations of production.

As an element of this process, the ISAs *contribute* to this reproduction. But the point of view of their contribution alone is still an abstract one.

It is only within the processes of production and circulation that this reproduction is *realized*. It is realized by the mechanisms of those processes, in which the training of the workers is 'completed', their posts assigned them, etc. It is in the internal mechanisms of these processes that the effect of the different ideologies is felt (above all the effect of legal-ethical ideology).

But this point of view is still an abstract one. For in a class society the relations of production are relations of exploitation, and therefore relations between antagonistic classes. The reproduction of the relations of production, the ultimate aim of the ruling class, cannot therefore be a merely technical operation training and distributing individuals for the different posts in the 'technical division' of labour. In fact there is no 'technical division' of labour except in the ideology of the ruling class: every 'technical' division, every 'technical' organization of labour is the form and mask of a *social* (=class) division and organization of labour. The reproduction of the relations of production can therefore only be a class undertaking. It is realized through a class struggle which counterposes the ruling class and the exploited class.

The *total process* of the realization of the reproduction of the relations of production is therefore still abstract, insofar as it has not adopted the point of view of this class struggle. To adopt the point of view of reproduction is therefore, in the last instance, to adopt the point of view of the class struggle.

2   The problem of the class nature of the ideolog*ies* existing in a social formation.

The 'mechanism' of ideology *in general* is one thing. We have seen that it can be reduced to a few principles expressed in a few words (as 'poor' as those which, according to Marx, define production *in general*, or in Freud, define *the* unconscious *in general*). If there is any truth in it, this mechanism must be *abstract* with respect to every real ideological formation.

I have suggested that the ideologies were *realized* in institutions, in their rituals and their practices, in the ISAs. We have seen that on this basis they contribute to that form of class struggle, vital for the ruling class, the reproduction of the relations of production. But the point of view itself, however real, is still an abstract one.

In fact, the State and its Apparatuses only have meaning from the point of view of the class struggle, as an apparatus of class struggle ensuring class oppression and guaranteeing the conditions of exploitation and its reproduction. But there is no class struggle without antagonistic classes. Whoever says class struggle of the ruling class says resistance, revolt and class struggle of the ruled class.

That is why the ISAs are not the realization of ideology *in general*, nor even the conflict-free realization of the ideology of the ruling class. The ideology of the ruling class does not become the ruling ideology by the grace of God, nor even by virtue of the seizure of State power alone. It is by the installation of the ISAs in which this ideology is realized and realizes itself that it becomes the ruling ideology. But this installation is not achieved all by itself; on the contrary, it is the stake in a very bitter and continuous class struggle: first against the former ruling classes and their positions in the old and new ISAs, then against the exploited class.

But this point of view of the class struggle in the ISAs is still an abstract one. In fact, the class struggle in the ISAs is indeed an aspect of the class struggle, sometimes an important and symptomatic one: e.g. the anti-religious struggle in the eighteenth century, or the 'crisis' of the educational ISA in every capitalist country today. But the class struggle in the ISAs is only one aspect of a class struggle which goes beyond the ISAs. The ideology that a class in power makes the ruling ideology in its ISAs is indeed 'realized' in those ISAs, but it goes beyond them, for it comes from elsewhere. Similarly, the ideology that a ruled class manages to defend in and against such ISAs goes beyond them, for it comes from elsewhere.

It is only from the point of view of the classes, i.e. of the class struggle, that it is possible to explain the ideolog*ies* existing in a social formation. Not only is it from this starting-point that it is possible to explain the realization of the ruling ideology in the ISAs and of the forms of class struggle for which the ISAs are the seat and the stake. But it is also and above all from this starting-point that it is possible to understand the provenance of the ideologies which are realized in the ISAs and confront one another there. For if it is true that the ISAs represent the *form* in which the ideology of the ruling class must *necessarily* be realized, and the form in which the ideology of the ruled class must *necessarily* be measured and confronted, ideologies are not 'born' in the ISAs but from the social classes at grips in the class struggle: from their conditions of existence, their practices, their experience of the struggle, etc.

April 1970

Notes

1 To my knowledge, Gramsci is the only one who went any distance in the road I am taking. He had the 'remarkable' idea that the State could not be reduced to the (Repressive) State Apparatus, but included, as he put it, a certain number of institutions from '*civil society*': the Church, the Schools, the trade unions, etc. Unfortunately, Gramsci did not systematize his intuitions, which remained in the state of acute but fragmentary notes (cf. Gramsci, *Selections from the Prison Notebooks*, Lawrence and Wishart, 1971, pp. 12, 259, 260–3; see also the letter to Tatiana Schucht, 7 September 1931, in *Letters from Prison*, Quartet, 1979, pp. 203–5).
2 The family obviously has other 'functions' than that of an ISA. It intervenes in the reproduction of labour power. In different modes of production it is the unit of production and/or the unit of consumption.
3 The 'Law' belongs both to the (Repressive) State Apparatus and to the system of the ISAs.

4 Truth, Power and Sexuality

Michel Foucault

From (a) *Power/Knowledge: Selected Interviews and Other Writings 1972–77* by Michel Foucault, 1977. Translated by Colin Gordon. Published by Harvester Press, 1980, and (b) *Sub-stance*, no.20 1978. Translated by Lawrence E. Winters. Reprinted by permission of . . .

(A) TRUTH AND POWER

1 The Discontinuity of Discursive Régimes

[In *The Order of Things*, (1970)] it seemed to me that in certain empirical forms of knowledge like biology, political economy, psychiatry, medicine, etc., the rhythm of transformation doesn't follow the smooth, continuist schemas of development which are normally accepted. The great biological image of a progressive maturation of science still underpins a good many historical analyses; it does not seem to me to be pertinent to history. In a science like medicine, for example, up to the end of the eighteenth century one has a certain type of discourse whose gradual transformation, within a period of twenty-five or thirty years, broke not only with the 'true' propositions which it had hitherto been possible to formulate but also, more profoundly, with the ways of speaking and seeing, the whole ensemble of practices which served as supports for medical knowledge. These are not simply new discoveries, there is a whole new 'régime' in discourse and forms of knowledge. And all this happens in the space of a few years. This is something which is undeniable, once one has looked at the texts with sufficient attention. My problem was not at all to say, '*Voilà*, long live discontinuity, we are in the discontinuous and a good thing too', but to pose the question, 'How is it that at certain moments and in certain orders of knowledge, there are these sudden take-offs, these hastenings of evolution, these transformations which fail to correspond to the calm, continuist image that is normally accredited?' But the important thing here is not that such changes can be rapid and extensive, or rather it is that this extent and rapidity are only the sign of something else: a modification in the rules of formation of statements which are accepted as scientifically true. Thus it is not a change of content (refutation of old errors, recovery of old truths), nor is it a change of theoretical form (renewal of a paradigm, modification of systematic ensembles). It is a question of what *governs* statements, and the way in which they *govern* each other so as to constitute a set of propositions which are scientifically

89

acceptable, and hence capable of being verified or falsified by scientific procedures. In short, there is a problem of the régime, the politics of the scientific statement. At this level it's not so much a matter of knowing what external power imposes itself on science, as of what effects of power circulate among scientific statements, what constitutes, as it were, their internal régime of power, and how and why at certain moments that régime undergoes a global modification.

It was these different régimes that I tried to identify and describe in *The Order of Things*, all the while making it clear that I wasn't trying for the moment to explain them, and that it would be necessary to try and do this in a subsequent work. But what was lacking here was this problem of the 'discursive régime', of the effects of power peculiar to the play of statements. I confused this too much with systematicity, theoretical form, or something like a paradigm. This same central problem of power, which at that time I had not yet properly isolated, emerges in two very different aspects at the point of junction of *Madness and Civilisation* and *The Order of Things*. [. . .]

This task [of analysing the mechanics of power] could only begin after 1968, that is to say on the basis of daily struggles at grass roots level, among those whose fight was located in the fine meshes of the web of power. This was where the concrete nature of power became visible, along with the prospect that these analyses of power would prove fruitful in accounting for all that had hitherto remained outside the field of political analysis. To put it very simply, psychiatric internment, the mental normalisation of individuals, and penal institutions have no doubt a fairly limited importance if one is only looking for their economic significance. On the other hand, they are undoubtedly essential to the general functioning of the wheels of power. So long as the posing of the question of power was kept subordinate to the economic instance and the system of interests which this served, there was a tendency to regard these problems as of small importance [. . .]

I wanted to see how these problems [about the conditions of possibility, modalities and constitution of the 'objects' and domains I analysed] could be resolved within a historical framework, instead of referring them back to a constituent object (madness, criminality or whatever). But this historical contextualisation needed to be something more than the simple relativisation of the phenomenological subject. I don't believe the problem can be solved by historicising the subject as posited by the phenomenologists, fabricating a subject that evolves through the course of history. One has to dispense with the constituent subject, to get rid of the subject itself, that's to say, to arrive at an analysis which can account for the constitution of the subject within a historical framework. And this is what I would call genealogy, that is, a form of history which can account for the constitution of knowledges, discourses, domains of objects etc., without having to make reference to a subject which is either transcendental in relation to the field of events or runs in its empty sameness throughout the course of history. [. . .]

2 Ideology and Repression

The notion of ideology appears to me to be difficult to make use of, for three reasons. The first is that, like it or not, it always stands in virtual opposition to something else which is supposed to count as truth. Now I believe that the problem does not consist in drawing the line between that in a discourse which falls under the category of scientificity or truth, and that which comes under some other category, but in seeing historically how effects of truth are produced within discourses which in themselves are neither true nor false. The second drawback is that the concept of ideology refers, I think necessarily, to something of the order of a subject. Thirdly, ideology stands in a secondary position relative to something which functions as its infrastructure, as its material, economic determinant, etc. For these three reasons, I think that this is a notion that cannot be used without circumspection.

The notion of repression is a more insidious one, or at all events I myself have had much more trouble in freeing myself of it, in so far as it does indeed appear to correspond so well with a whole range of phenomena which belong among the effects of power. When I wrote *Madness and Civilisation*, I made at least an implicit use of this notion of repression. I think indeed that I was positing the existence of a sort of living, voluble and anxious madness which the mechanisms of power and psychiatry were supposed to have come to repress and reduce to silence. But it seems to me now that the notion of repression is quite inadequate for capturing what is precisely the productive aspect of power. In defining the effects of power as repression, one adopts a purely juridical conception of such power, one identifies power with a law which says no, power is taken above all as carrying the force of a prohibition. Now I believe that this is a wholly negative, narrow, skeletal conception of power, one which has been curiously widespread. If power were never anything but repressive, if it never did anything but to say no, do you really think one would be brought to obey it? What makes power hold good, what makes it accepted, is simply the fact that it doesn't only weigh on us as a force that says no, but that it traverses and produces things, it induces pleasure, forms knowledge, produces discourse. It needs to be considered as a productive network which runs through the whole social body, much more than as a negative instance whose function is repression. In *Discipline and Punish* what I wanted to show was how, from the seventeenth and eighteenth centuries onwards, there was a veritable technological take-off in the productivity of power. Not only did the monarchies of the Classical period develop great state apparatuses (the army, the police and fiscal administration), but above all there was established at this period what one might call a new 'economy' of power, that is to say procedures which allowed the effects of power to circulate in a manner at once continuous, uninterrupted, adapted and 'individualised' throughout the entire social body. These new techniques are both much more efficient and much less wasteful (less costly economically, less risky in their results, less open to loopholes and resistances) than the techniques previously employed which were based on a mixture of more or less forced tolerances (from recognised privileges to endemic criminality) and costly ostentation (spectacular and discontinuous interventions of power, the most violent form of which was the 'exemplary', because exceptional, punishment). [. . .]

3   The State

To pose the problem [of disciplinary power] in terms of the State means to continue posing it in terms of sovereign and sovereignty, that is to say in terms of law. If one describes all these phenomena of power as dependant on the State apparatus, this means grasping them as essentially repressive: the Army as a power of death, police and justice as punitive instances, etc. I don't want to say that the State isn't important; what I want to say is that relations of power, and hence the analysis that must be made of them, necessarily extend beyond the limits of the State. In two senses: first of all because the State, for all the omnipotence of its apparatuses, is far from being able to occupy the whole field of actual power relations, and further because the State can only operate on the basis of other, already existing power relations. The State is superstructural in relation to a whole series of power networks that invest the body, sexuality, the family, kinship, knowledge, technology and so forth. True, these networks stand in a conditioning – conditioned relationship to a kind of 'meta-power' which is structured essentially round a certain number of great prohibition functions; but this meta-power with its prohibitions can only take hold and secure its footing where it is rooted in a whole series of multiple and indefinite power relations that supply the necessary basis for the great negative forms of power [. . .] I would say that the State consists in the codification of a whole number of power relations which render its functioning possible [. . .]

Along with all the fundamental technical inventions and discoveries of the seventeenth and eighteenth centuries, a new technology of the exercise of power also emerged which was probably even more important than the constitutional reforms and new forms of government established at the end of the eighteenth century. [. . .] What I find most striking about these new technologies of power [. . .] is their concrete and precise character, their grasp of a multiple and differentiated reality. In feudal societies power functioned essentially through signs and levies. Signs of loyalty to the feudal lords, rituals, ceremonies and so forth, and levies in the form of taxes, pillage, hunting, war etc. In the seventeenth and eighteenth centuries a form of power comes into being that begins to exercise itself through social production and social service. It becomes a matter of obtaining productive service from individuals in their concrete lives. And in consequence, a real and effective 'incorporation' of power was necessary, in the sense that power had to be able to gain access to the bodies of individuals, to their acts, attitudes and modes of everyday behaviour. Hence the significance of methods like school discipline, which succeeded in making children's bodies the object of highly complex systems of manipulation and conditioning. But at the same time, these new techniques of power needed to grapple with the phenomena of population, in short to undertake the administration, control and direction of the accumulation of men (the economic system that promotes the accumulation of capital and the system of power that ordains the accumulation of men are, from the seventeenth century on, correlated and inseparable phenomena): hence there arise the problems of demography, public health, hygiene, housing conditions, longevity and fertility. And I believe that the political significance of the problem of sex is due to the fact that sex is located at the point of intersection of the discipline of the body and the control of the population. [. . .]

4 The Politics of Truth

The important thing [. . .] is that truth isn't outside power, or lacking in power: contrary to a myth whose history and functions would repay further study, truth isn't the reward of free spirits, the child of protracted solitude, nor the privilege of those who have succeeded in liberating themselves. Truth is a thing of this world: it is produced only by virtue of multiple forms of constraint. And it induces regular effects of power. Each society has its régime of truth, its 'general politics' of truth: that is, the types of discourse which it accepts and makes function as true; the mechanisms and instances which enable one to distinguish true and false statements, the means by which each is sanctioned; the techniques and procedures accorded value in the acquisition of truth; the status of those who are charged with saying what counts as true.

In societies like ours, the 'political economy' of truth is characterised by five important traits. 'Truth' is centred on the form of scientific discourse and the institutions which produce it; it is subject to constant economic and political incitement (the demand for truth, as much for economic production as for political power); it is the object, under diverse forms, of immense diffusion and consumption (circulating through apparatuses of education and information whose extent is relatively broad in the social body, not withstanding certain strict limitations); it is produced and transmitted under the control, dominant if not exclusive, of a few great political and economic apparatuses (university, army, writing, media); lastly, it is the issue of a whole political debate and social confrontation ('ideological' struggles).

It seems to me that what must now be taken into account [is that] the intellectual is not the 'bearer of universal values'. Rather, it's the person occupying a specific position–but whose specificity is linked, in a society like ours, to the general functioning of an apparatus of truth. In other words, the intellectual has a three-fold specificity: that of his class position (whether as petty-bourgeois in the service of capitalism or 'organic' intellectual of the proletariat); that of his conditions of life and work, linked to his condition as an intellectual (his field of research, his place in a laboratory, the political and economic demands to which he submits or against which he rebels, in the university, the hospital, etc.); lastly, the specificity of the politics of truth in our societies. And it's with this last factor that his position can take on a general significance and that his local, specific struggle can have effects and implications which are not simply professional or sectoral. The intellectual can operate and struggle at the general level of that régime of truth which is so essential to the structure and functioning of our society. There is a battle 'for truth', or at least 'around truth' – it being understood once again that by truth I do not mean 'the ensemble of truths which are to be discovered and accepted', but rather 'the ensemble of rules according to which the true and the false are separated and specific effects of power attached to the true', it being understood also that it's not a matter of a battle 'on behalf' of the truth, but of a battle about the status of truth and the economic and political role it plays. It is necessary to think of the political problems of intellectuals not in terms of 'science' and 'ideology', but in terms of 'truth' and 'power'. And thus the question of the professionalisation of intellectuals and the division between intellectual and manual labour can be envisaged in a new way.

All this must seem very confused and uncertain. Uncertain indeed, and what I am saying here is above all to be taken as a hypothesis. In order for it to be a little less confused, however, I would like to put forward a few 'propositions' – not firm assertions, but simply suggestions to be further tested and evaluated.

'Truth' is to be understood as a system of ordered procedures for the production, regulation, distribution, circulation and operation of statements.

'Truth' is linked in a circular relation with systems of power which produce and sustain it, and to effects of power which it induces and which extend it. A 'régime' of truth.

This régime is not merely ideological or superstructural; it was a condition of the formation and development of capitalism. And it's this same régime which, subject to certain modifications, operates in the socialist countries (I leave open here the question of China, about which I know little).

The essential political problem for the intellectual is not to criticise the ideological contents supposedly linked to science, or to ensure that his own scientific practice is accompanied by a correct ideology, but that of ascertaining the possibility of constituting a new politics of truth. The problem is not changing people's consciousnesses – or what's in their heads – but the political, economic, institutional régime of the production of truth.

It's not a matter of emancipating truth from every system of power (which would be a chimera, for truth is already power) but of detaching the power of truth from the forms of hegemony, social, economic and cultural, within which it operates at the present time.

The political question, to sum up, is not error, illusion, alienated consciousness or ideology; it is truth itself.

(B)   THE WEST AND THE TRUTH OF SEX

What if there were [at the centre of 'sexual politics'] not a rejection and an occultation (mystification), but an incitement? What if the essential function of power were not to say no, to forbid, and to censor, but rather to bind coercion, pleasure and truth according to some indefinite spiral?

Think only of the zealousness with which, for several centuries now, our societies have multiplied all the institutions which are destined to extort the truth from sex, and which, thereby, produce a specific pleasure. Consider the enormous obligation to confess, and the ambiguous pleasures which simultaneously make it disturbing and desirable: confession, education, the relations between parents and children, between doctors and the sick, between psychiatrists and hysterics, between psychoanalysts and patients. It has been said that the West has never been capable of inventing a single new pleasure. Does the sensual delight in dredging, in hunting down, in interrupting, in short, the 'analytic pleasure' count for nothing?

Rather than as a society committed to the repression of sex, I see our society as dedicated to its 'expression', if I may be forgiven this devalued word. I see the West as bent on extracting the truth from sex. The silences, the barriers, the evasions should not be underestimated; but they could only have formed and produced their considerable effects on the basis of a will to knowledge which runs through our entire relationship to sex. A will to knowledge which is so imperious, and in which we are so enveloped, that we not only seek the truth of sex, but seek, through it, the truth about ourselves. We expect it to tell us about ourselves. From Gerson to Freud, an entire logic of sex has been constructed, a logic which organizes the science of the subject.

We willingly imagine ourselves under a 'Victorian' regime. It seems to me instead that our kingdom is the one imagined by Diderot in *Les Bijoux Indiscrets*; a certain, nearly invisible mechanism makes sex speak in a virtually inexhaustible chatter. We are in a society of speaking sex.

We might also, perhaps, have to question a society about the way in which the relations of power, truth, and pleasure are organized. It seems to me that we can distinguish two principal systems of organization. One is that of *erotic art*. Its truth is drawn from pleasure itself, collected as experience, analyzed according to its quantity, pursued throughout its reverberations in the body and the soul. This quintessential knowledge is transmitted by magisterial initiation, with the stamp of secrecy, to those who have shown themselves to be worthy of it, and who would make use of it at the very level of their pleasure, to intensify it, and to make it more acute and fulfilling.

For several centuries, Western Civilization had nearly no erotic art; it established the relations of power, pleasure, and truth in an entirely different mode – that of a 'science of sex'. A type of knowledge in which what is analyzed is not so much pleasure as desire; where the function of the master is not initiation, but interrogation, listening, and deciphering; where the end of that long process was not an increase in pleasure, but a modification of the subject (who, in this way, was pardoned or reconciled, cured or liberated).

The relations between this art and this science are too numerous for us to be able to find here the demarcation line between two types of societies. Whether in the direction of conscience or in the psychoanalytic cure, the knowledge of sex brings with it secret imperatives, a particular relation to the master, and a whole game of promises which still relate it to erotic art. How could one believe that without these confused relations someone would purchase so dearly the bi-weekly right to laboriously formulate the truth of their desire, and to wait patiently for the benefits of the interpretation?

My project would be to trace the genealogy of this 'science of sex'. I realize that this is not a novel enterprise; many today are devoted to it, showing how many denials, occultations, fears, and systematic misunderstandings have held back for so long the eventual knowledge of sex. I would like, however, to undertake this genealogy in positive terms, beginning with the incitements, the sources, the techniques and procedures which have made the formulation of this knowledge possible. Starting from the Christian problem of the flesh, I wish to follow all the mechanisms which have given rise to a discourse on the truth of sex, and have organized round it a mixed regime of pleasure and power. Recognizing the impossibility of globally following this genesis, I will try, in separate studies, to locate some of its most important strategies concerning children, women, perversions, and birth control.

The question which has traditionally been asked is this: why has the West censured sex for so long: and, on the basis of this refusal, or this fear, how have we come, with all reticence, to ask the question of its truth? Why and how, since the end of the nineteenth century, have we undertaken – with a difficulty which Freud's courage still attests to – to expose a part of the great secret?

I wish to undertake an entirely different interrogation: why has the West so continuously questioned the truth of sex and required that everyone formulate this truth for himself? Why has the West so obstinately wanted our relation to ourselves to pass through this truth? It is therefore astonishing that at the beginning of the twentieth century we were gripped by a great new guilt; that we began to undergo a sort of historical remorse which led us to believe that for centuries we had been wrong about sex.

It seems to me that what has been systematically misunderstood about this new guilt which we seem to crave is precisely that vast configuration of knowledge which the West has ceaselessly organized around sex, through religious, medical, or social techniques.

I suppose that many would agree with me on this point. But I will immediately be asked: 'Hasn't this great uproar about sex, this constant concern, had only one objective: to forbid the free utilization of sex?' Certainly the role of prohibitions has been important. But, from the start and above all, has sex been prohibited? Or, rather, aren't the prohibitions only snares within a complex and positive strategy?

Here we touch on a more general problem which we will have to treat thoroughly in counterpoint to this history of sexuality – the problem of power. When we speak of power, it is spontaneously conceived of as law, as interdiction, as prohibition and repression; and we are quite disarmed when we follow it in its mechanisms and in its positive effects. A certain juridical model weighs heavily on the analyses of power, giving an absolute privilege to the form of the law. We must write a history of sexuality which is not guided by the idea of a repressive power, nor of a censorial power, but by the idea of an inciting power, of a knowing power. We must strive to locate the regime of coercion, of pleasure, and of discourse which is not inhibitive but constitutive of the complex domain of sexuality.

PART II

Familial Ideology

5 Familial Ideology

Veronica Beechey

Introduction

'Familial ideology' is a fairly new area of enquiry which has been opened up for intellectual analysis, mainly by feminist writers, in recent years. A number of people have pointed out that the terms used to analyse domestic arrangements are confused and confusing, that 'the family' and 'the household' are often used interchangeably, for instance, and that 'the family' is used to refer both to all kinds of kinship and residential arrangements and to the more historically specific nuclear family, which leads to the incorrect assumption that the nuclear form of family which is the most common form in societies like contemporary Britain is universal in form and based on biological differences between the sexes. (See Harris, pp. 00–00 in this volume for further discussion of this.) Confusions are rife in this area, but linguistic muddles are not peculiar to studies of the family. Nigel Harris, pp.121–33 in this volume for further discussion of this.) Confusions are rife power implicit in the ambiguity of certain central concepts' like 'democracy' and 'socialism' (Harris, 1971, p.23), and Mannheim makes a similar point when he suggests that 'thought is a particularly sensitive index of social and cultural change' (Mannheim, 1960, p.74). Furthermore, linguistic confusions often reflect more fundamental struggles over the meaning of terms which reflect conflicts in the wider society. It seems clear that when a term like 'the family' becomes confusing and contested – when, for instance, a proposed White House conference on families planned for 1980 changed its name from singular to plural as it became clear that it was impossible to arrive at even a rudimentary consensus as to what 'the American family' was supposed to be – this not only signifies confusion about the term but also conflict about the social institution to which the term supposedly refers. It is partly because the family has itself become a site of conflict, and partly because of a growing awareness of the pervasiveness of 'familial' ideas in everyday life – in advertisements and soap operas, in medical and legal practices, in the operation of welfare institutions (like the social security system) and in management and trade union thinking, for instance – that familial ideology has become a subject of intellectual concern.

In this article I shall discuss a number of different analyses of familial ideology – Marxist and Foucauldian frameworks and analyses based upon semiology and Lacanian psychoanalysis. I shall also be concerned with the contributions made by feminist analyses in this area. I shall discuss a variety of examples of familial ideology, ranging from familial ideas within the welfare state and pronatalist thinking in post-war Britain to conceptions of 'the domestic' in different societies, and television soap operas and media representations of the Royal Family. Although, as will become clear in the course of the article, there is no general definition of 'familial ideology' which would be agreed to by everybody who is concerned with what might broadly be described as 'familial ideas' or 'familialism', as Donzelot calls it (Donzelot, 1979), a preliminary working definition of familial ideology might run as follows. Familial ideology refers to systems of beliefs which:

(i) describe a particular kinship system and set of living arrangements (the coresident nuclear family) and assert that this form of family is universal and normatively desirable, and
(ii) assert that the form of sexual division of labour in which the woman is housewife and mother and primarily located within the private world of the family, and the man is wage-earner and bread-winner and primarily located in the 'public' world of paid work, is universal and normatively desirable.

Although overt reference is by no means always made to biology or to the 'naturalness' of these arrangements, it is an underlying assumption of familial ideology that the form of family and the sexual division of labour within it are, at root, biologically determined. Although I have defined familial ideology as being comprised of beliefs, like other ideologies familial ideology may be expressed in a systematic way or be very much part of taken-for-granted commonsense assumptions. Likewise, it may be reproduced through social institutions (for example, the health service, or the state), either directly, through overt proclamations, or (as happens more often) indirectly, through institutional rituals and practices. Before proceeding with the main arguments about familial ideology which comprise the bulk of the article I want to make a few preliminary remarks about the sociology of the family, critical perspectives on the family, and the sociology of knowledge, in order to place the current discussion in a broader sociological context.

Early analyses of the family were conducted by the Chicago School, the most important school of American sociology in the inter-war years, not as a distinct object of study but as part of broader analyses of urbanization and modernization. Many of these studies emphasized the rootlessness of life in America's cities and the increasing isolation of the nuclear family. The effects of 'modernization' on the family were taken up again in the structural functionalist framework which became the dominant paradigm in studies of the family in Britain and the USA in the decades after the war.

Talcott Parsons, the principal structural functionalist theorist of the family, argued that the family was changing as a result of modernization, but rejected the view that it was facing dissolution or loss of function. Parsons argued that the family was becoming structurally differentiated and that its functions were being redefined. Thus, he argued, although it has lost its economic role as a unit of production, its significance in the system of political power and its function as a direct agency of integration within the wider society, the family has retained the function of socializing children (which it shares with the school) and has taken on new functions of stabilising adult personalities (Parsons, 1964). Parsons' theory was being formulated at a time when great emphasis was being placed on the importance of the woman's mothering role by psychologists like John Bowlby, but whereas Bowlby developed certain psycho-analytic insights into his theory of maternal deprivation (Bowlby, 1963), Parsons generated a macro-social theory of societal functioning and change. Like Bowlby, Parsons did not question the primacy of the mother-child relationship, nor did he consider why the woman's role as housewife and mother was being stressed in the post-war period. Parsons' theory reflected the prevailing beliefs that society was moving in some inexorable march towards progress, that the American middle class family was a success story (and the corollary of this that families which did not conform to this norm were 'failures'), and that the woman's primary role was a familial one. Parsons' model of society which represented the family (like the rest of society) as progressively evolving and depicted gender divisions as being determined, in the last analysis, by reproductive differences between the sexes, blinded him (as it has blinded many subsequent and far less sophisticated sociologists) to a range of important questions about the family and familial ideology and about the position of women. Instead of subjecting familial ideology and gender divisions to sociological investigation, Parsons incorporated conventional familial assumptions into his own framework of analysis.

Although structural functionalism continued to provide the dominant sociological paradigm for studying the family throughout the 1960s, there was growing pessimism about the state of the family among many writers on the subject, both conservative and radical. Some American sociologists commented on the isolation and inward-lookingness of the family which was becoming increasingly separated from kinfolk and traditional communities in the fast-growing American suburbs. And, although many sociologists found evidence of traditional communities and kin relations being recreated in the new towns and suburbs of Britain, other writers were less complacent. On the more radical front, the 'anti-psychiatry' writers R. D. Laing (1960 and 1971) and David Cooper (1972) engaged in a swingeing critique of the nuclear family, arguing that it produced 'schizophrenogenic' children, while Laing argued in *The Politics of the Family* that madness was the only sane response to an irrational world (a somewhat contradictory proposition). This theme was echoed by the anthropologist Edmund Leach in his BBC Reith Lectures when he suggested that 'far from being the basis of the good society, the family, with all its narrow privacy and tawdry secrets, is the source of all our discontents'. Reflecting on the different approaches to studying the family, the American sociologists, Brigitte and Peter Berger, point out in their recent book, *The War Over the Family* (Berger and Berger, 1983), that in the 1960s 'no longer were deviations in the norm seen as the problem but the norm itself – that is, the normative American family – was perceived and denounced as the real problem. In other words the problem was not maladjusted individuals or social groups but rather, the "sick society" of which the "sick family" was an integral part' (Berger and Berger, 1983, p.16).

Although alternative frameworks for analysing the family began to emerge from a variety of sources – for example, radical psychology and structuralist anthropology – it was feminism which provided the real impetus for a fundamental rethinking of the family in the 1970s and 1980s. Many feminists have identified the family as a major site of, if not *the* source of, women's oppression, and this critical approach to the family is one of the factors distinguishing the new feminism which emerged in the late 1960s from that of previous periods. In academic discussions feminists have generally been critical of both conventional sociological theories of the family like Parsons' and of many of the critical perspectives because they have generally ignored women's experiences of the family (both as individuals and as a group) and have seldom tackled the question of gender inequalities within the family or the possibilities for women attaining equality with men. Indeed, one might say that one of the criteria used by feminists to assess other perspectives on the family is what they say about women's experiences and the possibilities for women's emancipation/liberation.

The sociology of knowledge has traditionally concerned itself with analysing knowledge within a social context and with relating knowledge to groups in society who are conceived of as the holders or 'bearers' of this knowledge, whether these are social classes or other social groups. Forms of knowledge and cultural products have been conceptualized as matters of sociological enquiry because they have been seen as social constructs. Thus, in locating cultural products within a social context and linking them to groups in society, sociologists have generally subjected them to critical scrutiny. The sociology of knowledge is, as Terry Lovell has pointed out, an inherently critical enterprise (Lovell, 1980). Robert Merton argues in his classic statement on the Sociology of Knowledge that 'the term "knowledge" must be interpreted very broadly indeed, since studies in this area have dealt with virtually the whole gamut of cultural products' (Merton, 1957, p.456). However, despite the fact that familial ideology has undoubtedly been a powerful social force which has been quite explicitly articulated as part of the dominant political discourse in certain situations (e.g. Victorian Britain, and the contemporary United States, fascist states – cf. Mercer's article in Donald and Hall, 1985) and has been implicit in many other discourses, it has seldom been the subject of sociological scrutiny and has generally fallen outside the purview of the sociology of knowledge (an exception to this being a series of studies on the family produced by the Frankfurt School). Speculating a little, I would point to three reasons for this. First, although there have been critics of the family in previous periods (the Owenite socialists, for example), it is only relatively recently that the family has been more widely questioned and has become an arena of overt conflict. A second reason is that sociologists have generally accepted the prevailing view that the family embodies a 'natural' division of labour between the sexes. Since, with a few exceptions like Margaret Mead, they have not regarded beliefs about the family and the sexual division of labour as social constructs, they have not subjected them to sociological investigation. Finally, sociologists of knowledge have generally been concerned either with analysing so-called 'primitive' beliefs (as in Durkheim's analysis of primitive religions and Mauss' analysis of classification systems) or, when they have studied industrial societies, they have been preoccupied with forms of knowledge about the 'public' sphere (for example, the law, religion, the mass media, political beliefs), and have seldom analysed the 'private' sphere, let alone transcended the distinction between 'private' and 'public' spheres.

Since familial ideology has scarcely been analysed within the classical sociological tradition, there are no 'grand masters' to turn to. Nevertheless, as I hope will become clear in the course of this article, analyses of familial ideology have been concerned with similar sorts of questions to those which preoccupy students of beliefs and ideologies in other spheres, and the literature is riven with similar sorts of controversies, the most fundamental of which concern whether or not the term 'ideology' can be used at all. In this article I shall be concerned with two questions which, Stuart Hall suggests in his article in this volume, are central to the analysis of ideology. First, how does the ideological process work and what are its mechanisms? And second, how is 'the ideological' to be conceived in relation to other practices within a social formation? It should become clear in the course of discussion that work in this area is still in its infancy and that there is no generally accepted theory of familial ideology. I hope it becomes clear, too, that people writing in this area disagree radically with one another, and that answers to the second question of how the ideological is related to other elements of the social formation in particular differ widely.

The Influence of Marxism

Feminist critics have pointed out again and again that Marx himself had very little to say about the family. Nevertheless, the Marxist framework for analysing ideology has been extremely influential on analyses of familial ideology, much more so than the frameworks of other classical sociologists like Durkheim, Weber and Mannheim. There is some discussion of the family in *The German Ideology* where Marx and Engels criticize German idealist philosophers for adhering to an abstract universal 'concept of the family' and develop several arguments of their own: viz, that the bourgeoisie develops its general concept of 'the family "as such"' on the basis of its experience of the bourgeois family; that the form of family varies among different social classes and changes historically and should be analysed concretely in the context of an analysis of material social relations; and that as society develops, the family (which exists in the realm of 'civil society') becomes increasingly subordinated to 'the state' (Marx and Engels, 1965). Several aspects of the classical Marxist theory of ideology are evident in this discussion: first, the view that a distinction can be drawn between ideological conceptions and concrete social relations; second, that the former distort or obscure the latter; third, the notion that ideas can be linked to social classes, and finally the claim that the ruling class in any society proclaims its ideas as universal. Although he developed his theory of ideology further in his later writings, Marx never paid further attention to familial ideology, and his occasional references to the family (e.g. in *Capital*) suggest that he saw it in mainly biological terms. Likewise Engels did not concern himself with questions of ideology in *The Origin of the Family, Private Property and the State*. In this, which remains the classic Marxist text on the family, Engels restricts himself to an analysis of the role of the family in 'the production and reproduction of immediate life' (Engels, 1968, p.445).

It was Louis Althusser who developed a framework within which familial ideology began to be analysed in Marxist terms, especially by feminist workers although Althusser himself has very little to say about the family and familial ideology. He did, however, generate a distinctive and extremely influential framework for analysing ideology, which is discussed by James Donald and myself in the introduction to this volume. Althusser's analysis of ideology has influenced discussions of familial ideology in a number of rather different ways. The analysis in the first part of 'ideology and ideological state apparatuses' (the ISAs essay, see pp. 56–72) in which Althusser emphasizes the role of the dominant ideology in reproducing labour power and the social relations of production, has influenced writers like Elizabeth Wilson who, in *Women and the Welfare State* (Wilson, 1977), analyses the ways in which the welfare state reproduces the capitalist mode of production and women's dependence upon men within the family. And the more structural and psychoanalytic elements of Althusser's analysis, which are developed in the second part of the essay, have influenced writers like Juliet Mitchell. In *Women's Estate*, for example, Mitchell unravels the different structures determining women's position in contemporary capitalist societies (Mitchell, 1971), while in *Psychoanalysis and Feminism* (Mitchell, 1974) and her other essays on psychoanalysis (several of which are reprinted in *Women: The Longest Revolution*, Mitchell, 1984), she develops an analysis of feminine gender identity which is influenced both by Althusser's concerns in the second part of the ISAs essay and by Lacanian psychoanalysis. The critical contribution of the second part of the ISAs essay, and of Lacanian psychoanalysis, is that it provides an account of the constitution of subjectivity, something which has generally been missing from Marxist analysis of ideology. I shall briefly discuss Wilson's arguments and Mitchell's analysis in *Woman's Estate* next, and shall later return to the more psychoanalytic questions when I discuss representation of the family.

Women and the Welfare State

Women and the Welfare State is, as the title suggests, a book about how the welfare state defines women. Its central argument is that the welfare state embodies a set of assumptions about women which are expressed in its ideology and manifested in its policies and practices. The key to this ideology is the assumption that a woman's role is principally that of housewife and mother. Wilson argues that although its roots lie in the history of welfare in the twentieth century more generally, this familial ideology became particularly prevalent in welfare policies since the Second World War, a period marked by an intensification of state intervention in family life and in the life of children and by 'a heavy emphasis on the rebuilding of family life . . . (which) implied a return to traditional roles for women' (p.60).

Elizabeth Wilson argues that, the view that a woman's primary role is that of housewife and mother and that her proper place is in the family is expressed in a whole range of writings published in the 1950s and 1960s – for example, in sociological studies of family and kinship like those of Young and Wilmott and Townsend, in the writings of psychologists like John Bowlby whose 'maternal deprivation' theory received great publicity in the 1950s, and in psycho-analytic writings. She suggests that similar views were also expressed in many government reports – for instance, the Beveridge Report which laid the foundations for the national insurance system established in 1946, the 1951 Royal Commission on Divorce, and the Wolfenden Report, which, although heralded at the time for decriminalizing homosexuality, still 'seemed primarily concerned with the quality of family life' (p.67). Wilson also shows how a number of education reports – the Crowther Report, the Newsom Report and (to a lesser extent) the Plowden Report – emphasized the importance of educating girls into domesticity, because, as Sir John Newsom put it in a later article in *The Observer* newspaper, 'their main social function . . . is to make for themselves, their children and their husbands a secure and suitable home and to be mothers' (quoted in Wilson, 1977, p.83).

The welfare state, according to Wilson, 'is not just a set of services, it is also a set of ideas about society–about the family–and not least important, about women, who have a centrally important role within the family, as its linchpin' (p.9). She argues that the concept of the child in the nuclear family is central to the modern welfare state, and that the welfare state plays a crucial role in guiding and promoting the home and the school in their tasks of reproducing labour power. Wilson argues that while the welfare state controls 'the way in which the woman does her job in the home of servicing the workers and bringing up their children' (p.40) the ideology of welfarism (of which familial ideology is one component) masks the fact that women do housework unpaid and are used as an industrial reserve army of cheap and docile labour. In Wilson's view, then, the ideology of welfarism operates to distort the sexual division of labour. The welfare state is also important, she argues, in reproducing the social relations of production: it operates on universalistic criteria and fosters the belief that everyone is treated equally, yet continues to reproduce social classes and women's dependence (by treating married women as economic dependants on this husbands). Here again it distorts the real social relations which, in Wilson's view, are relations of class and gender inequality. Wilson argues that it is incorrect to analyse the dominant ideology in conspiratorial terms. Discussing the Beveridge Report she suggests that 'Beveridge's views did not express an overt state conspiracy to get women back to the kitchen sink at the end of the war', but 'to a great extent he simply reflected views commonly held at the time . . . (He) was not the only one to expect that, as before the war, marriage and work would continue to be alternatives to most women' (p.154). According to this analysis, part of the power of ideology resides in the fact that its operation is concealed, that ideologies construct themselves as being non-ideological.

Wilson's analysis of familial ideology has a number of strengths. It shows how familial ideology can be embedded in the operation of other, non-familial institutions (for example, the welfare state), it suggests that familial ideology can be held unconsciously – it does not arise as part of a conscious conspiracy, and it shows how familial ideology can play an important role in obscuring women's domestic labour and distorting the sexual division of labour and the operation of the welfare state. Furthermore, her analysis penetrates beneath the surface distinction between 'public' and 'private' spheres and analyses the relationships between them, and it suggests links between the family, the welfare state and the economic organization of the capitalist mode of production. However, some of the links made by Wilson are also the source of weaknesses within her analysis. For example, her analysis of the relationships between the family, the welfare state and the 'needs' of the capitalist economy is heavily functionalist and does not allow for contradictions between these institutions; while her model of the base-superstructure relationship is (like Althusser's) mechanistic and makes too rigid a separation between 'ideological' and 'economic' factors; and finally, her analysis of the family and familial ideology is monolithic and insufficiently historical. Some of these criticisms of this type of approach are developed farther by writers whose arguments I shall be discussing later in this article, particularly Denise Riley, who is also concerned with 'familial' ideas in post-war Britain, but develops a very different form of analysis.

Woman's Estate

In *Woman's Estate*, Juliet Mitchell places great emphasis on the role of ideology in representing the family as natural and in proclaiming ideal images of the family and of women. Mitchell follows Engels in arguing that the family was the economic basis of private property in feudal society, but suggests that under capitalism the family becomes the focus of the *idea* of private property. Familial ideology, she suggests, was an essential weapon in the armoury of the nascent bourgeoisie which used universalistic ideas to represent what was in fact a limited class interest. Mitchell's main arguments about ideology are not historical but structural, however. She argues that the position of women in industrial capitalist societies like Britain is determined not by any single cause, but by several discrete structures: production, (biological) reproduction, sexuality and socialization. These structures have developed independently from each other, according to Mitchell, but the ideology of the family imposes a unitariness and a universality on them which is otherwise absent. Like Althusser, Mitchell argues that this ideology is real and is not a matter of false consciousness. She also suggests that it is not simply a reflection of economic relations but has a relative autonomy from the economic level. Thus, Mitchell argues, 'the ideology of the family can remain: individualism, freedom and equality . . . while the social and economic reality can be very much at odds with such a concept' (Mitchell, 1971, p.156).

Mitchell's arguments have been very influential within feminist thinking. *Woman's Estate* goes some way towards unravelling the various elements of family life and conceptually breaking down the monolith of the family; Mitchell identifies familial ideology as a distinctive aspect of bourgeois ideology, and largely avoids the trap which so many Marxist writers have fallen into of assuming that the family simply reflects economic conditions; in emphasizing the contradictoriness of the relationship between familial ideology and the economy, she also suggests possibilities for change. If her adoption of a structuralist version of Marxism is one of Mitchell's strengths, however, it is also a source of difficulties. For a major problem with this approach is that the different structures determining women's position are analysed entirely discretely, and the relationship between production and the other structures which Mitchell identifies as part of the family are unexplored. Thus the analysis of socialization, for example, remains entirely divorced from the analysis of production. Furthermore, because she equates 'the economy' with 'production', Mitchell does not analyse the economic aspects of family-household relations. In many important respects, Mitchell's analysis reflects some of the difficulties which lie in developing a more sophisticated analysis of familial ideology within a broadly Marxist framework: of balancing the need to give due weight to ideology and not to see it as a mere reflection of economic relations with the need not to completely divorce ideology from an analysis of social and economic relations.

A consideration of Mitchell's and Wilson's answers to the question of how ideology is related to other elements of the social formation reveals that, while Mitchell allows for a greater autonomy of familial ideology from both production and other aspects of the family than Wilson does, they both see ideology as being ultimately determined by social and economic conditions. Mitchell shows how familial ideology emerged from the changing class relations of capitalist society. Wilson, in contrast, is not particularly concerned with the origins of the ideas she discusses, but with their institutionalization and particularly with their functions in reproducing the capitalist mode of production. Both Wilson and Mitchell see the role of familial ideology as being to obscure or distort social relations, especially the family structure and the social relations within it in which women are dependent upon men.

Historical and Cross-Cultural Perspectives

Analyses of the ways in which familial ideology is linked to social relations have recently been developed by feminists working in a variety of disciplines who have tried to integrate analyses of kinship and residential arrangements and the sexual division of labour derived from cross-cultural comparisons and from historical research into an analysis of familial ideology. Because cross-cultural and historical studies have shown quite clearly the diversity of forms of kinship system and residential arrangements and the variety of ways of dividing tasks between women and men in different societies, many feminists working in the social sciences have argued against 'the ideology of "the monolithic family" which equates the contemporary nuclear family with a breadwinner husband and a full-time wife and mother as the only natural and legitimate family form, [and] have challenged beliefs that any specific family arrangement is natural, biological, or "functional" in a timeless way' (Thorne and Yalorn, 1982, pp.2–3).

In *The Antisocial Family*, Barrett and McIntosh (1982) suggest that 'when we look at "the family" in detail we see that the naturalistic unit so widely referred to comprises many distinct elements, all of which vary, such as kinship, marriage, sexuality, household size and organization and so forth' (p.82). They conclude, therefore, that when speaking about 'the family' we ought to refer to 'a particular, historically and socially specific form of family since no general or essential category can be derived analytically from the many and varied elements commonly lumped together as the family' (p.81). Like a number of other writers today, Barrett and McIntosh argue that it is important to distinguish between familial ideology and family-household structures when analysing the family in industrial capitalist societies, although Barrett expresses the view in *Women's Oppression Today* (Barrett, 1980) that in practice it is difficult to separate out these two aspects of family relations. Like Mitchell, Barrett and McIntosh suggest that it is familial ideology which is hegemonic, and Barrett argues that 'the family-household constitutes both the ideological ground on which gender differences and women's oppression are constructed, and the material relations in which men and women are differentially engaged in wage labour and the class structure' (p.211). She goes on to suggest that 'women's dependence on men is reproduced ideologically, but also in material relations, and there is a mutually strengthening relationship between them' (p.211). Some writers – especially in the USA where women's situation and kinship relations have been changing more rapidly than in Britain, with more women entering paid employment, more families relying on at least two wage-earners, and the numbers of female-headed households, unmarried cohabiting couples, homosexual partners and single individuals not living in families continuing to rise – have suggested that the contradictions between familial ideology and the family-household are becoming ever sharper. This, it is suggested, is a major reason for the incorporation of familial ideology as part of the political philosophy of the American New Right which wishes to impose a form of family-household structure upon a population which is conforming less and less to the typical nuclear family. (See Petchesky (1984), chapter 7, for an excellent discussion of this phenomenon.)

In her article on 'Households as natural units', in this volume, Olivia Harris discusses the relationships between household forms and ideological assumptions about 'the domestic' in some detail. She draws on a wide spectrum of historical and cross-cultural evidence to show that the category of 'the domestic' contains all kinds of assumptions about the natural status of the activities and relationships within it, and argues that because of the strength and persistence of these assumptions, people continue to talk about 'the family' and 'the household' as universal institutions in ahistorical terms. A key argument is that the ascription of natural status to the domestic domain is a form of ideology through which the subordination of women is reproduced and their 'domestication' secured. Harris also makes the very important point that women are seldom completely subordinated to men, and suggests that the ideology of domesticity has remained so powerful and pervasive precisely because the situation of women is contradictory. Conceptions of ideology like Althusser's frequently present a very deterministic view of the social world in which individuals are completely subjected to, and enmeshed within, ideology. Harris' apposite conclusion that 'it is surely because the project of fully subjecting women to the control of men is so contradictory that an ideological definition of the domestic in terms of a natural finality has remained so powerful and persuasive' is an important corrective to the more pervasive, overdeterministic, versions of ideology which leave little space for contradiction, struggle or change.

In recent writings like Harris', and in many of the articles in an interesting volume of American essays called *Rethinking of the Family* (Thorne and Yalorn, 1982), a more sophisticated analysis of familial ideology and its relation to other practices within different social formations is gradually emerging. This analysis embodies one of the central principles of the sociology of knowledge that a distinction can be drawn between ideologies and social relations, and that ideologies distort or obscure social relations, often in quite complex ways. In some recent feminist writings, familial ideology is related quite precisely to family-household structures: it is argued that familial ideology functions to represent the nuclear family form as universal and as rooted in 'natural' differences between women and men, thereby obscuring the variety of household forms and forms of sexual division of labour. Others have emphasized the role of familial ideology within the organization of wage labour and have suggested that the ideological conception of 'the family wage' has frequently been used to distort men's and women's different relationship to the system of wage labour and to justify women's lower wages. I shall return to some of the implications of this mode of analysis later. Meanwhile I want to look briefly at the frame of reference provided by discourse theory which has recently provided an alternative framework for analysing familial ideas.

Discourse Theory: The Policing of Families

A rather different framework of analysis has been developed by writers who analyse familial ideas in terms of discourse theory. Although Foucault, the most influential discourse theorist, does not analyse the family in any systematic way, his conceptual framework has been developed to analyse the family by Jacques Donzelot, a French sociologist (Donzelot, 1979). Donzelot argues against any mode of conceptualization which takes the family as given on the grounds that such an approach is guilty of theoretical *a priorism*. In this respect, as Barrett and McIntosh point out, Donzelot's analysis of the family is radically deconstructionalist. Donzelot argues that the family should be seen 'not as a point of departure, as a manifest reality, but as a moving resultant, an uncertain form, whose intelligibility can only come from studying the system of relations it maintains at the socio-political level' (p.xxv). In other words, Donzelot suggests that the family should be analysed not as a static and unchanging institution, but as an ever-changing form, a mechanism through which other agencies operate. Donzelot analyses the family historically, and describes the variety of practices in which it is enmeshed – a plexus of public and private relations under the French *ancien régime*, for instance, and a set of external relations with medical, educational, legal and other discourses which regulate individuals in the nineteenth and twentieth centuries. Donzelot argues that the family has increasingly been 'policed' by discourses which are external to it. (That is, it has been shaped by these discourses and subordinated to them.) Thus what he calls 'familialism' – a discourse on the modern family summed up by the term 'happy family' – has become widely diffused throughout society: through educational, medical, legal and psychoanalytic discourses.

The Foucaultian framework of analysis which Donzelot develops has been very influential on recent writings, especially on sexuality, and its strengths and weaknesses as a framework have been hotly debated. (For further discussion of Foucault's perspective see the introduction to this volume and also Nancy Wood's article.) Its strengths as a framework for analysing familialism are that it recognizes, perhaps more fully than any other text, the diffuseness of familialism throughout modern societies and the ways in which this is articulated with other discourses. Donzelot also pays a great deal of attention to the ways in which familial discourses distinguish between different social classes so that there are different prescribed codes of conduct for different classes of family. A further strength is that Donzelot's approach is historical, thus giving a powerful sense of the changing ways in which the family has been shaped by other agencies. The Foucaultian approach used by Donzelot has also been welcomed as a means of sidestepping the thorny problems of the relationships between truth and ideology, and between base and superstructure. Donzelot's approach has also been sharply criticised, especially by Barrett and McIntosh who argue that he conceptualises the family as 'an empty vessel' which is devoid of any material content, and that he ignores sexual divisions within the family (Barrett and McIntosh, 1982).

The status of discourse theory so far as the analysis of ideology is concerned is somewhat difficult to determine. It can be argued that discourse theory and the classical sociological tradition are mutually incompatible forms of explanation since the classical tradition draws a sharp distinction between ideas and social relations while discourse theory regards all forms of practice – ideas, institutional rituals and practices and social relations – as discourses and does not allow for the existence of any 'real world' lying outside of discourse. On this interpretation, the concept of ideology has no place within discourse theory because it denies the existence of extra-discursive social relations. On the other hand, it can also be argued that discursive theory does not deny the existence of real social relations in the extra-discursive world, but that it merely refuses to legislate *a priori* about the form of relationships between ideas and other forms of practice. Clearly the view one takes about how familial ideology is to be analysed within this framework depends upon how one interprets the relationship between ideas and social relations within discourse theory, and in particular on the status of the concept of 'discourse' itself. If discourses are all pervasive, then it is difficult to see how one can talk about familial ideology, as distinct from 'familialism', because family-household structures and sexual and generational inequalities are assumed to exist only within discourse and there are therefore no material social relations to which ideas can be linked. If, on the other hand, discourses exist in a variety of historically changing relationships to the extra-discursive world, then the theoretical tools exist for distinguishing between, and linking, familial ideas on the one hand and the family and sexual relations, on the other. However, the notion that ideas may distort social relations (which is a crucial characteristic of ideology within the Marxist framework) disappears within this framework because social relations are not granted primacy within it.

Post War Pronatalism

Many contemporary feminist writers have been influenced by both the Marxist and Foucaultian frameworks for analysing ideology, while criticizing both for paying insufficient regard to gender divisions between women and men. Denise Riley's book, *War in the Nursery* (Riley, 1983), from which the extract called 'Post war pronatalism' (reprinted in this volume) is taken, is an interesting example of a text which starts off with a strong interest in questions which have conventionally been tackled within a Marxist framework, but ends up rather closer to discourse theory. *War in the Nursery* contains a number of different layers of analysis. Riley discusses biology, psychology and gender, seeking to find an alternative way of understanding how 'the gendered body' acts and is acted upon in the world – alternative, that is, to conventional biologistic and sociological explanations. She discusses how 'the biological' and 'the social' have been considered in developmental psychology, in child psychologies and in psychoanalysis (especially its 'popularized' forms), and she also analyses the operation of the labour market for women and policies on war nurseries in the Second World War and the immediate post-war years. Finally, in 'Post-war pronatalism', Riley reflects on some of the difficulties in interpreting women's situation after the war, and in weaving together the different strands of changing labour requirements, state suppositions about the family and the care of children, programmatic pronouncements, pronatalist rhetoric, etc.

The question of ideology is central to Riley's project. She takes a critical distance from the kind of interpretation of post-war thinking proposed by Elizabeth Wilson in *Women and the Welfare State*, an interpretation which has wide credibility within feminist thinking, but which Riley finds oversimplifying. She suggests that:

> Frequently treated as a device for negotiating the obscure gaps between politics and psychology, between biology and society, as well as generally constituting some account of the persistence of disabling ideas and their grip on the world, 'ideology' has been severely overstrained. Its invocation often serves to deepen the confusion it aims to alleviate. Socialist and feminist tendencies in particular have engaged with ideology as a key issue, but not much light has been shed on what it is, and whether there is a single 'it'.
> (Riley, 1983, p.10)

Riley goes on to suggest that both of the approaches to ideology contained in Althusser's ISAs essay have their problems, as do endeavours to understand the workings of particular ideologies. She suggests that in the post-war period 'the connections between government plans, the movements of women on and off the labour market, and the development of psychological beliefs were far more fragile' than feminist interpretations generally allow: and that 'there was, in fact, no concerted attack' (p.11). She therefore criticizes functionalist interpretations of post-war pronatalist thinking for implying too close a fit between rhetorical proclamations, state policies and the organization of the labour market.

Interestingly, however, Riley also distances herself from the Foucaultian framework of analysis, popular though it has been in the wake of these kinds of disenchantment with Althusserian functionalism. In particular, she criticizes Foucault's emphasis upon power which seems in his theory to be everywhere. And she critizes Foucault's analysis of the strategies which manage populations in *The History of Sexuality* which implies that these have no agency behind them, but 'work with causeless effects, their non-authorship the more remote and terrifying because their tracks are everywhere' (p.14). This criticism echoes Barrett and McIntosh's critique of Donzelot's analysis of 'policing'. How, if these strategies are omnipresent and yet authorless, Riley asks, can they be distinguished or resisted? Riley also takes issue with Foucault's exclusive emphasis upon discourses in studying sexuality, which, she argues, leads him to conclude not only that sexuality is described in language, but also that it is produced through language. Such forms of linguistic reductionism are no better, Riley suggests, than the biological and sociological reductionisms which Foucault wishes to circumvent.

Her article on 'post-war pronatalism' illustrates, in Riley's view, the difficulties of finding an alternative to functionalist accounts of ideology and discourse theory. Like Foucault and Donzelot, Riley places great emphasis upon language. She argues that 'the family', notwithstanding its widely assumed unity, is less an institutional reality than a reality in language. She also argues against the view that there can be a version of motherhood as such, true for all times and all places, which can be invoked in the service of feminist goals, arguing instead for an analysis of sexual-social difference which is not fixed under the guise of eternity (as 'motherhood' frequently is). Likewise, Riley places considerable emphasis on language in her discussion of the concept of ideology in Chapter 1 of *War in the*

Nursery. She suggests that in the later 1940s 'pronatalist ideology' became 'an orchestration of language, whose elements can be traced to their sources and disentangled'. Riley suggests that 'detecting ideology is more like taking the measure of the distances – or lack of distances – which obtained between politics, policies, and psychology, as they paid attention to each other, as they drew on each other's formulations to produce an apparently seamless fabric of self-confirming references, an unbroken mass of language'. Yet, she concludes, 'such a reliance on "language" . . . cannot finally close the account of the political' (p.15).

It can, I think, fairly be said that Riley poses many of the questions which one confronts when analysing ideologies concretely while refusing to provide any general or categorical answers to these. She places sustained emphasis on the different discourses within which 'the family' is constructed, and language has a central place within her analyses. Yet, she gives considerably more weight to the extra-discursive world than discourse theory usually does. The labour market, for instance, features strongly in her analysis, as does the whole question of nursery provision and policy during the war. Unlike Marxism, however, which presumes that ideologies are rooted in material social relations, either directly or 'in the last instance', *War in the Nursery* does not contain any theory about the nature of the linkages between different discourses and between discourses and other aspects of society. The form of relationships, it appears, varies from instance to instance. Riley's analysis also illustrates two central aspects of recent feminist analyses of ideology: firstly an insistence that gender should be foregrounded, and that an analysis of subjectivity should be concerned with gendered subjects. And secondly, a view that theories of ideology should have space for considering the possibilities of women struggling against conservative definitions of themselves, and that they should not represent the world in such a deterministic way that resistance and struggle appear to be impossible, as both Marxism and discourse theory frequently do.

Representation as a Process

One of the areas in which the analysis of familial ideology has been most fully developed has been in analysing the mass media. Feminists in particular have drawn attention to the objectification of women in many advertisements and in pornography, to the narrow range of roles created for women in many films and television programmes, and to the extent to which familial assumptions – that a woman's 'natural' role is that of housewife and mother – pervade the media. Early feminist writings about women and the mass media focused on images of women. The editors of a book called *Is this your Life?*, writing in this tradition, say that their aim is 'to identify the stereotypes which are still generally accepted in all the mass media, and to question whether they are relevant or in the best interests of women', to show how women's lives 'have been and continue to be circumscribed, and how this situation is reinforced by the traditional images of their roles as seen in newspapers, films and books, on radio and television, in advertising, and so on'

(King and Stott, 1977, pp.2-3). Many more recent writings, in contrast, have suggested that the concepts of 'stereotypes' and 'images' are too reductionist, and pay insufficient regard to the ways in which representations of women are constructed (as opposed to reflected) within the different media. Feminist analysis of the media has thus shifted from comparing 'images' with a supposed reality to analysing processes of 'representation' (cf. Hall, on the 'reality effect', in this volume).

Analyses of representation have taken a variety of forms. Some writers analyse representations of women and ground these in an analysis which is conceptualized in broadly Marxist terms. Janice Winship, for instance, analyses the visual and verbal forms and styles and modes of address employed in women's magazines, and relates this to an analysis of ideology which she conceptualizes as a set of common-sense and practical knowledge which offers a partial and selective (and sometimes contradictory) view of the social world, which constructs certain aspects of this world as natural and universal, and which obscures the fact that they are themselves a construction of social groups (Winship, 1983). Other feminist analyses of representation have focused upon the construction of subjectivity and have placed greater emphasis on the role of language, frequently developing a framework of analysis which uses insights gained from semiotics and from Lacanian psychoanalysis. In many respects they follow, in broad outline, the approach outlined by Stuart Hall in his discussion of 'the critical paradigm' in this volume. Rosalind Coward's article on 'The Royals', in this volume, is an example of this second kind of approach to the analysis of representations. This represents a rather different way of analysing ideology from the other approaches discussed so far in this article. Some understanding of semiology and Lacanian psychoanalysis is necessary in order to understand where Coward's framework of analysis comes from.

Roland Barthes outlines the aims of semiology – the general science of signs – in the introduction to his book, *Elements of Semiology*, in the following terms: 'Semiology . . . aims to take in any system of signs, whatever their substance and limits; images, gestures, musical sounds, objects, and the complex associations of all these, which form the content of ritual, convention, or public entertainment: these constitute, if not *languages*, at least systems of signification' (Barthes, 1967, p.9). Semiology uses a series of analytic concepts derived from structural linguistics (language and speech, signified and signifier, syntagm and system, denotation and connotation) to analyse cultural systems; and, as Stuart Hall points out, the question of signification is crucial to this method of analysis. Semiology rejects the referential conception of language 'whereby the meaning of a particular term could be validated simply by looking at what, in the real world, it referenced' (Hall, 1982, in this volume), and instead adopts a non-referential conception whereby language becomes the medium through which meanings are produced. Thus, in 'The Royals', Coward analyses the common concerns of family melodrama in terms of the concept of a 'narrative structure', and outlines the series of oppositions which occur in this narrative: rebel/conformist; promiscuous; faithful; good mother/bad mother: good son or daughter/bad son or daughter;

nobility/commoner; rightful (biological) heir/rival claim. What is crucial, in Coward's view, is not the 'real-life family behind the story', but 'the *way* the story is told, [with] some elements . . . [being] treated as highly significant, [and] others . . . not even dealt with'. As Hall points out, two rather different epistemological positions have been derived from the argument that language becomes the medium through which meanings are reproduced. On the one hand is a Kantian or neo-Kantian position which says that nothing exists except that which exists in the realm of language or discourse, on the other a position which assumes that the world does exist outside language, but claims that we can only make sense of it through its appropriation in discourse. The second position would seem to be Coward's position in her essay on 'The Royals'. She does not deny the existence of a 'real life Royal Family', but suggests that this is unimportant so far as media representations are concerned – 'seeing the Queen in the flesh isn't that different from seeing the actress who plays Miss Ellie' (p.164). Riley's position is also close to this.

If semiology provides one of the underpinnings of analyses like Coward's, interpretations of psychoanalysis which are influenced by the writings of the structural anthropologist, Lévi-Strauss, and the French psychoanalyst, Lacan provide a second. In an earlier book, *Patriarchal Precedents* (Coward, 1983), Coward suggests that what is distinctive about the psychoanalytic interpretation of social practices is that it reveals a radical approach to notions of representation and sexuality – radical because it resists the idea that symbolic practices simply reflect other social practices, because it is anti-functionalist, and because it transcends the dichotomies between the individual and society, and between biological and social forms of explanation. She suggests that structuralism can indicate how all societies are signifying systems, and can therefore provide a way of understanding how meanings are arrived at and function within a particular culture. Crucial to the structuralist analysis of meanings is Lacan's theory of the construction of subjectivity and sexual identity through language.

Hall points out that in theories influenced by Freudian and Lacanian psychoanalysis (like Coward's) the principle mechanism of ideology is how the speaker, the subject of enunciation, is positioned in language. And Coward and Ellis show, in *Language and Materialism* (Coward and Ellis, 1977), how a particular non-referential theory of language distinguishes the structuralist framework from Marxism and from Althusser's arguments in the second part of the ISAs essay, but suggest that it is necessary to develop the logic of Althusser's arguments further. They criticize Althusser for adhering to a notion of ideology 'as a cloud of ideas', (or false consciousness) as Marx did in *The German Ideology*, for adopting a conception of subjects as being the support for the meanings of ideology, and for regarding meanings as the product of distorted images of reality which function to reproduce existing social relations. Althusser, in Coward and Ellis' view, continues to utilize a distinction between ideology and social relations which they find unsatisfactory. They also object to the specific meaning given by Althusser to the notion that ideology is a material force, and suggest that he invariably interprets this as meaning that it is concrete and real and is manifested in institutions. According to Coward and Ellis, ideology provides the individual with a subjectivity and relates him/her to the social structure with its contradictory relations and powers. The underpinning for this theory of ideology is provided by Lacan's interpretation of psychoanalytic theory, and particularly by his theory of the relationship of subjects to signification.

Lacan argues that individuals only acquire a sense of individual identity through the acquisition of social position, and suggests that the acquisition of subjectivity and sexual identity occur simultaneously as the human infant enters into language (Lacan, 1966). Thus, for Lacan, subjectivity is acquired as the individual child learns to speak/is spoken to, and gendered subjectivity is acquired not through some intrinsic biological or sexual disposition, but is constructed through our entry into a culture which is polarized around anatomical difference. Subjectivity and the unconscious are thus produced in language.

Clearly the question of *why* human cultures are polarized around anatomical difference is a crucial question for this analysis, and here the writings of Lévi-Strauss provide an important underpinning. Lévi-Strauss claims that all societies have rules of kinship, and argues that these differentiate human societies from other primates, and in an important sense, therefore, constitute 'the social' (Lévi-Strauss, 1969 and 1972). Furthermore, he argues that it is not the biological family of mother, father and child that distinguishes human kinship structures, but a universal and primordial law which regulates marriage relations and which is expressed in incest prohibitions. Lévi-Strauss argues that it is always men who exchange women in the process of practicing exogamy, and that this exchange transforms natural families into cultural kinship systems. Juliet Mitchell suggests in *Psychoanalysis and Feminism* that this process of exchange constitutes the basis of patriarchy, or male power, within all human cultures, although this analysis is criticized by Coward in *Patriarchal Precedents* for being too reductionist. Coward argues instead for the introduction of a radical interpretation of signification, identity and the sign – that is, for a more fully developed theory of language and cultural meanings than exists in *Psychoanalysis and Feminism*.

To return to the question of familial ideology and 'The Royals', what are the implications of adopting this approach? The first implication is that 'the family' assumes a different importance from that ascribed to it by Althusser in 'Ideology and ideological state apparatuses'. It becomes an arena where subjectivity is produced in a particular relation to discourse and therefore to meaning. This approach also has implications for the analysis of processes of representation. It suggests that the speaker or author is positioned, within discourse, by language. He/she is less the individual originator of ideas than the executor of a story or film, the conventions for which exist outside of him/herself and affect what is produced. Thus, for example, the writers and producers of soap-operas or the authors of articles about the Royal Family in the popular press and women's magazines are, it is suggested, positioned by language. They may be drawing on the classificatory schemes of a society – schemes which construct the sexes and sexual divisions in a particular way – without necessarily being conscious of this. Likewise, we, the viewers of *Dallas* or readers of women's magazine stories about

'The Royals' are also positioned in a particular way. As Rosalind Coward puts it in the introduction to *Female Desire* (Coward, 1984) (the book of essays from which 'The Royals' is taken): 'I don't treat . . . cultural representations as the forcible imposition of false and limiting stereotypes . . . nor do I treat female desire as something universal, unchanging, arising from the female condition – I see the reproduction of female pleasure and desire as *producing* and sustaining feminine positions' (p.16). If we, the readers and viewers, identify with Princess Diana, or with Prince Andrew, or with Bobby Ewing, this is not because they appeal to some instinct in us (to be mothers or playboys or fathers) nor because we relate positively to their glamorous and idealized images, but because our identification is produced by the discourse within which we, as audiences of family melodrama, are constructed.

It is, I hope, clear by now that this framework of analysis places great emphasis upon language as a component of ideology. As in discourse theory language is analysed as being neither part of the base nor part of the superstructure but as an active constitutive part of social relations. Language, conceived of as a signifying practice within this framework, sets up the positions that enable social intercourse to take place. To a certain extent, then, how one assesses this framework must depend upon how one conceptualizes the relationships between language, ideology and social relations, and commentators have been sharply divided in their appraisal of this approach. Some people (e.g. Coward and Ellis) have argued that it provides a welcome means of avoiding the reductionism and functionalism so often found in classical sociology and Marxist theories, that it is a way of avoiding subjectivist accounts of ideology, and that it provides a much more thorough analysis of how the ideological process works and what its mechanisms are precisely because of the emphasis given to the role of language. Others have argued that this approach represents a move away from any attempt to analyse the relationship between ideas and social relations, that it provides a quasi-universalistic theory of the acquisition of subjectivity which is both asocial and ahistorical, and that it has an overly deterministic view of how subjectivity is acquired. Some critics have also argued that the particular interpretation given to Freud's theory by Lévi-Strauss and Lacan, on which the whole conceptual edifice is founded, is problematic and have suggested that Lévi-Strauss' account presupposes the subordination which it purports to explain. It has also been suggested by some commentators (e.g. Barrett, 1980) that Freud's theory is, at least in part, biologically deterministic, a view which is strongly repudiated by others (e.g. Mitchell and Rose, 1982) working within the Lacanian framework. These difficult and unsolved questions lead into more general questions about the analysis of ideology and the relationship between language and ideology which are the subject of the next and final section of this article.

Different Conceptions of Familial Ideology

I have discussed a number of rather different conceptions of familial ideology in this article – conceptions which are rooted in the problematic of classical Marxism, conceptions based upon the Foucaultian problematic, and finally, conceptions arising from a problematic which combines arguments from structuralist anthropology, semiology and Lacanian psychoanalysis and a variety of feminist approaches. Although there are important differences among people working within each of these problematics, and some cross-fertilization of ideas between the different frameworks of analysis, broadly speaking the different frameworks can be outlined as follows.

Within the Marxist framework, familial ideology is analysed as a system of beliefs about the family which (i) asserts that the co-resident nuclear family and sexual division of labour within it are naturally determined, universal, and normatively desirable; (ii) emerges in particular historical conditions and is determined by economic and social class relations, at least in the last instance; and (iii) functions to obscure or distort social relations, particularly the family structure and sexual division of labour within it. It is generally accepted by recent Marxist writers that ideologies are material forces (and are therefore not just false consciousness), that they may be inscribed in state institutions (as familial ideology is in Wilson's analysis), and some writers (Wilson, for instance, but not Mitchell) argue that they function not only to obscure or distort social relations but also to reproduce labour power and the social relations of production. The crucial point to recognize is that Marxist writers, following very much in the classical sociological tradition, make an analytical distinction between ideologies and social relations (even if some writers, like Barrett, accept that in practice it is difficult to distinguish between ideological and other factors).

People working within the Foucaultian problematic, in contrast, have developed a rather different mode of analysis. Within this framework beliefs about the family are not taken as given in the same way as they are within the Marxist framework. The question asked (by Donzelot, for instance) is not 'When did a given system of beliefs arise and why?', but 'How was it possible that a set of discourses aiming to restore the family through a variety of means – legal, medical, and later psychoanalytic – arose and what were their effects?' The concept of ideology is not generally used in this framework. Foucault argues explicitly against the use of the term on the grounds that it implies a contrast between 'ideology' and 'truth', that it refers to a 'subject' and that an ideology is always secondary in relation to something which functions as an economic or material determinant of it, and the concept does not figure in Donzelot's discussion of familialism. Within this framework the concept of discourse figures prominently although, as has been suggested above, the status of discourses *vis-à-vis* the extra-discursive world is uncertain.

Ideology has quite a different meaning again in analyses of processes of representation based on semiology and Lacanian psychoanalysis. Here, emphasis is placed on the ways in which subjects are constructed within language, and how they are given masculine and feminine positions and 'family' positions (as wife, mother, daughter, husband, father, son, etc.). Although this framework shares a common concern with language with some writers in the Foucaultian framework, the treatment of language within it is rather different. Whereas the Foucaultian framework tends to be historical, the semiological/psychoanalytic framework is often universalistic, making arguments about the acquisition of subjectivity in all human societies (a shortcoming which some commentators, for instance, Coward, have noted). Furthermore, whereas the Foucaultian framework does not make any presuppositions about universal psychological structures (indeed, Donzelot sees psychoanalysis as a key mechanism in 'policing' the family in twentieth-century western societies) the semiological/psychoanalytic framework relies, in the last instance, on a particular interpretation of Freud's theory which analyses societal structures in terms of universal psychological principles (see Hirst and Woolley's article in this volume for a summary of Freud's arguments).

Clearly, there are no clear-cut conclusions to be drawn about the rightness or wrongness of these different frameworks. In part, some of the differences between the frameworks can be accounted for by pointing out that the different frameworks have been concerned with different questions. The Foucaultian and semiological/psychoanalytic analyses are much more concerned with the first of the questions I raised at the beginning of this article: 'How does ideology work and what are its mechanisms?' and also with the question of how subjectivity is constructed. Marxist analyses, on the other hand, have been preoccupied with the second question: 'How does ideology relate to other practices in the social formation?' My own view is that in the end analyses of familial ideology (like analyses of other ideologies) need to concern themselves with both kinds of question, and that there is as yet no satisfactory theoretical framework available for combining these. It is, I think, essential to maintain the distinction between ideology and social relations because otherwise a good deal of the explanatory power and critical purchase of the theory of ideology get lost. It is very illuminating, for instance, to be able to distinguish between familial ideology and particular sets of household or sexual relations and to show how the former operates to distort or obscure the latter. In this respect, my own preference is for a theory of ideology rooted in the classical Marxist tradition. On the other hand, the other approaches have helped to identify areas where classical Marxist analyses are weak. Discourse theory has shown the importance of analysing the linkages between discourses and of not treating ideology or ideologies as monolithic entities, while psychoanalytic theory has shown how limited the Marxist analysis of consciousness is because it does not contain an analysis of ways in which subjectivity is constructed. The question of the relationships between language, ideology and social relations are key questions facing theories of ideology today, but they are difficult to resolve. If a non-referential theory of language is adopted, as in discourse theory and approaches based upon psychoanalysis, it is difficult to see how language can be related to social relations, except perhaps through an analysis of the effects of ideology (cf. Laclau, 1977). On the other hand, referential theories of language have tended to analyse language in highly reductionist terms, seeing it as a straightforward reflection of social relations, which is far too simplistic. It seems likely that over the next few years the relationships between social relations, language and ideology will continue to be hotly debated, as the relationship between 'economic' and 'ideological' factors were in an earlier period in the history of sociology.

It is interesting to note in conclusion that although feminists have worked with, and tried to develop, each of these frameworks, there are a number of similarities between feminist approaches which suggest that the categorization of approaches used here is perhaps too stark to take account of the complexities of feminist work. First, it is now generally accepted by feminist writers that the concept of 'the family' is too monolithic and ahistorical, and that it needs deconstructing. It is in the context of trying to unravel the components of the family that analyses of familial ideology have been developed. Recent discussions of familial ideology have suggested that this, too, has been conceptualized in too monolithic a manner. Thus Harris and Riley, who develop rather different frameworks for analysing the relationships between ideas and social relations, both emphasize the ways in which ideologies can be contradictory and dispersed. A second point upon which many feminists working in this area would agree is the importance of foregrounding gender in analyses not only of familial ideology, but in analyses of ideologies can be contradictory and dispersed. A second point upon which gender divisions and to inequalities within the family, the feminist writers considered in this article foreground gender divisions and gendered subjectivity in their analyses. Finally, some feminists are beginning to recognize that analyses of ideology are frequently overly deterministic, and that this is true of analyses which start from the classical Marxist framework (like Wilson's) and also of analyses which start from discourse theory (like Donzelot's) or psychoanalytic conceptions (like Coward's). Recent writers have begun to introduce discussions of contradiction and conflict into the analysis of ideology. Although such developments have so far occurred most frequently in analyses of familial or domestic ideologies, they are undoubtedly relevant to analyses of ideology more generally.

References

BARRETT, M. (1980) *Woman's Oppression Today*, London, Verso.

BARRETT, M. and McINTOSH, M. (1982) *The Anti-Social Family*, London, Verso.

BARTHES, R. (1967) *Elements of Semiology*, London, Jonathan Cape.

BERGER, B. and BERGER, P. (1983) *The War Over The Family*, London, Hutchinson.

BOWLBY, J. (1963) *Child Care and the Growth of Love*, Harmondsworth, Penguin.

COOPER, D. (1972) *The Death of the Family*, Harmondsworth, Penguin.

COWARD, R. (1983) *Patriarchal Precedents*, London, Routledge and Kegan Paul.

COWARD, R. (1984) *Female Desire*, London, Paladin.

COWARD, R. and ELLIS, J. (1977) *Language and Materialism*, London, Routledge and Kegan Paul.

DONALD, J. and HALL, S. (1985) *Politics and Ideology* Milton Keynes, Open University Press.

DONZELOT, J. (1979) *The Policing of Families*, London, Hutchinson.

ENGELS, F. (1968) 'The Origin of the Family, Private Property and the State', in Marx, K. and Engels, F. *Selected Works*, London, Lawrence and Wishart.

HARRIS, N. (1971) *Beliefs in Society*, Harmondsworth, Penguin.

KING, J. and STOTT, M. (1977) *Is this your Life?*, London, Virago.

LACAN, J. (1966) *Ecrits*, Paris, Editions du Seuil.

LACLAU, E. (1977) *Politics and Ideology in Marxist Theory*, London, New Left Books.

LAING, R. D. (1960) *The Divided Self*, Harmondsworth, Penguin.

LAING, R. D. (1971) *The Politics of the Family and Other Essays*, London, Tavistock.

LÉVI-STRAUSS, C. (1969) Elementary Structures of Kinship. London, Eyre and Spottiswoode.

LÉVI-STRAUSS, C. (1972) *Structural Anthropology*, Harmondsworth, Penguin.

LOVELL, T. (1980) *Pictures of Reality*, London, B.F.I.

MANNHEIM, K. (1960) *Ideology and Utopia*, London, Routledge and Kegan Paul.

MARX, K. and ENGELS, F. (1965) *The German Ideology*, London, Lawrence and Wishart.

MERCER, C. (1985) 'Fascist ideology', in Donald, J. and Hall, S. (eds.) *Politics and Ideology*, Milton Keynes, Open University Press.

MERTON, R. (1957) *Social Theory and Social Structure*, New York, The Free Press.

MITCHELL, J. (1971) *Woman's Estate*, Harmondsworth, Penguin.

MITCHELL, J. (1974) *Psychoanalysis and Feminism*, London, Allen Lane.

MITCHELL, J. (1984) *Women: The Longest Revolution*, London, Virago.

MITCHELL, J. and ROSE, J. (1984) *Feminine Sexuality*, London, Macmillan.

PARSONS, T. (1964) *Family, Socialization and Interaction Process*, London, Routledge and Kegan Paul.

PETCHESKY, R. (1984) *Abortion and Woman's Choice*, New York, Longman.

RILEY, D. (1983) *War in the Nursery*, London, Virago.

THORNE, B. and YALORN, M. (1983) (eds) *Rethinking the Family*, New York, Longman.

WILSON, E. (1977) *Women and the Welfare State*, London, Tavistock.

WINSHIP, J. (1983) 'Femininity and Women's Magazines', Unit 6 of *The Changing Experience of Women*, Milton Keynes, Open University Press.

6 Households as Natural Units

Olivia Harris

From *Of Marriage and the Market: Women's Subordination in International Perspective*, edited by K. Young, C. Wolkowitz and R. McCullagh, 1981. Reproduced by permission of the publishers CSE Books.

The sense that women are natural beings while men are able to transcend nature and become fully cultural is deeply embedded in European thought. The values attached to nature are not all negative, but whether viewed as a haven or a threat it is a force that is subject to control. The ideological basis of women's identification with a 'natural' sphere has been increasingly recognised and subject to critique; assumptions about nature and the natural are powerful metaphors that endow what are often quite transient states of affairs with an air of finality and eternity. Feminists have long been concerned to undermine the image of femininity as a natural quality; in particular the associations between physiological specialisation and a set of universal attributes that supposedly derive directly from them have been questioned, and shown to be culturally and historically specific – a means of guaranteeing the hierarchical organisation of gender relations. Nature as a concept is in fact a product of particular cultures, and ideas about what is natural, and the values assigned to it, vary correspondingly.

Naturalistic assumptions about femininity derive particularly from physiological characteristics and also from the organisation of family relations. It seems to me that similar naturalistic assumptions underlie also the way we think about the domestic domain, although here the assumptions are in general more concealed and less coherent. It has been generally accepted from Engels on that the key to women's subordination is to be found in their identification with the domestic sphere. Some have argued that domestic labour is a hidden form of exploitation; others that women's responsibility for the personal, emotional lives of household members structures their lives in such a way as to exclude their participation in social and political life; others have pointed to marriage as the key social relation by which women's subordination is secured; yet others have argued that women's status in the public domain can be positive only when there is little separation or differentiation between domestic and public spheres. Through a whole spectrum of arguments it is agreed that the domestic sphere is the site where gender subordination is produced and re-enacted.

In feminist discussions it is normal to talk of 'the' family, 'the' household, 'the' sexual division of labour, in a way that seems to impute some universal significance to these terms. Other writers are quite explicit about claims to generality. [. . .] A model of the sexual division of labour, as a division whereby women remain in the domestic sphere while men go out of it usually to do what is termed productive work, is deeply embedded in the literature. Both Marx and Engels take this to be the natural division of labour, and the same assumption resurfaces frequently even in contemporary feminist writing.

On the other hand, it is well-known that the division of tasks between women and men varies significantly from one culture to another and from one historical period to another. Anthropological research makes clear the enormous variety in kinship systems and residential arrangements; a spate of historical research on family and household particularly in Europe makes it possible to move away from some supposedly universal institution to perceived variation and its causes, and to reintegrate the variety of forms into a broader social and historical context.

Why then, given all we know about the variation in domestic arrangements, is it so common to find the domestic domain treated as a universal, or at least very widespread institution? Even those who recognise that the co-resident nuclear family is a historically specific idea will in the next breath talk of 'the' family, 'the' household in a way that surreptitiously reintroduces an assumption of universalism. Working as an anthropologist I have often noticed myself perform this same slippage and have wondered why it comes so easily [. . .]

One assumption which reinforces the image of the domestic domain as distinctive and universally recognisable is that household units coincide with families. [. . .] It is clear that the terms family and household are used interchangeably in many contexts, but they also refer to different sets of meanings. Feminist writers have pointed out that this confusion of terms is no mere accident; the prevailing familial ideology of capitalist society insists that members of a nuclear family should live together, and that people not related in this way should not live together [. . .] Even in a country, like Britain, where this ideology is deeply rooted and reproduced in social legislation, a surprisingly large percentage of households do not conform to the ideal nuclear family type [. . .]

The assumptions made today about the natural – and proper – organisation of family life can be shown to have arisen in particular historical circumstances. The definitions of motherhood, childhood, fatherhood, the representation of the home as a 'haven in a heartless world', have been forged out of veritable ideological and legal campaigns, and are subject to constant renegotiation as needs and circumstances change. However, the fact is that in most parts of the world recruitment to domestic groups does take place ideally through relations of kinship and marriage. Marriage may provide for the recruitment of new members to already existing units, or it may form the basis for the creation of a new unit, but it also provides a means by which families are reproduced from one generation to the next. Thus what is initially a contractual relation becomes absorbed into the language of genealogical (that is physiological) relations through the bearing of children. It is also common for household members who are not genealogically related to core members to be treated as kin, either through the formal process of adoption or simply by ascribing a kin status (for example, living-in servants are often treated as children of the house, albeit of a lower status; unmarried adults may be assigned the status of uncle or aunt, regardless of their real relationship to household members). Thus, while we know that kin relations have different meanings, different values in distinct situations, the fact that relations between members of a single domestic unit are thought of so often in terms of kin relations has important consequences. Kin relations, derived as they are from the biologically-founded ties of parent-child and siblings born of the same parents, are imbued in most cultures with ideas of natural behaviour, natural morality.

While the supposed coincidence of family and household presents the domestic unit as a domain in which relationships are based on natural law, I think there are other important dimensions in the assignation of natural status to the domestic domain. The English term household denotes an institution whose primary feature is co-residence; it is overwhelmingly assumed that people who live within a single space, however that is socially defined, share in the tasks of day-to-day servicing of human beings, including consumption, and organise the reproduction of the next generation. Co-residence implies a special intimacy, a fusing of physiological functions and a real distinction from other types of social relations which can be portrayed as more amenable to analysis. It is undoubtedly the case that whether or not it coincides with the family of procreation, household organisation is fundamental to ideologies of womanhood, and that households are in material terms the context for much of women's lives.

The Domestic Mode of Production?

In recent years several influential theories have been put forward of what is variously called a domestic or family mode of production. Fundamental to such theories is the assumption that as organisational forms the household or family transcend both historical and social boundaries, that they contain some inner logic separable from the context in which they are embedded. In the work of Christine Delphy the proposal of a family mode of production stems directly from her concern with how to interpret the subordination of women [. . .] However, some economic anthropologists have also developed theories of a domestic mode of production in an attempt to understand the logic of economic systems not dominated by commodity exchange and the law of value. The most elaborate formulation is to be found in the work of the anthropologist Marshall Sahlins (1974), and it has been developed in a rather different direction by another anthropologist–Claude Meillassoux (1981). Its intellectual roots are however far older. Sahlins in particular draws on the work of the Russian economist, A. V. Chayanov (1966) who in opposition to the prevailing Leninist orthodoxy of his time argued that the peasant economy was not based on the same calculations as a capitalist enterprise but rather was oriented to the consumption needs of a household. Since the aim of this family-based enterprise was continued subsistence, it would exploit its own labour until the needs of all its members were satisfied, and no more [. . .]

One aspect common to many theories of the household, is to treat this form of enterprise as an isolated unit whose functioning can be analysed without reference either to wider social or economic structures, or to the nature of relationships within the unit. It is premised on assumptions which are the more significant for rarely being rendered explicit. In particular, the supposed or ideal self-sufficiency of the individual household suggests a fundamental separation between this unit and the rest of society. This has various consequences: either society is construed as a series of identical units, held together in some ill-defined way; [. . .] or society is seen as being in some sense outside or in opposition to the household. This seems to underlie the distinction between domestic and public spheres and the theories that have been built on it; it is also the basis for the supposed anti-social tendency of the household, that is, that the interests of individual households are in opposition to the interests of more inclusive social groups [. . .]

Chayanov's theory in fact depends on something which is scarcely mentioned – the market. In the situation he discusses, that of the South Russian peasantry at the turn of the century, there was a market for both land, labour and produce, which set the parameters for the economic behaviour of the peasantry. This means that households have an *appearance* of autonomy since relations with other households are mediated through the abstract form of money. It is because the relations between peasant households were vitally affected by commodity exchange that the household as an individual unit appeared so distinct, and based on a unique structure of non-commodity relations.

The consequences of this supposed autonomy of the individual household, which in fact derives from dependence on the market, can be seen especially clearly in the work of Marshall Sahlins. His domestic mode of production, which is apparently held to characterise all primitive and peasant economics, is premised on two main assertions. First, that while households are never entirely independent, autonomy and self-sufficiency are ideals which affect economic behaviour – the 'centrifugality' thesis. Households will tend to self-sufficiency unless other countervailing forces prevent this centrifugality (such as, for Sahlins, political power). Secondly, and more important for his overall argument, Sahlins asserts that there is a difference in the form of circulation, or distribution of goods and of labour, that takes place *within* as opposed to *between* households. For him, intra-household economic relations are characterised by pooling and what he calls generosity, while those between different households are termed exchange, i.e. a two-way, balanced transaction [. . .]

This distinction in forms of circulation provides the justification for treating the household as an economically isolable and independent unit.If economic relations between household members were really so different from those with non-members, then that would give weight to the view of households as self-contained enterprises. However, this distinction in forms of exchange relies heavily though covertly on the categories of commodity exchange, which make possible the abstraction of objects exchanged from those who exchange them. It is in fact only in conditions of generalised commodity circulation that we can make a radical distinction between pooling, and the two-way transactions of the market-place. In such conditions though the individual household may well be isolated it is anything but independent, since it relies for its reproduction on the circuits of commodity exchange. On the other hand, in situations where commodity exchange does not prevail, for example in many peasant societies, the individual household is not more autonomous, but less [. . .]

With the development of generalised commodity exchange, there is a case for treating domestic units as economically distinct and related only through exchange; that is, for asserting a discontinuity between intra- and inter-household relations. This distinction is co-extensive with that between exchange-values and use-values in Marxist analysis. One of the defining characteristics of domestic labour under capitalism is that it produces use-values not exchange-values. Where commodity relations prevail, the circulation of use-values as use-values is effectively curtailed. Conversely where commodity exchange is absent, use-values are produced and consumed within an integrated circuit; this latter economic form is significantly termed in classical Marxism the 'natural economy'. For both Marx and Engels the natural economy, and the natural (sexual) division of labour, are characterised precisely by the absence of exchange relations. In their terms, then, the domestic formation is a natural one, and this would presumably include households within advanced capitalism.

Starting from assumptions about the discontinuity in forms of exchange within and between households under capitalism, it is easy to read backwards to other, non-capitalist economic systems and see the same discontinuity. This appears to be the basis of Sahlins' domestic mode of production. In even less explicit ways, it is also presumably a fundamental criterion by which the domestic domain can be assigned a transhistorical identity [. . .] An important consequence of the unacknowledged significance of commodity circulation in defining the boundaries of domestic units is that whatever economic activity is carried on within the household is given the same status. At worst it is characterised as 'natural', at best described as an absence – the absence of exchange relations, as though a polarised distinction between consumption and exchange could encompass the multitude of ways in which objects and labour circulate other than as commodities [. . .]

The Household Head

Ill-articulated assumptions about different forms of circulation are it seems to me fundamental in the ways that households are represented. If relations between households are characterised as exchange, distribution within households, where it is mentioned at all, is usually conceived as pooling, as for example in Sahlins' work. From his other writings (1974, Ch. 5) it is clear that pooling involves first centralisation and then reallocation. This process presupposes a centre from which redistribution is effected, though Sahlins himself never makes this explicit. In the case of Marx the structure is clearer though still vague since for him the agent who allocates both labour and the product of labour is what he calls the patriarch. The same term is used by Chayanov.

These writers are representative of many others in their unquestioned assumption that households are organised by and around a household head. They offer no suggestion of the multifarious forms of allocation within households. Often the unspoken assumption is that distribution is based on the criteria of sex and age. While Marx for example recognises that the reproduction of human beings includes a 'historical and moral element', many writers assume that consumption levels, defined according to sex and age, are constant in all circumstances (i.e. again given in nature). It is clear however that economic relations within a household do not always take the form of a centralisation of resources followed by their distribution by the household head. In agrarian societies men and women may own different sorts of property and control independently what is produced from it; or economic transactions between wife and husband can take the form of commodity exchange, as is found in parts of East and West Africa [. . .] Children too cannot be assumed to be under the direct, exclusive control of a household head. There are many examples of women's control of the labour of their children, a control which is jealously guarded.

Where all or most of household income takes the form of money it might be assumed that money, being more abstract and depersonalised than concrete products, would more likely be pooled and distributed by a single authority. However recent studies of family income in Britain show that the origin of money is often taken into account in how it is spent, and that there is considerable variation in how different portions of household income are allocated [. . .] This does not of course mean that the concept of household head is an illusory one. In many cases it obviously does involve real control; but the nature and extent of this control need to be investigated and specified, rather than assuming an undifferentiated autocracy, or even an undifferentiated communality, within domestic units [. . .] Shifts from household production for subsistence to household-based petty-commodity production to an economy based on the sale of labour-power, affect radically the structure of households, power relations within them, and the resulting changes in the power to command the fruits of one's own labour [. . .]

[Nevertheless], it would be mistaken to assume thereby that each economic system produces its own specific household form. It is highly misleading to talk without further qualification of the peasant household, the feudal or the capitalist household [. . .] Many other determinations must be taken into account – ecology, technology, precise inheritance rules, class position, and demography. While an appreciation of the complex ways in which household membership is determined is obviously relevant to an understanding of relations both within the domestic domain and between members of different domestic groups, it should be emphasised that a concern with formal structures and rules does not necessarily enhance the analysis of economic relationships.

On the other hand, the authority wielded by a household head should not be conceived solely through economic functions of production and distribution.

Meillassoux (1981) for example places great emphasis on reproduction as the determining structure of what he calls the domestic community. While the nature of the control exercised is in his theory quite specific, unlike the vague assumptions of many other writers, it is interesting that for him too the criterion by which the domestic unit is defined is via the identification of an authority-figure.

In the work of Christine Delphy we find what must surely be the apotheosis of concentrated focus on the household head. Delphy is fully aware of the pitfalls of discussing household organisation outside its historical and economic context. However, after enumerating carefully the many different ways in which work performed in the domestic setting is inserted into wider economic structures, she then goes on to treat these differences as insignificant for understanding women's oppression. Whatever the class position of the households in which their lives are constructed through birth or marriage, all women for Delphy have in common the unpaid domestic services they are obliged to perform for the household head. Her analysis thus turns on the power relationship between husbands and wives [. . .] 'Whatever the nature of women's tasks, their relations of production are the same' (1977, p.31).

In drawing attention to the power relation between women and men rather than trying to squeeze sexual divisions into the pre-existing categories of political economy, Delphy's analysis is important. But it is one thing to locate the subordination (or exploitation in Delphy's terms) of women in the domestic domain, and quite another to treat this as sufficient explanation. The absolute identification of the household with its head and the interests of its head is taken as given. She thus asks neither whether this power is uniform in different conditions, whether economic control always coincides with jural authority, nor whence the power is derived. Her analysis too is of *individual* households, *individual* women and their husbands.

While change and variation in household form, and their effects on the nature of authority within the domestic unit have been documented, this is rarely combined with an investigation of the *sources* of that authority. [. . .] To understand how the position of the household head is defined and reproduced takes us beyond the confines of the domestic unit itself. The authority located in a household head is not intrinsic to relations between household members, but must be sought in wider social structures. The sovereign body may be limited to a group of elders as in the West African societies dicussed by Meillassoux, or it may be the community of adult males who collectively take and enforce certain decisions affecting those who do not have formal access to the structures of power.

If we turn from decentralised agrarian societies to those effectively dominated by an organised state, many aspects of male power over other household members can be seen to derive from the nature of the state. In most state formations, household heads are made responsible for paying taxes and other dues to the state, and are answerable in law for other household members. It is usually a male household head who negotiates contracts, makes share-cropping arrangements, leases land or other property, and thereby exercises control over the lives of his wife, children and dependent kin. The very *activity* of census-taking, fundamental to state organisation, normally organises and defines households, precisely around the identification of a single person who is answerable for other members of the domestic unit. In the historical study of household forms this same criterion has generally been adopted in the identification of individual units [. . .]

The organisation of domestic units around household heads derives enormous impetus from the bureaucratic requirements of state organisation, and also from the partial devolution of power to adult males by different state systems. However the allocation of authority is made more effective by being identified with the *family* head [. . .] [Laslett (1949) describes the development in] seventeenth century England of a philosophy concerning the natural rights and authority of the patriarch. The family or rather the position of the father within the family, was thus taken as the natural source of authority which could then be applied to political authorities such as the monarch.

The unproblematic way in which in so many different contexts households are identified with their putative heads is, then, to be explained by the assumptions of patriarchal philosophy, combined with an assumption of discontinuity in forms of circulation within and between domestic units. What distinguishes patriarchal philosophy is the supposition that the authority of the father is or should be total. As a philosophy it makes little discrimination between different domains in which authority may be exercised, for example political versus economic; the identification of the household head with the father reinforces the identification of the household as a natural domain unified by the exercise of authority. In France under the *ancien regime* a contractual relationship between the state and the head of the family gave him the right to have his children imprisoned, and was preserved even in the Napoleonic Code. In England even the authority a man had over his wife was conceived on the model of the father, as was that over servants.

An instructive contrast can be made concerning who, in the absence of a father, takes on the role of household head. In most parts of Europe historically a widow has replaced her dead husband, thus asserting that criteria of age and the status of parenthood are prior to those of sex. In Japan however, a boy however young would traditionally be preferred to an adult woman. Again, it is important to understand under what conditions female-headed households form a significant proportion of the total [. . .] This is the case mainly among poor and marginal social groups which are anyhow excluded from the structures of power. Female-headed households appear to be common in situations of migration, urban poverty, and chronic insecurity; nonetheless ideological elements also intervene. Some cultures appear to accept the existence of female-headed households more easily than others. In Turkey for example it is virtually impossible for a woman however bereft and unstable her situation, to live in a domestic unit without a particular male head.

In formal terms, then, it is general to identify domestic units with a male head, and the identification is guaranteed by endowing this figure with the ideology of paternal authority. Both the source, the content and the effectivity of that authority must be investigated if we are not to fall here too into naturalistic assumptions that eternalise the concept of the household. Even in cultures where patriarchal ideology has been extremely fully developed, the household head only enjoys unwavering power in certain conditions. In pre-revolutionary China for example, it was only among the gentry that the authority of the patriarch was fully realised. Among poor peasants, the ideal was subscribed to, but practice did not match the ideal. In the legal system of contemporary Britain the authority of the male family head is not absolute even as an ideal. Married women still do not enjoy full civil citizenship, and in many contexts must be represented by their husband, but they did gain political citizenship fifty years ago. Thus whatever the ideology, the authority exercised by a male household head is rarely absolute. The conditions in which a complete conjunction of powers is located in the household head should be treated as the exception rather than the rule.

The Problem of the Domestic

While I have criticised the tendency of many writers to treat the household as a universal category, there are certain functions of the domestic unit which appear to be constant whatever the mode of production. These functions are frequently identified as 'reproduction'. [There are] substantial confusions in the use of this term [. . .] but in the context of discussion of the household what is generally meant is domestic labour. Regardless of what productive activities are carried out, households are always the site of reproduction in this sense. (This is clearly what underlies Meillassoux's assumption of the universality of the domestic unit.)

It is generally assumed, and indeed widely the case, that the way people live together is structured around the immediately physical needs of the human organism – food, sleep, cleanliness, clothing. Since these needs derive directly from physiology, it has been easy to separate off the servicing of the human organism in this way as a distinct kind of labour. Indeed the identification of this type of activity with the household as an organisational space is in a way circular, since the word domestic derives directly from the Latin word for house (*domus*). Insofar as people who inhabit a single physical space do not collaborate in these functions, they are thought to constitute at least partially separate households.

From this perspective too we find a close identification of the domestic unit with a set of activities construed as natural, in this case through their association with the human body. I suspect that it is also because of the base in physiology that such domestic activities have been virtually ignored by Marxists [. . .] Writers such as Meillassoux and Sahlins who are explicitly concerned with the domestic economy, never so much as mention this type of work. Since the human body is ideologically presented as a natural given, outside of history, it is easy to slide into treating domestic labour as a natural activity, also outside the scope of historical analysis [. . .]

The same approach has characterised assumptions about biological reproduction. The patently physiological process of procreation, birth and lactation has facilitated an entirely naturalistic approach to the place of these processes in social reproduction as a whole. Female fertility, and even infant mortality, are often treated, if they are mentioned at all, as invariant factors, or at best are thought to respond in some unspecified way to changes in the economy.

The ideological presuppositions that must be uncovered in order to reconstruct an analysis of domestic work on a firmer basis are extremely powerful ones. Their strength is further reinforced by the fact that it is overwhelmingly women, who naturally produce children, that also perform domestic tasks. This association of the fact of childbirth with housework is taken for granted by many writers. However while it would be folly to deny the association, it is equally mistaken to accept it as a satisfactory account. The assumption that all women perform domestic labour precludes an analysis of the forms of cooperation and division of labour that are found in this category of work. It is also clear that the nature of the domestic labour process changes radically with change in technology and size of household, as well as different forms of cooperation. Also human needs, while founded in undeniable physiological requirements, are also subject to cultural and social definition.

Again, even though domestic labour *is* overwhelmingly women's work, the degree to which it is oppressive and the ways in which it is burdensome differ greatly and must be taken into account. Quite apart from enormous variation in what work is entailed in the servicing of the human organism, the same tasks have quite different implications according to whether they are a basis for sociability and cooperation among women, or alternatively performed in virtual isolation with near-total dependence on the male household head.

One of the effects of analysing households as individual and autonomous units has been to miss the importance of the various forms of cooperation and collectivity in domestic work between households. While much of this type of work may well not involve a technical division of labour (that is, a complex division of skills), there are many variants of a social division of labour, for example where some women mind children and cook, leaving other women free to engage in wage labour. Whatever form cooperation takes, the degree of isolation on the one hand, collectivity on the other, will have important effects on women's position within their own households [. . .]

Whether or not it is assigned the status of reproductive work, domestic labour is overwhelmingly treated as distinct from productive labour. Under capitalism, as we have noted, the separation of domestic labour from socialised production coincides with the distinction between the production of use-values and the production of exchange-values in the form of commodities. The definition of use-values by Marx is closely associated with the idea of direct consumption (although not exclusively – for example the corn paid by a medieval peasant as rent and tithe is also seen as use-value). As a result the denomination of economic structures within which commodities do not normally circulate as natural, in contrast to the *social* relations engendered by commodity production and exchange, is further confirmed. The concept of consumption, modelled on the ingestion of food and drink, is deeply imbued with naturalistic assumptions, either derived directly from physiology, or in more sophisticated versions from differences between consumers based on sex and age, again treated as having universal applicability.

The domestic as a category is then defined in relation to a set of other concepts which mutually reinforce each other as natural, universal and not amenable to social analysis. These unspoken associations are important in that they continually reproduce the domestic as a separate, readily-identifiable domain. The very circularity by which the domestic is defined confirms the apparent transparency of this category – physiological needs, consumption, use-values inhabit a space whose identity emerged principally in contrast with another space defined by social rather than natural relations, exchange rather than consumption.

Domestic and Public Spheres?

[. . .] We have already noted the circularity by which the category domestic is defined. This is often extended to the way that women are identified with the domestic sphere, men with the public or social. Thus the sexual division of labour is often identified with a division whereby women remain in the home and men work outside the domestic sphere; the woman is identified with the house, the house with the woman. In another rendering, men do production, while women's primary responsibility is the 'sphere of reproduction', i.e. housework. The problem with such identifications is that they serve directly to confirm the dualism already present in the sexual division. Clearly there is an empirical foundation to this dualism but to approach it in this way is, at best, to give only a descriptive account of the way that women's activities are typically confined to the 'domestic sphere'. Too often, however, such identifications, move beyond the descriptive to the tautological; what women do is treated *by definition* as belonging to the domestic sphere, simply because women do it. One effect of this is to render invisible whatever activities women engage in that manifestly cannot be treated as domestic, for example wage labour. Anyone who has considered the problem of sexual divisions in capitalist society knows how easily women's waged work becomes invisible.

Since women and domestic units are so often mutually defining, any argument that women will be liberated by moving out of the domestic sphere must be viewed with caution. In many cases it may amount to no more than arguing that women will be liberated once they cease to be women. While domestic units are defined frequently in economic terms, the public sphere, in contrast to which the domestic has meaning, is not merely the domain of socialised production and exchange, but also the sphere within which structures of power are defined to the exclusion of women. Where this is the case, it makes little difference whether or not women participate economically in what is called the public or social sphere. There is, then, often a slippage from definitions of the domestic in economic terms, to assumptions about power. However, residential units do not always coincide directly with economic units, and still less do these necessarily correspond to politico-legal units, nor does women's involvement in social production necessarily correlate closely with high politico-legal status in the public domain. To base the division between the domestic and the public on economic activities cannot explain the unequal social value attached to these activities and gives too little attention to the diverse sources of male power. To look at the sexual division of labour, or a division between production and reproduction, is to omit the ways that males guarantee collectively, in many different types of groups, the power that each may wield in his own household.

Conclusion

[. . .] The domestic as a category contains all sorts of assumptions about the natural status of the activities and relationships contained within it. Because of these assumptions, rarely made explicit, we go on talking of the household as a universal institution, outside and separate from the long march of history, even though there is an abundance of evidence of variation in the content and organisation of domestic institutions. Having said this, I would not wish to conclude that we should abandon the category altogether, but that we should use it with a fuller understanding of its ideological context. [. . .]

While my discussion has been chiefly concerned with what is written *about* households, my argument is not that confusions in the term domestic are simply due to the myopia of historians, feminist writers, or social scientists. Nor do I think that they result from an unthinking application to all situations of the way the domestic sphere is continually reproduced under capitalism as a separate and privatised domain. On the contrary it is evident that a domestic domain is easily identifiable in a multitude of different contexts. If we ask why this is so, one answer will inevitably be couched in terms of physiological needs and the organisation of consumption for subsistence. However, it is equally clear that functionalist explanation of this sort is not conclusive. The constitution of a *sui generis* domain separate from the public or social world is also the means by which women are effectively controlled. The more households are organisationally separate, the more women are confined and isolated within the domestic space, the more total is their dependence on those men who represent them and speak for them in the world at large.

This means of subordinating women through the gender-typing of many activities and constraining those defined as female to a strictly circumscribed domain is found in many cultures and in widely-differing production systems. The ascription of natural status to this domain is certainly not restricted to western capitalist society, but is found also in other contexts – a form in which the subordination of women is ideologically reproduced and their 'domestication' secured. But equally it is important to recognise that this is an ideology – that is, women's subordination or domestication is never complete or guaranteed. Under capitalism the domestic domain is subject to continued intervention both directly through state agencies, legislation, welfare provision, and indirectly through the mass media, the structuring of wages, and through technological change that constantly alters the nature of work carried on within the home. In spite of this 'policing' of the household, only a limited number of units in fact conform to the ideal, as has already been noted. In other social and historical contexts too, whatever the power of domestic ideology, only a small number of units in practice approximate to it. Women can only be fully domesticated where men are wealthy and powerful enough to dispense with their abilities and labour and confine them to instruments of reproducing male stock. It is surely because the project of fully subjecting women to the control of men is so contradictory that an ideological definition of the domestic in terms of a natural finality has remained so powerful and persuasive.

References

CHAYANOV, A. V. (1966) *The Theory of Peasant Economy*, Homewood, Illinois, R. D. Irwin Inc.
DELPHY, C. (1977) *The Main Enemy*, London, WRRC.
LASLETT, P. (ed.) (1949) *Patriarcha and other Political Works of Sir Robert Filmer,* Oxford, Blackwell.
MEILLASSOUX, C. (1981) *Maidens, Meal and Money*, Cambridge, Cambridge University Press.
SAHLINS, M. (1974) *Stone Age Economics*, London, Tavistock.

7 Postwar Pronatalism

Denise Riley

From *War in the Nursery: Theories of the Child and Mother* by Denise Riley, 1983.
Reproduced by permission of the publisher, Virago.

[. . .] In asking whether the employment of married and unmarried women in the last war, including a proportion of mothers in both groups, made any differences to suppositions about 'women's place', we're entering a dense tangle of labour requirements, shifts in state suppositions about the family and the care of children, the nature of terms like popularisation, propaganda, ideology, and wants and needs. Did the reinstatement of the ideal of the woman at home with the child simply seal over a surface which had been only superficially scarred by the peculiarities of the war economy? One way into this thicket is to ask to what extent 'the free mothers' are an impossibility, a contradiction in terms, not only practically (the double burden of work in and out of the home) but also from the aspect of political theory. For women as mothers and potential mothers sit firmly within the illusory unity of the category of 'the family' – illusory in the sense that 'the family' is a complex object whose members possess different and sometimes antagonistic capacities and powers, and where money usually maps onto gender as well as age. There is no straightforward single recipient, 'the family', of family welfare measures. The lot of working mothers in wartime and after points up the incoherence built into social policy addresses to 'the family' which speak as if the interests and needs of women, men and children were always harmoniously unified. Mothers who work strain these assumptions of unity. 'The free mothers' of the 1940s were pinned down by that very status, both as war workers and after the war, in ways which were ultimately damaging from any liberationist or even egalitarian perspective.

Yet this rhetorical limiting took place against a myriad programmatic pronouncements, by a wide sweep of parties and interests, about freeing mothers, including by means of nurseries, from the intolerable drudgery of unrelieved childcare. But these 'free mothers' were to be released only into a more relaxed and whole-hearted support of the family – freed into having more children. Both during the war and most strikingly just after it, the reproductive woman at the heart of family policy was surrounded by the language of pronatalism. By pronatalism, I mean that despondency and alarm over the low birth rate, both past and as anticipated by demographers, which took the solution to the problem to be

134

encouraging women to have more children; four per family was a widely agreed target. Both this anxiety and this proposal for its remedy (as distinct from any economic analysis) had been building up throughout the 1930s and became more generally diffused towards the end of the war.

Pronatalist thinking generated a great deal of language about 'the mother', not all of which was decisively conservative, and much of which believed itself to be progressive. It filled bits of the world with sound, while the birth rate crept quietly upwards. But the ubiquity of this official nerviness about the falling population cannot in itself, without more evidence, be assumed to have affected women's reproductive behaviour one way or another. Rhetoric doesn't make women have more children through the sheer power of the word – the word narrowly conceived. Its presence matters, though, to put it mildly, and has to be assessed, irrespective of whether it 'works' in the most detectable sense. This has to do with the general difficulty of how we understand the acting of 'bad language' in the world; how it enters into and also forms – in Raymond Williams' phrase – 'structures of feeling'.

How, exactly, are we to grasp the full force of what can be loosely referred to as 'a climate of pronatalist opinion'? If we do not understand its impact in terms of its demonstrable effects (most obviously, fluctuations of the birth rate) or if we can't detect any such hard effects, how then do we make sense of its overall presence? Some might conclude – wrongly – that British pronatalism in the 1930s and 1940s was a lot of noise which hurt nobody. This conclusion could be reinforced by the fact that pronatalism itself was no smooth unity, but a ragged orchestration of differing origins. Certainly the mere presence in the world of certain ways of speaking and writing guarantees nothing. Yet to stop at merely noting the pervasiveness of a particular discourse is to stop too soon. I do not know how best to make sense of the vast conceptual gaps between the equally uninviting options of either just hailing the existence of a discourse, or only assessing its quantifiable effects. But understanding pronatalism demands thought about this. Here I edge towards a comment on a particular instance of pronatalism: that damage was caused by the timing of British postwar pronatalism, in that for a brief period it sounded as if it spoke to the same needs for the 'protection of motherhood' about which various women's labour organisations had been agitating for decades. But the sources of pronatalist anxiety were different, and transient. The temporary coincidence of verbal object – the mother – in the diction of population policies, of social-democratic 'progressiveness', and of women's labour organisations brought about an emphasis on the mother as real worker in the home, equal or indeed greater in 'value' than the waged woman worker. In all this, the mother who did go out to work, and who consequently had especial needs, became an impossibility, regarded by no-one. The possibility of speaking politically about women's *needs* became obscured by a passing rhetoric of their maternal *function*.

This suggestion is a hesitant one: to talk about rhetoric as having 'effects' needs some conception of just where the effects are to be detected, and how. Simply to say about postwar pronatalism, 'yes, such language was reactionary, but we can demonstrate that it didn't affect women's behaviour one way or another', only fights shy of the problems. But to move towards them is hard: how can we understand the spread of a particular rhetoric in relation to the more narrowly political discourses of the period? Can we accurately identify a dominant 'ideological' language, and then discover whether more limited forms of political speech engage head on with it, or exist quietly in its shade, or adopt its intonations? A political language possessed of any sensitivity but indifferent to such a socially overshadowing rhetoric as that of postwar pronatalism in Britain would be unlikely: then it's a matter of assessing the reasons for the *silences* of liberal, socialist, and feminist speech towards it; or what critical distances they took from it.

There is evidence of covert cynicism and some suspension of belief among respondents to sociological enquiries; but these traces of reserve can't alone guarantee resistance. An ideology is not reassuringly without 'effects' simply because it isn't wholeheartedly subscribed to. My sense of it is that, although in immediately postwar Britain there are a few traces of *direct* unease with pronatalism in the formal expressions of women's labour organisations – rather, some understandable determination to exploit a climate for what it might usefully yield – the effects of this unease are elsewhere altogether, and are less susceptible to being read off from conference and branch reports. Instead they are oblique: in the field of political speech as silence, absence of challenge, indirection. Because portrayals of postwar pronatalism were largely in key with other, apparently anodyne presentations of family, home and nation, it was easier for them to get away unchallenged. Their impact lies in what was not said: as if they had acted to cover over a space, make certain objections unable to be raised or articulated. But a rhetoric could only ever have this power if accidentally allowed it by a previous set of failures: failures, in this case of postwar Britain, of radical analyses of the family, the nation, the state and the sexual division of labour. 'Good reasons' can be found for these absences, certainly. But that's a different point.

An important question is that of possible sources for the metaphor of the mother as worker, which held such sway in 1945–6 and had such a dulling presence in the formulations of political organisations, including women's labour organisations. For its implications were rarely refined to expose its contradictions. My point is not that mothers aren't workers in the obvious sense – far from it – but rather that a strong separation, albeit at the level of language alone, between mothers (who are assumed to be always married and always at home) and women (who are assumed to be periodically at work) is both artificial and politically dangerous. Artificial, in that it overlooks the real drifts of the labour market (as it did in postwar Britain); and dangerous, in that it asserts 'motherhood' as a self-evident value, but at the same time works directly against any admission of the real needs of women with children. Doing this, it confirms the most conservative understandings of gender, family, work. It contributes, too, to the 'stages' idea of women's work – that women's lives are stratified into a spell of paid work, followed by motherhood, then maybe reentry into the labour market. But this presumption of neatly autonomous strata runs against fact; for the layers are constantly flooded into each other; the histories, pressures and needs of one shape and determine the others, and make the theoretical 'choice' to return to work utterly impossible in practice.

Post-1968 feminism has grown up with a depiction of a mass return of women to the home after 1945, engineered by governmental deployment of maternal deprivation theories. This depiction misleads not only in that it assumes a collusion between the state and psychology; the movements of the labour market, too, were not so simply homeward-bound. It also colours our understanding of the 'state' in relation to 'the family', so as to preserve a falsely unitary sense of both: for in an analysis of what went on between labour requirements, welfare, governmental departments and women's work or the lack of it, neither a unified state nor an undifferentiated family can usefully be assumed.

In the case of wartime nursery provision, for instance, the 'state' fragments into internal government politics, dissensions between the Ministries of Health, Education, and Labour, reactions to pressures from industrialists, and splits between central and local government authorities. As for 'the family' of immediately postwar family policy, the fiscal man and the reproductive women and the stock of children compose a multiple target; there is no symmetry between the man as wage earner and the woman as mother. Analogous, then, to other questions thrown up by the transitions of the war and postwar years (like, under what political conditions could forms of education in motherhood *not* appear reactionary?) is the question of the language in which a truly progressive family policy could voice itself. Would it refer to the family as such, and take it as the true unit of society; or would it instead shake family members apart, and speak about the needs and clashes of needs between children and parents, women and men?

The mother in 1945 stood side by side with her children in her own spotlight of planning and welfare. But how enlightened an illumination was in focus, after all? [. . .]

'The Mother' in Postwar Social Politics

The welter of proposed improvements in the lot of the postwar mother and the family is quite dazzling at first glimpse. Immediately after the war, 'comforts for free mothers' continued to be widely touted by social theories within a general social-democratic or liberal drift which crossed party boundaries. On the question of the mother, who was not a social democrat?

There is a huge literature, concentrated in 1945 and 1946, which argues for nurseries, after-school play centres, rest homes for tired housewives, family tickets on trains, official neighbourhood babysitters, holidays on the social services for poorer families, proper access for all to good gynaecological and obstetric help, a revolution in domestic architecture towards streamlined rational kitchens and a good number of bedrooms, more communal restaurants and laundries [. . .]

Examples of these mixes of practical improvements, domestic innovations, and pronatalist devices could be multiplied indefinitely: it is the tight meshing of these elements which is so noticeable in retrospect. By 1945 the universal tone of social-democratic policy on the family had been so often invoked that its repetitions begin to look flattened and exhausted themselves, like the housewives' lives they sought to improve [. . .] From a perspective of thirty-odd years on, contemporary feminism tends to assume that 'the postwar rehabilitation of the family' really was a concerted drive to revive traditional values after the demoralisation of war, to reinstate the nuclear family after the closing of war nurseries and the return of women to the home. But books and articles of the period make it clear that 'the family' was a preoccupation all through the war; that anticipation of postwar social reforms had a wider base than the immediate cluster of excitement around the Beveridge report on *Social Insurance and Allied Services* in 1942; and that there was no imposed and concerted drive to reinstate the family 'from above' at the immediate end of the war. The Reconstruction Priorities Committee was set up in 1943, to pursue Beveridge's proposals: in November of that year, a new Cabinet Committee on Reconstruction was announced, with Lord Woolton as Minister. Surveys and investigations on postwar reconstruction had been well established earlier, however, including for instance, the Nuffield College Social Reconstruction Survey which was instituted in 1941. The 'social reforms' introduced by the Labour government in 1945 were in this sense a consolidation of what had been established under the Coalition government.

In 1940, Orwell had written [in 'The Lion and the Unicorn'],

> There are wide gradations of income, but it is the same kind of life that is being lived at different levels in labour-saving flats or council houses, along the concrete roads and in the naked democracy of the swimming pools. It is a rather restless, cultureless life, centering around tinned food, *Picture Post*, the radio and the internal combustion engine.

But how accurate was this sense of a universal cultural flattening? My inclination now is to take 1945–7 as the moment of self-exhaustion of a particular social-democratic weighting on 'the family' which had been running through the war–as opposed to the more orthodox view that the pronouncements of 1945 were fresh moments of Labour family policy, a new end-of-the-war egalitarianism. In this light, that particularly intense concentration on the mother which got going in 1945–6 is a symptom of the impossibility of holding together, at the level of language, the doubtful unity of 'the family', once the end of the war had dissolved its rhetorical appeal. Orwell's fine phrase, 'the naked democracy of the swimming pool', ironically spins off from a rhetoric impossible to sustain for long after the war. The generality of 'the family', too, was less voiced after 1945.

For if you look for some uniform movement to 'rehabilitate the family', it cannot be traced. Instead a series of specialised agencies, such as the new psychiatric social work, 'open up' only certain kinds of families to corrective inspection, like the revived category of the 'problem family'; look for the responsibility of family members for breakdowns in family functioning; and settle increasingly on the mothers. Not that 1945 was in any way unprecedented in its growing emphasis on the mother: rather that it marks one of many watersheds in the periodic invocations of the family. Postwar welfare penetrated the traditional 'privacy' of the family by speaking more and more to the assumed needs of separate family members.

One of the strongest attempts to hold together the unity of 'the family' before 1945 is evidenced, I'd think, through the many metaphors of the family as a cellular organism in the body politic of the state and the community. Family health was a building block in the edifice of national health, spiritual or physical. (That extraordinary book written in 1943 by a woman doctor and a woman sociologist about a South London Health Centre, *The Peckham Experiment*, is one long metaphor of the family as a biological organism, a vital cell in the body of the national whole.) The predominance of the vocabulary of 'citizenship' in 1945 to 1947, especially in Fabian writings, had a similar neutral wholeness to that which 'the family' possessed. The blank face of 'the citizen' possessed neither class nor gender: as a political notion it simply refused all those differences, social and sexual, in its aspirations for an egalitarian democracy. These 'the family' also concealed.

But the bundle of pronatalist and ameliorative elements in postwar social policy on the family, taken together with the impossibility of sustaining a rhetoric of 'the family' as such after 1946, bring up a more solid possibility. That is, that 'family policy' is a contradiction: for the very good reason that the family does not exist as an entity. In so far as a 'family policy' has to do with children, and given that the bearing and rearing of children is by biology and custom respectively the province of women, then a main object of 'family policy' is women; the universally pronatalist climate of 1945–7 ensured that the true target of postwar social philosophy was the mother.

One of the clearest instances of this aiming at the mother is the manner in which the postwar retention of nurseries was argued. The very widespread pro-nursery sentiments of the late 1940s were perfectly congruent with familialism, enthusiasm for the family. Nurseries were advocated as key points for educating mothers through influence and precept, and as likely to raise the birth rate by lightening the burden of childrearing. Both conservatives and social democrats held that nurseries were an invaluable means for teaching 'mothercraft' to adolescent girls [. . .]

And state-provided childcare could cement marriages, since it would ease the tensions caused by overcrowding. Nursery demands fed into housing demands very neatly. For instance, in the House of Commons adjournment motion on the fate of the wartime nurseries, in March 1945, pro-nursery Members of Parliament argued that if they were retained, housing, 'the basis of responsible, healthy family life', would be made more bearable where it was bad. Nurseries would save the birth rate and marriage by taking the stress off the wife: the husband need no longer 'escape' to the pub or politics – 'one is as bad as the other if it splits the home' [. . .]

None of these considerations brought about a national network of postwar nurseries. The Government's interest in social need was merely rhetorical. It was not, in the end, swayed into action. Acute questions of childcare provision and other reforms central to the lives of women and children were decisively captured by a language in which the figure of the Mother was continuously produced as both cause and object of all these reforming movements.

It can be argued – and was argued at the time – that real progress was made out of this: access to contraceptive and obstetric services was improved and democratised to some extent; children in care received fresh consideration; family allowances were introduced. These were gains in line with the long-voiced demands of women's labour organisations and were significant advances, however imperfect and flawed their implementation. G. D. H. Cole observed about the new social security plans:

> The opinion of today credits women and children with individual rights and claims of their own. It is not so ready as its forerunners to say that the sins of the fathers shall be visited upon the children, or even upon the mother, or so sure that family life thrives best when women and children were offered up as victims to its sanctity. (Cole, 1947, p.542)

It was widely assumed by contemporary socialists and social democrats that serious humanitarian advances had been begun by postwar family policies, even if the material gains were in practice slight – as with family allowances, the principle was respected, while the five shillings a week was derided. This position, though, [. . .] depended on some conviction about the longer-term possibilities of a progressive capitalism. And although social policy developments did in some lights treat women and children as separate family members, women were mothers within and with reference to the family, socially and economically. Although mothers were indeed addressed in their own right, this was not in itself any guarantee of a political advance, even if it held the promise of practical gains. There's a crucial difference between invoking 'the mother' and speaking about the practical needs of women with children: the first is a rhetoric of function and static position, the second discusses sexual-social difference in a way which doesn't fix it under the appearance of eternity. To say this is perfectly compatible with acknowledging that some real, if circumscribed, aims were achieved in the lives of women with children. But postwar pronatalist opinion did not of itself produce such gains – even if it acted as a spur, they had other and older origins. And pronatalist speech imposed a double edge on the expression of these limited social gains, for it was always at risk of falling back into instrumentality [. . .]

Psychology, History and Reconstructions: Problems

The process of redescription of the wartime 'experiences' got well under way by the mid-1950s. Sociological commentaries stated that women had freely withdrawn from paid work, despite the fact that such a withdrawal was neither 'free' nor neatly occurring anyway. Popular psychological writings, drawing on the supposed evidence of war nurseries, evoked the dangers of separating mothers and children while claiming that the experiences of war had proved a vindication of the emotional health of unified family life. But references to the 'evidence' of evacuation and nurseries constituted a misleading history. Despite the hopes and retrospective claims made for the didactic value of the war experiences of mothers and children, the literature on it was limited. Appeals to the authority of the 'lessons of war' in fact hook up with the established prewar body of European and American psychoanalytic work on the dangers of institutionalising children in orphanages and hospitals. But the claim of the 1950s is for the irreducible evidence, derived from the 'facts' of the war years, of the dangers of women going out to work.

On the surface, the postwar literature of family sociopsychology that purports to draw on the experience of the war implies a series of smooth and rational transitions from psychological 'knowledge' to the practices of welfare policies, as if 'the state' acted on the family according to the dictates of child and maternal psychology, which had itself drawn on the evidence of the war years. But what actually happened was a constant mutual appealing from history to psychology and back, which resulted in a web of cross-reference. To take this as genuinely indicative of anything independently accurate would be misleading; what is needed instead is a means of understanding the construction and effects of that web.

The complication here is that the density of representations which we set about stripping down is, at the same time, both our inheritance from the 1950s and the means by which we form the questions which we turn back on the 1940s. For instance, in the question of the relation of the state to women and children, my approach was determined by attributions which it then turned out to be necessary to query. The legacy of a politics of socialism and feminism out of the late 1960s and 1970s is a set of suppositions about the standing of the state vis-à-vis the family – the idea, for example, that the postwar government used Bowlby's theory of 'maternal deprivation' to get British women out of their jobs and back into their kitchens. This received but inaccurate history, which has fuelled so much indignation among feminists over the collusion of science and state at the expense of women, has strengthened a picture of 'ideology' as more or less deliberately generated by the state – one which seemed able to claim the experiences of 1945 to 1947 as evidence for itself. The political attitudes which inspired that indignant curiosity were themselves necessarily founded on the same attributions which the 1950s had made about the 1940s, even if they were inverted in political tone. Undoing those attributions meant pulling apart some of the political axioms which had determined the questions in the first place: notably the assumption that you could start with a 'state' which 'acted on the family' from above in a straightforward manner.

One move, tempting to make in reaction to the inaccuracies of attributions about 'the experience of the war' and what it showed about 'the need for family life', is to use the same evidence for opposite ends. So, for example, one could take women's responses to the surveys for the Ministry of Reconstruction and Labour [which were conducted in 1943–4] and reinterpret them, rereading them so as to make them 'really' speak as one would prefer, picking up ambiguities and hesitations in women's replies and thus recapturing them for one's own side, drawing them across the line to rejoin 'us' where they really always were. This enticing enterprise can be helped along, too, by a seemingly 'materialist' method of working – that is, by answering questions about why, for instance, many young women cheerfully anticipated abandoning work for marriage, by pointing out all

Denise Riley

the practical conditions which surrounded their anticipation. One could describe the uninviting nature of the available work, the low degree of skill and unionisation, and the weight of the prospect of untrained years in the factory, offset by hope in the saving grace of marriage. Or one could even sidestep by commenting that really after all women did not withdraw from work anyway.

This sort of 'materialist' tack is a necessary one; some version of it is an essential starting point, but only if it is used in full recognition of its risks and limits. The anxiety I've felt about using it to undermine the surface obviousness of a response from 1945 like, 'I shan't want to work when I'm married,' lies in the inadequacy of its approach to the question of why and how people produce particular formulations about what they want (the considerations which, for example, the Italian historian Luisa Passerini discusses in her 'Work, Ideology and Consensus under Italian Fascism' (1979)); attitudes, behaviour, language, 'a sense of identity' and how these are susceptible to coercion.

In the absence of a solution to these considerations, I've sensed my work oscillating between two explanatory models: the one of saying, 'Women really did want to work, they did want nurseries; if we read the responses to these flat questionnaires correctly, we can surely decipher these wishes; or we can uncover the buried evidence of meetings, demonstrations and petitions to reveal their wants.' And the second of saying, 'Well, no wonder women were, on the whole, indifferent: what else, given these political conditions and these circumstances of work, could these women have done in 1945?' Both these explanatory models carry a certain amount of truth: but the truth can't comfortably be thus divided without being at risk of tearing apart. And it does seem to be divided; not because it's not possible to reconcile these paradigms in the abstract, but because in practice they stand and attract other attitudes.

On the one hand, the attempt to uncover real wishes can slip into presuming a clear and well-formed set of wants – of a 'progressive' cast at that – so that the struggle is to read correctly responses from the past, between the lines even, and give them a framework in which they can speak out unambiguously; as in the supposition that if you could only put the right questions to women industrial workers in 1945 about their work aims, then they would speak truly, demonstrating through their dissatisfactions their latent socialist consciousness. But the trouble with the attempt to lay bare the red heart of truth beneath the discolourations and encrustations of thirty-odd years on, is that it assumes a clear space out of which voices can speak – as if, that is, ascertaining 'consciousness' stopped at scraping off history. That is not, of course, to discredit what people say as such, or to imply that considering the expression of wants is pointless. The difficulty is that needs and wants are never pure and undetermined in such a way that they could be fully revealed, to shine out with an absolute clarity, by stripping away a patina of historical postscripts and rewritings.

But, on the other hand, some kinds of materialist explanation which skip the search for the nature of true need in favour of pragmatic accounts of the apparent conservatism of people's behaviour have serious deficiencies too. Explanations of the form, 'what else under these actually obtaining circumstances could people have done', are essential but incomplete, because they have nothing to say about desires, hesitations, cynicism, or self-conceptions on the part of the historical actors. Because of this silence, even explicitly and polemically socialist forms of this materialist approach invite in neighbours they wouldn't care for. The theory of collusion, for instance – exemplified at its simplest in 'women collude in their own oppression' – presents explanatory shortcuts of a dangerously psychologising kind. It's this kind of theory which can rush in with the air of filling the gaps left in those pragmatic materialist accounts which fight shy of considering why people 'act against their own interest'.

Versions of this collusion idea are occasionally raised as a refusal of the 'heroinisation' of women and as an insistence that women will only step into history if allowed to be fully marked by their culpability, which then has to be accounted for. The Italian Marxist writer, Maria-Antonietta Macciocchi, does this in her 'Female Sexuality in Fascist Ideology' (1979), where she treats the question of a seemingly gender-privileged 'consent' to fascism by Italian women. It might be thought that these suppositions could be contested by a materialist account, yet most materialisms tacitly support them by keeping quiet themselves about the fuller complexities of human actions: for instance, socialist versions of the 'home as refuge from the harsh world' school of apologetics might describe periods of retrenchment and the conservatising of daily life, as in post-Bolshevik Russia or National Socialist Germany, as inevitable given the rigorous material conditions of the time. Doing so, they are, with the best of intentions, and with the sanction of Trotsky in *The Revolution Betrayed* (1937, pp.140–1), acting as kindly variants of collusion theory. They seek to let people off from the charge of having 'reactionary' desires to go back to the warm privacy of the home, by redescribing them as materially based. For accusation, materialism is substituted, and an imaginative and sensitive materialism at that.

But the generosity of materialist pragmatics here is premature: its kindness can serve to mask the possibilities of real dissent, real resistances, voiced or not, on the part of those whose behaviour it seeks to excuse. It forgets that desires can be contradictory; and forgets, too, that 'the home' can hardly constitute a refuge for those who were always there, as providers and housekeepers and childcarers, at the heart of it anyway. It has nothing new to say to the problem of an apparent 'consent' to a reactionary social order. Instead it merely *writes all over it* – it covers it with elaborate descriptions of the historical details of how people acted. Ignoring the problems of why they acted, it leaves the way open for theories of collusion to be tacked, not inharmoniously, on.

I can only suggest that, to a materialist-realist explanation of seemingly conservative drifts in domestic organisation, two further steps could replace the home-as-refuge treatment. The first would be the refusal to take 'the family' as a unitary object for investigation. The second would be an attempt to examine the exact nature of the gaps at particular times, between, say,

psychology: social policy
social policy: social practices

propaganda: people's behaviour
policies: their enactment: people's acceptance.

Each of the colons in this sample list marks a point where derivation is conventionally claimed or assumed: policy flowing into practice, for example. But social practice cannot necessarily be read off from social policy, or even social consent from social practice. The whole range of speeches, articles, broadcasts to 'the family' does not guarantee any acceptance of, let alone a full complicity with, such notions on the part of their targets. Pronatalist rhetoric may flourish, and the birth rate may rise; but the former may not have brought about the latter.

'The feminine sex,' wrote Alva Myrdal, 'is a social problem' (1945, p.418). The dilemma is that of understanding social-sexual difference in 'progressive' or conservative ways: as transitionally produced and so susceptible to change; or as essential, guaranteed for all time. Human needs, too, can be understood as the volatile products of a complexity of production, speech, desires, consumption; or as the fixed products of social roles which guarantee them. One effect of the fixing and freezing of the Mother as a social category is to create an inflexible notion of needs as well to accompany this social role. So a double social-sexual fixity is set up.

There is no clear theory of need available to us. The insistence on the historically produced nature of needs in Marx is neither specific to Marxism nor enough to constitute a theory. I've said that people's needs obviously can't be revealed by a simple process of historical unveiling, while elsewhere I've talked about the 'real needs' of mothers myself. I take it that it's necessary both to stress the non-self-evident nature of need and the intricacies of its determinants, and also to act politically as if needs could be met, or at least met halfway. The benign if traditionally unimaginative face of 'socialist planning', is, at the least, preferable to its known alternatives, however much its objects will always tend to be in excess of it and slip away.

And, once on the terrain of family policies, socialist feminism will have to search for an understanding of need; this cannot be fully supplied by a kind of Fabian sociological thermometer for measuring, for example, the needs of mothers for nurseries. Nor, though, can needs be given transcendentally, to be fulfilled under some hypothetical communism of plenitude. For human needs may not be witnesses to the demands of some eternal human nature – but nor can they be expected to settle down to some final satisfiable form under a transformed mode of production. Yet once that unsatisfactory vision is rejected as exemplifying the 'sterility' of Marxism, the wish for something better, for some truly humane yet still specifically socialist good-heartedness, may well light on the old search for a 'socialist psychology'. But this is a doubtful goal; psychology cannot stand as a self-evident home of the humane (or for that matter the inhumane) fit to be translated into socialism by receiving new objectives, but otherwise keeping much as it is.

Such worries about what needs *are* does not mean that nothing can be done. For instance, even though it is true that arguing for adequate childcare as one obvious way of meeting the needs of mothers does suppose an orthodox division of labour, in which responsibility for children is the province of women and not of men, nevertheless this division is what, by and large, actually obtains. Recognition of that in no way commits you to supposing that the care of children is fixed eternally as female. What conclusions, of use for qualifying that supposition, might the narrative of the postwar government, of psychological theories and their languages yield?

Because the task of illuminating 'the needs of mothers' starts out with gender at its most decisive and inescapable point–the biological capacity to bear children–there's the danger that it may fall back into a conservative restating and confirming of social-sexual difference as timeless too. This would entail making the needs of mothers into fixed properties of 'motherhood' as a social function: I believe this is what happened in postwar Britain. Understanding social-sexual difference entails being alert to the real effects of existing differences, which must be acknowledged as effects–instead of being prematurely absorbed into neutral categories like 'citizenship'. Such categories, because they are systematically indifferent to gender, guarantee a return of that dominant order, the masculine, about which they are silent. And, on the other hand, taking social-sexual difference as something essential and to be celebrated can be equally misconceived–whether from the standpoint of the chauvinistic 'vive la différence', or of certain versions of feminism.

In the last war, women as workers and women as reproductive social beings were understood in the most conservative ways. Women's war work, even in presentations of their collective heroic capacities, was work done by *women*, marked through and through by the gender of its performers, and consequently by the especial temporariness of the work of women who were mothers.

In some obvious ways, all this weighing on gender is unsurprising. Only at an exceptional point of demand for all possible labour–the war economy–were all women, regardless of their reproductive status, made publicly visible as workers. But what could abstractly have been the moment to seize and push through the logic of sexual difference–through to the proper provision of childcare facilities and working conditions–was concretely impossible. Everything about the employment of married women in industry militated against their being taken seriously as real workers: by 1945 the dominant rhetoric held out an opposition between the mother and the woman worker.

The postwar collapse of the war nurseries only underlined the 'special nature' of temporary concessions to working mothers. The coincidence of pronatalism with the end of the war intensified the 'facts' that all women were mothers or potential mothers, that all women were marriage-prone, that no-one had children who was not married. Hence two marginal presences: the spinster, an isolated professional woman who might utterly legitimately work and who deserved equal pay; and the unmarried mother, who resurfaces in the psychosociology of the early 1950s as 'pathologically disturbed'. While it was 'transitionally' necessary to insist on better conditions of housing and money in which to have children in 1945, the coincidence of this with the prominent rhetoric of the 'value of motherhood' blurred the needs of mothers with the essence of maternity in a way fatal for any real approach to the meeting of need [. . .]

References

COLE, G. D. H. (1947) *The Intelligent Man's Guide to the Post-War World*, London.
MACCIOCCHI, M.-A. (1979) 'Female sexuality in Fascist ideology', *Feminist Review*, no. 1.
MYRDAL, A. (1945) *Nation and Family*, London.
PASSERINI, L. (1979) 'Work, ideology and consensus under Italian Fascism', *History Workshop Journal*, no. 8, Autumn.
TROTSKY, L. (1937) *The Revolution Betrayed*, London.

8   The Royals

Rosalind Coward

From *Female Desire: Women's Sexuality Today* by Rosalind Coward, 1984. Reproduced by permission of the publisher, Paladin Books.

'The Royals' is the longest-running soap opera in Britain. One branch of the media can always be relied on to carry the next instalment – one or other of the daily newspapers, a television news report, or a woman's magazine, invariably has something on the latest developments in the Royal family. We have become just as intimate with the doings of the folk from Buckingham Palace as we have with the folk from Southfork Ranch. The romances, weddings, births and deaths, the conflicts and rivalries, are all made available to us. And like any good soap opera, 'The Royals' has its ardent fans and its bitter opponents.

In the 1950s, the television soap opera found its feet. Using the fact of the permanent domestic presence of the television, a form of narrative developed which could, like life, go on almost indefinitely.

Each episode was to be a microcosm of drama and intrigue. And in that very period, the press began to treat 'The Royals' differently. Playing down 'statesmanship' and aristocracy, the public were treated to more and more intimate revelations and points of speculation about the young family of Queen Elizabeth. Is it just coincidence that in this postwar period, when anachronistic institutions might have been cleared away, the press produced a new-style monarchy – familial, more accessible and almost ordinary? Or was it that an infallible format had been discovered? Was it that 'The Royals', like a soap opera, offered a rich vein of intimate revelations, based 'roughly on reality', which never has to end, which never has to be the subject of political debate? Who, after all, is going to call for the abdication of Miss Ellie?

Royal soap is based on the same narrative structures as 'Dallas'. It offers all the pleasures of a good family melodrama. Like 'Dallas', it is the long-running story of an extremely wealthy and powerful family. The two soap operas share the same preoccupations: the unity of the family; family wealth; dynastic considerations like inheritance and fertility; sexual promiscuity; family duty; and alliances with outsiders/rivals/lower orders. The fact that 'The Royals' is loosely based on reality only adds to its fascination. Statements from the Royal press office attempt to check gross distortions; but this voice of truth only adds to the pleasurable activity of comparing reports, and building up a hierarchy of reliable sources. All our knowledge of the Royals is more or less fictional, based on media stories and the occasional sighting. We have no more direct knowledge of the Royals than of any other fictional TV character, and seeing the Queen in the flesh isn't that different from seeing the actress who plays Miss Ellie.

It doesn't matter that there's a real-life family behind the story. What matters is the *way* the story is told; some elements are treated as highly significant, others are not even dealt with. And the Royal family is presented exactly according to the conventions of a family melodrama. 'The Royals' doesn't just follow life as it is, because 'life as it is' is presented differently by different narrative genres. Narrative is, in general, the linear organization of events across time, and events are helped along by the functions or acts of various protagonists in the story. There are, however, wide divergences between genres as to what events are significant, how important the characters are in relation to the action, and so on [. . .]

A family melodrama is preoccupied with sexual relations, marriage, the unity of the family, internal conflict within the family, and the disintegration of the family which is usually embodied in the threat of 'outsiders' or 'the problem of the modern woman'. The story stays as close as possible to everyday [life . . .] And family melodramas do not deal with politics, workplace conflicts or social issues, except as they affect the family.

Some family melodramas have as their central aim the elevation of the particular family as representative of all human (or national) emotions. 'The Royals' have this position, just like the Ewings. The Ewings are elevated by extreme wealth; the Royals by extreme nobility. The function of this elevated status is the same for both though; it enables us to ask how are family conflicts and choices lived out in the family that has everything? The Archbishop of Canterbury gave an address at the wedding between Prince Charles and Lady Diana which made this archetypal function quite clear. The wedding, he said, may look like a fairly tale, but it is only the same step that everybody has to take; 'At the centre of a nation's life, there is a bewildering kaleidoscope of events, peopled by a huge and everchanging cast of politicians and personalities. We are fortunate in having at the heart of our national life another ingredient, the presence of a family, providing a sense of continuity and *pointing to the most profound themes of human life* which do not change from century to century' (Official Programme for the Royal Wedding, my emphasis).

The Ewings and the Royals may have an elevated status but their problems and conflicts are meant to be those which all families share. These conflicts and problems are expressed through a series of oppositions in the narrative. It is the function of the characters to carry one or other of the terms in the opposition. The oppositions in this kind of family melodrama revolve around: rebel/conformist; promiscuous/faithful; good mother/bad mother; good son or daughter/bad son or daughter; nobility/commoner; rightful (biological) heir/rival claim.

'Dallas' is able to offer fairly fixed functions for its characters. Thus JR can remain consistently rotten. In this authentic fiction, it is possible to have one really nasty character. After all, in the cut-throat world of big business, this is relatively plausible, perhaps even acceptable. The Royals, however, could not afford the luxury of a consistent rotter. Because their financial status is more ambiguous it would be dangerous to have one truly scheming member. Such a person in a world of extraordinary privilege, which is nevertheless granted by the goodwill of the people, would be far too problematic. The question might well be asked: why should we tolerate these people? Instead the oppositions between good and evil, deserving and undeserving, are distributed among a number of characters. The function of villainy, in short, is distributed among a number of characters who can then carry a single attribute of 'rottenness' – promiscuity, coldness, drunkenness. But no character in 'The Royals' is allowed to have all these characteristics at one time.

In fact the way in which the narrative functions are split up among the different Royal characters gives us a good idea about the structures and emotions to which the Royal appeal is addressed. Take the marriage of Prince Charles to Lady Diana. Lady Diana introduced a new element to the story of 'The Royals'; with her arrival several characters had to take a step sideways or change their narrative function. Princess Anne, from being basically a good sport, was promptly given the status of 'ugly sister'. Papers carried reports of her bitchy remarks about Lady Di and rumours were in circulation about the disintegration of her marriage. Mark Phillips, it was alleged, had gone off with a lady newsreader; hardly surprising, the papers continued, because Princess Anne was such a *bad* mother. The sudden indulgence of hostility towards Princess Anne (a hostility which has always been lurking beneath the surface) could suddenly appear because the Royals now had a truly charming, innocent, but sexually attractive Princess. Princess Anne was then transferred to the other side of the classic oppositions accruing to aristocratic women. Lady Di carried the gracious, gentle attributes; Princess Anne, on the other hand was arrogant, bitchy, ungainly. Clearly it became much safer to give Princess Anne these qualities once her children were displaced from the Royal succession.

Prior to the introduction of Princess Diana, the function of the undeserving Royal woman was fulfilled by Princess Margaret. The major opposition of good and bad was played out around the sisters, Elizabeth and Margaret. Margaret, at first a tragically thwarted lover, settled into her press position as a semi-alcoholic, difficult, divorced woman over whose sexual morality, it was alleged, hung a very large question mark. The Queen on the other hand was shy, dutiful, a good mother and a tactful woman–her only faults were the occasional signs of bad dress sense. So 'wicked' did Margaret become that even her commoner husband, the photographer Snowdon, was elevated to the position of patient, hard-working, long-suffering husband. Margaret for a long time has carried the connotations of the decadent and undeserving side of wealth. The splitting of the functions between characters is very apparent in the way her extended holidays in Mustique have been treated. These holidays are not worth so much as a mention when the other Royals go, but in Margaret's case they instantly symbolize the decadent and undeserving, the indulgent and weak side of wealth. Since the Charles and Di wedding, however, Margaret has been rehabilitated somewhat; we now see articles on how she has taken herself in hand, sorted out her life. This rehabilitation can probably last only while one of the other characters is carrying some of the attributes of decadence.

Margaret has also been a crucial figure in the speculation about whether royalty will make an alliance with an 'outsider'. And since her divorce from Lord Snowdon, she has been restored as a character able to bear speculation about what kind of sexual alliance royalty will make. Prior to his marriage to Lady Di, Prince Charles was the most important point of speculation on this subject. The Royal Wedding in fact produced a drastic change in the structural function of Charles. From Royal romancer travelling through the debutante set, he now takes up the position of Bobby Ewing, the faithful and devoted husband to the child bride. And once safely established as devoted husband and father, it was only a matter of time before questions were asked about whether he was also long-suffering, put upon by a wilful woman more concerned with getting her figure back than with her duties as a Royal mother: 'So shy Di became, first, the diet-obsessed anorexic Di, then hen-pecking, scolding Di, and now the little madam or fiend, or spoilt brat according to whom you read' (*Sunday Times*, 23 January 1983).

It is no coincidence that, as Charles is put through the possible options for good husband, another Royal romancer is brought to the centre of the stage. Known as 'Randy Andy', Prince Andrew was promptly cast as 'The Royals'' new Casanova. The Casanova function also becomes clear in his hands: will the Royals ever be tempted outside their ranks? Interestingly, Randy Andy obliges with another requirement which Prince Charles never properly fulfilled. Andrew, they say, does it with models and small-time pornography artistes whereas Charles remained largely within the aristocracy even if some of them were 'bad girls': 'The Royal dating game has never been easy. Not for any of the Queen's children. But, for Prince Andrew, with his chocolate box good looks, flashing smile and penchant for models and beauty queens, it has been the most complex of rituals' (*Daily Express*, 1 November 1982). The sexual alliances of these Princes have in essence hinged on the question of whether or not they will 'fall in love' with an outsider. All through Charles's hunt for an acceptable bride, there was speculation about whether love would get him into trouble – a Catholic, a divorcee, a commoner – we were all dying for it to happen. The narrative was just crying out for a trial in the name of love. Would he fall for someone and have to sacrifice everything, as the Duke of Windsor did before him? It is interesting to remember in passing that the Duke of Windsor's story readily adapted itself to an up-market soap opera.

This, of course, is a crucial element in a good family melodrama. A tension is required between the requirements of family duty and the wayward nature of love (so the ideology runs) which could strike any time and endanger the unity or survival of the family [. . .]

With Lady Di the media found a way of compromising the public desire for a love match with the actual constraints on Charles to marry an aristocratic virgin. Lady Di, with impeccable sexual and class credentials, was also sufficiently young and waif-like to satisfy the desire for a marriage to an outsider, or the girl next door. Deserted by her mother, in the shadow of her elder sister, sheltered and shy, Lady Di didn't have the overt appearance of a highly appropriate and eligible match. She could be seen as young, innocent and beautiful, loved for what she was rather than for her suitability.

In stories of family dramas and intrigues, there usually has to be one figure who represents stability, whose good qualities validate all the other comings and goings. In 'Dallas' there's Miss Ellie; in 'The Royals', the Queen Mother. These figures are the female heads of family. Now powerless, they are above the ambitions, promiscuity, and intrigue of the junior members. These characters have been in power at one time – they understand power – but they are now above it. The best and most worthy aspects of the family are invested in these figures. Gentle, kindly, understanding and humane, these are the characters who, in the end, validate the whole story.

These are the structural functions of the characters, but they don't fully explain why these family melodramas have such appeal. That appeal undoubtedly comes from the very successful combination of the 'cosmic' (Christian) themes of good and evil, deserving and undeserving, love and duty, and a very ordinary series of preoccupations. Even if the options facing these ideal families are somewhat rarefied, the family is presented as just an ordinary family confronting the options of modern life [. . .]

Family melodramas are now obsessed with the question of what options there are for the family, and this question is particularly centred on 'the problem of the modern woman'. The themes of contemporary melodramas are sexual promiscuity, divorce, remarriage, styles of parenthood, the working woman. Just as millions followed the struggle over the custody of JR's child, so millions followed with fascination the accounts of Lady Di's upbringing by her divorced father. The Wedding itself was a focus for speculation on changed attitudes to family ruptures: 'Diana will of course be given away by her father, although a few years ago this could have been a problem because he and her mother are divorced. In the past there may have been some hesitation in inviting her parents *and* their new partners. However, a precedent was set in 1960 – Lord Snowdon's parents were also divorced and even though Ronald Armstrong-Jones had married a third time, both he and his wife were at the ceremony' (*Woman's Own* Engagement Special).

Another series of options relate to the question of how the Royals will bring up their children. Will Lady Di have a Leboyer birth? Will she breast-feed? Will she be a formal or informal mother: 'Sharing and warmth will be the basis of Diana's style of motherhood. This child will benefit from the most tactile contact with his mother of any of the royal babies so far' (The Free Giant Royal Baby Poster, *Woman's Own*, 4 September 1982). Then there's the question of what role Prince Charles will play. Will he be a modern father and participate in caring for the child? Charles carrying his 'eight-week-old son' is sufficient subject-matter for a photo captioned 'Holding the Baby'. There's also the question of whether Diana should be with the child as much as possible or leave him while she carries out her public duties: 'Prince William may fly to Australia with his parents next spring . . . one of Britain's top paediatricians said: "I'm not talking specifically about the young prince, but as a generalization it's ideal for a child to be kept with his mother for the whole of the first year as much as possible."' (*Daily Express*, 1 November

1982). However remote the lives of the inhabitants of Buckingham Palace, their fictionalized lives are constructed around a number of dilemmas which are just as significant for people of entirely different social and economic groups.

In our very different ways, without the privileges and without the constraints of traditions, women are confronted constantly with family issues – marriage or not marriage, children or not children, divorce, custody, how to bring up children. These aren't trivial and unimportant issues. Women's opportunities and indeed often our happiness rest on how we resolve these questions. But having said that 'The Royals' addresses choices faced by all women, it is also quite true that it does so from a peculiarly 'traditionalist' standpoint. In the world of 'The Royals', there aren't really any options outside the family, nor is there any issue of female independence and autonomy. All the 'problems' faced by the modern woman are reduced to choices within the family. Divorce becomes merely a matter of how to be tactful at the next wedding, birth is reduced to an issue of breast-feeding or not rather than an event which might involve a loss of autonomy. Even 'Dallas' is slightly more open than 'The Royals' to discourses on female independence. For the Royals there's not a moment's hesitation in producing Lady Di as a modern heroine even though she married at twenty, was a mother by twenty-one, and had never had any sexual experience outside marriage.

Not only does 'The Royals' accomplish a repression of questions of female independence, it also accomplishes a repression of political and economic factors. The 'outside' of the Royal family is not working women and men who have little economic power and little control over their own lives. The 'outside' of royalty is aristocratic business men and show-biz. It is within this grouping that the Royals might make an alliance, as seen in the flirtations of Margaret and Randy Andy. The 'outside' of the Royals is the fashion world, the glamorous world of actresses, models, pop stars, and nightclub entertainers. These people are represented as somehow 'ordinary' in spite of the fact that they, like the Royals, represent an over-privileged, under-talented group. The 'outside' only ever intrudes into the unity of the family through sexual alliance; it is through love that the Royals are brought into contact with people of a lesser order, not through conflict between groups who have different economic and social realities. The centrality given to the sexual alliance obscures the other kind of relations which the Crown might have, relations of landlords and tenants, relations between those with power and privilege and those with nothing.

The centrality which sexual alliance has in the family melodrama isn't just a wilful plot thought up by 'The Royals'. It reflects a prevalent belief that people, especially women, can advance their social position through sexual alliance. Being a beautiful actress or top model is seen as a route to power; powerful men will be attracted by star qualities. Indeed this belief is one of the important ways in which real differences in material circumstances are obscured. Women can make it on the basis of their beauty. Again this theme is widespread; it is common in romantic fiction where girls with ordinary backgrounds and extraordinary beauty attract wealthy men.

'The Royals' as a family melodrama works over choices that are real for many women and does it in such a way as to guarantee narrative interest. But the problem is that the Royal Family isn't only fiction. It is sustained as a fiction when it also represents political and economic privileges, and political and economic preferences. The way in which the story is told means that we never have to deal with the Royal family as a political institution; we only have to think about human behaviour, human emotions, and choices restricted to the family. 'The Royals' eternalizes traditional values, glorifies women's route to power through individual sexual attraction, and defines women as exclusively bound up with these values.

PART III

The Regulation
of Sexuality

9 Foucault on the History of Sexuality: An Introduction

Nancy Wood

Rethinking Sexuality

'Popular opinion', wrote Sigmund Freud, 'has quite definite ideas about the nature and characteristics of (the) sexual instinct' (Freud, 1905, p.45). However applicable to his own times, it would be tempting to argue that Freud's observation has little relevance today. The frequency with which sexuality appears as a subject of public debate, and the intensity of feeling this debate arouses, would seem to indicate not only that our society no longer adheres to any 'definite ideas' on sexuality, but that virtually every dimension of sexuality has become the grounds for heated contestation. Mary Whitehouse, sexual libertarians, feminists, gays and various sexual minorities appear to jostle on a public platform to argue their case for alternatives to the sexual *status quo*. We might conclude that the only point on which popular opinion agrees is that the domain of sexuality is one of the most controversial arenas of social life.

This, at least, is one way of portraying the current climate of sexual politics. Another possibility would be to step back from this consensus concerning the controversial features of sexuality and re-examine the 'nature and characteristics' which are attributed to sexuality, whether these be found in sex manuals, popular novels, agony columns, medical and legal discourses or the conversations of everyday life. Here we might discover that although there are certainly disputes over what constitutes this entity called 'sexuality' there are, nonetheless, certain features which are commonly–often unquestionably–assigned to it. Taken together, *these* features form a composite portrait of sexuality–a set of 'definite ideas'–which are so widely and unhesitatingly embraced by our society, that it is hard from this perspective to justify all the battles which have been waged in its name. Let us consider just a few central features which are invoked most frequently.

By far the most common depiction of sexuality is that of a force, an impulse, an *instinct* which emanates from the inner biological recesses of the individual and is the natural expression of biologically governed processes. Secondly, this sexual instinct is not, by and large, portrayed as purposeless energy, but as an instinct invested with a biologically ordained *aim* (intercourse) and *object* (usually a person of the opposite sex). This profile of how the instinct functions is not only endorsed by social norms, but also seems to be guaranteed by umpteen studies of sexuality which have shed the light of scientific knowledge upon it. Thirdly, this instinct is usually viewed as *inherently rebellious* so that the paths of its expression must be carefully patrolled. The conflict between the sexual instinct and social life, it is assumed, is not created; it is given by the nature of the instinct itself which will inevitably come into conflict with the social, until a reconciliation is achieved. The issue then becomes one of deciding what *degree* of social intervention applied to sexuality is acceptable or desirable (hence the battles cited at the outset are often fought out over relative levels of social tolerance or constraint). Fourthly, even despite these quarrels, on the whole most of us might be inclined to adopt a view similar to that of one typical recent historian when he asserts that: 'We moderns stand at the end of a long ice-age, the first to enjoy the flowering of expressive egalitarian, non-reproductive sexuality'. To be sure, there are still unre-solved questions about sexuality, but it is precisely because we are more enlightened than our Victorian predecessors that such issues receive a public airing. Finally, we tend to accept that the struggle to achieve this emancipated state has been worth our time and energies precisely because of the *significance* sexuality can legitimately lay claim to in our personal lives and individual identities. If we believe that our sexual destinies are intimately linked to our personal destinies to some indeterminate degree, it is because we are convinced that sexuality alone offers access to that innermost reality of the individual. We may 'possess' a sexuality, but that sexuality, conversely, tells us who we are, in our very essence. It thus assumes the status of a 'thing-in-itself'; that is, it is seen as both a fixed essence of our existence as individuals and, at the same time, an indicator of our general well-being.

This is only a very schematic summary of certain 'definite ideas' which form part of our 'common-sense' notions of what sexuality is, and many of us might want to modify this description in its finer details. But even after such adjustments are made, what is left intact, and largely endorsed by 'popular opinion' is a definition of sexuality as biologically given, instinctually governed, and held in check by social and cultural mechanisms. Because these features of sexuality are assumed to be permanent and prescribed by the nature of sexuality itself, we shall call this view, in its broadest outline, a form of 'sexual essentialism'. This term is defined by Jeffrey Weeks as those approaches which conceptualize sexuality 'as an overpowering force in the individual that shapes not only the personal but the social life as well. It is seen as a driving, instinctive force, whose characteristics are built into the biology of the human animal' (Weeks, 1981, p.2).

In recent years, certain aspects of 'sexual essentialism' have come under attack from various quarters. Perhaps the most significant challenges have come from within the social sciences, and from social movements concerned to challenge the sexual *status quo* – especially the women's and gay movements.

It has now become a standard tenet of most disciplines in the social sciences that sexuality is shaped by social forces. Anthropology, sociology, social history and social psychology–to name but a few of these disciplines–have offered diverse descriptions of how these forces, ranging from kinship patterns, social norms and family structures to public policies, psychological formations and religious ideologies, shape sexual behaviour. The main thrust of these studies is to argue that the very range in forms of sexual expression over time and space confirms that sexuality is not the fixed entity described by biologistic accounts, but is a sphere mediated by social relations. As Ellen Ross and Rayna Rapp point out: 'Sexuality's biological base is always experienced culturally, through a translation, the bare biological facts of sexuality do not speak for themselves; they must be expressed socially. Sex feels individual, or at least private, but those feelings always incorporate the roles, definitions, symbols and meanings of the worlds in which they are constructed' (Ross and Rapp, 1981, p.51).

Attention to the social determinations of sexuality has also been given *political* impetus by the contemporary women's movement. A key slogan of the women's movement – 'The personal is political' – was an insight extended to that seemingly most intimate sphere of private life, that of sexual relations. Here, feminists found reproduced patterns of domination and subordination which prevailed in social relations at large. Moreover, these power relations, feminists noted, were sustained by *social* definitions of female sexuality disguised as descriptions of an 'essential' female sexuality. Various popular versions of this included the view that women were 'saturated' by their sexuality, and that its all-pervasiveness 'precipitated' sexual responses in men–even if women denied soliciting such responses. On the other hand, this continually active female sexuality was deemed to be profoundly mysterious and intractable–a 'secret' to be investigated (a persistent theme in various cultural forms – film, novels, etc.), or an unknown field to be uncovered progressively by scientific knowledge (the *Hite Report*, for example, was hailed as a major breakthrough in the excavation of female sexuality). Feminism has played a crucial role in contesting these popular conceptions of female sexuality and exposing the social basis of various definitions and practices. Most importantly, feminists have revealed the intertwining of sexuality and *power* and have thereby made 'sexual politics' a central aspect of both everyday life, and the social and political relations which organize it.

The gay movement of the 1970s and 1980s has also struck at one of the main bastions of sexual essentialism: the assumption that human sexuality is 'by nature' heterosexually-inclined. The impact of the gay movement has not only been the affirmation of homosexual object choice as a component feature of human sexuality, but the unmasking of a heterosexual bias sustained by sexual essentialism in virtually every sphere of social life. The activities of the gay movement have put this *norm* of heterosexuality into question, not only as it affects sexual preference, but as it pervades legal, economic and political relations as well.

Despite their rather different motivations and concerns, what these critiques of sexual essentialism have in common is their rejection of sexuality as primarily a biologically-defined domain, and their insistence that sexuality's meaning is determined within *social relations*.

Why Foucault?

The analysis offered by Michel Foucault in *The History of Sexuality* is also an attack on sexual essentialism, although his critique is more extensive in scope than the critics we have just considered and, arguably, more far-reaching in its political implications. The form of Foucault's critique may be divided into three broad lines of analysis.

First, Foucault identifies a form of sexual essentialism underpinning the conventional *history* of sexuality – a history which typically pits a repressed Victorian sexuality against its modern, and soon-to-be liberated counterpart. The evocation which I quoted above of an 'ice-age' of sexual repression from which we have emerged only recently is a good example of the conventional history to which Foucault is referring. Foucault believes that this sexual essenti-alism depends upon the theme of *repression* to characterize the historical relationship of power to sex. Consequently, Foucault's first concern is to expose the inadequacy of the conceptual foundation upon which this conventional history of sexuality rests.

Foucault also finds evidence of an essentialism in the way 'sexuality' is itself *defined* in this conventional history. For Foucault, it is not simply that sexuality should be conceived as a domain shaped by social and historical forces; rather, he insists that the entity 'sexuality' – understood as a *separate* and *central* domain of human existence – is itself a recent *historical construct*. Foucault insists: 'Sexuality must not be thought of as a kind of natural given which power tries to hold in check, or as an obscure domain which knowledge tries gradually to uncover. It is the name that can be given to a historical construct' (Foucault, 1979, p.105).

Finally, like feminists, Foucault also believes that the relationship between sexuality and *power* is one of vital importance. But unlike feminists, who tend to view this power as primarily an instance of patriarchal oppression, Foucault emphasizes the *administrative form* that power over sexuality has assumed historically. Here he finds terms such as 'regulation', 'management' and 'surveillance' more appropriate than 'male oppression' to describe how power over sexuality has been principally exercised. Moreover, in re-examining the past and present forms of power brought to bear on sexuality, Foucault is compelled to recast the character of power itself, as it has been traditionally understood in the social sciences. This reconceptualization of power in turn has implications for our understanding of past and contemporary struggles in the field of sexual politics.

Let us examine these three features of Foucault's study of sexuality in more detail.

The 'History of Sexuality' and the 'Repressive Hypothesis'

What are the main contours of the conventional history of sexuality which Foucault identifies? Do these stand up to closer inspection?

The modern history of sexuality, according to Foucault, is sketched as the chronicle of an increasing *repression*. It is a history firmly under the spell, in Foucault's terminology, of the 'repressive hypothesis'. What this history relates is a narrative in which, up to the early seventeenth century, sexuality was expressed fairly openly, and its various forms tolerated. A certain frankness ostensibly prevailed on sexual matters. No sharp division separated what an individual might do, say or think in relation to sex, and what was morally, legally and socially permitted. It was seemingly a period of 'direct gestures, shameless discourse and open transgressions'. In this conventional account, it is the Victorian era which is held responsible for bringing an end to sexuality's relative harmony with social life and imposing prohibitions on sexual discussion and sexual practices. The Victorian regime, it is claimed, installed a norm for sexual conduct modelled on the discreet behaviour of the conjugal couple whose ultimate goal was that of procreation. Victorians relegated their sexuality to the private sphere, we are told, and even there endured its strict submission to the function of reproduction. The only place where sexuality surfaced publicly was in clearly-demarcated quarters (the brothel, mental asylum, etc.), where social degeneration and sexual excess were seen to go hand in hand and foster each other.

Foucault claims that adherents of this history of sexuality are convinced that the modern world continues to suffer from the residues of this Victorian regime but believe they can progressively throw off these historical fetters by demanding that prohibitions on sex be lifted, by overturning antiquated laws and, above all, by *speaking out* publicly on the subject of sex–returning to sexuality its lost voice. This is a general minimum consensus adopted by all 'progressives' in the modern period but Foucault also observes that this modern quest for sexual emancipation has often been linked with radical political initiatives of the twentieth century on the basis of a presumed historical coincidence between the onset of sexual repression and the advent of capitalism. Wilhelm Reich, for example, is generally considered one of the first Marxists to incorporate a theory of sexual repression into a critique of the material conditions of life under capitalism – a marriage which launched the Sexpol movement in Germany in the 1930s (see, for example, Reich, 1972). According to Foucault, these movements for sexual freedom typically rely upon a 'principle of explanation' which highlights two bourgeois imperatives: the need to restrict sex to its procreative function in the interests of reproducing the labour force, and to cultivate individuals capable of directing the energy otherwise mobilized by sexual pleasure into the tasks of increased production. Having established such 'valorizing correlations' between sex and politics, the fate of the struggle against sexual repression and the struggle against economic domination are henceforth inextricably bound together.

In this context, sexual radicals who declare their intent to unleash the body's pent-up sexual energies claim not only to dismantle the legitimacy and permanency of conventional rules governing sexuality, but to undermine the libidinal basis of capitalism itself. For Foucault, however, the radical account of sexuality's repressed past is only distinguished from the more liberal conventional history by the causes which are seen to still impede sexual emancipation (unenlightment versus the logic of capitalism). What otherwise unites the liberal and radical account is the privilege both accord to the theme of *repression*. The shared reliance on the category of repression permits *both* accounts (a) to define sexuality as a force suppressed; (b) to represent the modern history of sexuality as an artificial and unhealthy tethering of a natural state; and (c) to chart a political itinerary for sexuality's eventual emancipation.

The Production of Sexuality

So how does Foucault begin to chip away at this historical edifice of repression that is widely accepted by liberals and radicals alike? First of all, he suggests that three assumptions of the 'repressive hypothesis' are less than self-evident:

(1)   that a regime of sexual repression dating from the seventeenth century can be historically validated;
(2)   that power over sex has been exercised primarily through the mechanisms of prohibition, censorship and denial;
(3)   that the vociferous condemnations of Victorian sexual repression adopted by sexual liberationist movements initiate a profound historical breach with the repressive era.

Foucault's aim in voicing these doubts is not to discount the critique of repression by asserting the opposite. He does not suppose that in the course of our modern history, sex has enjoyed unprecedented freedom, more tolerance, enlightened treatment, and so forth. Foucault's first dissatisfaction with the repressive hypothesis is prompted by what it *fails* to acknowledge: namely, that since the eighteenth century, sexuality has been continually and volubly 'put into discourse'. Far from being reticent on the subject of sexuality, the last two centuries have triggered a 'discursive explosion', a 'multiplication of discourses concerning sex', issuing from various institutions – medical, religious, legal, psychiatric, educational, etc. Indeed, certain public places have become the authorized locus of an 'incitement to speak about [sex] and to do so more and more; [there is] a determination on the part of agencies of power to hear it spoken about and to cause *it* to speak through explicit articulation and endlessly accumulated detail' (Foucault, 1979, p.18). At the same time, according to Foucault, it was the discourses produced by these various institutions which *constructed* a 'sexuality', residing in organs, endowed with instincts, and leading a separate life in the inner recesses of the individual. More precisely, out of these discourses, there emerged specific 'sexualities', which were more the creation of these efforts at specification and classification than a sexual 'condition' of the individuals to whom they were attributed.

These claims are difficult to comprehend on first encounter, but they are central to Foucault's entire project. By challenging the 'repressive hypothesis', Foucault is not denying that this proliferation of discourses on sexuality often had punitive or disciplinary effects upon the subjects who were encompassed by them. On the contrary, his discussion of the four 'figures' particularly targeted by these discourses – the 'hysterical woman', the 'masturbating child', the 'perverse adult' and the 'Malthusian couple' – demonstrates how the very designation of these figures as objects of knowledge by scientific discourse enabled certain disciplinary strategies to be directed at them. Foucault is, however, asking us to consider whether the general category of repression, and the image of a damming or suppression of an essential force which it tends to evoke, can adequately account for *how* such punitive effects come about, faced with evidence of the proliferating and inciting character of discourses on sexuality. Repression is only *one* mechanism through which the effects of punishment, control and regulation are achieved, and it is Foucault's contention that repressive strategies in this inhibitive sense have been less significant in the last two centuries than the productive and positive mechanisms through which power over sexuality has been exercised.

Nor is Foucault content with mere historical refutation of the type of force brought to bear on sexuality. Foucault questions the very nature of the object 'sexuality' whose fate adherents of the 'repressive hypothesis' claim to have traced. Indeed the notion of sexual 'repression' would seem to require as its correlate an energetic sexual force which continually strives for release – only to meet the preventive barrier erected by repression. The point, then, of maintaining that sexuality is an historical and 'discursive' construction is precisely to challenge the view that sexuality is a fixed biological essence, a self-sufficient unity, a 'thing-in-itself' which has invariable characteristics. For Foucault, 'sexuality' is the end-product of any and all the discourses which define it, analyse it, propose to control it, emancipate it, and so forth. For Foucault, sexuality has no 'reality', no subterranean core *outside* of these discourses.

It might be useful here to draw a parallel with what Foucault says on the subject of 'madness'. Foucault maintains that 'madness', which was claimed as an object of inquiry by the emerging discipline of psychiatry in the nineteenth century, should not be understood as a 'condition' which was 'discovered' by psychiatrists in particular forms of psychopathological behaviour. Rather, 'mental illness was constituted by all that was said in all statements that named it, divided it up, described it, explained it, traced its developments, indicated its various correlations, judged it, and possibly gave it speech by articulating, in its name, discourses that were taken as its own' (Foucault, 1972, p.32). Similarly, we might say that for Foucault, 'sexuality' was in fact *constructed* by all those discourses – religious, legal, psychiatric, educational, medical – which claimed merely to *describe* it. Foucault's proposed *history* of sexuality, then, is guided by the aim of analysing, not an essential sexuality, but *what* various discourses said about sexuality, *why* they emerged when they did, and some of the consequences of these pronouncements.

To exemplify the aims and themes of this Foucaultian project, consider how the figure of the 'homosexual' enters onto the stage of history. Common sense tends to lead us to assume that this term has a long usage in Western civilization to describe someone who has sexual relations with persons of the same sex. However Foucault, and following him Jeffrey Weeks (1977) and others, have demonstrated that the concept of the 'homosexual' is a relatively recent one, and one that emerged partly as a consequence of the re-classification of sexual 'crimes' which occurred throughout the eighteenth and nineteenth centuries. Foucault's historical investigations suggest that prior to the eighteenth century, sexual crimes were delineated as such on the basis of whether they transgressed or subverted the laws of marriage established by religious or civil authorities, which codified and sanctified relations between husband and wife. What was considered socially aberrant was *any* sexual practice which flaunted the marital code (homosexuality, bestiality, paedophilia, adultery, rape, infidelity, etc.), while the sexual 'crime' for which the perpetrator of such an act was judged was the *legal* infraction of the marital code. In the context of English law, for example, Jeffrey Weeks notes that although the penalty for sodomy devised by the 1533 Act of Henry VIII was death, the law was directed against the performance of the sexual act itself – an act which any individual could presumably commit. Weeks maintains that there was 'no concept of the homosexual in law, and homosexuality was regarded not as a particular attribute of a certain type of person but as a potential in all sinful creatures' (Weeks, 1977, p.12).

At the same time as the 'discursive explosion' of the eighteenth and nineteenth centuries, however, a new distinction begins to be drawn between sexual 'crimes' committed against the laws of the church or state on the one hand and, on the other, sexual crimes committed against nature itself. In Foucault's words: 'to marry a close relative or practise sodomy, to seduce a nun or engage in sadism, to deceive one's wife or violate cadavers, became things that were essentially different . . . there appeared on the one hand infractions against the legislation (or morality) pertaining to marriage and the family, and on the other, offences against the regularity of a natural function . . . ' (Foucault, 1981, p.39). In the course of making this distinction between moral-juridical crimes which transgressed the rules of sexual alliance and sexual offences purportedly stemming from an inherently 'defective' sexuality, new categories of sexual subjects appeared. The 'sodomite' (a figure who up until this period typified anyone from the undifferentiated sexual 'deviant' to the promiscuous libertine) is replaced by the figure of the 'homosexual' who is considered a *distinct species* in his own right and assigned *particular* characteristics. (Weeks scans the early sexology text-books and comes up with such features as inability to whistle, penchant for the colour green, adoration of mother or father.) In other words, out of this effort to re-classify sexual *acts*, there emerges a separate category of *individuals*. And where previously the individual committing certain sexual acts was simply the juridical subject of forbidden deeds, he now acquired the status of a personality – a *personage* – potentially culpable for his sexual desires.

Following Foucault, Weeks demonstrates how, in the English context, this re-classification was effected by several late nineteenth-century legal reforms which sought to distinguish various forms of buggery from sexual practices performed between men. Although the punishment for buggery was more severe, the enactment of new laws pertaining to all forms of male homosexual activity extended the application of the law to a distinct and identified sub-group of men – thus bringing a wider circle of people into the legal net. The trial of Oscar

Wilde was perhaps a turning point in this development in drawing public attention to the legal dimensions and effects of these juridical classifications. However, as Weeks also argues, the publicity such trials generated served at the time as a rallying-point for homosexual reformers out of which a self-affirmation of sexual choice and resistance to legal proscriptions could be simultaneously expressed.

It is interesting to note that this periodization of the emergence of a homosexual identity has become the subject of some debate. For example, the historian Alan Bray (Bray, 1982) situates the growth of a homosexual subculture and identity in a much earlier period than Foucault or Weeks. Bray contends that the 'molly houses' of early eighteenth-century England were the site of an *already-developed* homosexual subculture – and not an 'embryonic' one which only assumed its distinctively modern form in the late nineteenth century, as Weeks suggests. Bray maintains that the medical and legal discourses which 'identified' homosexuality in the nineteenth century proliferated against the backdrop of 'an identity and minority homosexual subculture that already existed – and had done so . . . for two hundred years' (Bray, 1982, p.137). Despite this histgraphical challenge to their periodization of the emergence of a homosexual subculture and self-consciousness, Foucault and Weeks nonetheless convincingly demonstrate that nineteenth-century legal and medical discourses introduced *new* conceptualizations of homosexuality which, in turn, instituted new forms of regulation and control over the homosexual 'subject' which these discourses had defined into existence.

If we take the emergence of 'homosexuality' as an exemplary moment in this recast history of sexuality, it is clear that the increased control brought to bear on sexuality was not one which derived its strength from institutional prerogatives to prohibit, exclude, suppress, or outlaw – a power which said 'no' to the expression of desire. On the contrary, this power was characterized above all by the mechanisms of *incitement* it deployed: identification, isolation, classification and hence an 'implantation' of diverse 'sexualities'. Consequently the historical subjection of homosexuality – i.e. the very real political, social and legal repression of homosexuals – should be sought, in Foucault's view, in those processes contributing to the creation of a 'homosexual subject' in the first place.

Sexuality and Power

If Foucault is insistent that the history of sexuality is marked by incitement rather than by a 'great machinery of repression, by volubility rather than silence', we can begin to see why Foucault does not believe that such a *production* of sexuality necessarily hailed the dawning of a new age of sexual freedom and enlightenment. Rather, Foucault believes that the aim and consequence of this 'discursive explosion' was the tighter incorporation of its new object – 'sexuality' – into the field of exercise of power itself. In other words, it is Foucault's view that the more 'sexuality' was taken as an object of analysis by public institutions and their attendant discourses, the more it was a 'target of intervention' upon which power could exert itself. And once again, the *form* this power adopted, according to Foucault, was not primarily one of repression – the rigid imposition of taboos – but essentially one of *administration*. A 'policing' of sex became the order of the day, says Foucault, but warns us that we must understand this term in its early modern sense, where 'policing' implied a programme designed to induce optimal social returns. Sexuality was not regarded merely as a thing to be 'condemned or tolerated but managed, inserted into systems of utility, regulated for the greater good of all, made to function according to an optimum. Sex was not something one simply judged; it was a thing one administered' (Foucault, 1979, p.24).

Since this notion of sexuality's 'regulation' is the linchpin of Foucault's entire study, and yet difficult to grasp immediately, let us take one of the examples which Foucault himself puts forward: the emergence in the eighteenth century of 'population' as a specific concern of government administration. What prompts this concern, suggests Foucault, was the recognition by governments that they not only governed over 'subjects', or even a 'people', but a *population*. From their perspective the 'population' was, among other things, a potential source of wealth and stability, or, alternatively, a drain on resources and a locus of unrest. However, Foucault concedes that even this linkage of the population question with the well-being and governability of the nation was less novel than the attempt to delineate the constituent elements of this potentially volatile entity and to find ways to bring these into the purview of state administration. What distinguished approaches to population in the eighteenth century, maintains Foucault, was the development of new knowledges, institutions and techniques of power designed to observe, monitor and *intervene* in all aspects of the phenomenon of population.

Foucault proposes that we might view the emergence in the eighteenth century of health, welfare, economic and other social policies, as well as the growth of fields like demography and statistics, as expressions of this new government concern with incorporating all aspects of the everyday *life* of the population into the administrative ambit. It was a matter, Foucault maintains, of developing techniques of power – a 'bio-politics' of the population – 'capable of optimizing forces, aptitudes, and life in general without at the same time making them more difficult to govern' (Foucault, 1979, p.141). In this volume, James Donald proposes that changes in educational policies in nineteenth-century England might be usefully analysed from the vantage point of Foucault's conception of 'bio-politics'. But even more than the health, morality, fitness for work and educability of the population, Foucault suggests that the *sexual* life of the social body was designated as a prime site for bio-politics. In this effort to develop and enhance a 'political technology of life', *sex* was constituted as a key area of investigation, since the vicissitudes of sexual performance and sexual practices gave rise to precisely those phenomena which the state felt compelled to monitor; birthrates, the age of marriage, legitimate and illegitimate births, the frequency and potency of sexual relations, the effects of celibacy, the use of contraceptive practices, and so on. Once sex was targeted as a topic for investigation by government bodies, and designated as a domain open to professional administration, it became a central point of mediation between governments and individuals: 'a whole web of discourses, special knowledges, analyses, and injunctions settled upon it' (Foucault, 1979, p.26).

It should be stressed, in addition, that this concern with the 'population' was not confined to governments. As Jeffrey Weeks documents in the article included in this volume, the neo-Malthusian and eugenics movements of the early twentieth century also took the 'problem' of population as their specific concern and aspired to influence state policy accordingly. Composed of various groups of citizenry – with middle class professionals and women highly represented in their ranks – neo-Malthusians and eugenicists shared the view that the national population could and should be subject to planning and control. Although these currents differed with respect to the perceived sources and solutions of the twin 'problems' of race 'degeneracy' and 'multiplication of the unfit', both identified the sexual 'irresponsibility' of the working and poorer classes as the prime target of reform. Eugenicists in particular were in the forefront of arguing (with uneven success, as Weeks notes) that social policy should develop national strategies designed to induce sexual 'responsibility' in the citizenry at large – but a 'responsibility' differentially interpreted according to class. Sexual responsibility for the lower classes meant practicing sexual self-restraint and limiting family size; for the rest of the population it implied an individual and national *duty* to procreate and enhance their overall numbers.

Foucault also maintains that a regulation of populations went hand in hand with the deployment of tactics whose objective was the disciplining of the *individual* body. Foucault concedes the 'Freudo-Marxist' argument mentioned earlier that such control was necessary within the development of capitalism for the 'controlled insertion of bodies into the machinery of production'. But he stresses that a bio-politics focused on the individual body was not merely concerned to render this body available and docile. To analyse – and to regulate – sexual practices and performance bio-politics required above all a body which *affirmed* its sexuality. Like Weeks, Foucault also finds a class distinction at work in this self-affirmation. The intensification of interest in one's own sexuality was above all displayed by the emergent bourgeoisie whose own bodies and sexuality continually came under the medical 'gaze'. Contrary to the claim of Freudo-Marxists, techniques of sexual scrutiny and control were levelled primarily at the bourgeoisie, rather than the working class. And conversely, the bourgeoisie came to regard this scientific interest as confirmation that their own sexuality was indeed distinctive and more valuable: 'a fragile treasure, a secret to be discovered at all costs' (Foucault, 1979, p.121). Foucault reminds us that it was in the bourgeois and aristocratic family 'that the sexuality of children was first problematized, and feminine sexuality medicalised; it was the first to be alerted to the potential pathology of sex, the urgent need to keep it under close watch and to devise a rational "technology of correction"' (*ibid.* p.120). Meanwhile, the working and poorer classes resisted a similar self-affirmation since they knew its effects only too well: eugenicist campaigns for limiting family size such as those cited by Weeks were one such effect, as were the campaigns for the 'moralisation of the poorer classes' which formed part of the social purity campaigns discussed by

Judith Walkowitz in this volume.

In Foucault's view, a further feature of this incorporation of sexual matters into an administrative network was the formidable role sex was henceforth designed to play: 'sex was constituted as a problem of truth' (Foucault, 1979, p.56). In conjunction with the nineteenth-century state's increasing preoccupation with the administration of sex, Foucault locates the emergence of a *scientia sexualis* - a science of sex - which embraced many fields of inquiry - medicine, psychiatry, sexology, psychoanalysis - which might in other respects be considered relatively disparate. What united these domains, in Foucault's view, is that each made sexuality an object of scientific knowledge, and couched knowledge of that sexuality in terms of an essential truth of the individual. *Scientia sexualis* cultivated the view that to penetrate the 'secrets' of an individual's sexuality was the means by which to procure the truth of that individual. In this respect Foucault identified *scientia sexualis* as the secular counterpart of the post-Reformation, Catholic confessional. The promises of individual atonement through the regular and frequent ritual of confession induced religious believers to disclose every detail of their lives - from deeds to furtive wishes. Similarly, Foucault argues, the therapeutic returns offered by the emerging scientific discourses on sexuality were premissed upon procedures which exhorted individuals to disclose the 'true' facts of their sexuality. Individuals, for their part, willingly responded to the injunction to 'confess' their sexual proclivities with the expectation of expunging the 'secret' of sex which they were told dominated them, but had hitherto eluded their conscious grasp. To make such disclosures, then, was to reach to the very root of one's subjectivity.

This 'interplay of truth and sex' is thus a fundamentally *historical* phenomenon, says Foucault, 'which was bequeathed to us by the nineteenth century, and which we may have modified, but, lacking evidence to the contrary, have not rid ourselves of' (Foucault, 1979, p.57). The modern period grants sexuality a central, definitive (some would say even terroristic) role in our lives, as if there was something inherent in sexuality which justified this eminence. But once again, Foucault counters this sexual essentialism with an account of how historical forces produced not only a *sexuality*, but produced a particular *significance for* sexuality, which it still enjoys today.

Sex and Sexuality

It is here that we can discuss one of Foucault's most radical propositions, and one which helps us to see the full extent of his anti-essentialist leanings. So far, this article has been using the term 'sex' and 'sexuality' interchangeably. But should we not make a distinction between the two? And if we were to make such a distinction, might it not be along the lines of conceding that if 'sexuality' is a historical construct, 'sex' is nonetheless that biological foundation which is resistant to the various historical transfigurations which 'sexuality' undergoes? While Foucault agrees that a distinction between 'sex' and 'sexuality' should be drawn, he resolutely refuses the basis proposed above. Sex, Foucault insists, is not a biological or somatic substrate and 'sexuality' the set of ideas formed around this bodily reality in time and space. He cautions: 'We must not place sex on the side of reality, and sexuality on that of confused ideas and illusions; sexuality is a very real historical formation; it is what gave rise to the notion of sex, as a speculative element necessary to its operation' (Foucault, 1979, p.157). Sex, Foucault seems to be arguing, is not the form of expression taken by a biological instinct, but an 'imaginary point' and a 'fictitious unity' imposed on what is otherwise only a disparate set of bodily sensations, excitations and responses which have no intrinsic unity or 'laws' of their own.

Foucault has himself been criticized for supposing that these bodily stimulations could themselves ever be outside the realm of discourse or beyond the grip of power. Jeffrey Weeks identifies in this depiction of the body a 'latent essentialism' in which the body itself appears 'as a final court of appeal' against a power which continually strives to invest it (Weeks, 1981, p.10). Peter Dews similarly suggests that Foucault's repudiation of naturalism throughout *The History of Sexuality* resurfaces in his own assumption of a 'corporeally-grounded' opposition to power (Dews, 1984, p.90). Finally, feminists such as Rosalind Coward, Lucy Bland and others have pointed out that the body of which Foucault speaks so loosely is not sexually undifferentiated, but necessarily enmeshed in a symbolic order in which the anatomical distinction between the sexes is continually *figured*, i.e. given form and meaning through systems and conventions of representation. Moreover, this figuration itself involves representations and definitions of the body and sexuality which have consequences for power relations between men and women. Despite these important criticisms, we can note what prompts Foucault to make this crucial distinction between 'sex' and 'sexuality'. The stress our culture attributes to the 'fact of sex' seems to gain credence from the widespread assumption that 'sex' is, after all, the natural response our body elicits to the basic biological drives. Foucault asks us to consider whether 'sex' has not instead been the historical outcome of the *idea* generated within 'apparatuses' of sexuality 'that there exists something else and something more' than bodies and their pleasures 'with intrinsic properties and laws of its own: sex.'

The Productivity of Power

How does Foucault's reconsideration of the relationship between sexuality and power prompt him to reconceptualize the character of power itself? To begin with, the analysis of sexuality which Foucault calls for must necessarily account for the paradox that while power over sexuality became increasingly exercised through 'regulative' measures, it nonetheless continued to be 'represented' in negative terms – that is, through notions like repression, prohibition, and censorship. The explanation which Foucault advances is that Western societies have been unable to disengage themselves from a representation of power which is grounded ultimately in the law. Western political analysis still clings to a repressive model of power in which the exercise of power is framed in terms of the laying down of laws and their enforcement. Foucault maintains that this repressive or 'juridico-discursive' model of power must be discarded since it is incapable of codifying the mechanisms through which power has been exercised in the modern era. It is Foucault's contention that the new *productive* mechanisms of power which have been set in motion since the eighteenth century have rendered the repressive model and practice of power increasingly obsolete. He argues that power in the modern period has operated more through the diffusion of *norms* than the imposition of laws, and its enforcement has been secured more by means of *regulation* and *management* than by submission to prohibitive dictates. Foucault is not denying that *subjugation* is the consequence of this form of power, but he is insisting that we revise our notions concerning *how* this subjugation comes about.

Once Foucault has rejected the adequacy of the repressive model of power to codify power's form and functioning, he then indicates how this productive model of power should be conceived. Here Foucault is led to reject altogether what we might call a *substantive* notion of power in favour of a *relational* one. Concretely, Foucault rejects the view that power can be localized only within certain institutions which 'seize' or 'hold' power and then deploy it in a negative or repressive way. Instead, Foucault proposes that we recognize (1) the fundamentally relational character of power (i.e. the way in which power is generated from shifting and unequal relations of force) and (2) the fact that power does not begin from a single source on high which then progressively filters down into its surroundings, but that power also comes 'from below'. It emanates from 'local centres' – families, groups, institutions – *because* power relations are immanent in all social relationships. This is not to deny that institutions, such as the state, are not major centres of power, but Foucault rejects an identification of the state and its ancillary institutions as the *privileged* locus from which power emanates. The state, according to Foucault, is the site of an 'institutional integration of power relationships' and the 'terminal form' which power assumes, but it is neither the source of all power nor its sole executor. On the contrary, Foucault maintains that the power relations invested in the state rely for their very operation on already-existing power relations, functioning 'outside, below and alongside the state apparatuses, on a much more minute and everyday level' (Foucault, 1980, p.60). And because these relations are typically organized and hierarchized, they generate relations of inequality, domination and subordination.

Finally, Foucault insists that the productive character of power may be seen at work in the very constitution of fields of knowledge concerning sexuality. The appropriation of sexuality as an object of knowledge, and the definition, identification and classification of diverse sexualities which this entailed, should not be seen as the mere application of objective methods of scientific enquiry to the domain of sexuality. Rather, Foucault maintains that the 'will to knowledge' which scientific discourses on sexuality exhibited *implied* a practice of power. Perhaps the example of scientific discourses on female sexuality in the nineteenth century is the most incisive in this regard. Once psychiatry and medicine decided that the female body was 'thoroughly saturated with sexuality', they could also claim to further diagnose the pathologies (especially hysteria) to which it was seen to be particularly susceptible. Since this female body had been socially designated as the reproducer of the species and the carer for children and family, a host of medical and psychiatric 'prescriptions' could also be administered as a 'cure'. The so-called 'knowledge' of female sexuality was thus inseparable from the practices of power intrinsic to such knowledge.

The introduction to this volume signalled various criticisms to which Foucault's view of power has been subjected (see pp.xvi–xvii). Perhaps the most crucial question facing further consideration of the regulation of sexuality is whether this enlarged and amplified conception of power implies that we are always and already subjected to its will. We might well ask: If power over sexuality has been exercised in this *productive* manner, ensuring in the process our *subjection* to the 'apparatus' that has been thus created, is there any point in making sexuality a terrain of struggle? And if we were to attempt at least to redesign the manner in which power is exercised in relation to sexuality, would we not be relegated to a role akin to players on a chessboard – implicated in the game of power, but as instruments rather than as agents of power's manoeuvrings?

It is here that Foucault's discussion of power's *necessary* correlate – resistance – is absolutely crucial: 'Where there is power' says Foucault, 'there is resistance'. Whereas in the repressive model of power, resistance can only be the 'other' of power, which emerges despite power's top-heaviness, in the productive model of power resistance is generated by power's fundamentally relational and productive character. Power relationships depend 'on a multiplicity of points of resistance: these play the role of adversary, target, support, or handle in power relations' (Foucault, 1979, p.95).

Despite this provocative suggestion to view power as the midwife of resistance, the elaboration of a theory or programme of resistance is one of the most undeveloped areas of Foucault's work. We have seen that Foucault is tempted to view the body and its manifold sensations as a key site of *individual* resistance, thereby leaving himself open to the charge of harbouring a residual naturalism. At the level of the *social* body, and possible forms of resistance, Foucault's conjectures are perhaps even more heretical. At several points, Foucault has proposed that only a 'desexualisation' of our identities can effectively break the monopoly which 'sexuality' has exerted historically over our lives (Foucault, 1980, pp.191, 220). Despite the suggestion of prudishness which such a term tends to elicit, this is by no means the Puritan rallying-call it would first appear to be. Foucault does not dispute the emancipatory potential of various forms of sexual politics, but he does believe that their potential can only be realised if their goal is 'a general economy of pleasure not based on sexual norms' (Foucault, 1980, p.191). Questions concerning who the 'agents' of this transformation might be, how they will pursue this goal, and what this goal even entails are far from clear in his account. Foucault does maintain, however, that those who call for the 'liberation' of sexuality wrongly assume that it has somehow an intrinsic nature and value, rather than seeing that it is precisely the historical apparatus of sexuality from which we need to be liberated. Movements based on the affirmation of sexual desires, sexual choices, and lifestyles hitherto denied social legitimacy – whether gay, feminist or otherwise – are therefore regarded by Foucault as more likely candidates for the task of effectively challenging prevailing definitions of appropriate sexual and social behaviour. However, Foucault is adamant that social movements seeking reform of the sexual *status quo* cannot base their programme of 'resistance' on a simple desire to reclaim a lost, suppressed or unrecognized sexuality. He insists that it is not a question of social movements laying claim 'to the specificity of their sexuality and the rights pertaining to it' but of breaking from those discourses 'conducted within the apparatuses of sexuality' (Foucault, 1980, p.219–20). Foucault warns that if such movements remain locked in an assertion that beneath their choices and desires lies an *essential sexual identity* – gay, feminist or otherwise – they risk slipping into the very sexual essentialism that has caused their discontents.

Strategies of Resistance

Such a warning, however apposite, does not dispense with the question of how to conceive of *concrete* strategies of resistance against the regulation of sexuality. What might such forms of struggle look like and how might we assess their strategies – be they historical or contemporary?

This is the interest and relevance of the articles by Judith Walkowitz and Frank Mort in this volume, whose respective analyses are informed by a Foucaultian perspective in a number of key respects.

Legal Regulation

In addressing the issue of how power over sexuality has been exercised in given socio-historical contexts (Britain in the late nineteenth century for Walkowitz, in the late 1960s for Mort), both writers point to the *regulatory* nature of the mechanisms brought to bear on particular social groups and sexual practices. Judith Walkowitz discusses legislative measures like the notorious Contagious Diseases Act in the 1860s and the Criminal Law Amendment Act (1885) which sought to manage or regulate (and not merely repress) the individuals and sexual practices which came within their purview. Beneath the ostensible medical, moral and other concerns motivating these pieces of legislation, Walkowitz identifies the sexual ideologies embraced by their supporters, the system of police surveillance over individuals and communities which they sanctioned, and the production of categories of 'illicit' sexuality which they helped to generate. Paradoxically, Frank Mort identifies a regulatory moment inscribed in a more contemporary piece of legislation generally hailed as 'progressive': the 1967 Sexual Offences Act which decriminalized sexual activity between adult male homosexuals in England and Wales. Mort argues that while the 1967 legislation appeared 'permissive' in decriminalizing homosexuality between consenting adult men in private, this very specification of the permissible in relation to homosexual activity and social spaces functioned to 'construct a new type of homosexual subject, understood as operating in the private sphere'. As a result, homosexual activity not confined to this sphere was considered 'irregular', an infraction against 'public order and decency', and punishable by law. Far from enjoying the fruits of permissiveness, Mort maintains that homosexuality was subsequently subjected to new forms of regulation and control and increased prosecution (evidenced in the higher number of convictions after 1967 for homosexual behaviour in so-called 'public' venues).

The Diffusion of Norms

Neither Walkowitz nor Mort assumes that the *legal* forms of sexuality's regulation, important as these were in codifying socially acceptable sexual behaviour, were the sole mechanisms for the exercise of power over sexuality. Both attach as much, if not greater importance to the less visible and tangible forms of regulation which Foucault identifies in *The History of Sexuality* as the *diffusion of norms*. These norms are above all embodied in the discourses on male and female sexuality which are in constant circulation in society and vie with each other for dominance.

As Walkowitz documents, in the case of the late nineteenth-century sexual reform campaigns, essentialist definitions of the nature of male and female sexuality prevailed in *both* the 'regulationist' and 'repeal' camps. The 'regulationist' discourse, for example, justified male recourse to prostitution by invoking an innately aggressive male sexual drive in need of regular 'outlets'. Walkowitz also highlights a fact which remains relatively obscured within Foucault's account. From her case study it can be seen that regulationist discourses on sexuality contained not only an administrative logic, they also wove into their discourses and practices forms of power in large part deriving from relations of sexual domination which endured within the Victorian household structure. Confinement of middle-class women to the familial domain and to particular definitions of femininity provided the basis upon which the servicing of male sexual 'needs' beyond the conjugal relation could be ultimately legitimized.

By virtue of their very participation in the repeal campaign, feminist repealers transgressed the private/public dichotomy and went on to adamantly reject the regulationist discourse on male sexuality as, among other things, a ruse legitimating the sexual double standard. However, their own discourse on female sexuality was in turn based upon a version of sexual essentialism. Rather than making a case in their moral reform efforts for a female sexual *agency* denied self-determination by regulationist and other practices, feminist reformers opted for a designation of female sexuality as essentially quiescent, necessarily bound to reproduction, and in any case subordinated to the needs of domesticity. Walkowitz proposes that this appeal to an essentially dormant female sexuality helps to explain the strength of the social purity campaigns of the late nineteenth century and the initial support feminists lent these campaigns. The outrage displayed by feminist repealers when confronted with tabloid tales of the 'traffic' in young working class women went beyond moral indignation at the sexual victimization it ostensibly documented. In so far as nineteenth-century middle class repealers (and their working class supporters) had attached themselves to notions of 'childhood' and 'adolescence' which presumed both sexual innocence and the necessary and prolonged dependency of children, any evidence to the contrary could only mean that working class girls had been inducted into a sexual knowledge and sexual activity which 'by nature' they would not otherwise have been party to. Failing to interrogate the socially and politically constructed basis of their own sexual norms, feminist repealers unwittingly participated in the late nineteenth-century production of a definition of 'illicit' sexuality – active, nonconjugal, and nonreproductive – which Walkowitz shows was soon to be 'ferreted out' and hounded by the combined forces of the law and social purity zealots.

Mort also argues that in the contemporary period, power over sexuality is not exercised by 'the direct operation of the law, but rather through the mobilization of a variety of non-legal practices'. Mort cites, as examples of these, the discourses and practices of medicine, sexology, psychology and sociology which all operate with implicit and explicit definitions of what constitutes sexual normalcy and deviancy. Apart from institutions linked to the state, Mort also notes the widespread and valorized link between heterosexuality and family life which forms the bedrock of a 'moral consensus' within popular opinion in contemporary Britain. The issue, Mort suggests, is not to collapse these definitions and practices into a single, all-embracing strategy of regulation, but to look at the various definitions produced and strategies sanctioned across a range of practices and institutions. Only by recognizing these specificities, Mort argues, can possibilities for change in either state institutions or civil society be realistically formulated.

Resistance

Arriving once again at that elusive but vital Foucaultian concept of resistance, it is important to recognize the positions of political engagement from which Walkowitz and Mort are respectively writing. Walkowitz's study of feminist participation in moral reform campaigns is partly motivated by feminist attacks on commercial sex and initiatives around sexual reform legislation in the present conjuncture. Walkowitz does not dispute that the nineteenth-century feminist repeal campaign was a movement of resistance with respect to the exercise of certain forms of power over female sexuality embodied in state policies, police measures, medical and military arguments or the behaviour of individual men. However, she locates the contemporary relevance of her historical analysis in the 'painful contradictions' which can accompany feminist sexual politics and thereby lend support to other strategies of power over sexuality; the brunt of those effects is borne by non-adherents to prevailing sexual norms: prostitutes, homosexuals, young people, and feminists themselves.

Mort similarly affirms the importance of the contemporary gay movement's efforts to resist and transform dominant definitions of sexuality, whether this be through legislative reform, 'coming out', or forming alliances with other sexual political movements. But he also issues the warning that 'general historical awareness of the social and cultural construction of homosexuality should make us cautious of developing a politics and a culture on the basis of any celebratory notion of an essential gayness'. Like Foucault, Mort proposes that the terrain of struggle of sexual politics should therefore revolve primarily around a 'disintegration' of fixed sexual categories and meanings 'rather than their reinforcement'.

References

BLAND, L. (1981) 'The Domain of the Sexual: A Response', *Screen Education*, No. 39, Summer.

BRAY, A. (1982) *Homosexuality in Renaissance England*, Gay Men's Press.

COUSINS, M. and HUSSAIN, A. (1984) *Michel Foucault*, London, Macmillan.

COWARD, R. (1978) 'Sexual Liberation and the Family', *m/f*, No. 1.

DEWS, P. (1984) 'Power and subjectivity in Foucault', *New Left Review*, No. 144, March/April.

FOUCAULT, M. (1972) *The Archaeology of Knowledge*, London, Tavistock.

FOUCAULT, M. (1979) *The History of Sexuality*, London, Allen Lane.

FOUCAULT, M. (1980) *Power/Knowledge*, edited by C. Gordon. Brighton, Harvester Press.

FREUD, S. (1905) 'Three Essays on Sexuality', *On Sexuality* vol. 7. of Pelican Freud Library, (1977) Harmondsworth, Penguin.

REICH, W. (1972) *Sex-pol Essays, 1929-1934*, New York, Vintage Books.

ROSS, E. and RAPP, R. (1981) 'Sex and Society: a Research Note from Social History and Anthropology; *Comparative Studies in Society and History*, Vol. 23, No 1, January.

WALKOWITZ, J. (1980) *Prostitution and Victorian Society: Women, Class and the State*, Cambridge, Cambridge University Press.

WEEKS, J. (1977) *Coming Out: Homosexual Politics in Britain from the Nineteenth Century to the Present*, London, Quartet Books.

WEEKS, J. (1981) *Sex, Politics and Society: The Regulation of Sexuality since 1800*, London, Longman.

WEEKS, J. (1982) 'Foucault for Historians', *History Workshop*, No. 14.

10 Male Vice and Feminist Virtue: Feminism and the Politics of Prostitution in Nineteenth-Century Britain

Judith R. Walkowitz

From *History Workshop*, No. 13, 1982. Reproduced by permission of the publisher, History Workshop Journal.

. . . In this [article] I am going to outline some of the historical precedents for the current feminist attack on commercial sex [. . .] Past generations of feminists attacked prostitution, pornography, white slavery, and homosexuality as manifestations of undifferentiated male lust. These campaigns were brilliant organising drives that stimulated grass-roots organisations and mobilised women not previously brought into the political arena. The vitality of the women's suffrage movement of the late nineteenth and early twentieth centuries cannot be understood without reference to the revivalistic quality of these anti-vice campaigns, which often ran parallel with the struggle for the vote. By demanding women's right to protect their own persons against male sexual abuse and ultimately extending their critique of sexual violence to the 'private' sphere of the family, they achieved some permanent gains for women.

Nonetheless, judging by the goals stated by feminists themselves – to protect and empower women – these campaigns were often self-defeating. A libertarian defence of prostitutes found no place in the social purity struggle; all too often prostitutes were objects of purity attacks. Feminists started a discourse on sex, mobilised an offensive against male vice, but they lost control of the movement as it diversified. In part this outcome was the result of certain contradictions in these feminists' attitudes; in part it reflected their impotence to reshape the world according to their own image.

The Contagious Diseases Act

In Great Britain explicitly feminist moral crusades against male vice began with a struggle against state regulation of prostitution. Parliament passed the first of three statutes providing for the sanitary inspection of prostitutes in specific military depots in Southern England and Ireland in 1864. Initially this first Contagious Diseases Act, as it was obliquely entitled, aroused little attention inside or outside of governmental circles. Public opposition to regulation did, however, surface in the 1870s, when a coalition of middle-class nonconformists, feminists, and radical working men challenged the Acts as immoral and unconstitutional, and called for their repeal. The participation of middle-class women in repeal efforts shocked many contemporary observers, who regarded this female rebellion as a disturbing sign of the times. The suffrage movement was in its infancy, and respectable commentators looked on with horror and fascination as middle-class ladies mounted public platforms across the country to denounce the Acts as a 'sacrifice of female liberties' to the 'slavery of men's lust' and to describe in minute detail the 'instrumental rape' of the internal examination. One troubled member of Parliament was moved to remark to Josephine Butler, the feminist repeal leader: 'We know how to manage any other opposition in the House or in the country, but this is very awkward for us – this revolt of women. It is quite a new thing; what are we to do with such an opposition as this?'

Under the leadership of Josephine Butler, the Ladies National Association (LNA) was founded in late 1869 as a separatist-feminist organisation. A 'Ladies Manifesto' was issued, which denounced the Acts as a blatant example of class and sex discrimination. The Manifesto further argued that the Acts not only deprived poor women of their constitutional rights and forced them to submit to a degrading internal examination, but they officially sanctioned a double standard of sexual morality, which justified male sexual access to a class of 'fallen' women and penalised women for engaging in the same vice as men.

The campaigns also drew thousands of women into the political arena for the first time, by encouraging them to challenge male centres of power – such as the police, Parliament, and the medical and military establishments – that were implicated in the administration of the Acts. Rallying to the defence of members of their own sex, these women opposed the sexual and political prerogatives of men. They rejected the prevailing social view of 'fallen women' as pollutants of men and depicted them instead as victims of male pollution, as women who had been invaded by men's bodies, men's laws, and by that 'steel penis', the speculum. This entailed a powerful identification with the fate of registered prostitutes.

Mid-Victorian feminists treated prostitution as the end result of the artificial constraints placed on women's social and economic activity: inadequate wages and restrictions of women's industrial employment forced some women onto the streets, where they took up the 'best paid industry' – prostitution. They also saw prostitution as a paradigm for the female condition, a symbol of women's powerlessness and sexual victimisation. Feminists realised that the popular sentimentalisation of 'female influence' and motherhood only thinly masked an older contempt and distrust for women, as 'The Sex', as sexual objects to be bought and sold by men. The treatment of prostitutes under the Acts epitomised this more pervasive and underlying misogyny. 'Sirs', declared Butler, 'you cannot hold us in honour so long as you drag our sisters in the mire. As you are unjust and cruel to them, you will become unjust and cruel to us . . . '

As 'mothers' and 'sisters' feminists asserted their right to defend prostitutes, thereby invoking two different kinds of authority relationships. A mother's right to defend 'daughters' was only partially an extension and continuation of women's traditional role within the family. It was also a political device, aimed at subverting and superseding patriarchal authority: it gave mothers, not fathers, the right to control sexual access to their daughters. But it also sanctioned an authority relationship between older, middle-class women and young working-class women that, although caring and protective, was also hierarchical and custodial. In other contexts, feminist repealers approached prostitutes on a more egalitarian basis, as sisters, albeit fallen ones, whose individual rights deserved to be respected and who, if they sold their bodies on the streets, had the right to do so unmolested by the police.

This was the radical message of the repeal campaign. It was linked to an enlightened view of prostitution as an irregular and temporary livelihood for adult working-class women. The regulation system, feminists argued, not prostitution as such, doomed inscribed women to a life of sin by publicly stigmatising them and preventing them from finding alternative respectable employment. 'Among the poor,' declared Josephine Butler, the 'boundary lines between the virtuous and vicious' were 'gradually and imperceptibly shaded off' so that it was 'impossible to affix a distinct name and infallibly assign' prostitutes to an outcast category. In fact, the young women brought under the Acts lived as part of a distinct female subgroup in common lodging houses, among a heterogeneous community of the casual labouring poor. They were both victims and survivors. The 'unskilled daughters of the unskilled classes', their lives were a piece with the large body of labouring women who had to eke out a precarious living in the urban job market, for whom sexual coercion was but one form of exploitation to which they were subjected. But prostitutes were not simply victims of male sexual abuse: they could act in their own defence, both individually and collectively, while prostitution itself often constituted a 'refuge from uneasy circumstances' for young women who had to live outside the family and who had to choose among a series of unpleasant alternatives.

Through their agitation, feminist repealers established a political arena that made it possible for prostitutes to resist, 'to show the officers,' in the words of one registered woman, 'that we have some respect for our own person'. LNA leaders and their agents descended upon subjected districts like Plymouth and Southampton, agitated among registered prostitutes and tried to persuade them to resist the regulation system. Feminists knew they were dealing with an ambiguous social underground – with lodging-house keepers who made profits out of renting rooms to prostitutes and with 'fallen' women who would 'rise' again.

Political expedience also pulled feminists in a different direction. On the whole the discussion of voluntary prostitution received far less publicity than exposés of innocent girls forced down into the ranks of prostitution by the 'spy police'. Feminist leaders used sensational stories of false entrapment or instrumental rape to appeal to all supporters of repeal – to working-class radicals and middle-class evangelicals alike. These accounts depicted registered women as innocent victims of male lust and medical and police tyranny – appropriate objects of solicitude, even for middle-class moralists who chiefly condemned the Acts for making 'vice' safe. Furthermore, feminist propaganda was still constrained by an extremely limited ideological vocabulary – constructed around the theme of female victimisation. Defences of prostitutes as women who were not yet 'dead to shame', who still had 'womanly modesty', were common. By mystifying prostitution and women's move into it, this propaganda imperfectly educated the LNA rank and file on the 'politics of prostitution'.

A politics of motherhood also structured the cross-class alliance between feminists and radical working men within the repeal camp. As mothers, LNA leaders called upon the sons of the people to join with them in a service rebellion against the evil fathers, clearly presuming that their working-class allies would follow their political lead. 'Our working men . . . are not unwilling to follow the gentle guidance of a grave and educated lady' or to 'devote the whole influence of their vote . . . when the right chord in their hearts and consciences is touched by a delicate hand'. Ironically, feminists encouraged working men to assume a custodial role toward 'their' women and frequently reminded them of their patriarchal responsibilities as defenders of the family. One LNA poster, for instance, warned 'Working Men!' to 'Look to the protection of your wives and daughters. They are at the mercy of the police where these Acts are in force'. Propaganda of this sort aroused popular indignation against regulation, but it also buttressed a patriarchal stance and a sexual hierarchy within the organised working class that feminists had vigorously challenged in other contexts. At the same time that Butler and her friends were trying to build bridges with the organised working class, they had to struggle with their new allies over proposals to restrict female employment. To feminists, a defence of free female labour and an attack on the 'slavery' of prostitution were part of the same work, but working-class leaders saw it otherwise. They countered libertarian and feminist arguments against protective legislation with a defence of the 'family wage' and with the view that prostitution resulted not from female unemployment but from the immiseration of the working-class family when adult male labour had to compete with the cheap labour of women and children. Feminists knew they were treading on dangerous grounds here. Despite her strong feelings against protective legislation, Butler hesitated from pressing the point at the annual meeting of the Trade Union Congress. 'I think it might be wise for us not to raise the question of the restrictions on female labour in the Trades Congress, this year . . . It is such a serious question for the future, that we must try to avoid that awful thing – a real breach between women and working men.'

LNA leaders did not entirely ignore their female constituency in the working class, but they tended to see working women principally as objects of concern rather than as active participants in the struggle. Although working-class women attended LNA lectures in great numbers and loudly voiced their indignation against 'those blackguard Acts', they were not effectively organised into their own repeal associations. In part this failure was due to the indifferent organising efforts and elitism of the LNA, in part to the practical difficulty of organising working-class women at that historical moment, given their economic dependence and exclusion from political culture.

Although capable of enunciating a radical critique of prostitution, feminist repealers still felt ambivalent about prostitutes as women who manipulated their sexuality as a commodity. And although they had joined with radical working men in an attack against elite male privilege, this cross-class, cross-gender alliance was fraught with contradictions. By and large these anxieties and contradictions remained submerged during the libertarian struggle against state regulation, but they soon surfaced in the more repressive campaign against white slavery.

White Slavery

After the suspension of the Acts in 1883, Butler and her circle turned their attention to the agitation against the foreign 'traffic in women' and the entrapment of children into prostitution in London. When Parliament refused to pass a bill raising the age of consent and punishing traffickers in vice, Butler and Catherine Booth of the Salvation Army approached W. T. Stead and the *Pall Mall Gazette* for assistance. The result was the 'Maiden Tribute of Modern Babylon', published in the summer of 1885 (see Gorham, 1978; Bristow, 1977).

The 'Maiden Tribute' was one of the most successful pieces of scandal journalism published in Britain during the nineteenth century. By using sexual scandal to sell newspapers to a middle-class and working-class readership, Stead ushered in a new era of tabloid sensationalism and cross-class prurience. New typographical and journalistic techniques were introduced to sell an old story, the seduction of poor girls by vicious aristocrats, one of the most popular themes of nineteenth-century melodrama, street literature, and women's penny magazines. The 'Maiden Tribute' resembled popular fiction and drama in that it contained a criticism of the vicious upper classes; but, as in the case of melodrama, this class criticism was immediately undercut by sentimental moralism, prurient details, and a focus on passive, innocent female victims and individual evil men that diverted attention away from the structural issues related to prostitution.

In lurid and prurient detail, the 'Maiden Tribute' documented the sale of 'five pound' virgins to aristocratic old rakes, graphically describing the way 'daughters of the people' had been 'snared, trapped and outraged either when under the influence of drugs or after a prolonged struggle in a locked room' (Gorham, 1978, p.354). The series had an electrifying effect on public opinion: 'By the third instalment mobs were rioting at the *Pall Mall Gazette* offices, in an attempt to obtain copies of the paper' (Bristow, 1977, p.249). An enormous public demonstration was held in Hyde Park (estimated at 250,000) to demand the passage of legislation raising the age of consent for girls from 13 to 16. Reformers of all shades were represented on the dozen or so demonstration platforms. For one brief moment, feminists and personal rights advocates joined with Anglican bishops and socialists to protest the aristocratic corruption of young innocents.

Recent research delineates the vast discrepancy between lurid journalistic accounts and the reality of prostitution. Evidence of widespread entrapment of British girls in London and abroad is slim. During the 1870s and 1880s officials and reformers uncovered a light traffic in women between Britain and the continent. All but a few of the women enticed into licensed brothels in Antwerp and Brussels had been prostitutes in England. Misled by promises of a life of luxury and ease as part of a glamorous demimonde, they were shocked and horrified at the conditions enforced upon them in licensed state brothels, a sharp contrast to what they had experienced in England. In most cases, then, it was the conditions of commercial sex and not the fact that deeply upset the women (Gorham, 1978, pp.376–378). Stead's discussion of child prostitution contained similar misrepresentations and distortions. There undoubtedly were some child prostitutes on the streets of London, Liverpool, and elsewhere; but most of these young girls were not victims of false entrapment, as the vignettes in the 'Maiden Tribute' suggest; the girls were on the streets because their other choices were so limited. 'Since sexuality in western culture is so mystified,' notes Gayle Rubin [in an unpublished essay (1981)], 'the wars over it are often fought at oblique angles, aimed at phony targets, conducted with misplaced passions, and are highly, intensely, symbolic.' The 'Maiden Tribute' episode strikingly illustrates both this mystification and its political consequences. Shifting the cultural image of the prostitute to the innocent child victim encouraged new, more repressive, political initiatives over sex.

Why then did feminist reformers endorse this crusade? Why did they ally with repressive moralists and anti-suffragists who were as anxious to clear the streets of prostitutes as to protect young girls from evil procurers and vicious aristocrats? Like the image of the instrumental violation of registered women under the CD Acts, the story of aristocratic corruption of virgins 'generated a sense of outrage with which a wide spectrum of public opinion found itself in sympathy' (Gorham, 1978, p.355). Feminist repealers undoubtedly believed they could manipulate this popular anger for their own purposes, first to secure the full repeal of the CD Acts (they were finally removed from the statute books in 1886) and then to launch a sustained assault on the double standard. They were also attracted to the radical message in Stead's exposé of aristocratic vice. The disreputable performance of MPs during the debates over the age of consent confirmed feminists' worst suspicions about 'the vicious upper classes'. During the debates, old rakes like Cavendish Bentinck treated prostitution as a necessary and inevitable evil, where others openly defended sexual access to working-class girls as a time-honored prerogative of gentlemen. One member of the House of Lords acknowledged that 'very few of their Lordships . . . had not when young men, been guilty of immorality. He hoped they would pause before passing a clause within the range of which their sons might come'.

Feminists felt obliged to redress the sexual wrongs done to poor girls by men of a superior class, but they registered the same repugnance and ambivalence toward incorrigible girls as they had earlier toward unrepentant prostitutes. For them as well as for more repressive moralists, the desire to protect young working-class girls masked impulses to control the girls' sexuality, which in turn reflected their desire to impose a social code that stressed female adolescent dependency. This code was more in keeping with middle-class notions of girlhood than with the lived reality of the exposed and unsupervised daughters of the labouring poor who were on the streets. Respectable working-class parents certainly shared many of the same sentiments toward female adolescents. Despite the fact that they often sent their own daughters out to work at 13, they nonetheless took pains to restrict their social independence and sexual knowledge and experience.[1]

Another sub-theme of feminist discussion was that females of all classes were vulnerable to male sexual violence. 'There was no place of absolute safety, neither in streets, nor parks, nor railways, nor in the houses, where the procuresses were often known to enter as charwomen, nor indeed in the very churches and chapels', one speaker announced at a meeting of middle-class women. Although female victimisation was a sincere concern of feminists, it also served diverse political interests. Whereas feminists identified the 'outlawed political condition of women' as the root cause of the crimes exposed in the 'Maiden Tribute', anti-feminists used the occasion to activate men into a new crusade to protect rather than emancipate women – a crusade that was, at times, overtly misogynist. 'Let us appeal to their manhood, to their chivalry, to their reverence for their own mothers and sisters – to protect the maidens of the land', declaimed one speaker, who rapidly acknowledged that the objects of such manly solicitude – 'those poor, silly, weak children who know not the frightful ruin they are bringing on their lives' – were not worthy of the ideals they had inspired.

What was the outcome of the 'Maiden Tribute' affair? The public furore over the 'Maiden Tribute' forced the passage of the Criminal Law Amendment Act of 1885, a particularly nasty and pernicious piece of omnibus legislation. The 1885 Act raised the age of consent for girls from 13 to 16, but it also gave police far greater summary jurisdiction over poor working-class women and children – a trend that Butler and her circle had always opposed. Finally, it contained a clause making indecent acts between consenting male adults a crime, thus forming the basis of legal prosecution of male homosexuals in Britain until 1967. An anti-aristocratic bias may have prompted the inclusion of this clause (reformers accepted its inclusion but did not themselves propose it), as homosexuality was associated with the corruption of working-class youth by the same upper-class profligates, who, on other occasions, were thought to buy the services of young girls (Weeks, 1977, pp.18–20).

Despite the public outcry against corrupt aristocrats and international traffickers, the clauses of the new bill were mainly enforced against working-class women, and regulated adult rather than youthful sexual behaviour. Between 1890 and 1914, the systematic repression of lodging house brothels was carried out in almost every major city in Great Britain. In many locales, legal repression

dramatically affected the structure and organisation of prostitution. Prostitutes
were uprooted from their neighbourhoods and had to find lodgings in other areas
of the city. Their activity became more covert and furtive. Cut off from any other
sustaining relationship, they were forced to rely increasingly on pimps for
emotional security as well as protection against legal authorities. Indeed, with the
wide prevalence of pimps in the early twentieth century, prostitution shifted from
a female- to a male-dominated trade. Further, there now existed a greater number
of third parties with a strong interest in prolonging women's stay on the streets. In
these and other respects, the 1885 Act drove a wedge between prostitutes and the
poor working-class community. It effectively destroyed the brothel as a family
industry and centre of a specific female subculture; further undermined the social
and economic autonomy of prostitutes; and increasingly rendered them social
outcasts.

Social Purity

But prostitutes were not the only objects of reformist attacks. In the wake of
Stead's 'shocking revelations', the National Vigilance Association (NVA) was
formed. First organised to ensure the local enforcement of the Criminal Law
Amendment Act, the NVA soon turned its attention to burning obscene books,
attacking music halls, theatres, and nude paintings. It condemned the works of
Balzac, Zola, and Rabelais as obscene and successfully prosecuted their British
distributors; it attacked birth control literature and advertisements for 'female pills'
(abortifacient drugs) on the same grounds. To these moral crusaders,
'pornographic literature', thus broadly defined, was a vile expression of the same
'undifferentiated male lust' that ultimately led to homosexuality and prostitution
(Weeks, 1977, p.18). The fact that pornography was now available in cheap
editions undoubtedly heightened middle-class concern over the emergence of a
degenerate and unsupervised urban popular culture.[2]

While the social purity movement served middle-class interests, it is a common
error among historians to assume that working-class support for social purity was
ephemeral or that both before and after the summer of 1885 social purity remained
an almost exclusively middle-class movement. Middle-class evangelicals may
have predominated in the National Vigilance Association, but the values of social
purity seem to have penetrated certain portions of the working class.

By the mid-1880s, Ellice Hopkins, the female pioneer in social purity, had
already organised hundreds of male chastity leagues and female rescue societies.
Besides counselling working-class mothers on how to avoid incest in their homes,
she regularly delivered speeches on purity before meetings of working men, and
she and others successfully recruited thousands of respectable working men
throughout the nation into White Cross armies, which were dedicated to
promoting the single standard of chastity and attacking public and private vice.
The prescriptive literature distributed by social purity groups also seems to have
influenced the child-rearing practices of the time. Edwardian working-class

parents were notable for their strict schedules, puritanical treatment of masturbation, and for the severe restrictions they placed on their teenage daughters' social and sexual behaviour. Although the late-Victorian and Edwardian years represented a 'germination' period for the formulation of a 'new sexuality', the available facts about sexuality – the general decline in both venereal disease and prostitution; the high age of marriage and low illegitimacy rates; the apparently limited use of contraceptives among the working classes – seem to support the hypothesis that 'sexual restraint' was indeed 'spreading down through society'.

But sexual restraint could also serve women's interest. In a culture where women were often the victims of sexual coercion yet blamed for crimes committed against them (Edwards, 1979), and where it was difficult even to conceive of female sexual agency as long as women lacked agency in other vital areas, defenders of women's rights could and did regard the doctrine of female passionlessness and male sexual self-control as a significant advance over traditional assumptions of a dangerous and active female sexuality.[3] Whatever its drawbacks, this sexual strategy resulted in some permanent gains for women: it made it possible for women to name incest and rape as crimes against their person (rather than as crimes against the property of men). Most particularly, through the Incest Act of 1908, young women were offered legal recourse against sexual violence by male family members for the first time. By insisting that women had the right to refuse the sexual demands of husbands, and by widely propagandising this view in the early decades of the twentieth century, feminists within social purity laid the foundation for the new egalitarian code of marital relations still to be fully realised in the contemporary era. In feminist hands, desexualisation could empower women to attack the customary prerogatives of men. It could also validate a new social role for women outside the heterosexual family. The 'New Women' of the late nineteenth century, as Carroll Smith-Rosenberg has noted, strove to achieve social autonomy, but at the cost of sexual identity, to legitimise their social and economic dependence at the 'price of donning the mask of Victorian [sexual] respectability' (Smith-Rosenberg and Newton, 1981).

Since middle-class women elaborated these ideas, it is hard to know what working-class women thought of them. Labouring women did participate in mothers' meetings, and they may have found the moral authority imparted to desexualised women attractive, as it reinforced the power of mothers and female collectivities. In the dense urban neighbourhoods of late-Victorian and Edwardian England, where female neighbours shared space and services, and where female relatives sustained the bonds of kinship, social and sexual norms were often articulated at 'street level' through hierarchical female networks. The mothers of Plymouth, Lancaster and Salford, for example, enforced incest taboos, socialised their daughters into a fatalistic and dependent femininity, and increasingly shunned 'bad women' (often at the instigation of purity agencies). On the whole, the activities of neighbourhood matriarchs sustained social hierarchies and divisions, particularly along generational and sex lines. Female sexual respectability in these neighbourhoods was purchased at a high price, with little promise of social independence. The 'New Woman' option was simply not available to working-class daughters: they could not aspire to a future outside heterosexual domesticity – for working-class women, such a future could only forebode a life of hardship and homelessness. As a result, the contradictory nature of the power imparted to women through 'passionlessness' appears even more apparent for working-class women. However much this doctrine mitigated the powerlessness of dependent wives, it left working-class women alienated from and ignorant of their own sexuality and body, and unable to control reproduction – a disabling condition, to judge from the depressing letters collected by the Women's Co-operative Guild in their volume, *Maternity*.

Social purity presented working men with a different set of implications and opportunities; it could bolster their authority as responsible patriarchs if they were willing to submit themselves to a certain domestic ideology. In general, sexual respectability became the hallmark of the respectable working man, anxious to distance himself from the 'bestiality' of the casual labouring poor at a time when increased pressure was being placed on the respectable working class to break their ties with outcast groups. The social purity movement itself provided an avenue of social mobility for some men, like William Coote, a former compositor who became the national secretary of the National Vigilance Association. Changing employment patterns also seem to have reinforced patriarchal tendencies among skilled sectors of the working class by the end of the century, as the proportion of married women working outside the home declined and the family wage for male workers became an essential demand of trade unions. In this context, social purity – which called upon men to protect and control their women – may have served as the ideological corollary of the family wage, morally legitimating the prerogatives of patriarchy inside and outside the family.

What was the subsequent relationship between feminism and social purity? Initially, prominent feminists filled many of the committee positions of the National Vigilance Association, but Butler and her circle resigned when the prurient and repressive direction of the NVA became apparent. Throughout the late 1880s and '90s, Butlerites warned their workers to 'beware' of the repressive methods of the social purity societies who were 'ready to accept and endorse any amount of coercive and degrading treatment of their fellow creatures in the fatuous belief that you can oblige human beings to be moral by force . . . ' But their warnings were too late. The new social purity movement had passed them by, while absorbing a goodly number of the LNA rank and file.

Moderate suffragists like Millicent Fawcett and Elizabeth Blackwell remained within the ranks of social purity, and feminist purity reformers, most notably Laura Ormiston Chant, were prominent in the attack on theatres and immoral public entertainments. Feminists still maintained a voice within social purity after 1885, but they were in constant danger of being engulfed by positions far removed from their own. To be sure, feminist repealers had earlier faced a similar dilemma, but the problem of social purity feminists was compounded by the fact that social purity was by no means an explicitly feminist or libertarian cause, nor dominated by a forceful feminist leader like Josephine Butler. The reactionary implications of social purity, for feminists and prostitutes alike, are illuminated by the public controversy surrounding the Jack the Ripper murders.

The Ripper Murders

In the autumn of 1888, the attention of the 'classes' as well as the 'masses' was riveted on a series of brutal murders of prostitutes residing in lodging houses in the Whitechapel area of East London. Public response to the murders was widespread and diverse, but the people who mobilised over the murders were almost exclusively male.

An army of West End men, fascinated by the murders and bent on hunting the Ripper, invaded the East End. Meanwhile, a half-dozen male vigilance committees were set up in Whitechapel – by Toynbee Hall, by the Jewish community, by the radical and socialist workingmen's clubs. These male patrols were organised to protect women, but they also constituted surveillance of the unrespectable poor, and of low-life women in particular. They were explicitly modelled on existing purity organisations already active in the area that had helped to close down 200 brothels in the East End in the year before the Ripper murders. As we have seen, the message of social purity to men was mixed: it demanded that men control their own sexuality, but it gave them power to control the sexuality of women as well, since it called upon them to protect their women and to repress brothels and streetwalkers.

These generalisations are borne out by the Ripper episode, when a number of men ostensibly out to hunt the Ripper harassed women on the streets while husbands threatened wives with 'ripping' them up in their homes. Female vulnerability extended well beyond the 'danger zone' of Whitechapel: throughout London, respectable women, afraid to venture out alone at night, were effectively placed under 'house arrest' and dependent on male protection. Despite the public outcry against the 'male monster', 'who stalks the streets of London' in search of fallen women, public attention inevitably reverted to the degraded conditions of the Whitechapel victims themselves. 'The degraded and depraved lives of the women,' observed Canon Barnett of Toynbee Hall in the *Times*, were more 'appalling than the actual murders'. Men like Barnett finally manipulated public opinion and consolidated it behind closing down lodging houses where the murdered victims once lived and replacing them with artisan dwellings. Through the surveillance of vigilance committees the murders helped to intensify repressive activities already under way in the Whitechapel area and to hasten the reorganisation of prostitution in the East End.

During the Ripper manhunt, feminists were unable to mobilise any counter-offensive against the widespread male intimidation of women. Josephine Butler and others did express concern that the uproar over the murders would lead to the repression of brothels and to subsequent homelessness of women; but these were isolated interventions in an overwhelmingly male-dominated debate.

Feminism

Although some feminists still maintained a national presence in the purity crusade, all in all, by the late 1880s feminists had lost considerable authority in the public discussion over sex to a coalition of male professional experts, conservative churchmen, and social purity advocates. On the other hand, social purity left a permanent imprint on the women's movement through the First World War. Both the 16-year campaign against state regulation and later sexual scandals such as the 'Maiden Tribute', ingrained the theme of the sexual wrongs perpetrated against women by men on later feminist consciousness. After the 1880s, the 'women's revolt' became 'a revolt that is Puritan and not Bohemian. It is uprising against the tyranny of organised intemperance, impurity, mammonism, and selfish motives.' On the whole this attack on male dominance and male vice involved no positive assertion of female sexuality. Although a small minority of feminists like Olive Schreiner and Stella Browne were deeply interested in the question of female pleasure, they were far removed from the feminist mainstream, where the public discussion of sexuality and male dominance was still couched within the terms of a 'separate sphere' ideology, implying that women were moral, 'spiritual' creatures who needed to be protected from animalistic 'carnal' men, and demanding, in the words of Christabel Pankhurst, the Edwardian militant suffragist, 'votes for women', and 'chastity' for men. Moreover, the obsession with male vice again sidetracked early twentieth-century feminists into another crusade against white slavery (1912), while obscuring the economic basis of prostitution. It even prompted the most progressive women of the day to advocate raising the age of consent to 21. Finally, it led to repressive public policies. Commenting on the enforcement of the White Slavery Act of 1912, Sylvia Pankhurst remarked, 'It is a strange thing that the latest Criminal Amendment Act, which was passed ostensibly to protect women, is being used almost exclusively to punish women'. As late as 1914, first-wave feminists were rediscovering that the state 'protection' of young women usually led to coercive and repressive measures against those same women.

These then are the early historical links between feminism and repressive crusades against prostitution, pornography, and homosexuality. Begun as a libertarian struggle against the state sanction of male vice, the repeal campaign helped to spawn a hydra-headed assault on nonmarital, nonreproductive sexuality. The struggle against state regulation evolved into a movement that used the instruments of the state for repressive purposes. It may be misleading to interpret the effects of these later crusades solely as 'blind' repressive attacks on sexuality; in many ways they clarified and identified whole new areas of sexuality. According to Michel Foucault (1979), this elaboration of new sexualities was a strategy for exercising power in society. By ferreting out new areas of illicit sexual activity and sometimes defining them into existence, a new 'technology of power' was created that facilitated control over an ever-widening circle of human activity. But power is not simply immanent in society; it is deployed by specific historical agents, who have access to varying sources and levels of power. The reality of a hierarchy of power severely impeded feminists' efforts to use purity crusades to defend and empower women. Through rescue and preventive work, feminists and other women were certainly implicated in the regulation and control of sexuality. But there were others whose access to power was more direct. Rescue work, mothers' meetings, and moral suasion by no means carried the same authority as a morals police under the CD Acts, male vigilance committees, or an emerging 'science of sexuality' controlled by male professionals. The feminist challenge to male sexual prerogatives was a major historic development, one necessary precondition for the ideology of egalitarian heterosexual relations: but when they tried to use the powers of the state to protect women, particularly prostitutes who had been the original objects of their pity and concern, feminists usually came face to face with their own impotence.

What are the moral lessons to these moral crusades? If there is a moral lesson, it is that commercial sex as a locus of sexual violence against women is a hot and dangerous issue for feminists. In their defence of prostitutes and concern to protect women from male sexual aggression, feminists were limited by their own class bias and by their continued adherence to a 'separate sphere' ideology that stressed women's purity, moral supremacy, and domestic virtues. Moreover, they lacked the cultural and political power to reshape the world according to their own image. Although they tried to set the standards of sexual conduct, they did not control the instruments of state that ultimately enforced these norms. There were times, particularly during the anti-regulationist campaign, when feminists were able to dominate and structure the public discourse on sex and to arouse popular female anger at male sexual license. Yet this anger was easily subverted into repressive campaigns against male vice and sexual variation, controlled by men and conservative interests whose goals were antithetical to the values and ideals of feminism [. . .]

Notes

1 For reformers, 'girlhood' was a stage in life marked by dependency but not any specific psychosexual development. Accordingly, debates over the age of consent rarely included reference to the actual sexual development of the girls they were seeking to protect. The age of consent was arbitrary; indeed, many reformers wanted to raise it to 18, some to 21. Moreover, many of the same assumptions about protecting and controlling female adolescents ultimately led to the definition and incarceration of sexually active girls as 'sex delinquents'.

2 Similarly, purity reformers were concerned about the pernicious effect of music hall entertainment not only because they deemed many of the acts obscene, but because the acts encouraged working men to emulate the parasitic, licentious life of the 'swell'.

3 I am following Nancy Cott's (1978) use of the concept of passionlessness to 'convey the view that women lacked sexual aggressiveness, that their sexual appetites contributed a minor part . . . to their motivations, that lustfulness was simply uncharacteristic. The concept of passionlessness represented a cluster of ideas about the comparative weight of woman's carnal nature . . . ' 'Passionlessness: an interpretation of Victorian sexual ideology, 1790–1850', *Signs*, No. 4.

References

BRISTOW, E. (1977) *Vice and Vigilance: Purity Movements in Britain since 1700*, Dublin, Gill and MacMillan.

EDWARDS, S. (1979) 'Sex crimes in the nineteenth century', *New Society*, No. 49, 13 September.

FOUCAULT, M. (1979) *The History of Sexuality*, Vol. 1, London, Allen Lane.

GORHAM, D. (1978) 'The "Maiden Tribute of Modern Babylon" reconsidered', *Victorian Studies*, No. 21, Spring.

SMITH-ROSENBERG, C., and NEWTON, E. (1981) 'The Mythic Lesbian and the New Woman', conference paper presented at Berkshire Conference.

WEEKS, J. (1977) *Coming Out: Homosexual Politics in Britain from the Nineteenth Century to the Present*, London, Quartet.

11 The Population Question in the Early Twentieth Century

Jeffrey Weeks

From *Sex, Politics and Society: the Regulation of Sexuality since 1800* by Jeffrey Weeks, 1981. Reproduced by permission of the publisher, Longman.

By the beginning of the twentieth century, the sexual question was being inextricably linked with the politics of population. The problem of 'population' recurs in all the major discussions of the time, from the 'social question' to the threat of national decline, from issues of unemployment to the threat of war.

At the heart of the debates was the increasing belief that the health, hygiene and composition of the population were the keys to progress and power. And sex was the key to the question of population. It was the point of access both to the health and status of the individual and to the future of the population as a whole. The political and theoretical debates over personal morality and national fertility, physical deterioration and a differential birthrate, major topics in the early decades of this century, all raised the twin questions of the population and the role and significance of sexuality. Sex, wrote Patrick Geddes and J. Arthur Thomson in their little book of that title (1914), is 'a cardinal fact of life and one of the prime movers of progress.' Consequently, irregularities of sexual behaviour had to be judged not just by their influence on the individual, 'but by their influence on the race' [. . .]

The issue of population was not, of course, new in the twentieth century. The concern with the population, in the sense of an organised, regulated and policed domain, and as a major concern of political theory, can be traced back at least to Plato. [. . .] But from the late eighteenth century the population takes on a new significance, because it begins to be quantified: it becomes an object in its own right, an entity that can be measured and described.

From the first census in 1801, and with growing strength from the 1830s, with compulsory registration of births, marriages, etc., statistics in ever growing numbers could indicate changes, chart trends and pinpoint problems. Birth and death rates, life expectancies and fertility rates, all could be laid out to show the population trends.

Coinciding with this was a politicisation of the question of population associated with the work of Thomas Malthus and his supporters. Malthus's argument, in reply to Godwin's, that as food suppliers move in arithmetic progression while the population moves in geometric progression, the population would soon overshoot the food supply, to be swamped by vice and misery, had clear political, social and sexual connotations. It suggested that because no social remedy was possible, the poor were responsible for their own poverty, the major cause of which was therefore moral: reckless overbreeding. Charity or reform were valueless: the only conceivable remedy was to educate the workers in the secrets of political economy and in particular to get them to see the importance of sexual self-restraint and of deferring marriage [. . .]

The fundamental purpose of Malthusian doctrine, it has been well said, was to establish 'a new moral economy'. Its peculiar strength came from its basic belief that the laws of population (like the laws of political economy) were inscrutable, and from its claim to be based on objective and scientifically proven facts. Social life could only be satisfactorily established on the basis of subservience to the facts of social existence, and these could not be changed by lay interference. The result was an inherent pessimism in Malthusianism proper. Its function was to instil awareness of these 'facts', not fruitlessly to try to change them [. . .]

The population issue remained a significant undercurrent from the 1830s but it was not until the 1870s, with the revival of the debate over contraception, that it again became a central political question. One major sign of this was the re-emergence of neo-Malthusianism in an organised form (the Malthusian League was formed in 1877) attempting to induce in the educated classes a conviction of the truth of Malthusianism with the hope that this awareness would penetrate to the feckless. Another sign was the development of theoretical arguments, which were to crystallise in eugenics at the beginning of the new century, about the possibilities of direct intervention in the planning of population. We can observe, in other words, a more generalised move away from *laissez-faire*, with its pessimism over population, to a new interventionism, often wildly utopian and scientistic. Its aim was control over the population.

A number of closely related themes recur throughout the population debates of the late nineteenth and early twentieth centuries: the problem of 'degeneracy'; the multiplication of the 'unfit'; the question of a differential birthrate. And these themes were given a peculiar reverberation because of external referents to which they were thought to be linked: poverty and urban problems; and the fear of national decay.

The theme of degeneracy was evoked in the 1880s to try to explain the results of urban change. Behind it was a fear, particularly amongst the urban middle class, that Britain might have taken a major wrong turning in becoming an urban, industrial society. Commentators looked with alarm at the casual labourers and the slum inhabitants of the big cities – almost another race – who were increasing at a disturbing rate and were refusing to respond to legislation and charity to improve them. Degeneration was, as Gareth Stedman Jones has put it, 'a mental landscape within which the middle class could recognise and articulate their own anxieties about urban existence' (1971, p.151), but it became an explanatory tool to justify the existence of a residuum of people who did not seem to respond to the blandishments of self-improvement.

The social investigation of Charles Booth and Seebohm Rowntree from the 1880s pinpointed the problem: many believed that what was happening was a reverse natural selection, producing a distinct subspecies of people, unable to accept the social norm, a residuum of the 'unfit' (Searle, 1976, pp. 22 ff.). Of course, the perception of class inequality and of poverty could as easily lead to political theories arguing for radical social change, but it was within a hereditarian discourse that many of the debates were actually played out.

Degeneration represented a falling away from type. It was a general condition of a section of the population which nevertheless manifested itself in many different forms of individual behaviour. In this context sexual variations could readily be seen as part of the same core problem as poverty. Dr Rentoul of Liverpool, one of the more extreme eugenicists, could easily lump together lunatics, neurotics, kleptomaniacs, alcoholics and sexual perverts as all being examples of degenerate stock. *Reynolds' Newspaper* made the relevant connection in commenting on Tarnowsky's book, *The Sexual Instinct*: 'A perusal of these pages will reveal the fact that many so-called sexual "crimes" are simply irresistible impulses of degeneracy, an illustration of the doctrine of heredity, a theory which none more than British scientists have done so much to popularise.' It went on to suggest that 'the earnest seeker after the truth' should present these facts to the public, 'in the interests of his species'.

The major perceived problem was the rapid multiplication of 'unfit' people producing more and more inadequates [. . .] As the National Birth Rate Commission, an unofficial body set up to study this question, pointed out, amongst the upper and middle class there were around 119 births per 1,000 married males under 35, while for the skilled workmen the figures were 153, and the unskilled 213. The result, Karl Pearson argued, was that 25 per cent of the population threatened to produce 50 per cent of the next generation. Consequently, the racial mixture of the population was undergoing a fundamental change: the worst stock were reproducing busily, while the best were dying out.

Even when the arguments were not taken to this extreme, the larger size of the working-class family (with an average of over 4 children) was seen as being a major source for the perpetuation of poverty. One leading neo-Malthusian could not understand how Parliament could enact a legal minimum wage, without at the same time enacting 'a Legal Maximum Family', while Havelock Ellis believed there to be a correlation between large families and abnormalities: large families tended to be degenerate. What was inevitably taking place was a slide in the argument, from questions of quality of the population as a whole to a rough equation of genetic worth with social standing. It was the working-class which was breeding over-rapidly, and within that the unrespectable who were reproducing most quickly. And as Lord Rosebery suggested, 'in the rookeries and slums which still survive, an imperial race cannot be reared'. These debates crystallised around the turn of the century precisely because they seemed to touch on the question of national survival: 'an empire such as ours requires as its first condition an imperial race'.

The impact of the Boer War gave this issue a special centrality, for the war brought to light what was perceived as the drastic unfitness of the imperial race. The reports of the Inspector General of Recruiting, which suggested that 3 out of 5 men presenting themselves for enlistment in Manchester in 1899 had to be rejected as physically unfit, aroused widespread concern, and he commented in his 1902 report on the 'further gradual deterioration of the physique of the working classes' [. . .]

The Interdepartmental Committee set up to investigate physical deterioration in 1904 in fact decided that actual deterioration remained unproven, though working-class health and the appalling infant mortality figures left much to be desired. It made 53 recommendations, most of which dealt with the environment (overcrowding, the lack of open spaces, pollution, bad housing) or with working-class conditions (unemployment, adulteration of food, insurance). Overwhelmingly, however, these environmental issues were ignored in the ensuing debates (see Davin, 1978). The recommendations generally endorsed and underlined both the hereditarian as opposed to the environmentalist flavour of the discussions, and the new stress on the role of motherhood, especially those covering the instruction of girls and women in cooking, hygiene and child care.

Maternalism

What was taking place, indeed, was a partial shift in the dominant ideology, away from the nineteenth-century stress on woman as wife towards an accentuated (though not of course new) emphasis on woman as mother. Women's traditional domestic responsibilities were being ideologically reshaped to accord with new perceived problems. A good index of this is an observable change in the recommended reasons for marriage at the turn of the century. A representative manual of the 1860s, for instance, stressed the need for a young woman to find someone to support her, to protect her, to help her, and who was qualified to guide and direct her. There was no mention of children. A 1917 book, concerned with young women and marriage, on the other hand, offered three main reasons for marriage: mutual comfort and support; the maintenance of social purity; and the reproduction of the race. Motherhood, it seemed, was a major key to a healthy population. As the Swedish feminist Ellen Key put it, 'as a general rule the woman who refuses motherhood in order to serve humanity is like a soldier who prepares himself on the eve of battle for the forthcoming struggle by opening his veins'. The new ideological inflection was undoubtedly a cross-class phenomenon. As Havelock Ellis put it: 'Woman's function in life can never be the same as man's, if only because women are the mothers of the race . . . the most vital problem before our civilisation today is the problem of motherhood, the question of creating human beings best suited for modern life'. But it had a particular nuance when directed at the 'unfit' working class, with its high infant mortality and arguable physical deterioration. It was not poverty that was seen as the cause, but poor maternal training. What were needed were better mothers. Bad hygiene, dirty bottles and dirty homes, and the general question of working-class ignorance were tackled with a fervour by the host of unofficial voluntary bodies that sprang up in the years before the First World War often directed at working-class mothers [. . .]

Child rearing was no longer seen as just an individual moral duty: it was a national duty, and this was reflected in the new spirit of interventionism on the part of the state. Compulsory education had already undermined the pure doctrine of parental rights, and the Poor Law Act of 1899 had given the Guardians power to remove children from unsuitable parents. Measures in the early twentieth century, many associated with the Liberal reforms after 1906, accentuated the trend. The provision of school meals for the needy in 1906; medical inspection in schools; the 1907 requirement for the notification of births within six weeks, so that health visitors could be sent round; the Children Act of 1908, making detailed provisions regarding child welfare, and the introduction of maternity insurance in the 1911 Health Insurance Act; all these betokened a new state intervention in the regulation of maternal duties, with particular regard to questions of health and hygiene (Davin, 1978, p. 13).

This new interventionism was not a full-scale state assumption of responsibility. It offered, rather, a generalised supervision and the provision of a safety net. The real everyday responsibility still belonged to the mother. Nor was it the product of a conscious adoption of a national policy for motherhood. Most of the policies adopted were *ad hoc* responses rather than part of a national strategy. Continuance of older policies, such as the Poor Law with its less eligibility clauses, meant that at no time before the Second World War did the state assume direct responsibility for the health of the population as a whole. Nevertheless, the new policies, whatever their source, did contribute to an improvement in health, particularly underlined by a reduction in infant mortality and the growth of child-welfare centres after the war.

But what also has to be measured is the balance between the improvement in health, and the subtle tightening of the ideology of motherhood that accompanied it. The improvement of medical care in childbirth went side by side with the loss of control by women over its management. The elevation of the professional expert involved the denial of the neighbourly amateur. Science extinguished the benefits of tradition. Above all, the triumph of medicine represented in practice the assumption by men of many of the traditional responsibilities exercised by women, which in turn could easily mean the imposition of professional middle-class values over working-class traditions.

These new ideological and political interventions are clearly reflected in the specification of female sexuality. At its most extreme, the implication was that sexual intercourse was a racial duty. Havelock Ellis believed that every healthy woman should at least once in her lifetime exercise the vocation of motherhood. Those, like Beatrice Webb, who rejected, for various reasons, individual motherhood, could easily accept the notion of 'racial motherhood', particularly given the expanding opportunities for women in health and social administration. For Mrs Webb, as for many others, the alternative to physical motherhood was celibacy and social activity, 'so that the special force of womanhood – motherly feeling – may be forced into public work'. The period indeed saw a significant reassessment of female sexuality, and the accentuated ideologies of motherhood were to be of prime significance in this redefinition. It is no accident that the influential work of Marie Stopes in the 1920s should be simultaneously a celebration of female sexuality, a paean to parenthood, and a rehearsal of eugenics' arguments. Her intellectual formation was precisely during this period.

Eugenics

If maternalism was one stream feeding population policy in the early decades of the century, eugenics was another which more coherently attempted to transform national policy and intellectual debate, though its degree of success is open to doubt. Many eugenicists were in fact maternalists as well. Havelock Ellis and C. W. Saleeby are two important examples. Other leading eugenicists, such as Karl Pearson, were more worried about the possible dysgenic effects of preserving too many infant lives, particularly the lives of the offspring of the unfit. Such views remained influential for decades, and as late as the end of the 1920s the *Eugenics Review* could comment that 'from every point of view, we can best afford to lose the lives of infants', for by their very death they 'offered a strong possible presumption of inherent worthlessness'.

It was never an undifferentiated approach. But there was a unifying belief behind eugenics, a conviction that it was possible to intervene directly in the processes of producing the population. It was, as its earliest leading proponent, Sir Francis Galton, put it, 'the study of agencies under social control that may improve or impair racial qualities of future generations either physically or mentally'. And as Havelock Ellis added, it was 'the effort to give practical effect to those agencies by conscious and deliberate action in favour of better breeding'. The perceived problem was how to induce in the population a new sense of 'sexual responsibility' so as to direct sexual selection into appropriate channels to serve racial progress.

Behind this was no mere dispassionate belief that 'science' could take over where individuals or 'stocks' had failed (though this was present). Science in the eyes of the leading advocates of eugenics was married with a messianic optimism and fervour. Galton called for a 'Jehad', a holy war, to be declared on the survival of ancient dysgenic customs, and urged that eugenics – 'a virile creed' – should become a 'religious tenet' of the future. Ellen Key, no less an enthusiast, believed that men and women would eventually devote the same religious fervour to propagating the race as Christians devoted to the salvation of souls. The National Council of Public Morals ('for Great and Greater Britain') adopted a similar note of millenarian hope in introducing its 'New Tracts for the Time': 'The supreme and dominant conception running through these Tracts is the Regeneration of the Race. They strike, not the leaden note of despair, but the ringing tones of a new and certain hope. The regenerated race is coming to birth; the larger and nobler civilisation is upon us.' The titles in the series underlined the complex concerns within eugenics, marrying public morality with the higher 'science'. C. W. Saleeby's *The Methods of Race Regeneration* and Havelock Ellis's *The Problem of Race-Regeneration* marched arm in arm with J. A. Thomson and P. Geddes's *Problems of Sex*, the Rev F. B. Meyer's *Religion and Race-Regeneration*, Mary Scharlieb's *Womanhood and Race Regeneration* and Sir Thomas Clouston's *Morals and Brains*. Social purity, sex reform, racial hygiene and scientific advance could all find a home with eugenics.

Eugenics was a particular social strategy which while drawing on pre-existing beliefs effectively transformed them into a new approach (see Searle, 1976; Rose, 1979; Mackenzie, 1976). Hereditarian beliefs were not absent from social reform before eugenics, particularly with the adoption (for example by the philosopher, Herbert Spencer) of Lamarckian beliefs in the inheritance of acquired characteristics. But such beliefs were used to argue for environmental reform; bad conditions, drunkenness and drug abuse, for instance, were held to have bad effects on the next generation. Social reform, Spencerians believed, could improve the next generation.

But behind eugenics, giving it practical impetus, was the conviction either that social reform had failed, or that it was totally insufficient to improve the race. What was needed were policies designed to produce a new sense of citizenship based on the planning of sexual behaviour. Ellis, always a sound weathervane, observed that the progressive movement was beginning to see that comparatively little could be affected by improving the conditions of life of adults. The need was to switch from concentration on the point of production to the source of the problem: 'the point of procreation', 'the regulation of sexual selection between stocks and individuals as the prime condition of life'.

This activism also distinguished eugenics from neo-Malthusianism, which still adhered to the strict economic arguments of its founder, and therefore believed that all that was necessary was to demonstrate the validity of Malthus's arguments, making recourse to social controls unnecessary (though in practice and quite logically Malthusians were to be more activist than early eugenicists in promoting contraceptive knowledge). Eugenicists like Karl Pearson felt that whatever its pretensions, Malthusians directed their effective propaganda at the middle classes (who after all had already limited their birthrates) and bypassed the poor.

Leading neo-Malthusians, on the other hand, claimed that the Malthusian League had always in fact been eugenically minded, in as much as its main goal was to limit the birth of the poor. But whatever the considerable overlap, both in policies and personnel (several leading neo-Malthusians joined the Eugenics Education Society), the theoretical origins of eugenics were quite different.

Eugenics in any recognisable form, can be said to have originated with Charles Darwin. His central concept, that Man is a product of natural selection, led in an 'age of science' quite logically to the hope that Man could participate consciously in the evolutionary process. Darwin's response to the developing eugenics ideas of his cousin, Sir Francis Galton, was in fact cautious. He stopped short of endorsing them in his *Descent of Man* (1871), where he discussed some of the ideas. In other ways, however, eugenic ideas could be said to be in the air. Many eugenicists later claimed to have come to their ideas before Galton publicised them [. . .]

Galton had been working on eugenicist lines since the 1860s (his *Hereditary Genius* was published in 1869) but it was not until the end of the century that eugenics as a programme of scientific breeding achieved a degree of plausibility: until, in fact, biologists had gained a sufficient grasp of heredity to be able to explain how parents could transmit their genetic qualities to their offspring. First of all there was the break with Lamarckian theory of the inheritance of acquired characteristics, a break associated with the theories of the German biologist August Weismann on the continuity of the germ plasm. Adumbrated in the 1880s, it rapidly became the starting point for further studies. The basis of Weismann's arguments was the distinction he drew between the germ cells which controlled reproduction, and the body or somatic cells. Germ cells were independent of somatic cells and could not be attracted by any modification caused by disease or injury. From this, eugenics drew the conclusion not only that acquired characteristics could not be inherited but that environmental reforms could only have a limited effect: only selective breeding could improve quality.

The second major theme was Galton's development of the concept that the laws of heredity were solely concerned with deviations expressed in statistical units. From this emerged the biometric approach, which sought to measure mathematically the genetic variations, and which was destined to be vastly influential in the growth of statistics and of intelligence testing. He was able to demonstrate, to his own satisfaction at least, a rigorous statistical relationship between heredity and degeneration. For Galton eugenics always meant applied biometrics, and under his closest supporter, Karl Pearson, this became a central element of eugenics (see Rose 1979).

The third major breakthrough was the rediscovery in the late 1890s of Mendelian genetics; though Galton never felt much enthusiasm for this aspect. A group of biologists led by William Bateson observed that certain physical traits in human beings observed the simple laws of gametic segregation which the Abbé Mendel had analysed in sweet peas in the 1860s. This was seen as a key to the unlocking of the genetic structure of human life, which in turn offered the possibility of applying genetic engineering to individual lives: the aim was not so much to change individuals as to change the balance of the stock. Eugenics was therefore conceived of as applied genetics.

Theoretically then, eugenics welded together a hereditarian theory of population, population statistics and population genetics to develop a distinctive theory of population regulation. This was to find various forms of institutional expression in the first decade of the century. A Eugenics Records Office was set up in 1907 which became the Eugenics Laboratory under Pearson's direction, and this was accompanied by a chair in eugenics, endowed by Galton's will, at University College London in 1911. Pearson was its first incumbent, and he was widely influential. The Eugenics Education Society was founded in 1907 to propagate eugenic views, and this published its own review. By 1914, it had a membership of 634, including a number of highly influential intellectuals, though Galton held aloof for a while, and Pearson remained hostile.

The eugenics movement thus institutionalised was to have a wide, but diffuse, influence. It was probably more important in setting the context for policy making than in influencing detailed policies themselves, but a wide spectrum of people, from far right to socialist left, worked until the 1930s and even beyond within a eugenics framework, or at least with a eugenics terminology. As befitted the prevailing social mood of its period, and as a response to the anxieties that gave it its resonance, clear imperialist and patriotic themes can be discerned. Galton himself spoke of the need to arrest a 'very serious and growing danger to our national efficiency' in the growth of the feeble-minded, while F. S. Schiller argued that 'the nation which first subjects itself to a rational eugenical discipline is bound to inherit the earth'. Pearson went further, accepting the full logic of social imperialist views (as early as the 1880s): 'If child-bearing women must be intellectually handicapped, then the price to be paid for race-predominance is the subjection of women'. But it would be wrong to see eugenics simply or straightforwardly as an apologia for imperialism. Many supporters of eugenics, like Havelock Ellis, were not imperialists, arguing that what they were after was not population quantity but quality. Nor were all eugenicists in agreement with Pearson's view that a nation could be 'kept up to a high pitch of external efficiency by contest, chiefly by way of war with inferior races, and with equal races by the struggle for trade routes and for the sources of raw material of food supply'. Many felt that war was a waste of 'germ plasm', and was fundamentally dysgenic.

Nor was the heart of eugenics its constant evocation of the language of race. There was undoubtedly an unthinking assumption that the white races were superior to the coloured, and many explicit racists, like Arnold White, could inveigh against 'Rule by foreign Jews' or the influx of 'diseased aliens'. But others, like Ellis, stressed that they were talking not about specific races, but about the human race.

More central than any of these factors were the class connotations of eugenics. There is a problem here. It is tempting to see eugenics straightforwardly as the ideology of a particular social stratum, which on the basis of the social background of most of its supporters would be the professional middle class, and particularly what could be termed its 'modern' sector. We then have to face the question of whether it is the *expression* of the social needs of that class: whether, in fact, eugenics was little more than a class-specific ideology, limited in its effectiveness by that very fact. There is undoubtedly an emphasis in eugenics on the social importance of the middle-class expert, that is the very type who gave eugenics allegiance, and from Galton's *Hereditary Genius* onwards there is a suspicion both of inherited wealth and of the titled nobility, as well of course as of the working class. But we cannot explain eugenics simply in these class reductionist terms, because though eugenics ideas may have had a class-specific origin, they were presented as a strategy for the whole ruling class to adopt, and support was gained from outside the professional classes, just as opposition to eugenics came from within it.

Nevertheless, the class origins or locations of most active eugenicists are clear and important, and they help to explain some of their assumptions. The bulk of the active members of the Eugenics Education Society were from the new professional middle class, that is from the intellectual, creative and welfare professions: they were university teachers and scientists, writers and doctors. 'Sociologists' were prominent (the inaugural meeting of the Sociological Society had been addressed by Galton in 1904), and the majority of biologists were also members of the Society. On the other hand, business men and the aristocracy were not prominent, no more than were the working class. The older professions, such as law and the churches, were also sparsely represented. Women, however, were highly represented, constituting more than half the total membership of the Society in 1913.

Given this balance, not surprisingly, the heroes of the eugenicists were generally professional people, and at various times the Eugenics Education Society clearly took up the interests of the professional middle class. They protested, for instance, at the burden of income tax on professional people, arguing that it discouraged parenthood, and they advocated rebates for each child. On the outbreak of war the Society helped in the setting up of a Professional Classes War Relief Council. Eugenicists were, however, rather uninterested in business: business acumen did not figure in their criteria of mental ability, and they often attacked the plutocracy as well as the hereditary aristocracy. They were also, by and large, and not unexpectedly, hostile to *laissez-faire* capitalism. Galton was generally highly conservative politically, but Karl Pearson had described himself as a socialist from the 1880s (though social imperialist might be a more appropriate description). The general assumption was that eugenics as such was a neutral, scientific doctrine, and the adoption by the state of eugenic policies was to the general good of the body politic. Nevertheless, it was clear that a eugenic society would, necessarily, be administered by eugenic experts, that is by people similar to the middle-class professionals who were putting forward eugenic views.

From their point of view, the task of state policy was to encourage methods to induce a sense of sexual responsibility in the population at large. Theoretically, there were two ways to do this: by encouraging the best to breed, or by discouraging the worst. But in practice, social policy had to be directed at the latter – who, as we have seen, were inevitably seen in class terms.

Eugenics not surprisingly made a strong appeal to many Fabian socialists, many of whom came from a similar social background and who shared the same distrust of the masses and faith in professional administrators as many leading eugenicists. H. G. Wells had a burst of enthusiasm on hearing Galton and advocated the 'sterilisation of failures'. Sidney Webb, more soberly, as was his *métier*, warned that unless the decline of the birthrate was averted the nation would fall to the Irish and the Jews. What Fabians and eugenicists shared then, and what is characteristic of their appeal, is their belief in planning and control of population.

It was inevitable that the Fabians would extend their beliefs in social regulation to fertility: reproduction was obviously too important to be left to individuals, and Sidney Webb believed it could not safely be left to the residuum to regulate their lives with Malthusian prudence. In 1907 a Fabian Tract on *The Decline of the Birth Rate* (the product of a sub-committee set up in 1905) had warned of the dangers of the differential birthrate, where the thrifty limited their families, and the residuum did not. Webb had argued that the state should adopt social policies, which would induce the right sort of people to assume parenthood. Eugenics might be useful in eliminating the biologically feeble, but only social policies could enable the socially disadvantaged to improve their lot. So there was an important difference between the Fabian approach and the eugenic, whatever the class, and rhetorical similarities. Webb advocated policies–such as the endowment of motherhood–which eugenicists thought were dysgenic, while the main thrust of the Fabian approach was to differentiate between the thrifty and the residuum in order to encourage the *social* advance of the former. George Bernard Shaw's call, in his inimitable way, for the 'elimination of the mere voluptuary from the evolutionary process', and his advocacy of a State Department of Evolution to pay women for their child-rearing services, and if necessary to regulate a 'joint stock human stud farm', had social efficiency as their purport. Pure eugenicists on the other hand were uninterested, as we have seen, in such fripperies or in reform. Their aim was to purify the stream of life at the source, to eliminate not so much the social causes of evil, but the core biological defects. Hence the twin poles of their arguments, 'positive' and 'negative' eugenics, the centre of their efforts to control the processes of procreation.

Positive eugenics stressed the need to breed a better race, a race of Shakespeares and Darwins. Beatrice Webb, though feeling she and Sidney could contribute little to the process themselves, believed 'the breeding of the right sort of man' to be the most important of all questions. Few eugenicists actually went so far as to recommend breeding experiments, however.

Galton feared that in man's present state of ignorance, attempts to arrange eugenic marriages would do more harm than good. There was a realisation that human life was somewhat different from the stock yards, despite the verbal flourishes. Moreover, some eugenicists realised that if it became possible to breed supermen, it might also become possible to breed mutants.

There was the further problem of selecting the criteria which were to be developed [. . .] But the core question was who was to decide which groups to control, and how? Havelock Ellis felt that the state had no more right to ravish a woman than a man, but Galton's faith that each group would regulate their own fertility policies was scarcely practical. So as C. W. Saleeby argued, 'the *positive* methods of regeneration, at any rate under anything like present social conditions, will be mainly educative'. He rejected therefore compulsory mating, 'and anything else that involves the destruction of marriage'. But this acceptance of conventional morality meant that in the end he was left with little besides education for parenthood, and the encouragement of eugenic marriages [. . .]

The problem that eugenicists faced was that many efforts to encourage better breeding, such as subsidies for motherhood, might actually encourage the unfit to breed even more. Similarly, proposals for the penalisation of bachelors might actually encourage undesirable single people to enter dysgenic relationships. Consequently, the most favoured approach was to alter the tax system in favour of married couples with dependent children. The beauty of this was that as only the middle class generally paid substantial income tax, it would not needlessly encourage the unfit. The Liberal Government's introduction in 1909 of an allowance of £10 to income-tax payers for every child below 16 was heralded as a major triumph for eugenic principles.

Positive eugenics, however, offered a double problem: it was both technically difficult to achieve, and it did not tackle the core problem: the multiplication of undesirables. Hence the greater emphasis, particularly from the early 1920s, on negative eugenics, the elimination of the unfit. Galton had foreshadowed this possibility as early as his 1906 Huxley lectures. In Britain few actually advocated their actual physical destruction [. . .]

The other drastic remedy was compulsory sterilisation of the unfit, advocated in particular by Dr Robert Reid Rentoul of Liverpool. Few were prepared to support him, though many were prepared to back voluntary sterilisation, especially of those suffering from hereditary defects. It would, it was pointed out, be cheaper than custodial care.

The prohibition of marriage or its limitation to those with medical certificates, was another possibility floated. But this, it was pointed out, would not prevent degenerates from coupling. Segregation, therefore, 'the permanent care under humane medical supervision' of defectives, seemed a possibility.

But as with positive eugenics, so with negative: education in eugenic principles seemed the only practical way forward. Out of this was to come the beginnings of genetic counselling. But another logical step was the advocacy of deliberate birth control. Many of the leading supporters of birth control in the 1920s and 1930s, like Stopes, had strong eugenic backgrounds. But many felt contraception was dysgenic, as it was the middle class who generally controlled their fertility, and *that* was the major problem. Others felt that by so directly entering the sexual debate, rather than maintaining a scientific stance, the whole moral tone of eugenics was threatened. Still others, however, like Ellis and the socialist feminist F. W. Stella Browne, were quite prepared to use eugenic arguments to garner support for birth control, and their influence passes through into later debates.

The Influence of Eugenics

. . . What eugenics fundamentally wanted was the adoption of a national policy for the population which would regulate sexual behaviour in the interests of the race. But Britain never during this period adopted anything that could be termed a formal population policy. This does not mean of course that informal population policies did not exist. A host of government actions, from its taxation and housing policies to its attitudes to birth control, had vital effects on decision making. But these were *ad hoc* policies rather than the result of strategic planning. In these, eugenic notions often played a significant, but by no means decisive, part. It is as a current of thought, colouring a variety of debates, that the real influence of eugenics has to be sought.

References

DAVIN, A. (1978) 'Imperialism and motherhood', *History Workshop*, No. 5, Spring.

MacKENZIE, D. (1976) 'Eugenics in Britain', *Social Studies of Science*, No. 6.

ROSE, N. (1979) 'The Psychological Complex: Mental Measurement and Social Administration', *Ideology and Consciousness*, No. 5, Spring.

SEARLE, G. R. (1976) *Eugenics and Politics in Britain 1900–1914*, Leyden, Noordhof International.

STEDMAN JONES, G. (1971) *Outcast London*, Oxford, Clarenden Press.

12 Sexuality: Regulation and Contestation

Frank Mort

From Gay Liberation Collective *Homosexuality Power and Politics*, 1980. Reproduced by permission of the publishers, Allison and Busby.

[The report of the Wolfenden Committee on Homosexual Offences and Prostitution, published in 1957], with its reformist implications and its liberalism, remains a forgotten text for the gay movement of the 1970s. Yet if it is possible to locate a particular moment which marks a radical shift in the regulation of sexuality in general, and homosexuality in particular, we should turn to the period of the late 1950s and to the debate around the subsequent Sexual Offences Act of 1967. We should be aware that politically we continue to occupy a space which is very much formed in the aftermath of Wolfenden. In terms both of the lived relations within the gay community, and in the formation of the identities of gay men, we are very heavily structured by the dual strategies of regulation and tolerance which govern homosexuality in the Wolfenden Report.

Legally, the recommendations of the Wolfenden Report still define the current position of gay men. The changes enacted by the 1967 Sexual Offences Act, as a result of ten years of parliamentary struggle, decriminalised sexual activity between adult male homosexuals in England and Wales. But the real significance of that legislation lies in the precise *way* in which it changed the law, and more widely, the implications this has had for the political strategies developed by the gay movement, and for the ways in which gayness is constructed as a category. The legislation introduces a new development in the regulation of sexuality and morality – it marks a shift in the exercise of the power to legally punish or not to punish, to regulate by law or to leave to the self-regulation of individuals. For Wolfenden the law's function in the field of sexuality is defined as essentially public: 'to preserve public order and decency, to protect the citizen from what is offensive and injurious, and to provide safeguards against the exploitation and corruption of others'. But the Report is also explicit that 'it is not the function of the law to interfere in the private lives of citizens, or to seek to enforce any particular pattern of behaviour'. And later it states categorically: 'unless a deliberate attempt is to be made by society acting through the agency of the law, to equate the sphere of crime with that of sin, there must remain a realm of private morality and immorality which is not the law's business'. In making this distinction, the Report and the subsequent legislation introduce a new relation between what is legally defined as public, and what is private and to be left to individual self-regulation (though, as we shall see, still subject to non-legal forms of control). It is a relation which has had real effects on defining the space in which we are able to operate – politically, culturally and sexually.

The 1967 legislation on homosexuality can be defined as permissive inasmuch as it constructs an area of private, individual consent, while at the same time often strengthening the controls on the public appearance of 'irregular' sexuality. In the introduction of this new set of legal principles Wolfenden should be seen in the context of the subsequent 'permissive reforms' of the late 1950s and 1960s, which focus around a concern with the family, sexuality, morality and procreation. These include the Obscene Publications Act (1964), the Abortion Act (1967), legislation on divorce (1969), on theatre censorship (1968) and on the law governing Sunday entertainments (1968). Also, in the degree of attention given to a form of non-procreative sexuality, and in the intimacy of its enquiry, Wolfenden marks an expansion of concern on the part of the law in relation to questions of sexuality and morality. The 1885 Act which prohibited all homosexual activity between males, was a three-line amendment. In fact, homosexuality and homosexuals are isolated as the main focus for a sustained set of legal, medical, psychological and religious debates in the 1950s and 1960s, as well as being constructed as the source of repeated moral panics over sexuality [. . .]

Legislation and Norms

Given the central place occupied by legal debates it is not surprising that the law becomes a privileged terrain on which struggles around sexuality and morality take place. The early homosexual groups were, for good reason, transfixed by the law, which was identified as the principal source of the regulation of sexuality, and the oppression of particular sexualities. The permissive legislation provides certain of the political and cultural conditions possible for the re-emergence of feminism and sexual politics in the late 1960s and 1970s. Often the political strategies and tactics developed involved attempts to push the legal boundaries of the legislation beyond its legally defined parameters. Feminist struggles around legislation on abortion, and over legal definitions of female sexuality and dependence, together with the various and continuing campaigns for lowering the age of consent for gay people – all these political developments take as their point of departure and contestation the ground gained by these liberal reforms. And in the struggles over redefinitions, legal liberalism and tolerance come to be labelled as merely partial, and as ultimately oppressive. In fact, some of the sharpest political engagements in struggles over sexuality have involved pushing the contradictory tendencies implicit in much of the legislation to their extremes.

More generally, we should be aware that throughout the nineteenth and twentieth centuries the rule of law has occupied a central place in the construction and regulation of sexual and moral definitions – as much as it has in the sphere of capital-labour relations. Fresh legislation in the field of sexuality (such as the recent Bill on child pornography) or significant legal reversals (for example the *Gay News* Trial of 1977) act as a sensitive register of the moral climate. The law occupies a quite particular relation to debates and struggles around sexuality, in that if a specific form of sexual practice is seen to break the law it crystallises and concretises what have previously been constructed as *moral* debates [. . .]

But if the law remains a central factor in the regulation of sexuality – with a particular history and importance for homosexuality – we should not be 'trans-fixed' by its operation. A theory and a politics which bases its analysis too centrally on the forms of legal prohibition and censorship can easily remain unaware of the complexity of the strategies of regulation which address sexuality in its modern form. A juridically based understanding of the operation of power works with a largely negative conception of the power-sexuality couplet, which also often relies on assumptions of an innate or essential sexuality. That is to say, in such a model power relations are seen to exclude, block or refuse a basic and underlying sexuality. Moreover, the regulation of sexuality is assumed to be uniform in its operation throughout all apparatuses, institutions and social and cultural practices: from the patriarch in the family to the state apparatuses power is exercised through a coherent strategy.

In contradistinction to that model we would maintain that power, or sets of power relations addressing sexuality, operate through a multiplicity of practices and apparatuses (for example: medicine, psychology, sociology, education), each of which is distinguished by its specific structures of regulation, which are non-reducible to a uniform or single strategy. Also, we should be aware that power operates 'positively' – it does not merely repress or prohibit, but is actively engaged in the construction of particular forms of sexuality which will not necessarily remain constant *across* a set of social practices (for example, the construction of homosexuality in the media may well be very different from its construction in law). It is an understanding which draws much from the work of the French theorist Michel Foucault – particularly his recent work on *The History of Sexuality* (1979).

Foucault's theory of discursive practices and their power to regulate insists on the specificity of particular institutional sites and social and cultural practices in the forms of knowledge-power relations which are integral to them, the types of subjects which they construct and the strategies of resistance which are possible. Furthermore, it is a conception which differs not only from a notion of power as merely repressive, but also from current Marxist understandings of ideology. In his insistence that power relations work not only ideationally (i.e. on consciousness or mental processes) but also that they are effective in shaping and regulating the physical space of the body with its attendant sensations and pleasures, Foucault draws our attention to the sophisticated and multifaceted dimensions of regulative techniques in what he terms a 'disciplinary society'. Within that theorisation, the law is seen to operate not necessarily as the single or central form of regulation, but rather as a 'norm' – Foucault maintains that the legal apparatuses are increasingly incorporated into the general expansion of regulative structures and practices, which form a whole 'microphysics of power'.

How far do Foucault's general statements on the construction of sexuality help us to form a more complex picture of the regulation of homosexuality in the contemporary period? Moreover, can such an analysis provide us with a more adequate understanding of the way in which we, as gay people, have been constructed – personally, sexually and culturally – by the structures of regulation which address us? Finally, does Foucault's theory enable us to review our political strategies in a different light, and to construct new forms of political intervention in the overall struggle to transform dominant sexual meanings and definitions? It is to that set of questions that we now turn.

Regulating the Homosexual Subject

As we have seen, the legal changes introduced in the 1967 Act construct a new type of homosexual subject, understood as operating in the private sphere; a subject who in matters of sexuality and morality is defined as consenting, privatised and person-focused. In effect, what the reformed version of the law does is to continue to reproduce the structures through which the male gay subculture had developed over the previous hundred years, while now decriminalising it. One can speculate here that the structuring of the law across this public/private divide may have had much to do with the particular ways in which the gay subculture, and latterly the commercial gay scene, has developed from the late nineteenth century onwards. Clearly the divorce of physical sexual pleasure from marriage and procreation, together with the high degree of economic and personal freedom (though only really for middle-class men) has done much to determine the development of gay culture in the direction of leisure, pleasure and consumption. But legal structures have also been influential in that development; the legal confinement of gay people to a privatised space may have done much to structure the person-focused, pleasure-seeking and often apolitical nature of our present commercial culture.

It is that type of regulation through confinement which the gay movement, with its stress on the public process of coming out, has sought to contest. But, and I think it is here that the strategies we have developed have been caught within the historical and political structures and contradictions which define homosexuality, resistances are never external to the power relations they seek to challenge. They take as their necessary point of departure and contestation the specific structures and definitions of a particular historical moment. To accept that is to acknowledge the terms on which realistic political strategies can be developed. The specific problem is that political strategies which are merely based on an affirmation of gayness can serve to reproduce in a curious way the constructed definitions of homosexuality which it was Wolfenden's implicit aim to reinforce.

Generally, in the development of a theory and a politics of homosexuality, we should be attentive to a historical perspective. We should be aware that the homosexual subject is a socially and culturally constructed category, emerging at a particular historical moment in the late nineteenth century, and that emergence is the product of shifts and transformations in various discourses (medicine, psychology, sexology), apparatuses and institutions (the courts, the Church, social work and so on) and social and cultural practices (for example, popular culture and common sense meanings). Also, implicit in the construction of the new homosexual identity is the operation of discrete principles of regulation – as is also partly the case with the construction of the categories of 'mother' and 'child' in the same period. For Foucault, the processes of objectification and identification form one of the principal mechanisms for the exercise of power relations within a particular discourse or practice. In the general shift away from notions of criminality and deviance which were constructed around the *act* of transgression, the deviant subject (madman, sexual pervert and so on) comes to be awarded a particular identity, with a specific biography and set of instincts, and, in the case of the homosexual, with a differentiated anatomy and physiology.

The proposals contained in the Wolfenden Report operate with that type of strategy. If the Report advocates the decriminalisation of certain homosexual practices in the private sphere, it does not envisage the total abandonment of strategies of regulation. Power is no longer to be exercised through the direct operation of the law but rather through the mobilisation of a variety of non-legal practices. Henceforward, medicine, 'therapy', psychology, and forms of applied sociology are all envisaged as forming new principles of regulation. The dominant and institutionalised forms of those disciplines have indeed served to confirm the construction of homosexuality through the definitions of social deviancy, sickness or maladjustment. For example, the homosexual patient in orthodox medicine is only allowed to speak from the position of sickness or mental illness. Moreover, in the various 'academic' and popular debates which proliferated after Wolfenden most of the arguments rest on an assumed and radical difference between heterosexuality and homosexuality. Much of the sexology, psychology and sociology of the 1960s and 1970s, with its stress on the personal history and aetiology of the sexual deviant, insists that the difference between the homosexual and the heterosexual goes much deeper than the choice of object gratification, and that it involves differences in the total personality. Almost all the discourses hierarchise and distribute the various categories of sexual deviance around the norm of marriage, the family and procreation, which provide the particular 'régime of truth' for the classification of 'other' sexual and moral practices. Wolfenden characteristically defines homosexuality as being 'reprehensible from the point of view of harm to the family', and questions whether buggery should not be retained as a separate offence in that 'it is particularly objectionable because it involves coitus and thus simulates more nearly than any other homosexual act the normal act of sexual intercourse'. A parallel theme in the classification of deviant sexualities has been the linking of homosexuality with ideologies of nationalism and imperialism. The relation between definitions of sexual perversity and ideologies of national imperial decline has an extensive history, dating back in Britain at least as far as the 1880s and 1890s, with the panic over national efficiency and degeneracy, class-specific underpopulation, and debates over the proposed sterilisation with a renewed power to classify non-procreative sexualities.

Sexual Politics

That general historical awareness of the social and cultural construction of homosexuality should make us cautious of developing a politics and a culture on the basis of any celebratory notion of an essential gayness. As gay people we are placed in a privileged, though often painful, position in this respect. An awareness of the historical construction of our own identity and emergence must lead us to insist that sexual meanings are neither biologically nor socially fixed, but are involved in a continual process of construction and re-formation – both over long historical periods, and at the level of one's own individual constituted identity. Obviously it is crucially important for gay people to organise politically to defend their own sexuality and culture; and in moments of political crisis it may be as much as we can do to achieve that defence. Moreover, strategies which emphasise coming out and the general public manifestation of one's sexuality are important in the struggle to challenge and shift definitions within the dominant heterosexual culture [. . .] But, and the qualification is a large one, we should also attempt to maintain a political perspective of a longer duration which involves a recognition that 'freedom' for gay people cannot come solely from a greater assertion of gay rights, but must come from far wider social and cultural shifts involving the transformation of *all* sexual meanings and definitions. In the present conjuncture we can only begin to achieve this by organising politically around the historically given sexual categories and meanings. But we should be aware that our ultimate aim is the disintegration of those categories rather than their reinforcement.

The contemporary gay movement emerged out of the political and cultural climate of the late 1960s as a specific and autonomous form of struggle. In Britain, as in other metropolitan countries, its forms of appearance owed much to the general cultural and moral crisis of the period, where revolt was directed as much at the civil structures of society as at the economic point of production. A renewed emphasis on the effectiveness of ideology, and the necessity of exposing and contesting its operation through forms of cultural and ideological struggle, made it possible to develop new types of analysis and new strategies of political intervention. In the forms of its political engagement the gay movement and the women's movement have differed profoundly from existing political structures. Their origins and early strategies were often spontaneist and counter-cultural, which in retrospect we can see were developed out of the very structures of oppression which confined women and gay people.

The dialogue which has subsequently been constructed in the 1970s between sexual politics and the established forms of socialist organisation has formed one of the major political developments in the period. Theoretically, it has encouraged certain tendencies within the gay movement and the women's movement to develop a form of analysis premised on examining the relationship between the structures of sexuality and capitalist economic, political and ideological organisation. Socialist feminism attempts to provide a theory (and a politics) of the construction and regulation of sexuality, by developing Marxist categories in areas which have hitherto remained undertheorised or largely ignored. As has often been indicated, this new departure has been made possible by a number of related influences: the general critique and move out of economism in the post-1968 period, together with an understanding of the 'relative autonomy' of the ideological or cultural level which is seen to possess its own specificity, a revival of interest in work on and struggles around the state (with an emphasis, via Althusser and Gramsci, on the crucial ideological and cultural work performed by the state apparatuses) and more generally, an acknowledgement (often through the insistence of feminism) that certain forms of struggle are in no way reducible to the basic class contradiction at the level of the mode of production.

Yet this dialogue between Marxism and feminism over sexuality has provided as many new questions as answers. Certainly, it has fruitfully challenged Marxism as a coherent and defined body of knowledge. But we should be aware that these questions are not *merely* academic and theoretical; they relate crucially to the types of political intervention that we attempt to make as gay people. Questions which focus on the relation between the structures of sexuality and capitalist organisation, or on the forms and sources of power which regulate sexuality, will influence the type of political questions we formulate in developing a politics around sexuality – together with the way we envisage our own struggles relating to a more general conception of socialist politics.

Reproduction/Construction

Theoretically, the development of a theory of sexuality in relation to Marx's analysis of the history of capital accumulation has been made possible by the use of the concept of *reproduction*. The task of reproducing the work-force for capital, both biologically and through the forms of domestic labour historically performed by women, was seen as the point of departure for an understanding of the subordinate economic, legal and ideological position of women, and the construction of definitive forms of sexuality across a rigid male/female gender division. In certain versions of this type of analysis, capital is seen to 'need' or 'require' a specific form of the family and sexual organisation to secure the reproduction of labour power, the maintenance of social and political stability and the preservation of the work ethic. Those needs and requirements are met, it is argued, largely through the strategies of state intervention, whereby the state, working as 'the ideal social capitalist' attempts to preserve the reproductive conditions necessary for the continuation of capital accumulation. The construction of the welfare state, with its strategies of intervention directed at the family, together with the body of legislation developed to legally regulate sexual practices are both analysed on the basis of a theory of reproduction. Moreover, given the insistence that the forms of state intervention must be seen to operate not only legally but also ideologically, the state is viewed as instrumental in the reproduction of the dominant sexual ideologies. These ideologies, it is maintained, serve to reinforce women's subordinate position in the reproductive sphere, both as mothers and domestic labourers, and help to channel sexuality into its heterosexual procreative norm, and thus to regulate other forms of sexuality as deviant or perverse. Sexual ideologies are, therefore, also understood in a basically functional or reproductive way; they are seen to act as 'props' or supports for the material sexual divisions within production and reproduction. The construction of childhood, motherhood, domesticity and the structures of heterosexual morality are seen to exist in a more or less direct articulation with the needs and requirements of industrial capitalism.

More generally, such accounts of sexuality and its regulation insist that it is the relation *between* the structures of sexuality and capitalist organisation which should be examined, and which should ultimately form the basis for a politics of sexuality. From that type of analysis certain basic conclusions tend to be drawn. Namely, that the various practices and institutions which legally and/or ideologically contribute to the regulation of sexuality both 'inside' and 'outside' the state (the law, welfarism, medical practice, and so on) are unified in an overall strategy which exists in a definite relation to the forms of state intervention in the capital-labour contradiction. Hence *patriarchal relations*, the collective term used to describe the historically specific forms of sexual oppression, are seen to exist in articulation with the history of capitalist relations.

Two central and related problems are posed by this type of analysis. The first of these is the assumption, as a precondition for theoretical and political work, that the structures of sexuality and capitalist organisation necessarily exist in some articulation. The second concerns the identification of a unified and overall strategy which functions to regulate sexuality in an identifiably coherent way across a whole range of practices and institutions. Clearly, capitalist organisation in historically specific periods does have particular 'conditions of existence' which will be influential in determining the construction and regulation of sexuality and morality – though we should be aware that there is no guarantee that those conditions will be met. Furthermore, it should be stressed that sexual oppression predates capitalist development, and exists in cultures which are not capitalist in their organisation.

But ultimately the question is a broader one, and concerns the focus of our political and theoretical attention. An analysis of sexuality which takes the history of capitalist organisation as its central point of reference will necessarily attempt to integrate the structures of sexuality into that history, whereas an analysis which begins from an attempt to understand historically the *construction of sexuality* may produce a quite different set of conclusions. Homosexuality presents very much a 'test case' in this respect. It is fundamentally misguided to explain the construction and regulation of homosexuality solely in terms of the demands and requirements of capitalist organisation. More generally, we should be aware of the dangers of applying a theory, originally developed to understand the nature of *class* society, to explain the structures of sexuality.

Tentatively at this stage, we can say that the types of sexual meanings and the power relations which are produced in a particular historical moment will be dependent on the balance of relations between the various discourses, practices and apparatuses addressing sexuality, together with the forms of resistance to those structures. However, and the qualification is important, our analysis will be simplified if we impose a model derived from classical Marxism, with the determination 'in the last instance' being effected by the economic mode of production. In a similar way, the sets of power relations which are seen to oppress gay people should be seen as *specific* to particular practices (for example, the law, medicine and psychoanalysis). That is to say, the specific structures of oppression implicit in these practices should not be attributed to an external cause, which can be seen to inform or 'shine through' each and every social and cultural institution. Too often, accounts of the regulation of sexuality are premised on an understanding that the power relations contained within a particular institution are derived from a primary or first cause. The specific structures of power are attributed to 'capital', 'capitalists', 'men', or 'heterosexuals' – individuals who are seen to have defined interests, and whose position the structures of power are thought to maintain. Politically, we should of course stress that the majority of cultural practices and institutions continue to define gay people in a subordinate relation to the structures of heterosexuality, but we should be cautious in deriving those structures from the single conspiratorial interests of capitalists or heterosexuals. Everything depends on the complex way in which particular practices and institutions are linked historically.

Strategies

Politically, in what ways does the theoretical analysis have implications for the strategies we attempt to develop in the moral climate of the early 1980s and beyond? We have already focused on the law as a principal mechanism in the construction and regulation of sexuality, and stressed the importance of mobilising struggles in that area. The rule of law is central to the exercise of state power, and we should be continually alert to attempts to shift sexual and moral definitions through the use of legal strategies. Consequently the law must remain a central arena for struggle and contestation over sexuality. Furthermore, unless we hold to a simple anti-statism or libertarianism, we must be aware that the effort to shift legal definitions around sexuality involves an engagement with the law, on the terrain of the law. We need to campaign to support legislation which attempts to shift the law in a progressive direction; and to make alliances with those radical liberal and social democratic tendencies which have, in the past, helped to achieve some measure of sexual law reform.

But the potential for progressive legislation being carried through the parliamentary machinery is not merely dependent on the composition of the legal profession, or the police, nor for that matter does it depend solely on the balance of forces within the arena of parliamentary politics. It depends ultimately on the overall state of the particular historical moment, or *conjuncture* – and for us, as gay people, on the particular position occupied by morality within that conjuncture. We need to devote much more of our attention to identifying precisely and complexly the moral climate or consensus of the period of the early 1980s. The problem *is* a complex one, and again can easily invite simple or reduced theoretical-political analyses.

First, as an overall point of insistence, we should continue to stress the specificity of sexual and moral definitions and their related struggles. They possess their own history, which is not reducible to other social, cultural or economic developments, and they do not exist in any clear relation to other progressive political movements. A common response to the problem is to directly link political and economic shifts with moral and sexual transformations. An economic recession, so it is argued, is not only 'expressed' by a political shift to the right, but also by a cultural regression and a moral hardening of the arteries [. . .]

But the problem is that moral and sexual emphases do not, as yet, occupy a central place in the policies and strategies of the new Thatcherist right [. . .] What we should be aware of is the set of unsung moral and sexual assumptions which form the ground on which the more prominent political issues are articulated and debated. We are dealing here with the identification of a climate or atmosphere, rather than any clearly definable moral shift rightwards. The case is most clearly illustrated in examining the Labour Party and its programme for social democratic reform, from the 1960s onwards. Progressive statements and legislation on sexuality and morality enacted during Roy Jenkins's period as Home Secretary were often articulated to a wider set of concerns over leisure, welfare, and the general cultural climate of Britain. But they were subtly downplayed in the type of consensus that Wilson attempted to construct – a consensus which increasingly incorporated the older structures of a 'moral methodism' (both in its style and mode of address) with its general stress on technological and scientific revolution. Callaghan consolidated that repertoire, with subjects always implicitly addressed through the structures of the family and family life.

Those are the terms on which sexual and moral questions are raised and debated within the political arena, and within the apparatuses of the state. Such an analysis does not rule out the possibility of a period of increasing moral and sexual reaction, but it does stress that such a movement, coming from within the sphere of 'orthodox politics', would mark a radically new type of political intervention, which has only a limited set of precedents. One would suspect that an actively endorsed legal and political shift to the right on sexual and moral questions might run into conflict with certain of the unvoiced liberal moralities of the social democratic repertoire.

Where, of course, sexual and moral debates are massively carried, and where both progressive and regressive political shifts are often first noted, is in the complex web of regulatory disciplines, practices and institutions (to which Foucault among others has drawn our attention), together with the popular discourse of common-sense assumptions, meanings and definitions. The various apparatuses and practices (education, welfare, probation, social work, medicine, psychology, criminology, genetics and so on) stand in varying relations to the centrality of state power – some forming an integral part of the state apparatuses, others existing in a more mediated relation. What is clear is that it is in the day to day operation of these practices – in their practical rituals – that particular sexual and moral definitions are constructed and enforced, and local political struggles are fought out [. . .]

PART IV

Schooling: Norms and Differences

13 Beacons of the Future: Schooling, Subjection and Subjectification

James Donald

I Introduction

In Arthur Conan Doyle's 'The Naval Treaty', first published in the *Strand* magazine in 1893, Sherlock Holmes and Dr Watson are on a train heading back to London from a case in the home counties.

> ... Holmes was sunk in profound thought and hardly opened his mouth until we had passed Clapham Junction.
>   'It's a very cheery thing to come into London by any of these lines which run high and allow you to look down upon the houses like this.'
>   I thought he was joking, for the view was sordid enough, but he soon explained himself.
>   'Look at those big, isolated clumps of buildings arising up above the slates, like brick islands in a lead-coloured sea.'
>   'The board-schools.'
>   'Light-houses, my boy! Beacons of the future! Capsules with hundreds of little seeds in each, out of which will spring the wiser, better England of the future. I suppose that man Phelps does not drink?'

What were these board schools that so captured the imagination of the usually cynical detective? They had been established only a couple of decades earlier, in 1870, by the Elementary Education Act introduced by W. E. Forster during Gladstone's first Liberal administration. Their express purpose was to extend education for working-class children by 'filling in the gaps' in the schooling already provided by a number of religious societies. They were administered by locally elected school boards which had, for the first time, the power to levy a rate for education. Attendance did not finally become compulsory until 1880. Nor were the schools free; it was only in 1891 that boards were given the discretion to do away with the 'school pence'. In short, the board schools introduced universal, state-funded, compulsory elementary education to England.

For Holmes, though, they seem to represent something more significant. Look at the imagery. The schools are more than mere 'clumps of buildings'. They are 'brick islands', recognizable and reassuring landmarks breaking up potentially dangerous enclaves as they rise out of the 'lead-coloured sea' of working-class London. Nor is it just physically that they open out these apparently impenetrable areas. As 'light-houses' they bring moral illumination into the proletarian murk. As 'beacons of the future', they are mechanisms of progress. As 'capsules with hundreds of seeds in each', they are catalysts of a political and ethical evolution towards 'the wiser, better England of the future'.

What intrigues me is that these utopian images should present themselves to Conan Doyle in 1893 as no more than common sense. What had been happening in debates about education and in the provision of schooling over previous decades which made it possible for such imagery to appear, apparently as a matter of course, in this widely read piece of fiction?

I pose the question in that somewhat roundabout way to underline the point that my concerns here are as much methodological and theoretical as they are historical. I am not just trying to answer the deceptively innocent question, what happened? Indeed, one of my premises is that history is not a coherent and agreed set of facts or data against which social scientists can measure their interpretive models. Histories are always written from particular theoretical perspectives, using different concepts and methodologies which highlight certain features of the narrative and obscure others. My aim here is to consider how, or whether, concepts like 'ideology', 'discourse', 'power' and 'subjectivity' might help us to write a history of popular schooling in nineteenth-century England and, at the same time, make sense of the massive presence of education in our contemporary culture. To be specific, I want to see how illuminating it is to analyse that history using a number of ideas deriving from Michel Foucault's work. That does not mean I would accept all of them uncritically. Indeed, in the implicit debate between Foucault and Althusser outlined in the introduction to this volume (pp. xi–xviii), it seems to me right to hold onto something like Althusser's conception of interpellation and also his more Gramscian insistence on the inscription of class relations in state apparatuses. These concepts have already been taken up productively in sociological analyses of education. Sometimes, though, a partial appropriation of the ISAs essay concentrating only on a simplification of the argument about reproduction, has also led to a view of education as a cog within a rather functionalist model of state and society. It is in countering this tendency, and in attending to the detailed texture of educational activity and change, that a critical deployment of Foucault's approach seems to me potentially useful. I shall try to demonstrate this by concentrating on three overlapping topics.

First, we might study *educational ideologies* as such – particular statements in which competing sets of beliefs, perceptions, propositions, values, grievances and aspirations are articulated around the term 'education'. It was during the nineteenth century, I would argue, that 'education' took on this ideological currency within the sphere of political debate. As evidence, consider the sheer range and diversity of educational programmes produced – from the Anglican Dr Bell's 'Madras system' for the efficient indoctrination of religious and patriotic beliefs among the poor in the first decades of the century to the utopian schooling provided by the socialist Robert Owen in his experimental community at New

Lanark; from the attempts to create a rational, secular society by Chartist autodidacts like William Lovett to the elitist social engineering of public school advocates like Dr Arnold; from the anti-reformist Robert Lowe's reluctant acknowledgement that the extension of the franchise in the 1860s meant that 'it will be absolutely necessary to compel our future masters to learn their letters', to the Fabian Sidney Webb's meritocratic vision at the turn of the twentieth century of an educational ladder enabling clever children to escape from the working class.

This profusion of educational argument was, no doubt, related to the expansion of popular education, initially through local religious or philanthropic initiatives and eventually, as in the board schools, through provision by the state. This, in turn, was tied up with a number of other changes in the division of labour and the labour process (especially those which released children from the workforce), in family legislation and welfare provision, in housing and urban development and so forth. *How* all these things were connected is by no means self-evident, though. Taken along with the other changes, the various educational proposals can be read as symptomatic of new strategies for social regulation. But we should be careful to treat them as what they are – which is less descriptions of existing institutions than prescriptive statements about *why* schooling should be provided and *how* it should be organized.

What we are dealing with, in short, is an example of the political struggles within and about language analysed by Volosinov and Gramsci, and summarized by Hall (this volume, pp.42–45). To use Volosinov's distinction, these nineteenth-century educational ideologies did not reflect the existing reality. They refracted that reality through a range of conflicting perspectives, values and strategies. Or, to take a step further along the logic of the 'reality effect' (this volume, pp.41–2), they constituted attempts to impose particular meanings on reality by defining the purposes, practices and nature of education. Thus the very word 'education' became an arena of struggle and contestation.

From this point of view, it is possible to study the systematic relationships between the terms, categories and propositions within the ideologies; to extrapolate the shifting discursive field defined by their dialogue; and so to chart the fluctuating battle of philanthropic, political and professional ideas within which the school in a recognisable modern form came into being.

What makes it possible to construct this field retrospectively is the common usage of that term 'education' to denote an institutional process capable of producing specifiable social and political outcomes. On what those outcomes could and should be, the various participants in the dialogue differed radically. And in reality, of course, schooling achieved none of them; it never could. Indeed, to underline this simple but important point, it is the *failure* of education to be functional for any one strategy that not only explains the rise and fall of educational ideologies, but also provokes shifts in policies, new strategies for organizing schools and learning, new (or recycled) visions of what education might utopianly do.

Educational ideologies, in this context, might therefore be defined as clusters of concepts, beliefs and values, organized in certain linguistic codes, and circulating historically within particular discursive fields – government reports, parliamentary debates, journalism, treatises on pedagogy and even popular detective fiction. This is, admittedly, a narrow definition of ideology, but useful insofar as it allows a distinction between these educational ideologies and my second topic for investigation. This is the deployment of what Foucault calls human sciences in the practices of schooling – I am thinking, for example, of theories of child development and changing pedagogic techniques. These are just as much constituted by forms of knowledge and discourse as educational ideologies, but they are something rather more than representations. The distinction is not between discourse and practice, but between the discourses embodied in ideological representations and those embodied in these sciences and techniques. These latter are integral to the routines of schooling in ways that cannot altogether be explained in terms of ideology. They are comparable to other regimes of knowledge studied by Foucault. In *Madness and Civilization* (1965), for example, he showed how the principles evident in the organization of asylums were formalized in the discipline of psychology; in *Discipline and Punish* (1977), he examined how the new science of penology determined the design of prisons, the activities of the agents working in them, and the ways in which their inmates were categorized and treated. These forms of knowledge were not so much representations of the institutional practices as their very motor.

'When it is exercised through these subtle mechanisms', Foucault argues, power 'cannot but evolve, organize and put into circulation a knowledge, or rather apparatuses of knowledge, which are not ideological constructs' (1980, p.102). My concern is therefore with the *implication of apparatuses of knowledge in the subtle mechanisms of schooling as a form of social regulation.*

But does such a conception of social regulation provide a sufficient answer to the question implied by a conception of ideology broader than the one I have been using so far? This question has been posed by Althusser (though not only by him, of course): how is it that individuals take up particular positions within a social world that always already exists? Foucault argues that this process of subjectification is achieved through the subtle mechanisms of power within institutions and apparatuses of knowledge. It does not rely on the manipulation of the ideas and beliefs that constitute consciousness, and therefore – given this rather polemical definition – the concept of ideology is redundant. Others, following Althusser for example, would reject Foucault's definition of ideology in terms of false consciousness. They would argue instead that any explanation of the process must take into account psychic mechanisms (such as interpellation) as well as cultural ones. This remains a difficult and disputed area: even to pose the problem in terms of 'individual' and 'society' means using categories which have been much criticized for pre-empting the argument (see Henriques *et al*, 1984). In identifying my third topic of study, therefore, it is probably clearest at this stage to say that it involves what has conventionally been posed in psychological and sociological studies as the role of the school in socializing the child. Rather than talking in terms of socialization, though, I shall be drawing on theories of subjectivity which attempt (by no means definitively) to understand the connections between the individual psyche and the symbolic orders of the culture within which it is formed and operates. In shorthand terms, I shall be looking at *schooling as a process producing certain forms of subjectivity*.

Of course, these three topics – educational ideologies, the disciplines and theories governing education as a technique of social regulation, and education as a process producing subjects – are not the only ones that can be studied in an analysis of nineteenth-century schooling. Indeed, one reason for emphasizing them is that they often seem to be overlooked in studies which concentrate on the relationship between education, the state and the economy or between education and the vicissitudes of the working-class movement. The main reason for this focus, though, is that these questions seem to be the crucial ones raised by the debate about ideology opened up by the work of people like Althusser and Foucault.

What I take from Foucault in my account is not a ready-made historical analysis, but a certain way of posing questions, a conceptual map with which to chart apparently inchoate events. To repeat, what follows is not a history (let alone *the* history) of education in nineteenth-century England. It is an attempt to write histories for a number of educational themes, each with its own logic and rhythm of development. The first theme concerns the formulation of educational strategies and policies in terms of a new conception of population as the object of social and political concern – what Foucault calls 'bio-politics'.

II Bio-Politics and Educational Strategies

Apart from the provision of workhouse schools for the children of paupers, it was not until the 1830s that the English state became formally involved in the provision of schooling for working-class children. Earlier schemes for providing such education had come primarily from religious organizations, most notably the Anglican Dr. Bell's National Society and the non-conformist Dr. Lancaster's British and Foreign School Society. In the first two decades of the century, they introduced their monitorial schools – a cheap and supposedly efficient method whereby a single master or mistress surveyed and controlled a whole schoolful of children. The younger children were taught by the older ones, who were responsible to an elite of monitors, who were in turn answerable directly to the master. What they were taught was limited to the most basic instruction in literacy, computation and morality. The non-conformists were more restrained in their religious indoctrination and encouraged the skill of writing. The Anglicans were deeply suspicious of the idea that working-class children should be able to write. As the Evangelical Hannah More put it, the aim was to steer a course between 'the Scylla of brutal ignorance and the Charybdis of a literary education'. However attractive the system may have been to social reformers, the dismal reality was contemptuously denounced by the radical journalist William Cobbett as 'heddekashun', an imposed and constraining form of discipline and instruction that was inimical to learning.

Nevertheless, when the social tremors caused by the Reform Act of 1832 and the waxing of Chartism as a coherent political programme in the 1830s gave the question of how to manage the population a new urgency, the first steps were taken by the state to help and control these schools. In 1833 Parliament voted funds of around £20,000 to be paid in unconditional grants to the two voluntary societies. In 1839 the Committee of the Privy Council on Education was set up, with Dr. James Phillips Kay (who later became Sir James Kay-Shuttleworth) as its first Secretary. Its job was to administer the grants and to introduce a system of inspection along the lines laid down in the factory legislation of the time. But Kay-Shuttleworth had a more radical vision. He saw state-funded education as a bulwark against social chaos.

> We confess that we cannot contemplate with unconcern the vast physical force which is now moved by men so ignorant and so unprincipled as the Chartist leaders ... It is astonishing to us that the party calling themselves Conservatives should not lead the van in promoting the diffusion of that knowledge among the working classes which tends beyond anything else to promote the security of property and the maintenance of public order ... If they [the working class] are to have knowledge, surely it is the part of a wise and virtuous government to do all in its power to secure them useful knowledge and to guard them against pernicious opinions.
> (quoted in Simon, 1960, p.338)

Conventional enough stuff in many ways, but there were significantly new elements in Kay-Shuttleworth's strategy. First, although he was himself an active philanthropist, it is important that Kay-Shuttleworth insisted on the need for *state* intervention. Although such demands go back to the beginning of the century, it was only in the 1830s that the principle was accepted – in part because the provision of education by the state increasingly became a central feature of the political demands of Chartists and their successors. Secondly, Kay-Shuttleworth insisted on certain reforms to the existing forms of educational provision. The coercive forms of control and indoctrination exercised by the monitorial schools were bound to be ineffective. His more subtle version of regulation would therefore involve changes in what children were taught. In his report on *The Moral and Physical Condition of the Working Classes Employed in the Cotton Manufactures in Manchester* (1832), for example, he concluded that 'the education offered to the poor must be substantial'. If a degree of political unrest could be ascribed to 'a people only partially instructed', this was because the little knowledge they were forced to memorize in the monitorial schools was indeed a dangerous thing. Kay-Shuttleworth, the Benthamite rationalist, was at one with a socialist educator like Robert Owen in seeing such crude indoctrination as counter-productive. Education must involve *understanding* – though, of course, he differed from Owen as to what would constitute such understanding. Kay-Shuttleworth wanted to see 'elevating' secular knowledge introduced into the curriculum – those parts of the exact sciences connected with occupations, 'the ascertained truths of political economy' and '*correct* political information' about the relationship between capital and labour. The drive for understanding would also require new forms of pedagogy, to replace the imposed docility of the monitorial system.

Underlying both the political rationale and the educational proposals of Kay-

Shuttleworth's reforms, it is possible to detect a more fundamental strategy, a way of defining what came to be called the social question that itself constituted a new technique for characterizing and regulating the population. Kay-Shuttleworth was one of a new breed of intellectuals and state administrators addressing the impact of industrial capitalism on English society. Many, like himself, were physicians. Even those who were not shared a primarily medical paradigm in developing what Lucy Bland and Frank Mort (1984, p.132) term the 'moral environmentalism' that characterized this first phase of social intervention by the state (roughly from 1839 to 1860). These professional reformers saw the dense concentrations of the lower classes created by industrialization and urbanization as a potential source of contagious disease and also of moral and social corruption. To pre-empt this, the reformers proposed a programme for *social hygiene*, breaking up these enclaves, getting detailed information about the lives of their inhabitants, improving their welfare and at the same time their morality. The aim, in short, was to civilize and socialize them (see Rose, 1979, p.24).

This strategy also created a particular genre of Victorian writing – the social explorer's account of his investigations into dangerous and mysterious quarters. Like Charles Booth's *Life and Labour of the People of London* (1897) more than sixty years later, Kay-Shuttleworth's own Manchester report of 1832 is presented – to use Bland and Mort's striking image – as a 'nightmare journey to the centre of corruption':

> He whose duty is to follow in the steps of this messenger of death [cholera] must descend to the abodes of poverty, must frequent the close alleys, the crowded courts . . . and behold with alarm, in the hot bed of pestilence, ills that fester in secret at the very heart of society.
> (quoted in Bland and Mort, 1984, p.134)

These 'ills' and 'pestilence' refer not only to disease, but also to the chain of imagery linking susceptibility to contagion with criminality, moral and physical depravity, and political sedition. Against this metaphorical network of corruption, Kay-Shuttleworth counterposed a particular representation of the family and a strategy of state intervention in its support.

Both the representation and the strategy embody the same axioms and principles – in particular, the family is seen as both object and mechanism of intervention and the working-class child is seen as endangered by disease and corruption and therefore as a potential danger to society. It is in such formulations that Kay-Shuttleworth's ideas are strikingly similar to those of the contemporary French strategies studied by Jacques Donzelot in his Foucaultian analysis of *The Policing of Families*. For example, Donzelot identifies a number of techniques aimed at 'shepherding the child back to spaces where he could be more closely watched: the school or the family dwelling' (1979b, p.47).

In what sense does Donzelot's identification (and Kay-Shuttleworth's advocacy) of the working-class family and the school as agencies for carrying the norms of the state into the private sphere constitute a strategy of 'policing'? Clearly, Donzelot is not using the term just in its modern sense of enforcing laws in order to keep the peace. He means more the use of political power to investigate the details of the population's everyday life and to secure its well-being and happiness – its fitness for work, its morality and discipline, the quality of its health and housing, and so forth. In this he is following Foucault's appropriation of the usage current in the seventeenth and eighteenth centuries, which is when he identifies a fundamental shift in the state's concern with its citizens – away from a consideration of subjects only in terms of their rights and duties *vis-à-vis* the state to this new concern with the growth and care of the population as a whole and then, increasingly, the monitoring and welfare of individuals. This conception of policing or regulation he also refers to as 'bio-politics' or 'bio-power'.

The major shift that Foucault describes in terms of bio-politics refers primarily to the French context, to that far-reaching political and cultural split between the *ancien régime* and post-Revolutionary bourgeois society which is also one of Donzelot's major points of reference. In England, the form and timing of such changes were quite different and were linked to other historical develop-ments – particularly the growth of industrial capital at the expense of the landed bourgeoisie, the development of the factory system and urbanization. Nevertheless, although the focusing of political concern on the population seems to have developed later in England, what is evident in the moral environmentalism of the mid-nineteenth century is the fusion of welfare and control in the exercise of power by an increasingly extensive and watchful state that characterizes Foucault's conception of 'bio-power'.

The discourse of social hygiene, ascribing pathology to environmental factors, marked an important change from the characterization of the 'dangerous classes' in the terms of pauperism, criminality and sedition which were evident in earlier proposals for monitorial schools. Equally important, though, were the resistances which the policies of reformers like Kay-Shuttleworth ran into when they were put into operation through state apparatuses which had already developed their own rationalities and practices.

The Cash Nexus

One result of the state's increasing (though still fairly marginal) financial involvement in education was that its funding became increasingly subject to the rules (and political battles) governing the budgeting of public expenditure. (By the time Kay-Shuttleworth retired in 1849, the yearly grant to the Committee of Council had increased sixfold to £125,000 and within another decade, by 1858, the newly established Science and Art Department was disbursing over £663,000.) Along with this increased expenditure went increasing monitoring of the recipients' activities, and during this time the system of inspection created by Kay-Shuttleworth to ensure minimum standards was made more systematic and rigorous.

The 1850s and 1860s also saw an unprecedented series of Royal Commissions investigating aspects of educational provision – especially for the children of the bourgeoisie in the universities of Oxford and Cambridge, the public schools (Clarendon) and the endowed schools (Taunton). The only one of the Royal

Commissions not to result in major legislation was the Newcastle report on the elementary schools. This had been charged to 'enquire into the present State of Popular Education in England, and to consider and report what measures, if any, are required for the Extension of sound and cheap elementary instruction to all classes of the People'. The Commission's support for the idea of a county rate for education (while leaving the voluntary system intact) was not taken up. Its proposal that teachers' salaries should be made partly dependent on children's results was greeted more warmly by politicians committed to cutting public expenditure. The technique for implementing this system of 'payment by results' was the Revised Code, introduced in 1862 by Robert Lowe, then Secretary of the Education Department, and finally put into operation in 1863. This led to a decrease in the level of grant disbursal (from £800,000 in 1861 to £600,000 in 1865), an increased degree of central inspection and control and a curriculum restricted to rote learning and the '3 Rs'. 'I cannot promise the House that this system will be an economical one,' Lowe told the Commons, 'and I cannot promise that it will be an efficient one, but I can promise that it shall be one or the other. If it is not cheap, it shall be efficient; if it is not efficient it shall be cheap.'

Lowe simply did not accept (at this stage anyway) the premises of a bio-political strategy. Taking a more *laissez-faire* view of the state, he remained sceptical about the power of education to ensure either the welfare or discipline of the population. In taking this position, he provoked the hostility not only of Kay-Shuttleworth, who from his retirement reiterated that education was the necessary corollary of democracy, but also of Anglican bishops like 'Soapy Sam' Wilberforce and non-conformist clerics (who feared the Code might be the prelude to the withdrawal of funding for their schools) and of school inspectors like Matthew Arnold, who bemoaned the excessive reliance on the 'mechanical examination' required by the Code. The Revised Code, in short, highlighted a problem within the bio-political strategy. As responsibility for the provision of welfare assistance shifted from philanthropic to state agencies, so its actual fiscal costs as well as its potential social benefits came into the calculation. The problem was exacerbated because promises that education and schemes of social hygiene would reduce crime and pauperism in the cities had not been fulfilled.

Population, Race and State

This failure of moral environmentalism led to a modulation in the ways that the social question was posed from the 1860s onwards. Increasingly, the focus of attention shifted from the social and moral environment of the population to the inherent aptitudes and/or inadequacies of the individual. The danger that was now identified was the possible deterioration in the quality of the population, a fear intensified by the passage of the second Reform Act of 1867 which further extended adult male suffrage. Such fears once again placed the population question explicitly on the political agenda in the 1870s and 1880s (Weeks, this volume).

In terms of the individual, concern focused on mental deficiency and degeneracy; this was given a scientific footing through the psychologist Francis

Galton's assertions about the inheritability of intelligence. In terms of the population, especially the urban population during the so-called 'Great Depression' of these decades, attention was directed to a newly identified social grouping with specific characteristics – the unemployed and/or the unemployable (Rose, 1979, p.24). Although this concern was often expressed in terms of public order rather than the alleviation of distress, the explanation provided in Charles Booth's *Life and Labour of the People of London* (1897), for example, was posed less in terms of a static conception of natural viciousness than of a dynamic theory of a process of urban degeneration.

> The residuum of unemployables becomes the focus of all those forms of vice that infect the towns and flourish in the margins of civilization – vagrancy, crime, prostitution – linked around the defect in character of the unemployable individual, a defect both physical – poor eyesight, bad hearing, small size, scrofula, phthisis – and mental – in both intellectual and moral faculties.
> (Rose, 1979, p.26)

One outcome of this concern was a shift of emphasis during the last decades of the century from fears about the 'fitness' of the population to the aspiration to breed – and educate – an 'imperial race'. As the military humiliation of the Boer War coincided with increased industrial competition from Germany, America and Japan, it became clear that the stupefying routines of schooling under the Revised Code were inadequate to that task.

The watchword now was National Efficiency – a floating term which integrated a number of discourses (around government, industry and social organization as well as education) in a programme for reorganizing the existing power bloc and extending the powers of the state. In the sphere of education, campaigns were launched for a broader curriculum which would not only beat the nationalist drum through newly established subjects like history and geography, but would also provide training for citizenship (through systematic instruction in social duty or lessons in civics), physical exercise and military-style drill for boys, and instruction in the responsibilities and techniques of domesticity and motherhood for girls (see Reeder, 1977, p.78; Davin, 1979).

The concern with the physical and domestic well-being of children is evident across the political spectrum, from jingoism to socialism. On the far right can be found the imperialist schemes and reactionary polemics of Lord Brabazon, Earl of Meath. In the 1880s and 1890s, he lobbied for colonies for the unemployed, open spaces in cities, school playgrounds, the Children's Ministering League, state feeding of children and compulsory physical training. He was also involved with the Northern Union Schools of Cookery, the Housewifery Association, the National League for Physical Education and Improvement and the National Educational Union for harmonizing home and school training (Reeder, 1977, p.81). At the same time, socialists on the school boards, like Margaret McMillan in Bradford and Annie Besant in London, were in the vanguard of campaigns for school welfare provision – free meals, detailed medical and dental examinations and reports by School Medical Officers, fumigation of verminous clothing, access to public baths, special provision for mentally deficient children, and so forth (Simon, 1965, p.156–8).

Once again, the provision of welfare went hand in hand with the extension of surveillance and the gathering of information about the population – the strategy of policing families. One of the most interesting formulations of the strategy, in that it also displays clearly a new conception of the organic state (a state which would penetrate into all areas of social life), can be found in the 'social imperialism' of the Fabian leaders Sidney and Beatrice Webb. For them, national efficiency required a number of interlocking changes: a rationalized administrative machinery, the improvement of industrial production by the application of scientific expertise (and hence the extension of scientific and technical education) and, again, the improvement of the nation's physique and the fitness of its population. In achieving them, education would be crucial. In 1901, for example, Sidney Webb argued that in the new century the primary duty of Government would be considered 'the prevention of disease and premature death, and the building up of the nervous and muscular vitality of the race'.

> As such, it must necessarily form the principal plank in any Imperial programme that will appeal to the Progressive instinct of the century. But it is not enough that we rear a physically healthy race. The policy of National Efficiency involves a great development of public education.
> (Webb, 1901, pp.79–80)

For Webb this meant neither the board schools nor a return to 'the "common school" of our Radical grandfathers', but a rationalized and integrated system of public education, from primary schooling through selective secondary education to the universities. The key element here, in line with the eugenist thinking of the time (from which he differed in other important ways) was selection. The man in the street, he wrote, 'will wake up if he is told that the whole system is to be so reorganized that every clever child, in every part of the country, shall get the best possible training that can be devised' (1901, pp. 18–2). Every *clever* child, notice, not every child – for most children, he foresaw higher elementary schools which would not 'lead up to any higher *school*, but to the counting house, the factory, or the kitchen' (cited in Simon, 1965, p. 206).

His vision of 'a number of specialized schools each more accurately fitting the needs of a particular section of children' is interesting because of both the political programme it implies and the psychological assumptions it embodies. As chairman of the London Technical Education Board, Webb considered that his plans for a system of secondary schooling based on scholarships were incompatible with what he saw as the mechanical elementary education provided by the board schools. He also thought the Boards themselves were inefficient and too open to the influence of the teachers and Progressives, who found his commitment to selection uncongenial. He therefore made common cause with the Conservatives in Parliament, the Anglican wing of the Church and fellow enthusiasts for national efficiency, like the civil servant Robert Morant, in campaigning against the Boards. The result was their abolition and the incorporation of education into the ambit of County Councils by the 1902 Balfour Education Act, which Morant steered through the Education Department. Webb's arguments for selective educational institutions were not based just on political grounds, though. It was his assumptions about the psychological needs and capacities of individual children, and how these are distributed statistically through the population, that were pivotal. The outcome was a system based on segregating bright children (as diagnosed by mental measurement) from other children perceived to be potentially dangerous or in danger (to borrow Donzelot's terms), and therefore needing other forms of care and control.

The State as Educator

In this section, I have looked at changing strategies for providing mass education in England during the nineteenth century. In studying the internal logic of programmes like those of Kay-Shuttleworth and Webb, the differences between them and some of the resistances encountered when they were put into practice in the form of policies, I have been treating them as educational ideologies in the sense I defined above (p.216). This does not imply that they were covering up or obscuring the real purposes of education. On the contrary, what they were doing – quite openly – was to articulate certain strategic objectives and thus render them intelligible.

To say that people like Kay-Shuttleworth and Webb gave voice to these strategies does not mean that they originated them. As Foucault points out, strategic objectives do not require expression in this intentional form – 'the logic is perfectly clear, the aim decipherable, and yet it is often the case that no one is there to have invented them, and few who can be said to have formulated them' (1979, p.95). In the case of English strategies for schooling, there actually seem to have been a good number who did, and despite the many differences between these formulations, I have suggested that it is possible to extrapolate a common thread. This seems to be close to the conception of 'policing' or bio-politics developed by Foucault and Donzelot, a concern to moralize the working class – disciplining it, studying it, diagnosing its ills and inadequacies, tending to its welfare.

Another general feature was that such interventions should be subsidized or, increasingly, conducted by agencies of the state. Most of the initiatives for popular education were actually philanthropic or religious in the first instance, and were only gradually, often grindingly, incorporated into a state apparatus. In this sense, the state, especially in its extended, organic form, should be thought of as the outcome of such discourses and strategies, rather than their origin. Nevertheless, by the turn of the twentieth century, it would be hard to disagree with Gramsci's diagnosis that 'the state must be conceived as an "educator", in as much as it tends precisely to create a new type or level of civilization' (1971, p.247).

This formulation is strikingly reminiscent of the strategy of 'moralizing the working class' emphasized by Foucault. Such similarities of interpretation should not be used, though, to obscure their theoretical differences about the state, and especially whether it has a specifiable relationship to the formation of classes through the division of labour. For Gramsci it is axiomatic that the aim is always that of 'adapting the "morality" of the broadest popular masses to the necessities of the continuous development of the economic apparatus of the state' (ibid, p.242)–so that, for example, the new level of civilization promoted by the state 'corresponds to the needs of the productive forces for development, and hence to the interests of the ruling classes' (ibid. p.258). But note that this is the *aim* of the state's role as educator. There is no guarantee that it will be achieved; at best its hold will be contradictory and precarious. It is certainly not automatic. It is less clear whether Foucault's conception of the state as 'the codification of a whole number of power relations which render its functioning possible' (this volume, p.92) is an extension, bracketing or denial of that proposition; what it seems to lack is Gramsci's anti-deterministic feel for the logic or tendential pattern of political struggle.

That debate remains open, but the substantive question that it raises for any historical analysis is why strategies and practices change. Condensed there are two questions–Why do they change *when* they do? and; Why do they change *in the particular way* they do? I have already tried to show how political, economic and fiscal crises can provoke new demands on, and programmes for, education–it is worth noting in passing that significant changes in educational policy have generally occurred in periods of social unrest, after major wars or during depressions rather than in periods of economic expansion. But the nature of such changes cannot be derived from such events: this has to be explained with reference to the discursive fields within which educational ideologies circulate. For example, Kay-Shuttleworth's policies were articulated in terms of moral environmentalism–terms which became disarticulated when in practice they collided with the budgetary logic of fiscal policy. These uneasily synthesized discourses were later rearticulated as residual elements in the organic collectivism of National Efficiency.

The point is that the discursive field within which the battle of educational ideas took place did not have fixed boundaries, but was criss-crossed by other fields. Ideological change came about through the processes of articulation, resistance and negotiation which I have tried to outline. A similar process can, I think, be identified in the institutional practices of schooling. I therefore want to turn now from the strategic objectives formulated within educational ideologies to my second topic of study, to the subtle mechanisms of regulation and control operating in education.

III Mechanisms of Power

To illustrate these mechanisms, I shall have to rerun the history of nineteenth-century schooling from a different angle, concentrating now on techniques which rendered individual children the object of various forms of control, knowledge and concern.

This was not a covert or mysterious process. On the contrary, it was clearly visible in the very structure and routine of the schools. Going back to the beginning of the nineteenth century, for example, consider the design of the monitorial schools and the forms of discipline and pedagogy it implied. Figure 1 shows a Lancastrian school. The master is on the right. The 'general monitor of order' stands on a stool in the centre, controlling some 365 boys all seated in long, fixed rows of desks. At the left-hand end of these are the 'monitors of class'. Figure 2 shows Bell's Madras system, in which the central area is kept clear. Classes are being given in three-sided, almost military formations, with pupils either standing or sitting on movable benches (Seaborne, 1971, pp.137–9).

Despite these differences, both are organized to allow instruction and control to pass through a series of relays – from master or mistress through the monitors to the pupils and back again. It is also clear that this form of discipline depends on the visibility of the pupils to the master – the sort of surveillance that Foucault argues is crucial to the disciplinary technologies of the institutions he studies in *Discipline and Punish*. Thus the monitorial schools exemplify an architecture designed, in Foucault's words, 'to permit an internal, articulated and detailed control – to render visible those who are inside it; in more general terms, an architecture that would operate to transform individuals: to act on those it shelters, to provide a hold on their conduct, to carry the effects of power right to them, to make it possible to know them, to alter them' (1977, p.172).

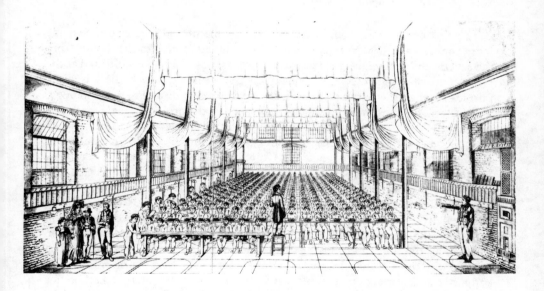

Figure 1 Southwark, London, Central School of British and Foreign School Society, Borough Road, early nineteenth century.
Source: The British and Foreign School Society's *Manual of the system of primary instruction*, 1831 (by permission of the Society)

Figure 2 Central School of the National Society, Baldwin's Gardens, London, early
nineteenth century.
Source: J. Hamel, *L'enseignement mutuel*, Paris 1818

This link between Foucault's analysis and the monitorial schools can be made
more concrete. In *Discipline and Punish*, Foucault attempted to show how, from
the seventeenth and eighteenth century onwards, power has been directed at the
production of regimented and self-policing subjects – 'docile bodies' is his
phrase – through the pervasive, localized operation of a disciplinary technology.
To illustrate the forms this technology had taken by the turn of the eighteenth and
nineteenth centuries, Foucault refers to English reformers like Patrick
Colquhoun, who was Chairman of the Committee for Dr. Bell's Free School in
Orange Street, Westminster, and the Utilitarian philosopher Jeremy Bentham.

From Bentham he takes the central image of *Discipline and Punish* – the
Panopticon, a scheme for an ideal penitentiary in which a single observer in a
watch-tower could watch over a circle of tiered, individual cells without being
observed by the prisoners. The system was designed to produce an effect of
constant, omniscient surveillance (though not all the prisoners would actually be
watched all the time) and thus instil a regime of individual self-regulation. The
parallel with the monitorial schools is clear – indeed, Bentham was an enthusiastic
supporter and was active in an ultimately fruitless scheme to found a school for
middle-class children using monitorial methods and to be built according to 'the
Panopticon principle of construction'.

In the monitorial schools, the system of *hierarchical observation*, which Foucault
identifies as one of the definitive techniques for implementing the new
disciplinary power, was instituted in their design, the use of monitors and the

Figure 3   Stow's model infants' school, 1836.
Source: D. Stow, *The training system,* 1836

systematic organization of pupils' time. But just as important as those forms of surveillance were new ways of studying, classifying and treating the inmates of the rationalized institutions. These established the *norms* of behaviour from which incarcerated individuals were held to deviate. Thus the physical punishment of prisoners gave way to confinement and, increasingly, to programmes of rehabilitation based on information gathered about each case history – the technique of *normative judgement*. Similarly, the monitorial schools operated a detailed economy of punishments and rewards not only for pupils' ability to memorize their lessons, but also for their behaviour, attitude, time-keeping, cleanliness and so on.

It was this coercive focus on the individual child that was criticized by educators like Robert Owen, Kay-Shuttleworth and David Stow (who wrote about teaching methods and ran a model school for training teachers in Glasgow). For them it was not enough to produce docile bodies. They believed that the civilizing goals of elementary education required pupils who could understand their lessons (Hamilton, 1981, p.2). Their practical solution was a move away from the individualism of the monitorial schools towards the simultaneous instruction of a whole class by the teacher.

As a corollary, the design of school rooms also began to change. Whereas the desks in a Lancastrian school were often arranged in a slight incline to make all the pupils visible to the master, Stow introduced galleries designed to focus the attention of children on their teacher. Figure 3 shows an infant school-room,

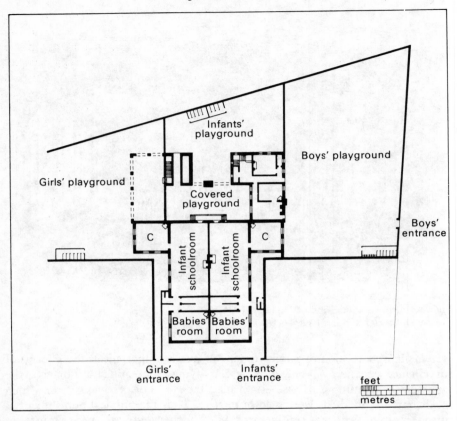

Figure 4 Wornington Road Board School, Portobello, London; infants' department on the ground floor, 1874
Source: Seaborne and Lowe (1977)

designed by Stow, in this transitional phase. The boys and girls are seated on a gallery, with a wooden rail dividing them. In front of them stands the master, next to his chair and lectern. In the central part of the room are lesson-posts with pictures or objects attached to them. When not being taught in the gallery, the children would cluster around these in groups to be taught by a monitor (Seaborne, 1971, p.144).

What emerged under the name of simultaneous instruction was a new combination of interrogatory methods with the grouping of pupils using criteria which emphasized the similarities between pupils in 'classes' rather than their individual differences. Through these new methods, with pupils being asked questions randomly by the teacher or being invited to indicate their readiness to answer by putting up their hands, it was hoped that the minds of children would be perpetually engaged and under the influence of the master (Hamilton, 1981, pp.5–6).

By the time of the Board Schools in the 1870s the idea of the school-room had been replaced – or at least supplemented in larger schools – by the characteristic design of a school consisting of a school hall surrounded by a number of separate classrooms. The London School Board was one of the first to appoint an architect, E. R. Robson, and in 1872 he laid down a number of principles and rules. Each group or 'standard' should be taught in a separate classroom although 'as each school is under the supervision of one master or mistress, this principle must in some degree be subordinate to the necessity for such supervision' (quoted in Seaborne and Lowe, 1977, p.25). All classrooms had to be entered from the central schoolroom. (A concern with the supervision of pupils' sexuality also led to the requirement for separate playgrounds for boys and girls and for separate entrances placed as far apart as possible – preferably on different streets.) These principles are visible in the Board School Robson designed in Wornington Road in the Portobello district of London in 1874, which also incorporated two infant schoolrooms and two babies' rooms in an elaborate ground-floor extension. The boys' and girls' schools were on separate floors above; they show Robson moving towards the design based on a central hall with classrooms off it (see Figure 5). (Seaborne and Lowe, 1977, pp.29–30.)

The Science of Pedagogy
This separation of classrooms went hand in hand with the appearance (in the phrase that first appeared around this time) of classroom teachers (Hamilton, 1981, p.10). These adult teachers, often women, were qualified, but under the control of the head teacher. Many were drawn in by the unprecedented demand created by the 1870 Education Act, although the creation of a professional teaching force had begun earlier with another of Kay-Shuttleworth's schemes. In the 1840s he had initiated a state-financed pupil-teacher system and a network of teacher-training colleges. But teaching did not become fully professionalized until the last decades of the century, when the first university departments of education were set up and a number of professional journals began to appear.

It was in these new contexts that the reaction against simultaneous instruction (especially after the introduction of the Revised Code in 1862) was given its clearest expression. In his *Principles of Class Teaching* (1902), for example, J. J. Findlay (who was to become Professor of Education at Manchester University) expressed his belief that the '*unit* in *Education* is not the school, or the class, but *the single pupil*'. Thus the professional academic discipline of education was marked from the beginning by an allegiance to the 'New', 'Progressive' or 'Child-centred' educational movement. According to Hamilton, it took shape as a rejection of 'the claimed mechanization of simultaneous instruction; just as the work of Stow and Kay-Shuttleworth represented a reaction against the arbitrary nature of pre-nineteenth-century individualized instruction' (1981, p. 11).

Feeding into this new science of pedagogy were two other discourses concerned with the scientific classification of children: child study and mental measurement (Walkerdine, 1984, pp.169–73). The vogue for child study represented an attempt to chart systematic patterns of growth in children; the studies often took the form

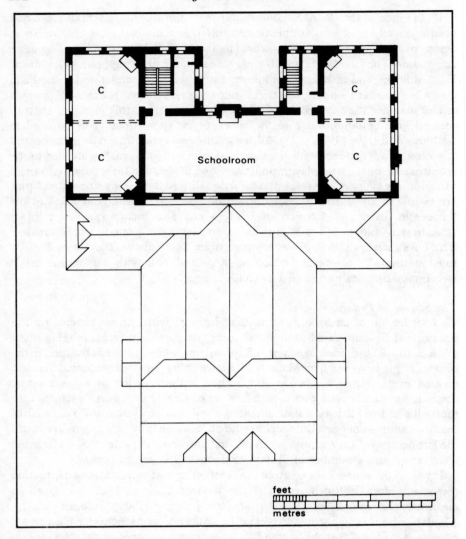

Figure 5 Wornington Road School; boys' department on the first floor
Source: Seaborne and Lowe (1977)

of detailed accounts by scientists of their observations of their own children's
'development'. Although the most influential text was Wilhelm Preyer's *Die Seele
des Kindes*, which appeared in English as *The Mind of a Child* in 1881, the most
widely quoted English example was Charles Darwin's *A Biographical Sketch of an
Infant*, published in 1887 on the basis of notes made in the 1840s. What is
important about these and other studies is not only that they impute a normal
process of growth to children, but above all that, as Valerie Walkerdine observes,

'children *as a category* were being singled out for scientific study for the first time and the discourses which produced children as the objects of that study were drawn from biology and topography, and everyday-life common sense' (1984, p.171; my emphasis).

Whereas child study was concerned with all aspects of children's growth – their physical growth, their beliefs and habits, their play, and so on – mental measurement focused solely on the development of intellectual capacity (or 'intelligence') and its distribution across a population. For the psychologist Francis Galton, the leading exponent of this new science, the impetus for such work was the eugenist fear about degeneracy and a desire to protect and improve the quality of the English population. Once again, we are confronted with that sea-change in the modes of understanding and political action in the decades around the turn of the century, in which the capacities of individual children, as defined by the new psychological sciences, feed into a new pedagogy and ever more pervasive forms of social welfare, investigation and surveillance.

Examination, Inspection, Records
The various techniques for individuating and regulating pupils, which required the apparatuses of knowledge described above, were also productive of knowledge in another sense. 'Hierarchic surveillance' involved breaking down the anonymous mass of a population into individual cases. 'Normalizing judgement' then regrouped these cases around certain statistical norms, which can act coercively on those who deviate from them. For this normalizing process to work, each prisoner, student, inmate or citizen had to be given an individual history, which took the material form of detailed institutional records and reports. This was part of what the historian Carlo Ginzburg has called the imposition of 'a close-meshed net of control on society', which involved 'attributing identity through characteristics which were trivial and beyond conscious control' (Ginzburg, 1980, p.24). It was in the massive written archive produced in this process that people were classified and categorized. Here the ordinary individuality which had previously remained 'below the threshold of description' (Foucault, 1977, p. 191) became the object of investigation and record.

In education (and elsewhere) one tactic which was central to this strategy was what Foucault calls the 'slender technique' of the examination (1977, pp.184–94; Hoskin, 1979). The examination, this 'mechanism of objectification' (1977, p.187), ceased to be simply a final certificate of educational competence. Instead, it became a routine method of testing pupils' performance and establishing a hierarchical order among them. Written examinations and the records of their results also constituted a 'proliferating network of writing' in which individuals were captured, their aptitudes defined and their qualifications fixed.

This, at any rate, seems to have been something like the logic behind the Revised Code of 1862. In part, it no doubt represented an attempt to establish more effective control over individual schools by the state – every school receiving a government grant was required to keep a log of its daily life, for example. But its detailed definition of educational *standards* that had to be met was also a clear (although often ineffectively crude) mechanism for subjecting both schools and pupils to common norms (see Figure 6).

	Standard I	Standard II	Standard III
Reading	Narrative in monosyllables.	One of the Narratives next in order after monosyllables in an elementary reading book used in the school.	A short paragraph from an elementary reading book used in the school.
Writing	Form on black-board or slate, from dictation, letters, capital and small manuscript.	Copy in manuscript character a line of print.	A sentence from the same paragraph, slowly read once, and then dictated in single words.
Arithmetic	Form on black-board or slate, from dictation, figures up to 20; name at sight figures up to 20; add and subtract figures up to 10, orally, from examples on blackboard.	A sum in simple addition or subtraction, and the multiplication table.	A sum in any simple rule as far as short division (inclusive).

	IV	V	VI
Reading	A short paragraph from a more advanced reading book used in the school.	A few lines of poetry from a reading book used in the first class of the school.	A short ordinary paragraph in a newspaper, or other modern narrative.
Writing	A sentence slowly dictated once by a few words at a time, from the same book, but not from the paragraph read.	A sentence slowly dictated once, by a few words at a time, from a reading book used in the first class of the school.	Another short ordinary paragraph in a newspaper, or other modern narrative, slowly dictated once by a few words at a time.
Arithmetic	A sum in compound rules (money).	A sum in compound rules (common weights and measures).	A sum in practice or bills of parcels.

Figure 6   Definition of standards by the Revised Code, 1862 (Maclure, 1979, p.80)

Detailed records also started to be kept on individual pupils – particularly those considered to be in danger morally or potentially dangerous socially. The models for such work were doubtless the files kept by the police and by prisons, in which an identity (in terms of physical characteristics, including the use of fingerprints introduced into Britain by Galton in the 1880s) and a case history (in terms of a past record) were imposed on individual prisoners. But these records were also incorporated into more therapeutic and pastoral strategies. As John Tagg has shown in an article on the complicity of photography in this spreading network of power, the photographic image was invested with the power to show the true nature not only of criminality, but also of insanity, poverty, poor housing, and so forth. In the 1860s, for example, the Stockport Ragged and Industrial School commissioned a local photographer to compile an album of each of the teachers and children in the school (see Figures 7 and 8). In 1874, Dr Barnardo opened a Photographic Department in his Home for Destitute Lads in Stepney. The role of the pictures was quite clear (see Figure 9):

> . . . to obtain and retain an exact likeness of each child and enable them, when it is attached to his history, to trace the child's career . . . By means of these likenesses children absconding from our Homes are often recovered and brought back, and in not a few instances juveniles who have been stolen from their parents and guardians or were tempted by evil companions to leave home, and at last, after wandering for a while on the streets, found their way to our Institution, have been recognised by parents or friends and finally restored to their care.
> (cited in Tagg, 1980, pp.43–4)

This interweaving of surveillance with pastoral care and welfare provision is a familiar characteristic – earlier, for example, I noted the monitoring and recording of individual pupils' medical and social well-being. The school was becoming a relay in extending this strategy into the community. The progressive London School Board, for example, appointed a network of Visitors to 'police' the families of working-class children by providing information (not only about educational matters) which could be tapped by local and national government authorities. As early as 1875, the Visitors were asked to prepare a census of the wife desertion they discovered in the course of their duties (Rubinstein, 1977, pp.232–3). Again, care for individuals is linked to the monitoring and control of the population.

In this section, I have tried to demonstrate some of the 'subtle mechanisms' through which education was designed to individuate people, discipline them and render them the objects of power and knowledge. I stress *designed*, because it should not be assumed that these mechanisms actually worked. The usefulness of a Foucaultian approach, it seems to me, lies in its power to reveal the principles governing the organization of schooling and its forms of discipline and pedagogy – those aspects sometimes referred to as 'the hidden curriculum'. It is a curious phrase, because, far from being hidden, they are the most obvious part of the experience of schooling: perhaps it is this that makes it possible to overlook them. Rather more mysterious, it seems to me, is the question of what is going on in the curriculum proper. What symbolic categories and hierarchies does this embody? How are these organized and transmitted through the school and what

Figures 7 and 8   The Stockport Ragged and Industrial School. Cartes-de-visite, c. 1865.

Martha Berry

Source: Stockport Library Local History Department

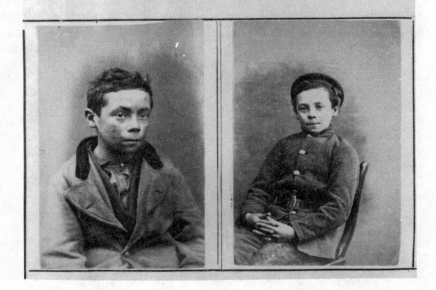

Admitted January 5th, 1876.

Aged 16 Years.

Height, 4-ft. 11-in.

Color of $\left\{\begin{array}{l} \textit{Hair, Dark Brown.} \\ \textit{Eyes, Brown.} \end{array}\right.$

Complexion, Dark.

Marks on body—None.

If Vaccinated—Right Arm.

If ever been in a Reformatory or Industrial School ? No.

Figure 9 Section of a *Personal History* of a child at Dr Barnardo's Homes, 1874-83.
Source: Dr Barnardo's

forms of subjective investment do they produce? Above all, how does this
management of knowledge institute a complex pattern of cultural differences?
This leads back to the Althusserian definition of ideology as a process producing
subjects. In other words, it means switching from the production of the individual
as an object to the production of the individual as a subject – in Foucault's terms,
from *subjection* to *subjectification*.

IV Subjectivity and the Management of Knowledge

The political importance of the classification of knowledge and the management of the symbolic did not escape those concerned with popular education in the nineteenth century – 'Knowledge is power' was, after all, a widely used radical and Chartist slogan. Particularly revealing, though, are the arguments of Robert Lowe after his conversion to the need for popular education. As I noted earlier, he doubted whether the strategy of moral environmentalism could produce the social harmony its proponents promised. But faced with the extension of male suffrage in the 1860s, he became a supporter of universal and (in contrast to someone like Kay-Shuttleworth) compulsory education. Why the change?

Lowe spelt out his logic in *Primary and Classical Education* (1867). If the lower classes are to have *political* power, he argued, then the higher must develop a different mode of *cultural* power. They must use their 'greater intelligence and leisure' to ensure that they 'know the things the working men know, only know them infinitely better in their principles and in their details'. In this way they might 'conquer back by means of a wider and more enlightened cultivation some of the influence which they have lost by political change' (quoted in Simon, 1960, p.356). In other words, Lowe was proposing a strategy for what, in a lecture delivered in 1970, Foucault called 'the social appropriation of discourses' along lines 'marked out by social distances, oppositions and struggles'. 'Any system of education', comments Foucault, 'is a political way of maintaining or modifying the appropriation of discourses, along with the knowledges and powers which they carry' (1981, p.64).

What might these knowledges and powers be? It is noticeable that Lowe's strategy did not propose an absolutely separate content for children from different classes, but a different *manner* of education and a different *orientation* towards knowledge. How such differences were instituted in French education has been the subject of several Althusserian studies. Baudelot and Establet (1971) identified two networks of education – instrumental forms of knowledge imposed on working-class children on the one hand and, on the other, the idealist rationalism of bourgeois academicism. Similarly, Renée Balibar has argued that the post-Revolutionary bourgeoisie, having imposed a uniform national language, asserted its cultural superiority by retaining (and transforming) the elite school system of the *ancien régime* and its distinctive literary language. In the two-tier education system established in France in the nineteenth century, children in secondary schools were offered some conceptual framework for understanding how language works, whereas working-class pupils in the elementary schools were instructed in the mechanical rules of the language. Thus for the subordinate classes, argues Balibar, the language imposed through the education system was experienced as an external discipline and as an exclusion from a superior, literary language.

Although the English case was different from the French, the fixing of a particular variant of the language as 'standard English' and the institutionalizing of certain texts as the canon of English literature in the second half of the nineteenth century do seem to be symptomatic of a far-reaching reorganization of cultural relations. They meant that the appropriation by the bourgeoisie of the categories of language, perception and taste embodied in an academic (or national) culture could be passed off as the result of natural aptitudes instead of a class-based training. Thus while children in the elementary schools were subjected to a language supposedly reflecting the everyday physical world (Rose, 1984, p. 7), middle-class boys in public schools learned to speak the languages of classical civilization. Greek and Latin were so important because it was *distinction* and *cultivation* that were at stake, not economic utility. Professional training could not be the guiding principle for public schools, insisted Edward Thring, headmaster of Uppingham. It would be 'absolutely impossible to direct the studies of a great school to this end beyond a certain degree, without destroying the object of a great school, which is, mental and bodily training in the best way, apart from immediate gain' (quoted in Wiener, 1981, p. 19).

Similar patterns of differentiation are evident in the academic disciplines of History and Geography that were established in universities and schools at this time. Along with standard English, elementary school pupils were subjected to an identity defined in terms of nationalism and imperialism. This was not just a matter of political propaganda, though. As Benedict Anderson shows in *Imagined Communities* (1983), it is the construction of a national past in terms of a specific narrative conception of time that allows for subjectification within the discourses of nationalism – whether as the subjects of national destiny or as a subject to the sacrifices it demands. Similarly, Edward Said (1979, p.55) argues that 'imaginative geography and history help the mind to intensify its own sense of itself by dramatizing the distance and difference between what is close to it and what is far away' – in his example, between the West and the Oriental or, in this case, between England and the colonial. What matters is that the definition of the former in terms of its distinction from the latter (its Other) allows the rhetorical elision of differences and antagonisms within its fictional unity or identity.

In such ways the school curriculum embodies a hierarchy of forms of knowledge, to which access is socially distributed. This pattern is historically and culturally specific, being governed by the rules of what Foucault in his earlier work called a 'cultural unconscious' – rules that are unformulated and also generally unrecognized by those who operate them, but which define what is true, what is relevant and who has the authority to give voice to a particular discourse. If the curriculum is a mechanism for instituting patterns of social differentiation, then it operates not through its content but by regulating the circulation and appropriation of symbolic codes for classifying knowledge and representing reality.

This sort of approach has, in a rather different way, been at the core of Basil Bernstein's work on education. His early distinction between restricted and elaborated linguistic codes prefigured Baudelot and Establet's networks of education. In his later works, Bernstein has proposed a number of increasingly complex models to demonstrate how the classification and framing of knowledge in the curriculum, along with different forms of pedagogy, produce specific subject positions for different social groups (Bernstein 1977; 1982). It was also this question of how relations of power are inscribed in the organization of knowledge in the curriculum – and the struggle for this symbolic power – that Robert Lowe was concerned with. He wanted to institute clear ideological boundaries between the bourgeoisie and the newly enfranchized lower classes. That is why the latter should 'be educated that they may appreciate and defer to a higher cultivation when they meet it; and the higher classes ought to be educated in a very different manner, in order that they may exhibit to the lower classes that higher education to which, if it were shown to them, they would bow down and defer' (Simon, 1960, p.356).

The questions begged by Lowe's formulation, of course, are *why* the 'lower classes' should 'bow down and defer' to this higher cultivation and, indeed, whether they did. It is here that Foucault's account of subjection and subjectification, however useful in linking the organization of the symbolic to the operation of disciplinary technologies, may be less productive than Althusser's conception of interpellation. What is at stake is how the cultural unconscious determines the individual unconscious – or rather, given that this way of putting it might reproduce the duality between 'society' and 'individual', how subjectivity is produced within the terms of the symbolic.

The important point to stress here is the *production* of subjectivity. In thinking about schooling, this means breaking radically from the idea that education is concerned with the natural intellectual development of the child. Subjectivity is alway historically and culturally specific; the 'nature' of the child is itself a norm defined in disciplines like psychology and imposed through pedagogic techniques. Subjectivity is also different from the idea of socialization. The school does not socialize the child in the sense of pouring certain myths, values and attitudes into its more or less receptive consciousness. Rather, it helps to secure unconscious structures which make people responsive to certain representations, and so enable them to recognize themselves as subjects addressed in ideology. Subjectivity is therefore not seen as an indentity, but as a particular imaginary ordering of the symbolic.

What often seems to be missing from Foucault's work is not only an alternative theorization of such processes, but also a sense of how problematic, how *difficult* they are. Education, he asserts (1981, p.64), establishes 'a qualification and a fixing of the roles for speaking subjects', but says nothing about how subjects fill these roles. In his more recent work on 'the way a human being turns him- or herself into a subject' he states that people 'have learned to recognize themselves as subjects of "sexuality" ' (1982, p.208) – but without really specifying what is involved in that recognition.

Althusser's theorizing of interpellation through the speculary mechanisms of ideology does at least tackle this problem directly (see Introduction, pp.xiii–xiv). But does he provide a more adequate account of the difficulty of subjection/subjectification? Here there seems to be a tension between the two strands in his ISAs essay. On the one hand, the axiomatic link between ideology and the reproduction of the relations of production presupposes that the process works – that the forms of interpellation instituted in the mirror phase and secured through the ISAs sustain the existing social order. But on the other hand, he derives his account of the mechanisms of interpellation from Lacanian psychoanalysis, whose very starting point is that such an internalization of norms does not and cannot work. The ordering of subjectivity as an identity is a precarious fantasy, whose 'failure' is constantly revealed by the operations of the unconscious (Rose, 1983, p.9).

It is the first strand of Althusser's work that has generally been taken up in sociological studies of education. The result has been a step back from the unstable, fragmentary subjectivity of interpellation to the coherent, self-conscious subject of an unruffled socialization functioning to reproduce the social order. What is needed instead, I would argue, is an account of subjectivity which comprehends its aggressivity, and which does not reduce it to an identity or to the passive reflection of an external order. In studying education, this might help to explain both the hold of the symbolic categories embodied in the hierarchy of the curriculum and at the same time why, *contra* Lowe, subordinate groups do not simply 'bow down and defer' to them. In short, it raises the question of resistance.

V Conclusion

How might a conception of resistance be properly integrated into the sort of approach I have been developing here? The danger of focusing on how certain disciplinary, pastoral and symbolic regimes have been set in place through the schools is that a sense of the daily struggle and muddle of education can disappear even from the margins of the story. When accused of producing too neat and conflict-free an analysis of bio-power, Foucault acknowledged the problem and suggested a defence:

> Oh, I quite agree. Judiciary and psychiatry join hands, but only after such a mess, such a shambles! Only my position is as if I were dealing with a battle: if one isn't content with descriptions, if one wants to try and explain a victory or a defeat, then one does have to pose the problems in terms of strategies, and ask, 'Why did that work? How did that hold up?' That's why I look at things from this angle, which may end up giving the impression the story is too pretty to be true.
> (Foucault, 1980, p.209)

Partly, then, how you see resistance depends on your angle of vision – and, indeed, there are already histories of nineteenth-century schooling organized around the struggle for working-class education (Brian Simon), popular alternatives and resistance to the forms in which it was provided (Richard Johnson) and the less politically coherent recalcitrance of the pupils themselves (Stephen Humphries). The existence of histories written from these different angles does not solve the question of how to incorporate resistance here, though.

Foucault himself suggests that resistance is the inevitable corollary of power – 'where there is power, there is resistance' is his slogan. That is true enough. The policies and pedagogies I have examined were not implemented without being fought, rejected and negotiated at every turn. The problem with Foucault's linkage of resistance with power in this way is that he sees them *both* as infinitely diffuse, as coming from everywhere. If that logic is followed through, then resistance can easily be reduced to the status of 'noise' or interference in communications theory. Foucault does not really distinguish between types and forms of resistance: for him, it remains always plebeian and pre-political. In other words, he emphasizes resistances to the localized exercise of power rather than the articulation of such instances into political programmes and strategies.

If such articulation is possible, this suggests an approach to power and resistance organized around Gramsci's conception of hegemony. By this I mean not 'consent' in a rationalistic or manipulative sense, but the way that the field of power relations is organized around certain imaginary unities and oppositions – Englishness/alien cultures, masculinity/femininity, class solidarity and so forth. These nodal points are not identities in an essentialist sense – they are created only in the historical flux of social relations – but they do provide the terms through which individual 'identities' are precariously established. This approach therefore hangs onto the central importance of interpellation, but without suggesting that all the diverse forms of interpellation can be explained in terms of a single antagonism (the class struggle, the division of labour or whatever.) From this point of view, then, ideology can be conceived in terms of practices and mechanisms aimed at mitigating the instability of both social relations and subjectivity by representing them as functioning totalities and fixed identities.

What does this definition imply for the study of education? Negatively, the approach I am suggesting is incompatible with a number of general assumptions. It would not start from the principle that schooling is a mechanism for slotting children into the niches required by the division of labour – not because people don't want it to but because there are only weak theoretical or empirical grounds for supposing that it has the capacity to train people for specific occupational roles. For similar reasons, it would not see schools as agencies of socialization, if that implies an individual identity imprinted by a social order so as to turn children into docile workers. Not would it accept an instrumental conception of either power or the state.

Instead, I would begin by asking how schooling contributes historically to the production or organization of social relations and subjectivity – rather as Gramsci conceived the importance of language to the formation of a national culture:

> Every time the question of the language surfaces, in one way or another, it means that a series of other problems [is] coming to the fore: the formation and enlargement of the governing class, the need to establish more intimate and secure relationships between the governing groups and the national-popular mass, in other words to reorganise the cultural hegemony.
> (Gramsci, 1985, pp.183–4)

For Gramsci, classes – certainly classes as formations with some degree of cultural identity – were not given, but had to be made. Similarly, the *form* of the relationships between classes had to be fought for in political and cultural struggle.

So, for example, the creation of the public schools in the nineteenth century, however marred by their nostalgia for aristocratic culture and their disdain for science and industry, was undoubtedly symptomatic of the recomposition of the English bourgeoisie. Similarly, the various strategies for providing working-class schooling were all concerned with establishing particular relationships between rulers and ruled – this applies just as much to those in working-class political movements who demanded such provision as to politicians like Lowe who tried to ensure that the form in which it was provided would take the sting out of the extension of the suffrage.

In what sense were the relationships established by these educational initiatives 'intimate and secure'? They were intimate in the sense that both the disciplinary and pastoral modalities of power which they operated focused on the individual child with unprecedented rigour and precision. Pupils were subject not just to the formal routines of the schools, but also to their criteria for classifying children, their detailed records of the child's development and home life, their provision of welfare and so forth. (It is the detailed texture and hold of these practices that a Foucaultian approach illuminates with such clarity: it provides a method for showing just how the individual subject is, in Gramsci's words, 'a product of the historical process to date, which has deposited in you an infinity of traces, without leaving an inventory' (1971, p.324).) Just as important as such techniques of subjection, though, is the way that subjectivity is formed in relation to the symbolic orders of the culture – hence, for Gramsci, the emphasis on language. Hence, too, my arguments earlier about the symbolic hierarchies of the curriculum.

How the curriculum embodies a particular ordering of the symbolic, and how this then plays into the ordering of subjectivity, remain perhaps the most tantalisingly underexplored question in the study of education. In thinking about how resistance and struggle might be tied into these processes, therefore, my comments can only be speculative – indications of possible lines of inquiry, rather than a conclusion.

The first point to stress, again, is that, rather than having their own separate symbolic orders, different social groups relate differently to normative orderings of the same symbolic categories. This, I think, is the implication of Bernstein's work. It was certainly the premise of Volosinov's work on language in the 1920s, where he presents this common symbolic or semiotic system as both the precondition for ideological struggles and their stake.

> Class does not coincide with the sign community, i.e. with the community which is the totality of users of the same set of signs of ideological communication. Thus various different classes will use one and the same language. As a result, differently oriented accents intersect in every ideological sign. Sign becomes an arena of class struggle.
> (Volosinov, 1973, p.23)

This provides a clue, I think, to the way that the curriculum works ideologically. It is not a question of filling different people's heads with different contents. What the curriculum does is to establish hierarchical relations between different forms of knowledge. At the same time, this symbolic organization also generates a network of subject positions in relation to these hierarchies – it defines what it is to be educated, cultivated, discriminating, clever, literate and so forth. It therefore differentiates not only between forms of knowledge but also between *people*. And it also makes it possible for this system of differentiation to be presented not in terms of social conflict and antagonism, but as the natural consequence of the psychological and intellectual aptitudes of the people who occupy those subject positions.

This, perhaps, is how the curriculum is implicated in the struggle to secure 'intimate and secure' social relations – intimate because it feeds into the ordering of subjectivity, secure because of the apparent naturalness of its categories. In this sense, the approach I am suggesting repeats the arguments of people like Baudelot and Establet about the different networks of education or Renée Balibar about different orientations to language. But it also undermines any idea that the organization of schooling and the curriculum simply reproduces in the sphere of education the fundamental class antagonism generated through economic relations. It is not as though the only subject positions produced by schooling are the public schoolboy spouting Greek verse and eager to take up the reins of Government and Empire, and the oppressed, alienated elementary pupil browbeaten by some latterday Gradgrind. The specific patterns of cultural differentiation produced through schooling are much more complex and diverse than that.

Take for an obvious example the differences created around gender – not just in terms of working-class girls being instructed in housewifery or sex stereotyping by teachers, but in presuppositions about the natural aptitudes of girls and boys and in the definition of subjects like science and mathematics as 'masculine' in contrast to the more 'feminine' arts subjects. How would it be possible to challenge a commonplace like 'girls are less talented at maths than boys'? What that takes for granted – or, more precisely, as natural – is the definition of differential subject positions for women and men in relation to the discursive field of the curriculum (the masculine connotations of mathematics). The implication is that, here as elsewhere, women are naturally subordinate or inferior to men. If that implication is to be resisted, it is the premise that has to be challenged. Only by stepping outside this way of formulating the problem is it possible to show that what is at stake is not a natural difference between boys and girls, but the exclusion of women from prestigious forms of knowledge – an instance of oppression rather than one of subordination. That alternative becomes possible, I would argue, if one starts from the premise that schooling is concerned not with developing natural aptitudes, but with the diffusion of norms which institute specific patterns of cultural differentiation.

That at least seems to be the underlying logic or strategy of education, however shambolic it might turn out to be in practice. It also suggests, I hope, how schooling operates at what Gramsci calls the 'intimate' level of subjectivity – without implying that this necessarily or automatically fulfils the 'need' for 'secure' social relations. Both subjectivity and social relations are characterized not by security but by tension and instability. The production of subjectivity, as I have already argued, involves not the reflection of a social order by the passive individual, but the precarious ordering of symbolic categories. This is an active, even aggressive process – not least because such categories are never encountered in the abstract, but always as they are formulated in discourse and deployed in social interaction. The *difficulty* of appropriating language, for example, is well expressed in this observation by the Soviet theorist M. M. Bakhtin:

> The word [or discourse] . . . exists in other people's mouths, in other people's contexts, serving other people's intentions: it is from there that one must take the word, and make it one's own. And not all words for just anyone submit equally easily to this appropriation, to this seizure and transformation into private property: many words stubbornly resist, others remain alien, sound foreign in the mouth of the one who appropriated them and now speaks them; they cannot be assimilated into his context and fall out of it; it is as if they put themselves in quotation marks against the will of the speaker. Language is not a neutral medium that passes freely and easily into the private property of the speaker's intentions; it is populated – overpopulated – with the intentions of others.
> (Bakhtin, 1981, pp.293–4)

This underlines the main point that I am trying to make about resistance and education. This should not be pictured in terms of an oversimplified conflict between the authenticity of working-class (or whatever) experience and the imposed ideology of the school—not because I think experience is unimportant, but, on the contrary, because the concept of experience is much more difficult than such an image acknowledges. It entails the complex set of issues I have been dealing with in this article – the forms of power and knowledge deployed in schools, the symbolic categories organized in the curriculum, the ordering of subjectivity in relation to both of these, and so forth. In this view, resistance cannot be the irruption of some essential subjectivity which has escaped these networks of power and culture. Instead I would see it as an integral component in the strategic exercise of power through which subjectivity and social relations are produced and the diversity of social antagonisms are regulated. Only through this sort of approach, it seems to me, is it possible to understand both the strategic logic of education and the many different tactics that pupils have for negotiating the experience of school and appropriating its culture.

Finally, a methodological point. In his article on the affinities between the investigative methods of Freud, Sherlock Holmes and the art historian Giovanni Morelli, Carlo Ginzburg identifies two epistemological models for the human sciences that became visible around the middle of the eighteenth century. One was the anatomical metaphor, in which society or the state is seen as an organism with all its different parts contributing to the functioning of the whole. This is the model presupposed by functionalist accounts of education, whether sociological or Marxist. The alternative paradigm, suggests Ginzburg, was the *semiotic*. Instead of imputing functional needs to society and then identifying the institutional means for their fulfilment, this tries to understand the significance of often unnoticed or apparently trivial details of social life in order to diagnose their underlying rationale.

> In a social structure of ever-increasing complexity like that of advanced capitalism, befogged by ideological murk, any claim to systematic knowledge appears as a flight of foolish fancy. To acknowledge this is not to abandon the idea of totality. On the contrary, the existence of a deep connection which explains superficial phenomena can be confirmed when it is acknowledged that direct knowledge of such a connection is impossible. Reality is opaque; but there are certain points – clues, signs – which allow us to decipher it.
> (Ginzburg, 1980, p.27)

Clearly, Foucault for one does question the idea of a pre-given totality – although not the idea of mechanisms for totalization. Despite this crucial difference, though, his genealogical approach clearly falls within this paradigm. Indeed, Donzelot has compared it explicitly with the detective story.

> In the detective story reality has an enigmatic quality. It is the *a priori* incomprehensible, the surprising, that which upsets comforting, serene representations, a crime of disappearance which throws a new light (but which?) on a person, a house, a city. The procedure followed is not a search for a general causality but the identification of clues. Clues are not causes, not even minor ones. They are traces of a passage, and in following the thread which links them one is able to establish the line or lines of a transformation which leads to the reality of the investigation's point of departure.
> (Donzelot, 1979a, p.78)

In our case, following this sort of semiotic investigation, I have attempted to identify certain clues to the transformations in popular education which might make it possible to understand the operation of modern schooling. And this metaphor of detection leads us back to where we began, with Sherlock Holmes heading towards Victoria. No doubt the drinking habits of that man Phelps would turn out to be a clue of some kind; but a less significant one, I suspect, than the Board Schools on the London horizon.

References

ANDERSON, B. (1983) *Imagined Communities*, London, Verso.

BAKHTIN, M. M. (1981) *The Dialogic Imagination*, ed. M. Holquist, Austin, Texas, University of Texas Press.

BALIBAR, R. (1974) *Les Français Fictifs*, Paris, Hachette.

BAUDELOT, C. & ESTABLET, R. (1971) *L'École Capitaliste en France*, Paris, Maspero.

BERNSTEIN, B. (1977) *Class, Codes and Control, Vol. 3* (2nd edn.), London, Routledge and Kegan Paul.

BERNSTEIN, B. (1982) 'Codes, modalities and the process of cultural reproduction: a model', in M. W. Apple (ed) *Cultural and Economic Reproduction in Education*, London, Routledge and Kegan Paul.

BLAND, L. & MORT, F. (1984) 'Look Out for the "Good Time" Girl', in *Formations of Nation and People*, London, Routledge and Kegan Paul.

DAVIN, A. (1979) '"Mind that you do as you are told": Reading books for Board School girls, 1870–1902', *Feminist Review*, no. 3.

DONZELOT, J. (1979a) 'The poverty of political culture', *Ideology and Consciousness*, no. 5.

DONZELOT, J. (1979b) *The Policing of Families*, London, Hutchinson.

FOUCAULT, M. (1965) *Madness and Civilization*

FOUCAULT, M. (1977) *Discipline and Punish: The Birth of the Prison*, London, Allen Lane.

FOUCAULT, M. (1979) *The History of Sexuality, Volume 1*, London, Allen Lane.

FOUCAULT, M. (1980) *Power/Knowledge: Selected interviews and other writings*, ed. C. Gordon, Brighton, Harvester Press.

FOUCAULT, M. (1981) 'The order of discourse', in R. Young (ed), *Untying the Text*, London, Routledge and Kegan Paul.

FOUCAULT, M. (1982) 'The subject and power', Afterword to H. L. Dreyfus & P. Rabinow, *Michel Foucault: Beyond Structuralism and Hermeneutics*, Brighton, Harvester Press.

GINZBURG, C. (1980) 'Morelli, Freud and Sherlock Holmes: Clues and scientific method', *History Workshop*, no. 9.

GRAMSCI, A. (1971) *Selections from the Prison Notebooks*, ed. Q. Hoare & G. Nowell-Smith, London, Lawrence and Wishart.

GRAMSCI, A. (1985) *Selections from Cultural Writings*, ed. D. Forgacs & G. Nowell-Smith, London, Lawrence and Wishart.

HAMILTON, D. (1981) 'On simultaneous instruction and the early evolution of class teaching', mimeo, Glasgow, University of Glasgow.

HENRIQUES, J., HOLLOWAY, W., URWIN, C., VENN, C. and WALKERDINE, V. (1984) *Changing the Subject*, London, Methuen.

HOSKIN, K. (1979) 'The examination, disciplinary power and rational schooling', *History of Education*, vol. 8, no. 2.

HUMPHRIES, S. (1981) *Hooligans or Rebels?*, Oxford, Basil Blackwell.

JOHNSON, R. (1979) 'Really useful knowledge', in Clarke, J., Critcher, C. and Johnson, R. (eds) *Working Class Culture*, London, Hutchinson.

JOHNSON, R. (1981) *Education and Popular Politics*, Milton Keynes, Open University Press.

MACLURE, J. S. (1965) *Educational Documents: England and Wales 1816 to the Present Day*, London, Methuen.

REEDER, D. A. (1977) 'Predicaments of city children: late Victorian and Edwardian perspectives on education and urban society', in Reeder (ed), *Urban Education in the Nineteenth Century*, London, Taylor and Francis.

ROSE, J. (1983) 'Femininity and its discontents', *Feminist Review*, no. 14.

ROSE, J. (1984) *The Case of Peter Pan, or the Impossibility of Children's Fiction*, London, Macmillan.

ROSE, N. (1979) 'The psychological complex: mental measurement and social administration', *Ideology and Consciousness*, no. 5.

RUBINSTEIN, D. (1977) 'The London School Board, 1870–1904', in P. McCann (ed) *Popular Education and Socialisation in the Nineteenth Century*, London, Methuen.

SAID, E. (1979) *Orientalism*, New York, Vintage Books.

SEABORNE, M. (1971) *The English School: Its Architecture and Organisation 1807–1870*, London, Routledge and Kegan Paul.

SEABORNE, M. and LOWE, R. (1977) *The English School: Its Architecture and Organisation, Vol. 2 1870–1970*, London, Routledge and Kegan Paul.

SIMON, B. (1960) *Studies in the History of Education, Vol. 1: The Two Nations and the Educational Structure, 1780–1980*, London, Lawrence and Wishart.

SIMON, B. (1965) *Studies in the History of Education, Vol. 2: Education and the Labour Movement, 1870–1920*, London, Lawrence and Wishart.

TAGG, J. (1980) 'Power and photography', *Screen Education*, no. 36.

VOLOSINOV, V. N. (1973) *Marxism and the Philosophy of Language*, New York, Seminar Press.

WALKERDINE, V. (1984) 'Developmental psychology and the child-centred pedagogy', in HENRIQUES *et al.*

WEBB, S. (1901) 'Lord Rosebery's escape from Houndsditch', in *The Nineteenth Century*, reprinted in E. J. T. Brennan (ed) (1975) *Education for National Efficiency*, London, Athlone Press.

WIENER, M. J. (1981) *English Culture and the Decline of the Industrial Spirit*, Cambridge, Cambridge University Press.

14 Peter Pan, Language and the State
Captain Hook goes to Eton

Jacqueline Rose

From *The Case of Peter Pan or, the Impossibility of Children's Fiction* by Jacqueline Rose, 1984. Reproduced by permission of the publishers, Macmillan.

In 1925, J. M. Barrie wrote a short story called 'Jas Hook at Eton, or The Solitary' for inclusion in an anthology of short stories for children, *The Flying Carpet*. Instead of being published in that anthology, the story was delivered as a speech to the First Hundred at Eton on 7 July 1927, and published in *The Times*. It was replaced in the anthology by a sequel to 'The Blot on Peter Pan'[1] a short story called 'Neil and Tintinnabulum' which describes how the male narrator loses his godson when he is absorbed into the life of a public school – the title reflects the loss as the little boy's name is changed at school from Neil to Tintinnabulum, from English to Latin. Latin is the element which connects the two stories. The autograph manuscript version of Barrie's 1927 story is accompanied by a leaf of manuscript in an unidentified hand which gives the following Latin inscription for James Hook: 'Gratissimus Almae Matris filius magistro inform. et alumnis omnibus avete hoc ivto Iunii die MDCCC? ex Moluccis Iacobus Hook Floreat Etona'.[2] The sequence from the earlier story 'The Blot on Peter Pan', which turns on the child's use of language as picture puzzle, to 'Neil and Tintinnabulum', therefore, describes the passage from the most elementary of child's play in language to the most elevated of linguistic/cultural norms.

The story 'Jas Hook at Eton' is presented by Barrie as evidence for the Latinate and public school credentials which are given in Hook's dying words – 'Floreat Etona' – which he utters as he jumps off the edge of the ship in the last sequence of the play. The reference goes back to *The Little White Bird*[3] which ends when the public school master, Pilkington, steals (that is how it is expressed) the boy David and his friend Oliver from the narrator of that story and carts them off to school. In the 1911 *Peter and Wendy*, Barrie spells the association out in the form of a revelation or scandal – as the ultimate and most carefully guarded secret of his story:

Hook was not his true name. To reveal who he really was would even at this date set the country in a blaze; but as those who read between the lines must have guessed, he had been at a famous public school.

By writing a story (or giving a speech) to Eton about Hook at Eton, Barrie is going over the traces of his story, elaborating (confessing, exposing) its cultural code, bringing out into the open something which, prior to this, had operated purely at the level of allusion or aside. Making Hook's cultural allegiance explicit is, therefore, a little like drawing back the veil on a mystery, or else breaking into a sanctuary, with the implication that neither the hitherto protected scenario nor the onlooker will survive the revelation. The story Barrie tells of Hook's relationship to Eton describes just such a violation – it is not the story of his schooldays, but the story of how he broke into the school one night after 'Lock Up time' to destroy all record of his ever having been there. This cleverly disposes of two problems at once – the fact that the infamous Captain Hook would threaten the good name of the school had he indeed once been its pupil, and the fact that (as the records will show) the whole idea is a fantasy, or lie.

The idea of breaking and entering also has a history which goes back to the first Peter Pan story in *The Little White Bird* when Maimie Mannering broke the rules and stayed in Kensington Gardens overnight, where she (and we as readers) met Peter Pan for the very first time. Thus there is a second circuit which overlays the passage from language as play to language as privilege with the notions of exclusion, barriers and taboo. At the simplest level the overlapping of these two moments suggests that the desire to get back to the beginning and make everything perfect takes the form of the familiar desire for better opportunities, and a fantasy of public school life. That the secret Latin reference is as much a risk to the purity of *Peter Pan* as the partly spoken fantasies about origins and birth is confirmed, however, by the fact that in 1915, when the London County Council's Books and Apparatus Sub-Committee accepted Barrie's *Peter and Wendy* as a reader for use in the schools, every vestige of this reference was systematically cut.[4] In 1915, the public elementary school child, object of compulsory education since 1880 and recently redifferentiated from the middle-class child by the second Education Act of 1902, did not speak Latin but English, and an English which was carefully distinguished [in a 1912 Board of Education Circular on teaching English in elementary schools, for example] from literary language by its reference to experience, to the 'sights and sounds, the thoughts and feelings of everyday life'. Against this language was set not only Latin, but literary language in general or, more specifically, the language of the literary trope. Matthew Arnold, HM Inspector of Schools from 1852–86, offered the following two extracts in 1867 to illustrate the gulf which then separated the privately educated middle-class child from children in the elementary schools.

> My dear parents, – The anticipation of our Christmas vacation abounds in peculiar delights. Not only that its 'festivities', its social gatherings, and its lively amusements crown the old year with happiness and mirth, but that I come a guest commended to your hospitable love by the performance of all you bade me remember when I left you in the glad season of sun and flowers.

Dear Fanny, – I am afraid I shall not pass in my examination. Miss C says she thinks I shall. I shall be glad when the Serpentine is frozen over, for we shall have such fun; I wish you did not live so far away, then you could come and share in the game.

The pseudo-classicism which Arnold is commenting on in the language of the privately educated middle-class child is picked up by Barrie in his 1927 story about Captain Hook: 'But even so, what ardour to excel, how indomitable is the particle man'. It also appears at various points in *Peter and Wendy*: 'O man unfathomable'; 'the elegance of his diction, even when he was swearing, no less than the distinction of his demeanour, showed him one of a different caste from his crew'. Along with all mention of Hook's educational history, this language is edited out of *Peter and Wendy* when it is accepted by the schools. Thus the censorship does not only apply to the explicit references to the institutions of schooling. Equally, and more crucially, it takes out any signs of their associated forms of linguistic style.

For *Peter Pan* to become a *reader*, the overconscious signs of its status as *literature* must be erased. The distinction is one which was written into state educational policy on language in the first decades of the century, when the state faced a potential contradiction between an increasingly generalised policy of state aid to schools (the 1902 Education Act provided state aid for the first time to the previously private domain of secondary education),[5] and the need to secure a differentiation between classes of child.

The Language of the Child

The language of the child – the language which it speaks, the language it reads, and the relationship between the two – was one of the central arenas within which this contradiction was played out. Here, the question of language becomes the question of *literacy*, and the question of literature hands over to that of *literary language* (how and what to speak, what to read and to what end?). By this almost imperceptible shift, both language and literature are released as objects of *policy* – policy by means of which the child's relationship to its culture can be defined. Language is not simply there to be spoken, any more than literature waits to be read, like matter almost to be imbibed by the child ('When you give your child a bath, bathe him in language' – the exhortation of the 1974 Bullock Report on literacy, *A Language for Life*). Both the language and the literature available to the child fall inside institutions which constitute them differentially and with different values and meanings at different times. The point of examining *Peter Pan*'s encounter with the schools is not, therefore, so much to demonstrate an outrage – the repressive educational machinery clamps down on the book for the child – as to show how both language and literature are constituted by just such 'machinery' in the first place. In this context, natural language or the idea of language as naturally expressive – a concept which [has been] so central to writing on children's literature – appears not as something outside the range of these determinations, but as one pole of a fully structural opposition between natural and cultured language in the schools.[6]

This is how the Board of Education Circular of 1912 on the teaching of English in the public elementary school concludes its final section on English teaching for its senior classes:

in teaching children, failure to use a direct, simple, unaffected style is doubly harmful: it makes the teaching more difficult for the child to understand and remember, and it corrupts his natural taste ... To preserve and develop naturally the unsophisticated virtues of children's language is worthy of an effort and will indeed require an effort on the part of a grown-up teacher. He need not revert to 'childish' language, but if he can recover some of the directness and simplicity of thought and expression which education too often impairs, he will find that his effort has been of as great advantage to himself as to the children.

This from the opening section of the 1910 Board of Education Circular on English teaching in the secondary schools:

It would only be wasting words to refute the view that knowledge of English in any real sense of the term will be 'picked up' naturally, or that though systematic instruction is necessary in such subjects as mathematics or foreign languages, the mother-tongue may safely be left to the occasional direction and influence of home, or to the rare chance of spontaneous liking for its study. The instruction in English in a Secondary School aims at training the mind to appreciate English literature, and at cultivating the power of using the English language in speech and writing. These objects are equally important, and each implies the other. Without training in the use of language, literature cannot be fully understood or properly appreciated. Without the study of literature there can be no mastery over language.

We should remember that the relationship between these two types of school was not one of a sequence – a journey through the educational system of an individual child (elementary *then* secondary). The age groups of the two schools partly overlapped (10 to 14 for the senior classes of the elementary school and 12 to 16 for the secondary school). The elementary school stopped at 14 because this was considered the appropriate educational span for the working-class child; and the secondary school made it clear that its methods should also be used for the elementary training of its pupils ('the whole spirit of the Circular must be regarded as applying equally to pupils of this more elementary stage'). The differences between these recommendations on language – an unsophisticated language on the verge of 'childishness' versus literature as the precondition for mastery over language itself – cannot therefore be resolved into the stages of a continuous development or growth. They remain, precisely, a difference.

The language of the elementary school child was to be natural – which meant a vocabulary based on concrete objects, and written composition constructed on the basis of speech ('No attempt should be made to impose a difference in style in written and oral composition'; 'Written composition should be subordinate to oral'). It meant literature based on physical actions, and on facts which could be added to the child's stock of information. The child should read literature for its story, poetry for its matter rather than its form. If literary taste was to be developed, it too should 'grow naturally by feeding on the best'–although the child will not be fully cognisant of the process ('they will rarely be able to show reasons for their preference'). In the secondary school, the priorities are almost exactly reversed. Since literary language predominates, so the child's speech is encouraged towards cadence and quality, its composition towards structure and style. Books of fiction are the one form of writing to be excluded from its reading. In the final stages, the study of literature leads to the analysis, appreciation and mastery the classicism of Milton's style. Literature is to be selected for its 'specially fine passages' which the child commits to memory by learning them by heart ('not so much a method as the presupposition of all methods'). Literary language therefore becomes the fully internalised model of the child's own mental processes which reflect not everyday concrete experience, but 'remembrances', 'unconscious associations' and a 'widening experience of life'. The image is that of a subjecthood which 'ripens' in accordance with the truly organic nature of a literate culture ('nature' appearing with opposite connotations on either side of the educational divide).

Thus the secondary school remained, even after it had been taken partly under state control, the repository of a notion of literacy, whose objective was the classicism which Arnold's quotation (p.251 above) shows us so slavishly imitated by the middle-class child. Meanwhile, the public schoolboy was himself learning English for the first time (a 'new subject' in 1906 according to the Assistant Master of Harrow School), but English as 'pure literature', with composition taught on the earlier models of Latin prose. In this context, therefore, Barrie's Latin reference places *Peter and Wendy* in the midst of a struggle about the appropriate ownership, patronage and reproduction of linguistic and cultural privilege in the schools. Even for Matthew Arnold, who pleaded for a 'humanising' influence to be exerted on the raw, uncultivated information of elementary education, Latin literature represented the one cut-off point of his cultural *largesse*: 'we do not want to carry our elementary schools into Virgil or Cicero'.

Elementary language is, however, no more natural than this classical prose. When *Peter Pan* was written, elementary language, with its emphasis on natural expression, can clearly be seen as something in the process of being *constructed* as one half of an opposition whose other term it necessarily evokes. As if symptomatically, the 1912 Board of Education Circular recommends *Tom Brown's Schooldays* along with the more predictable *Robinson Crusoe* and *Masterman Ready* as reading for the elementary schools. The first (which was first in a long line of books for children written in the second half of the nineteenth century about public school life) demonstrates the uneasy but always present relationship between the different sectors of the educational system (their constant reference to each other); the second two are the wholly appropriate representatives of an old empiricism of language and a colonialism of adventure whose long association with childhood was now to receive the sanction of the linguistic-educational policy of the state.

Elementary and Literary Language

This can be seen most clearly in a new synthetic method for teaching English which was devised in 1914 in direct response to the 1912 Government Circular by R. Wilson, whose *Progress to Literature* had already revealed something of *Peter Pan's* problematic relationship to the world of children's books (see Rose, 1984, pp.85–6). Its objective – which it defined against the previous analytic method of teaching English by grammar, spelling and dictation – was to teach the child language by means of the visual image, in such a way that language should be seen to arise directly, and without interference, out of the objects of the visible world:

1   To name in turn various objects represented by the artist, e.g.: I see a horse.
2   To close book and name objects from memory, e.g. I saw a horse, or, I have just seen a horse.
3   To say what he will see when he opens the book, or, what his companions will see, e.g. I shall see a horse, etc. He will see a horse, etc.
4   To name 'actions' or 'states' represented by the artist, eg. Grazes in the field . . .

The method was appropriate for a child whose future was most likely to involve the physical manipulation of objects in manual work. (This has in turn produced a new crisis of literacy since this form of language is now considered unsuitable for a workforce no longer employed predominantly in manufacture, agriculture and mines.) But the stress on the visible and manipulable aspects of physical experience, on concrete impression and on language as the direct extension of the visual sign, can also be seen as the linguistic prototype for a late nineteenth-century imperialism (increasing control of an empirically knowable world) which was simultaneously bringing subjects like geography, religion and comparative ethnography for the first time into the elementary schools. The paradox was that the social group which actually serviced the Empire (the public school élite) was prevented by the counterweight of their own classical-linguistic privilege from allowing, other than with the greatest difficulty and reluctance, either the newly celebrated mother-tongue or the subjects appropriate to the ideology of imperialism into their schools.[7]

There is a long colonial history which lines up under one banner childhood, the beginnings of language and the origins of the race – with *Robinson Crusoe* often serving as the link between the three (it was the one book recommended by Rousseau for children) (see Rose, 1984, ch. 2). *Robinson Crusoe* is appropriate not just for its fantasy of a primary and natural state of man, but also because it presents language as a record which directly captures experience much as physical labour puts man in immediate contact with the land. Accordingly, the Government Circular of 1912 takes this text as its image for the most proper, that is, physical and concrete, relationship between literature and the elementary school child:

a child should not be expected to write a single composition upon a whole book or story, eg on *Robinson Crusoe*; it will be found far more profitable to call for a description of some particular scene or incident which is specifically interesting, or even to frame two or three pointed questions on some portion of the book; eg., what were the difficulties which Crusoe found in building his boat, and by what means did he overcome them.

We can compare this with the use of literature in the secondary school, where the child's consciousness is directed at the language of the author (whose words 'express the meaning better than any other words' can do'); the aim being to produce an attention to language itself rather than to by-pass it in the name of the concrete event which it records.

This moment of educational history is, therefore, particularly helpful in allowing us to bring into sharper focus what it is we mean when we talk about language for the child. Children's language is not a concept which comes as readily and easily to mind as that of children's literature, although it is clear from the encounter between *Peter and Wendy* and the schools that they are inseparable, in so far as what is allowable to the child as fiction – its literature – is in part an effect of what it is permissible at any one moment for the child to speak. 'Children's language' tends to be a differential term, meaning 'not adult' and associated with babbling, rhythm, puzzle or play. But the one moment when this language of puzzle or play surfaces in the history of *Peter Pan* ('The Blot on Peter Pan') has conspicuously been discarded by the myth. For the elementary schools in 1912, there is no doubt that any trouble which children's literature might pose at this level of impossibility and/or nonsense is to be subsumed under the correctness of the child's mother-tongue:

> *Lesson XXIV 'Who'*
> Write down two sentences.
> Alice was a little girl. She had many adventures in Wonderland.
> Now join them by substituting *who* for she. Note that *who* comes near to the noun for which it stands.
> Now offer the following for similar treatment.
> Red Riding Hood was a little girl. She met a wolf in the wood.
> Tom was a boy sweep. He was turned into a water baby.
> Peter Pan was a little boy. He did not wish to grow up.

There is an obvious repressiveness involved in turning all these unlikely or miraculous characters (metamorphosed – Tom, in danger – Red Riding Hood, or desiring the impossible – Peter Pan) into familiar people 'who . . . '. But this deflation of the content conceals the more important transformation, which is the fundamental *ordering* of the language through which it takes place.

It would, therefore, be misleading to describe the relationship between elementary and cultured language as an ideal sequence from linguistic underdevelopment into literate civilisation – a sequence which, at the turn of the century, was only available to one class of child. First, because the same child did not attend the elementary and secondary schools, and secondly because to conceive of the differences between them as a sequence can give the impression that the more simple language is uncorrupted and true, or else simply deprived – with the idea of the elementary as something lacking, or left out, as far as these educational determinants are concerned. The 1912 circular ends, indeed, by recommending the teacher to put back the clock on her language and to start speaking almost like a child. But the fact that this statement comes at the end of a document designed to lay down the principles of natural language, plus the fact that it has to sidestep so carefully the more incoherent of children's speech, suggests that the idea that there could ever be a natural language is a myth. Rather there are two ideologies *of* language – one based on the visible, knowable and controllable of the physical world, the other based on the more numinous reaches of our higher cultural life. The most rudimentary laws of how to organise narrative fall under the rubric of each: for the elementary child [in Wilson's Lesson Book], actions and their immediate consequences ('What happened and what happened next'); for the secondary school, [according to the Board of Education] the circular motion of a fully integrated teleology of prose ('the end would be in view from the beginning . . . the whole piece of composition shall be an organic whole in which each portion is related to all the rest').

Barrie's *Peter and Wendy* belongs on both sides of this cultural division. The confusion of tongues between adult and child on the part of the narrator (Rose, 1984, ch. 3) carries with it an oscillation between these extremes of language, between elementary English and the periodic cadences of a more Latinate prose:

> Wendy came first, then John, then Michael.
>
> It was just at this moment that Mr and Mrs Darling hurried with Nana out of 27.
>
> He was a little boy and she was grown up.

> Fell from their eyes then the film through which they had looked at victory.
>
> The elegance of his diction, even when he was swearing, no less than the distinction of his demeanour, showed him one of a different caste from his crew.
>
> That passionate breast no longer asked for life.

The Latin style is conspicuous; the elementary English fades into the invisibility of an apparently natural and universally comprehensible linguistic form. But, as educational policy at the turn of the century makes clear, the most natural of languages only has a meaning in relation to that other stylistic quality against which it is set. There is no natural language (least of all *for* children); there is elementary English and cultured prose, evoking each other, confronting each other, or else coming together as here, only to be carefully orchestrated apart.

School Readers

When *Peter and Wendy* comes up against the schools, it therefore reveals, almost accidentally, that it is speaking to two different children at once, and that its language is not cohered but divided down the middle. But, at a time when the state was particularly concerned to secure a differentiation in the language of its subjects-to-be, such a conflation was impossible to accept and every sign of it therefore had to be edited out.

The effect of that editing is to take with it almost all the other forms of disturbance which have been described so far in relation to Barrie's text of 1911. The authorised school version removes:

all syntax (periodisation, inversion) or tropes (metonymy, synecdoche) which are resonant of a classical literary style;

all specific cultural and material references (not just to Hook's educational history, but also the more middle-class associations of the nursery: Mr Darling's stocks and shares, and Mrs Fulsome's kindergarten for the children);

all signs of play or parody of its own language, especially those which comment on language as institution or practice ("'I, George Darling, did it. *Mea culpa. Mea culpa.*" He had had a classical education'. 'Feeling that Peter was on his way back, the Never Land woke into life. We ought to use the pluperfect and say wakened, but woke is better and was always used by Peter'; the implication here seems to be that language must not be seen to comment on itself;

all those moments when the sexuality of the text becomes explicit (in the Lagoon sequence, when Hook is being taunted by an invisible Peter, 'He felt his ego slipping from him . . . In the dark nature there was a touch of the feminine, as in all the great pirates' – Hook then resorts to a guessing game with Peter; the text drops the 'ego' and the 'feminine' but keeps the game, which was the one 'judicious form of play' recommended by the 1912 circular;

all episodes which disturb the logical narrative sequence of the story (*Peter and Wendy* describes the children's escape retrospectively, that is, it gives the outcome and then leads up to it; the school version picks out the story of what happened but drops the frame which gave it the status of a memory).

Above all, the school version cuts out virtually all signs of the presence of an identifiable narrator – that narrator who so uncomfortably forces on the reader's attention the question of who is telling the story (with all the instability in language that this implies). The school version is told almost entirely by an anonymous third person narrator who never appears explicitly in the text to trouble its linguistic norms or its utterly sustained cohesion of address. Thus, after dropping the first ten pages of Barrie's text completely, it opens 'The children were in bed', a sentence which it lifts clean out of this one from the original: 'On the night we speak of all *the children were* once more *in bed*' (my italics).

Barrie's text is not the only version of *Peter Pan* accepted after alterations for use in the schools. Three years before *Peter and Wendy* was approved, D. O'Connor's *Keepsake*[8] had been admitted as a reader. The complexity of the operation carried out on this text is less because its challenge is less. It was, after all, a summary version of the play which went into circulation largely because of the difficulties of Barrie's own relationship to his text (in which context it is significant that O'Connor's text should be accepted before Barrie's own, which had appeared the year before). The *Keepsake* is not so much dramatically cut as corrected and its vocabulary simplified where this is too ponderous or literary: 'voracious saurian' to 'greedy crocodile', 'weird apparation' to 'strange figure', 'became inaudible' to 'died away'. Above all its syntax is simplified, which means that for a sentence like this one 'he was the best father who never forgot to be a little boy', which grammatically can be read in at least three different ways ('of those fathers who never forgot to be a little boy, he was the best', 'he was the best father because he never forgot', 'he was the best father and never forgot') the easiest and most banal is the meaning which is retained: 'He was the best of fathers; and he never forgot to be a little boy' (the separation of the two clauses breaks the otherwise total and perhaps uncomfortable identity between fathers and little boys).

Barrie's text is never *rewritten* in this way. It is *abridged*, which means that the form of language desired by the schools can be extracted out of the most recalcitrant of Barrie's prose. Unlike O'Connor, whose faulty grammar is corrected on a number of occasions, Barrie never makes a mistake. It is precision in relation to both forms of language, which he so skilfully meshes together, that is the scandal.

In educational terms, Barrie's personal history can suggest why he might have been particularly well placed to produce something which appears in *Peter and Wendy* as a type of condensation of these forms of speech, which for the schools were rapidly coming to be seen, and increasingly being defined, as incompatible. In relation to linguistic policy at the turn of the century, Barrie's text was full of interference or noise. In relation to Barrie, however, this can be seen as the logical outcome of a fairly remarkable educational history which stretched from the learning situation of a small domestic economy in Scotland, through the Dumfries Academy (Barrie's elder brother was, like Arnold, an HM Inspector of Schools, and the Independent Scottish Academies were renowned for their cultural standards), to Edinburgh University and then London.[9] The public school education which Barrie provided for the Llewellyn Davies boys, whom he finally adopted, is well known (Eton of course). But it only makes sense in relation to *Peter Pan*, when seen as the termination point, or fantasy, of a linguistic trajectory which runs right across the spectrum of educational institutions and practices at that time. Barrie spoke almost all their forms of language – and desired perhaps above all the one that he did not speak. But the biographical reference is important here only because it shows up the complex institutional determinants – at the level of language and education as they bear most directly on the child (Barrie included) – of a work which has given to childhood the transcendant and ahistorical status of a myth.

The alterations carried out on *Peter and Wendy* suggest that it is not just the stylistic features of literary language which clash with the linguistic demands of the elementary school. The cutting out of the narrator's comment on Mr Darling ('He had had a classical education'), and of the more infantile voice which rebels against correct grammar in the name of Peter Pan ('we ought to use the pluperfect and say wakened, but woke is better and was always used by Peter'), removes from the text any linguistic self-consciousness, any drawing attention to the language as something whose origins are never safely anonymous (a third person narrator who just *speaks*), nor single, but stem from what might be a multiple and contradictory source. One of the main achievements of many works which are successfully classified as literary (amongst which *Peter and Wendy* cannot really be included) might, therefore, be the extent to which they smooth over these differences, and integrate our own divisions in language into a coherent form. The demand for stability in language (which has been central to one strand of children's literature since the eighteenth century and which appears in so much criticism of children's books) would, therefore, carry a double burden: the securing of our identity as subjects in the world, and a suppression of those aspects of our linguistic-educational history which, because of its cultural divisiveness, give that myth of identity in language so thoroughly the lie [. . .]

Notes

Notes numbered in square brackets have been added by the editors.

[1] Barrie's short story 'The Blot on Peter Pan' was published in 1926 in an anthology for children, *The Treasure Ship*, edited by Cynthia Asquith. (The original title, 'The Truth about Peter Pan', was changed for publication.) In this story, the narrator tells a group of children about how he based the play *Peter Pan* on his relationship with a little boy, Neil. The 'truth' about, or 'blot' on Peter Pan is his cockiness in vying with the narrator and trying to outdo him as a writer by producing his own play, which involves a play on language, on the opening night of *Peter Pan*.

2 'A most grateful son of our Dear Mother to the headmaster and to all her pupils. Greeting! this 4th day of June 18—, from the Moluccas, James Hook, Eton for ever.'

[3] *Peter Pan* had a complicated textual and publishing history. The story first appeared as an interlude in a novel for adults, Barrie's *The Little White Bird* (1902), where it is told by the narrator to a little boy whom the narrator is trying to steal. In order for it to become a work for children, therefore, it was extracted from this source and transformed into a play, first performed in 1904–5. A number of other authors rewrote *Peter Pan* as a narrative for children, but it was not until 1911 that Barrie published *Peter and Wendy* – which, because of the way it exposes the ambiguous position of the narrator and the problem of identity in language, still 'constitutes something of an attack on, or at least an affront to, the very concept of children's literature with which it is most often linked' (Rose, 1984, p.86).

4 'Report of the Books and Apparatus Sub-Committee, July 19, 1915', Greater London Record Office and Library, London County Council Education Minutes, 1915, 2, 28 July 1915, p.164. Originally set up in 1872 under the School Boards to give instructions to local school managers (and then teachers from 1899) on the selection of books for use in schools, the policies of this Committee were adopted by the County Council in 1904.

5 The Taunton Commission of 1864–8, investigating 'middle' (that is non-public) schools, recommended a class-based tripartite division of the educational system (upper and professional, mercantile and higher commercial, upper working class). Despite the inclusion of secondary education in general state policy after 1902, it is clear that the three types of school – public, secondary and elementary – correspond to and reinforce such a division. Sir Francis Sandford makes the distinction between elementary and secondary education the basis of his introduction to Matthew Arnold's *Reports on the Elementary Schools 1852–82* (1899): 'Education should be based upon three principles – the mean, the possible, the becoming, these three. The term "mean", used here in the ordinary Aristotelean sense, seems, as applied to elementary education, to be equivalent to what Mr. Forster called "a *reasonable* amount of instruction"; not confined to the three R's on the one hand, not trenching on the domain of secondary education on the other'.

6 For further discussion of this issue and of the general argument on which this chapter is based, see Renée Balibar's examination of national educational policy on language in post-revolutionary France (Balibar, 1974).

7 This whole question has to be seen in the context of resistance to new utilitarian concepts of education on the part of the public schools. Gladstone had written to the Clarendon Commission criticising the 'low utilitarian argument in matters of education'; Rev. T. L. Papillon specifically criticises the public schools for the low level of teaching relevant to Empire (geography, English history and literature, ethnology and religions) as part of his general exhortation 'learn to think Imperially' (*The Public Schools from Within*, 1906, p.284).

[8] O'Connor's *Peter Pan Keepsake*, 'the story of *Peter Pan* retold from Mr Barrie's fantasy', with a foreword by W. T. Stead, was first published in 1907.

9 Barrie's educational history was even more complex than this. It includes a Free Church School, a number of private schools, a seminary, the Glasgow and Forfar Academies as well as the Dumfries Academy which he attended before going to Edinburgh University in 1878. Many of these changes were determined by his elder brother's career (he was classics master at Glasgow Academy from 1867 to 1817).

References

BALIBAR, R. (with the collaboration of G. Merlin and G. Tret) (1974) *Les Français Fictifs*, Paris, Hachette.

ROSE, J. (1984) *The Case of Peter Pan or, The Impossibility of Children's Fiction*, London, MacMillan.

Index